WOMEN IN THE WORLD OF RELIGION

WOMEN
IN
THE WORLD OF
RELIGION

by Elsie Thomas Culver

DOUBLEDAY & COMPANY, INC.
GARDEN CITY, NEW YORK
1967

Library of Congress Catalog Card Number 66-14928
Copyright © 1967 by Elsie Thomas Culver
All Rights Reserved
Printed in the United States of America
First Edition

TO THE MEN—
in the hope that, as men and women together
rediscover our God-given oneness,
we may also find and achieve
God's purpose for the World.

ACKNOWLEDGMENTS

I am grateful to many persons who have helped assemble the diverse material which has gone into the preparation of this book, including all who have been kind enough to send pertinent press releases, clippings, bibliographic references, conference programs, or who have graciously taken time out of busy schedules to give expert answers to persistent questions.

I must specially mention several members of the faculty of Pacific School of Religion, for comments and suggestions about the material in the manuscript stage. By the very nature of the material, we could not ask them to verify our research or to espouse all our ideas. The mistakes, as well as the interpretation of facts, are entirely the responsibility of the author. Substantial parts of the manuscript have been read by Dr. Georgia Harkness, Dr. Harland Hogue, Dr. Stilson Judah, and Dr. Charles McCoy. I would like also to thank Dr. James Muilenburg, who, as my major professor when I was a student at P.S.R., many years ago, first introduced me to the joys and disciplines of Biblical research; I sincerely hope that the path down which it has led me will not disturb him unduly.

For assistance with the chapters on the role of women in the church today, I am grateful to many staff members of the World Council of Churches, and the National Council of Churches, especially to Miss Frances Maeda, who has kept me supplied with clippings and copies of pertinent material from New York ecumenical circles, and to Dr. Madeleine Barot and members of her staff who have kept me abreast of developments from Geneva, Switzerland. Leaders of United Church Women and the heads of women's work in several American denominations have been helpful. Dr. Cynthia Wedel and Dr. Margaret Shannon brought me up to date on National Council of Churches plans to encourage co-operation between men and women. Mrs. Ethlyn Ross of the YWCA has been good enough to read and improve paragraphs about the YWCA. Dr. John and Anne Bennett of Union Seminary gave me hospitable shelter while I completed the last chapters of the manuscript.

To the University of California San Francisco Medical Center, and Dean Seymour M. Faber, I am tremendously grateful for the opportunity to attend various conferences, especially the one in 1963 on "The Potential of Women." The use of the facilities of Holbrook Library at Pacific School of Religion, of St. Margaret's House, U.C. Library, Berkeley, the Oakland and Berkeley public libraries, the Union Theological Seminary and National YWCA libraries in New York are greatly appreciated; I could write a special chapter on the knowledge and helpfulness of women librarians encountered at many places.

Members of the Women's Bureau, U. S. Department of Labor, in both Washington and San Francisco, have been encouraging, and reports from the President's Commission on the Status of Women have been invaluable. Mrs. Eleanor Roosevelt, during a visit by the author to Hyde Park in 1949, was one of the first to give encouragement to undertaking such a survey.

For a special genius of some sort for finding valuable reference books on the subject of women, hidden in uncharted archives, I especially thank my daughter, Mrs. Helen Peterson; also Miss Hazel Gillette who has helped with the reading. I also thank my granddaughter, Miss Valerie Peterson, for helping me read parts of the manuscript, as well as for her stimulating enthusiasm in regard to the subject matter. The first copy is for her, in the hope that the women of her generation will find a satisfying and creative role in the world of religion.

CONTENTS

INTRODUCTION

This is a book of record—an attempt to set down the main outlines of the story so far, and the dialogue to date, in regard to women in religion. We cannot be exhaustive; there have been too many interesting women in this field for that to be possible. We shall try to be comprehensive and furnish guideposts and references for those who wish to carry the study forward.

People anxious to establish once and for all the superiority of either sex are bound to be disappointed; it is only fair to warn them. We shall certainly discuss the relative roles of men and women, and consider the discrimination against as well as the favoritism for, either men or women in both religious and secular callings, at various times and places in the world's history; and we shall look for some sort of a pattern. We shall not talk about man versus woman, in organized religion or elsewhere, but of the potential service to God and society of both men and women working together. We shall not emphasize rights, but responsibilities.

We shall question, as pointedly as we can, why Christianity, which quite rightly boasts of its basic concern for women as persons, has often been so reluctant to accept their service to the Church on a par with that of men.

We shall find some very interesting women in the Bible, especially in the Gospels, but we promise not to hold up as an example *par excellence* for today's housewife that virtuous but overworked lady of Proverbs 31. We shall talk quite a bit about Paul, and how his actions speak far louder than some of the words attributed to him, of his good will toward women.

Our survey of the women of the major faiths other than Christianity must be sketchy at best, but will perhaps suggest further exploration. We acknowledge that our vantage point has been with American women of the Hebrew-Christian faith, but a glance at women in the history of other religions will help us see our own in perspective.

In regard to recent and current times, especially, we sincerely hope our readers will help us fill the gaps and add new material. The picture is changing so rapidly, and in general all for the good, that no volume can aspire to be definitive. Hopefully, we shall be able to find interest and inspiration—and perhaps a few warnings—in the picture to date.

We shall delve only very incidentally into the attractions and distractions that men and women seem to bring out in each other, leaving the psychologists to tell us why the clouds of envy and exploitation seem to have outweighed the joys of mutual appreciation, that day when the man first noted that the woman had soft, pretty curves (which the baby seemed to prefer to his own sinuous arms) and the woman noted that the male did have good strong muscles which would be mighty useful to have around the cave for lifting rocks, felling trees, and the like.

We shall ask whether we are, as some think, at the end of an historical cycle of male dominance, with the pendulum starting to swing much too briskly in the opposite direction. If so, is renewed ecclesiastical conservatism concerning women in religion going to help? Or is it possible that as men and women of good will study the matter together, we may find a way, in this new and challenging world of ours, to reinterpret the concept of our oneness, so that with neither man nor woman dominating or trying to dominate (by force or by wiles) we may live and work in harmony? Can we establish patterns of co-operation between the sexes in the churches that will suggest a pattern for all areas in which men and women work together, be it home, school, factory, office, laboratory, the realm of art, politics, or leisure-time fun?

This is no casual or temporary problem, and it is as important that we solve it as it is that we, pertinently, find a cure for cancer.

For the tensions and jealousies of one half of mankind in relation to the other half does have a cancerous quality that sends its tentacles into all our human relationships and is making it impossible for mankind (men and women together) to reflect our Creator-God and be worthy instruments in fulfilling his design here on earth.

In our day science is discovering its own rationale for equality (by no means identity) of men and women, and industry is rethinking its policies to make more use of the full economic potential of women. Established religious institutions of whatever faith have never been famous for initiating new and revolutionary patterns. They are more apt to put their stamp of approval and lend their strength to causes for which reckless individuals (within or without their membership) have already wagered their necks, their fortunes, and their reputations. Often the religious group offers such persons sanctuary. Often, in time, it adopts and defends their ideas. On the other hand, there is the recurring criticism, sometimes valid, that the religious institutions of the world fail to speak with anything like their potential authority, partly because they speak without first putting their own houses in order; partly, too, because, aware of the position in which this places them, they find rationalization for not speaking at all. The point has often been made by both Roman Catholics and Protestants that a divided Church has found it difficult to speak with authority to a divided and warring world. Non-integrated churches have been embarrassed in speaking on the question of racial equality. Most churches would find it very embarrassing to speak out on the place of women in today's secular world, a question to which the secular world is, however, addressing itself.

The trend toward better understanding and co-operation between men and women in our daily life and community seems to be established, reinforced by the findings of science and demands of industry. It is, however, in the less tangible field of human rights, interpersonal relations, and, most of all, perhaps, in religion, that the most is lost when women are not permitted to make their full contribution to society.

Obviously the study of "women in religion" presents some problems. The first, certainly formidable, problem is to define our terms. Anyone who ever tries to describe either women or religion in terms which will be universally acceptable is just too much of an optimist. We know a woman when we see one. We know religion when it touches our lives.

Obviously the more of an enigma woman is (like the Sphinx or Mona Lisa), the more durable and universal her popularity is likely to be. Similarly, religion which veils itself in the mystery of antiquity often seems to have a wider appeal than that which emphasizes contemporary relevance or a personal moral imperative. We like women, and we like religion, especially if they do not become too demanding. They are both "nicer" when pliable, and perhaps just a little vague.

Yet anyone who has been subjected even slightly to the spirit of modern science knows we should not try to carry on a discussion about the relation between two unknown factors. One, at least, should represent a stable frame of reference, from which to move on into unexplored areas. What can we say with conviction about (a) women, (b) religion?

What Is a Woman?

A century ago we had only what would now be considered elementary knowledge about biological chemistry, the workings of the human mind, sources of energy, and the mysteries of outer space. Today, comparatively speaking, we know a lot. In view of this demonstrated agility of the human mind, it seems we might be expected to know a good deal about women, who have been with us from the beginning, when we had considerable more time for interpersonal relations than we seem to have in the space age. Yet who would be so bold and foolish as to claim to know "all about women"? Until recent years, a great deal of what we "knew" was without much validity. Much was sentiment, some pure sentimentality. Some was diatribe. A lot was based on old wives'—or old husbands'—tales. As for women, as women, being suitable subjects for theological study, you cannot, even today, find the word woman in the index of most theological works. If you do, the references are usually negative. The Reverend A. Maude Royden of England, in her book *The Church and Woman*, speaks of the fact that "one must dig so deep to find so little" on the subject; "One searches through a volume to find it in a footnote." On the other hand, we have recently had word of a ten-year research project carried on by twenty-one scholars of a major denomination; they will, it seems, publish six volumes on marriage and family problems; but not one of the contributing writers or editors is a woman! Have women no competence in this field?

Because of the ambiguity of the English word "man," it is often difficult to find out whether we are talking about the male animal or the human being. Male scribes through the centuries have apparently not felt called upon to clarify the matter, so they have perpetuated semantic uncertainty which crops up even as we read the Bible, search for references in the Concordance, or try to find out what the early church fathers or present-day theologians have to say.

Hearsay is as much of a problem as this ambiguity. Dr. Royden herself follows the popular notion that "in no time and no country have women been seriously regarded as the equals of men." However, historian Mary Beard, in *Woman as a Force in History*, thinks this supposition is just one of those ideas that "everybody knows" and that the search must be carried far back into history to get the true picture of women's fluctuating status over the centuries, as related to current cultural patterns.

Moreover, where one hopes for history or objective analysis, one often finds outright propaganda, substantiated only by references to other equally enthusiastic propagandists. This, therefore, is a field in which an especially critical evaluation of the sources of authority is essential, if one is to achieve even reasonably objective findings. To quote even usually reliable sources may have the aspect of taking a "calculated risk."

What Is Religion?

In speaking about "religion," we have chosen the broadest possible terminology and hope it will always be evident whether we are speaking of (1) man's personal relationship to God, (2) his reflection of that relationship in dealings with his fellow men, (3) established institutional religion, (4) a semi-magic force to coerce nature and society, (5) an exclusive social group who have common ideas of decency and ethics, (6) a (frequently superstitious) belief in the efficacy of certain symbols and rituals, (7) a fellowship of the "righteous" in an evil world, (8) maintenance of contact with and tapping the power of the dead, (9) return to source of existence—loss of selfhood in the infinite, (10) a spiritual approach to co-ordinating all the values of life; or any combination of these or parallel definitions. Both men and women of various faiths will be found in most categories. Who will say what proportion of sociology and mysticism, boldness and meekness, authoritarianism and the prophetic voice, austerity and the aesthetic, syncretism and exclusivism, and a hundred other pairs of qualities, must be held in tension within our minds as we grope for some acceptable concept of religion?

Are Women First-class Christians?

If the idea of saying anything definitive about either women or religion is baffling, the idea of trying to discuss the two subjects together is appalling. Yet doing so may throw considerable light on both, and at least help to clear up a most puzzling and persistent prejudice: organized religion's apparent doctrine that women, while lovely and useful creatures, and certainly children of God in being bound by his moral and ethical laws, are *not* on the same basis as men when it comes to being first-class citizens of the religious community.

Men and women are both beginning to realize that a "battle of the sexes" is foolish and destructive for both sides. The more chivalrous as well as the more self-confident males are taking the matter seriously and admitting that somehow, soon, men and women must learn to do genuine teamwork, and they can only do this through mutual respect and appreciation, never by a program of coercion. The human race is, as a matter of fact, divided by another major cleavage which is on a par as to pervasiveness with the physical cleavage of male and female.

At least as important is the question of whether the individual's attitude toward religion and life is one of ethical co-operation or coercive domination. Coercion is, of course, not necessarily by physical strength. Each group and each individual has its own method of making other people do things its way: guns, money, power manipulation, social pressures, ridicule, flattery, the "economic squeeze," appeal to exclusive personal or group loyalty, snobbery. Women are inclined to pride themselves on being less coercive in their human relations because they do not use physical force. But herein (i.e., in their reliance on "maneuvering" others) we encounter a question of ethics of major proportions.

One of the most persistent myths in regard to man-woman relationships is that certain kinds of work and play are innately suitable for boys or girls, men or women, simply on the basis of sex, and that there is something "wrong" with an individual who cannot fit his or her talents into the "proper" category. However, the relatively new science of genetics seems to indicate quite different conclusions. We cannot go into the complicated though very fascinating science of genetics at this point, but a statement by Professor J. A. Jenkins, Department of Genetics, University of California, will make clear how very fallacious much of the "common knowledge" about inherited characteristics, and so-called male and female inherited traits, has been. It would now seem that there is very little difference in the potential tastes and talents which the infant boy or the infant girl may bring into the world; Dr. Jenkins explains the genetic inheritance in this manner:

"Each individual comes into the world with his or her own set of genes (thousands of them) that direct the individual's development from the fertilized egg to maturity. These genes are arranged in a linear sequence on 23 different pairs of chromosomes. One member of each chromosome pair is contributed by the mother and one by the father. As a consequence, each new individual receives two complete sets of genes, one member of each gene pair from the mother and one from the father. Of the 23 chromosome pairs, only one, the XY pair, is in any way related to sex. Males have an X chromosome that always comes from their mother and a Y chromosome that always comes from their father. Females, on the other hand, inherit one X chromosome from each parent, as is true for any other chromosome pair. Thus, with the exception of the relatively few of the genes located on the XY pair, each individual receives an equal contribution of genes from both parents."

The overwhelming majority of traits are no respecters of one sex or the other. Either the new boy or the new girl may come up with a happy combination of traits, probably any one of them contributed by either parent, which traits, together, afford a potential talent for music, knack for teaching, genius for scientific research, nose for news, or even an aptitude for religion.

Boys and girls start life about equal, physically. Girls develop somewhat faster at first, and language skills seem to come somewhat easier to them. In their late teens the boys tend to overtake the girls in physical development. This timing process is apparently sex-related.

Meantime, however, from the first day of life, family, friends, and the whole social structure begin to bring the pressures of conformity—according to that particular society's established pattern—to produce the prototype of what a "little man" or a "little lady" is expected to be. What would we think of a fond uncle who brought his favorite nephew a sewing basket, and his little niece a tool chest? Yet it is quite unlikely that ability to handle a needle or a saw are in any way sex-related traits which were inherited!

All this we need to consider before we say that women do or do not have a "natural talent" for religion. There is almost no possibility that either man or woman as such inherits a sex-linked package of genes that would insure his or her success in a religious career (whatever we mean by that!). At birth the number of boys and girls endowed with a reasonable number of traits useful in a life devoted to some sort of religious service would be about the same. But the social pressures that determine that the boys shall become preachers, elders, and trustees, while the women make the meat loaf for the church dinner, are deep-rooted and potent and are constantly strengthened by the reiteration that it has *always* been that way.

In 1963, at a conference at the University of California Medical Center in San Francisco, thirty-odd experts from various disciplines discussed "The Potential of Women." The reports, now available in book form, say very little about religion *per se* but furnish the scientific background which might well supplement this survey of the *history* of women in religion. Beyond what has already been said, we pause to mention only one specific finding:

An "animal behaviorist" on the conference program reported that the mother monkey who is made to feel insecure passes this feeling of insecurity on to her baby, whether male or female. This creates a climate of social frustration degrading to the whole troop. Let this, the conference was told, be a lesson to the human race. One cannot, we might surmise, downgrade women without downgrading the whole social structure in which they move—family, church, or state.

It is very interesting, from this standpoint, to trace the attitude of religion in general toward women, through the ages, and speculate on the psychological effects on human culture.

The Orante

To conclude our introduction on a more "spiritual" note, and recalling that a woman of mystery always has a special appeal, let us turn for a moment to a finding of archaeology.

One of the most persistent symbols found in the catacombs is a volatile little figure—always feminine—which appears on the tombs of both men and women. She is referred to as the Orans, or "praying one," and seems to represent the soul of the departed (man or woman) probably praying for those who remain. At first the praying ones were often Biblical figures—Noah, Moses, and Daniel were favorites. However, the Christian tombs of the first four centuries show some 150 of these unidentified little female figures, with the arms outstretched to the sides, forearms raised parallel to the body, the fingers spread wide, as if receiving power from an unseen source. Often the figures appear in association with Jesus as the Good Shepherd. In one case there are twin Orante.

Scholars frankly admit they do not really know the significance of the Orante, but for the early Christians, to whom the symbolism of the Resurrection was tremendously important, the Orans must have had very special meaning. Some writers have identified the Orans as the Virgin Mother. Another suggestion is that she represents the Holy Spirit, who, like the earlier Biblical figures, is defending the soul of the departed. The fact that they appear so often in association with the figure of Jesus as the Good Shepherd gives plausibility to the suggestion that the Holy Spirit was, in the first century, considered the feminine element in the Trinity by the Roman Christians. Or does the Orans represent the Church, likewise referred to by the feminine pronoun?

At any rate, why was practically all record of this popular and apparently very significant symbol lost? Was that her penalty for being feminine?

Chapter 1

THE AWAKENINGS

When did the human race become religious?

When did we first begin to think of our own strength in relation to the strength of the forces of nature which we saw about us and wonder, vaguely, if there was a connecting pattern? When did a person first feel the strange new sensation of gratitude for the starry stillness of the night or the warmth of the morning sun? When did he notice the dependability of seedtime and harvest? When, in some hour of dire need, did he first cry out to some unseen force outside himself? And were these first glimmerings of religious insight not granted to both men and women?

Religion has taken as many forms as there are things in the universe at which to marvel: the tree swaying in the wind, a gushing stream, a great stone, a mountain, a carved stick or a molten piece of metal, the sun or the moon, the stranger of unfamiliar size or complexion, a concept of a political state, or an economic regime. Many and varied have been the persons whom men have recognized as God's representative on earth: the priest who made the sacrifice (and provided the communal meal), the medicine man, the king, the conqueror, the soothsayer, the astrologer, the moral prophet, the Buddha, the Christ.

Many and devious have been the paths of religion, but the search for the knowledge of God, and the effort to discover the ways to his approval, the desire to relate ourselves to a beneficent force beyond our comprehension but in whose omniscience and omnipotence we can trust, and whose loving kindness we can experience and emulate—this quest is a common heritage of mankind. Theologically we may say that the Creator-God wills our return and we respond.

Quarrels over turns in the road, shattered hopes, less than worthy performances, weariness over the length of the climb, the rival lures of sensual indulgence, wealth, power, false idols or false prophets met along the way, the temptation to inertia or to accepting the *status quo*, quarrels over the source of revelation, are a few of the many causes which slow us down and send us on regrettable detours.

In spite of our differences, however, the desire to know our ultimate relationship to God and express our gratitude to our Creator is a compelling force that unites us, whatever diverse paths we take.

For all living creatures, there are two survival instincts—self-preservation and procreation. Man and beast and microbe find nourishment and develop a way of race or strain survival. Many and complicated are the patterns, but the basic instincts of the amoeba, fruit fly, mealy bug, or the human being are essentially the same. Primitive man finds a cave, the swallow builds a nest, the snail grows a shell, all to essentially the same purpose. And each, according to his own pattern, meets and breeds with its own kind, and in differing ways, and with varying degrees of success, attempts to secure the survival of its successors in the line of creation.

However, self-survival, or species survival, does not carry life very far along the evolutionary road. When did fear and awe begin to give way to trust—love—faith—worship? At what point are we aware of the Lord's presence walking in the garden in the cool of the evening—or traveling beside us in the early morning traffic rush? When does myth evolve into symbol, and rite into awareness of moral imperative? When does altruism begin to supplant acquisitiveness in human consciousness? When does man, emerging from the clay of isolation, first learn to think of God as a loving parent? When does he learn to call his neighbor "brother"?

We cannot reconstruct the first patterns of developing religious thought with any certainty as to time or place or exact circumstances. We do know, however, that reverence for and reliance upon some concept of deity has, since before the dawn of history, been the common heritage of mankind. No matter how benign his environment, man has never found himself sufficient, without such support, to cope with the universe in which he lives.

And, so far as we know, no religious insight has ever been the exclusive gift of one sex or the other.

From the earliest times, mankind probably lived in families. Woman bore the young, and it was she who stayed home and took care of them while the father went out to hunt for food. It was, therefore, usually the woman who had the task of tending the fire, which archaeological findings tell us was most often just outside the cave entrance. Around the fireplace, where the food was cooked, was, in effect, the family living room. When members of the family died, they were, often as not, buried in a circle around this same fireplace. Sociologists give various reasons for this, but the simplest one seems most likely—to keep them as part of the family circle.[1]

There is no one pattern, any more than there is any one timetable for the development of religion in different countries, but around the hearths of the world there was a coalescence and an attrition of many of the elements which grew into the various patterns of which we speak when we talk of primitive religious practices: the communal meal, the emphasis on family solidarity and continuity, ancestor worship, necromancy, the altar with its continuous flame, the ritual of family worship to ward off evil spirits and enlist the help of beneficent ones, the offerings to the spirits, the development of the communal meal into the ritual service, acts of thanksgiving for favors received from unseen sources combined with requests for the continuance of such kind treatment, and the hope for added favors.

It was undoubtedly the woman, home with the children, who kept the flame of the altar—center of a developing religious sense—alive.[2]

It was probably the woman, too, who at first accidentally, then with growing purposefulness, discovered that if a bit of grain was scratched into the ground near the cave with a stick, and left there, a miracle happened.[3] Her act of faith was rewarded by the grain she planted being multiplied many-fold. The woman, rearing the children, planting the grain, tending the fire, communicating with the children and the neighboring women by words, which still came hard to her husband (who did not have as much opportunity to practice speaking)—this woman surely had *mana*. She was magic, like the tree or the spring, or the flame itself. She was wonderful. She knew the way of unseen powers. She was the first priestess. She was also the witch!

But man had his own sort of *mana*. He had a strong voice, and wonderful physical strength. When he had learned to domesticate animals, and sacrificial creatures came from the stock pen instead of being trophies of the hunt, the idea of a male priest, strong enough to kill the creature ceremonially, came into vogue. The man's more mobile life brought him into contact with many new facts and experiences, which his mind struggled to correlate.

Communal religion is the aggregate of millions upon millions of human experiences lost in the mists of antiquity: the moment of individual awareness which cannot be shared with another, experience with one other person or in a family circle, group experiences related to primitive human culture, a developing sense of ethics, and the mutual trust which makes trade and commerce, and even conversation and written communication, possible.

When did mankind become *consciously* religious? Was it, as the primitive story of Noah implies, at a time when, saved by providence from some terrific natural calamity that threatened all mankind,[4] the handful of survivors, taking refuge on the mountaintop, spontaneously raised their arms in supplication and thanksgiving to some dimly perceived source of strength which had saved them when they knew they could not have saved themselves? Who can say?[5]

The Fertility Cult

Out of this background of primitive religion emerged simultaneously in various parts of the world two related developments of special interest for our present study: the fertility cult and divine kingship.

The fertility cult is not one special religion, but a very widespread and persistent way of looking at life. It seeks to force or bribe deity to "join our side."[6] Sympathetic magic, incantations, identification with a totem animal or plant famed for its fecundity or other admired trait—this is the way primitive man tried to charm good fortune to work on his behalf, to bring him good harvests and plentiful flocks.

The priest who served such a "religion" soon discovered that there were ways to make this calling profitable. The ceremonies and incantations became increasingly complex. Only the professional priest, properly recompensed, could do *exactly* what was required.

Elaborate magic formulas were devised to assure the fertility of the herds and the fields. Festivals became the occasion for sexual liberty between human beings, aimed—or at least rationalized—at assuring, by the process of sympathetic magic, a good crop of grain or grapes, in the field or vineyard where the human act took place.

In Canaan, where the food supply was largely dependent upon erratic weather, the fertility cult, with Baal and Anath as its chief god and goddess, had become firmly entrenched long before Moses led the Israelites from Egypt, and the older Scriptures are largely a record of the struggle between developing ethical monotheism of the Hebrews and the fertility worship of Baal and Anath of the Canaanites. Protest against fertility cult type of thinking was basic to the prophetic message.[7]

To what extent the "temple prostitute" found in many countries over a long period of time was an instrument for sympathetic magic to produce good crops and flocks and business, to what extent this practice was primarily a source of revenue for corrupt priests, and to what extent the temple prostitute was rationalized as a religious symbol, we do not know. Most ethical religions from a very early day frowned upon the practice, but it still persisted and was prevalent in many forms.[8] Could the attitude of revulsion which some churchmen feel concerning women taking part in a church service be a subconscious psychological protest against a racial memory of this ancient institution of the temple prostitute?

There is, however, no evidence whatever that all women connected with the temple were prostitutes; many seem to have been prophetesses, and in earlier days priests, musicians, healers, and teachers.

Nor should we think of all fertility cult rites as necessarily sex-related. The god Moloch, in the Near East, demanded the sacrifice to him, through fire, of the first-born, as a suitable offering to assure a stable foundation of a house or a city. In Carthage great walls have been unearthed with inscriptions that attest to a mass sacrifice of infants to this demanding god.[9] Of course this may have been related, sociologically, to population control.

A recent television documentary showed an amazing survival of a fertility ritual from a remote region of North Burma. In a mountain cave decorated with ancient paintings of the still-current ritual lives a giant cobra. On his good will, the primitive people of this area believe, depends the food supply and prosperity of the near-by valley. So once a year the people pay the snake a visit. He is served by a small, honored cult of virgin priestesses, some of them very aged. Only by a woman can the snake-god be propitiated. The oldest of the women offers fruit and milk at the entrance of the cave. When she has lured the snake out, she and the cobra go into a weird sort of ceremonial dance, swaying and twisting back and forth, while the rest of the villagers watch in charmed fascination. The priestess, displaying amazing agility, must actually kiss the cobra's head three times to insure fertility of the land. Two priestesses have lost their lives in the ritual in recent years, but the cult continues.

By its very nature the fertility cult found its greatest acceptance in those areas which were either agricultural or where the people were settled breeders of livestock. Moreover, where the fertility cult persisted, though the feminine principle may at times have been perverted, it was certainly not ignored. At its best it gave way to the concept of the great, beneficent, sustaining and all-embracing mother-goddess, who has taken so many forms in so many parts of the world, but who felt most at home in the softer climates, where established homes and agriculture prevailed, and where woman's homemaking and garden cultivation were prized. Later the fertility cults often developed into "mystery religions."

Kingship

Meanwhile, the migratory peoples of the world, the Bedouins, the hunters, the people on the march, war-minded tribes relying on physical strength or use of weapons, tended naturally to exalt the male. In the popular mind, their god took on the attributes of the male potentate. Out of their need for a strong and decisive leader and ruler, able to hold his own in battle, to give and enforce laws and regulations, maintain discipline in the camp, and when necessary invade the fertile lands and appropriate their produce to feed his own people, developed the institution of kingship—almost from the first *divine* kingship.[10]

The king became the symbol of his people; as he prospered, they would prosper; as he was virile, so also would his people and their flocks be virile. If he got too old, if the forays for food into the fertile lands failed, if, in general, things just went wrong, it was proper to kill him and get another king. This danger to his life was lessened as all things belonging to him became taboo, and as he became, himself, identified as a god. This pattern of kingship became almost global in its spread, and we shall see that it was not—for various reasons—a role in which woman was apt to be at her best.[11]

Mythology

Mythology had its beginnings in primitive—often fantastic—legends. In some countries it did not grow much beyond this point. In others it became a most intricate and sophisticated system of theology, including in its scope the most widespread materialistic interpretation of natural phenomena, sociology, psychology, and anthropology of a pre-scientific era. The vehicle, however—supernatural stories about anthropomorphic gods in their daily relationships—lacked the essential stability that a valid interpretation of the world of ideas demands. From the beginning, the ideas the philosopher-theologians were trying to express got mixed up with what human beings *do*. The characters were always getting out of hand and doing things at once more unpredictable and more interesting than their assigned roles in the family of gods called for. This was undoubtedly a humanizing if humiliating influence on theology. The problem came in the fact that then, as now, the average person seems to have been considerably more interested in the unpredictable, "spicy," and more or less irresponsible actions of the minor gods and "bad guys" than in the lofty sentiments of their more noble superiors. The "old gods," though honored, were likely to be considered pretty stuffy by the younger generation of mortals, who created a newer generation of gods with divine scruples more in tune with their own. "Reform" was likely to take the way of return to the "old gods." But somehow the younger gods had the appeal of being more vital and powerful, and more able to do special favors for the current crop of worshipers. It was not infrequent for gods who were doing well in one community to be imported and honored by a neighboring people.

The first myths were probably stories to explain local landmarks or customs, natural phenomena, place names, events in the clan's history worth commemorating and in which it seemed there might have been supernatural intervention. Why is the great rock in the middle of our village? (It is the dwelling place of a special goddess, who watches over our people.) Where does the sun go when it goes down? (Into a magic rowboat that takes it around the rim of the earth, to rise again in the east.) Who made mankind? (Men and women hatched from one primeval egg.) Why is this city called Hormah (Destruction)? (It was here that the god of the invading people handed over the cities of the land to their invaders for destruction.)

Charles Mills Gayley classified myth as (1) explanatory—e.g., of natural phenomena, (2) aesthetic—for amusement and often romantic, (3) interpretive—historic, philological, allegorical, theological (inculcating moral ideas).[12] A feature of the more developed myth is often the central hierarchy of gods, based on concepts of the human family and the culture of the community. Sometimes there is only one god or goddess (especially at the beginning) strictly attached to and responsible for the local community or the wandering tribe.[13]

One of the most persistent concepts of deity in human form was the concept of the primitive female being—"the Mother of the Gods."

Of the world's mythologies, the Greek is probably both the most familiar to Western ears and the most consistent. It is also one of the most sophisticated. There is little doubt that the Greeks—and the Romans also—knew precisely the true nature of mythology.

Far more impressive than the amorous tales of later, complicated days
are the early myths of "the beginning"—though these may impress one
as being much closer to pre-science than to religion. Gayley tells us that
in the earliest Greek myths, as presumably sung by Orpheus himself,
"Time was in the beginning—yet [Time] had no beginning." From
Time preceded Chaos, a yawning abyss of night and mist and fiery air.
Time, spinning mist around the fiery air, produced the huge world
egg. This egg divided into heaven and earth, while from its very
center emerged Eros, Love.

The Greek poet Hesiod says that after Chaos came "Broad-bosomed
Earth and Beautiful Love, who should rule the hearts of men." From
Mother Earth came "the starry vault of heaven," where the gods were
to take up their abode. Earth also brought forth mountains and
fields, the sea, plants, and animals. Then, as love stirred in the heart of
creation, things male and female came into being. Uranus (Heaven)
married Gaea (Earth) and they produced the Titans and Cyclopes.[14]
Furies, serpents, monsters, and nymphs followed in frenzied profusion.
Finally Cronus, a Titan, urged by his mother, Gaea, overcomes his
father, marries his sister Rhea, and they reign through innumerable ages,
bringing forth three daughters: Hestia—who became the Roman goddess Vesta (virgin goddess of the hearth and home); Demeter—Roman
Ceres (goddess of earth and crops); and Hera—the Roman Juno (prototype of the ideal wife and protector of women); they also have three
sons: Hades—Roman Pluto (Underworld); Poseidon—Roman Neptune
(Sea); and Zeus—Roman Jupiter (whom the gods themselves chose to
be their supreme representative). Zeus and his sister-wife, Hera, and the
other gods are installed on Mount Olympus. Hera and Athena (Minerva) help to overcome the giants who, like the Titans and other
monsters, are finally buried in the abyss of eternal darkness.

The "Great Gods" of Rome (before myth became popular fiction
too complicated to follow and too sex-submerged to elevate the mind)
were:

Jupiter and Juno;
Minerva, virgin goddess of wisdom, who sprang full-grown from
Jupiter's head;
Mars (war), Vulcan (fire), and Hebe (youth), children of Jupiter
and Juno;
Apollo (sun) and Diana (moon and chase), children of Jupiter and
Latona;
Venus (love and beauty), Jupiter's daughter by Diana;

Mercury (communications), Jupiter's son by Maia;

Vesta, Jupiter's eldest sister and first of the older generation of gods.

Vesta had a special place of honor and was served the choicest morsels on Olympus. It was from her altar, kindled by rays of the sun, that all the other gods received their fire. The earthly counterpart of her altar in Rome was tended by six vestal virgins—a very high honor. Vesta was reverenced as the oldest and worthiest of the Olympian deities and was served first at every feast. None of the normal celestial gossip was permitted concerning Vesta. The fires of her altar were extinguished by Emperor Theodosius in 380 A.D.

Gaea or Ge (Mother Earth), was also honored as the primitive mother of the pre-Olympian period; with her were associated her daughters Rhea (mother of the most important Olympian gods), her granddaughter Ceres (harvest), and her great-granddaughter Proserpina (the seasons).

Certainly anyone looking for hints of an early matriarchal element in Indo-European history will be interested in the above list.

There is no end of myths and they tell us a great deal about the status of women in the country where a particular myth prevailed.[15] In Sumeri, for instance, Inanna of Breck was particularly well known for her sexual love, fertility, and procreation. Her admirers got the idea of celebrating her marriage each New Year's Day—to the current ruler. One of her temple attendants stood in for the goddess.

The story of Lilith, so far as we can at present discover, came to Palestine from Babylon, where she was a powerful night demon. Probably some early theologian, toying with the concept of duality, introduced her into literature as Adam's first wife, before Eve came on the scene. She was cast out—or flew away—because she insisted on full equality with Adam.[16] Like Lucifer in another story, she became an evil spirit, her specialty being injuring newborn babies and children.

In Egypt, unusually complete records make it possible to compare the various beginnings that were eventually synchronized into one generally accepted myth.[17] There was one story that concerned Re, the sun-god, his Eye, the goddess Hathor, and the Heavenly Cow. Or there was the myth of the primeval ocean from which emerged the primeval earth hill, out of which crawled a beetle and a frog, earth's first life—a drama repeated yearly as the flood waters of the Nile receded. There was Hathor of Upper Egypt and the Heavenly Bull. There were local deities, and symbolic animals. And out of all this emerged the great myth of Horus the Elder, the force behind Egyptian civilization. Horus was generated through Atum, "the Hidden One," who also generated the male Shu and the female Tefnut, the air and water which support the sky; and from their union came Geb and Nut, earth and sky respectively, and their four children, the familiar Osiris, Isis, Seth, and Nephthys. Horus the Younger, the falcon, was the child of Osiris and Isis. He became, after many adventures, the true king and god, about whom the body of early Egyptian myth clusters. Not until his time do we see the male become dominant in Egyptian mythology. But in all the myths, the female gods, especially Isis, play an important and intelligent, if somewhat ruthless, role. However, new gods were now emerging and Amon-Re, who could be at once male and female, took on the aspects of the sun-god of the *universe*.

A tale of the Middle Kingdom tells of the ancestry of a line of rulers through Re and the wife of one of his priests. Queen Hatshepsut, standing squarely in the way of a trend toward male domination, claimed that Amon-Re, disguised as her mother's husband, had sired her. The child was fashioned, she said, on a potter's wheel, and Hathor, the cow-goddess, presented her to Amon-Re, who called her *king*. Special royal apartments for the birth of potential king-gods helped keep the royal birth myths alive till a late date.

There is a story, perhaps itself a myth, that it was Ikhnaton's emigrée mother who inculcated a monotheistic religion into her son at an early age and made him the first great monotheistic king in history, rejecting all mythology. At any rate, up until this time—shortly before the Hebrew Exodus—the Egyptian mythology certainly shows no particular desire to subjugate women; neither did the mother-goddesses over-emphasize their fertility aspect, as goddesses frequently did in Asia and Eastern Europe.

We cannot stop longer for even a casual look at the ancient myths. They are as varied as the people of the world are varied. Moreover, they are not of equal antiquity or equally serious value, so close comparison is not especially useful for our present study. Myths grow out of the experience of people. It should be noted that new archaeological studies are being made available so rapidly that it is certainly the part of wise scholarship to keep open minds till the experts give us more definitive conclusions.

A quick survey of available material, however, seems to indicate that the early myth of the main cultural groups honor perhaps first of all the great mother-goddess, often in her local manifestation,[18] and secondly the sun-god. Extreme honor paid to the older goddesses—notably Vesta of Rome—reinforces the speculation, being made with increasing frequency by reputable scholars, that there was, in an earlier period, if not a matriarchy, at least a civilization which gave precedence to women, in the Indo-European homeland from which so many migrations started. It was when migrations started that male leadership took over.

It is altogether possible that we have now passed the end of the pendulum swing to the male side. We hope that with less emotion and more sanity we may retard the accelerated swing toward female domination, but we doubt if the way to do this is to put new and heavier restraints on the females. The urge to dominate is a cultural phenomenon which intelligent men and women ought to be willing jointly to renounce, and the Church, at every level, could help.

The Goddesses

In *Hastings Encyclopedia of Religion and Ethics* is a most interesting treatment of "The Female Principle" by Dr. Edwin Diller Starbuck.[19] One fears that under such a title it may unfortunately have been overlooked by many scholars. Goddesses as patrons of cities, Dr. Starbuck tells us, rose and fell and sometimes, after a goodly rule, lost popularity and became extinct. This "twilight extinction," he says, occurred especially often in early Babylon, Syria, and among other nations that "entered upon an heroic program of world conquest." Such goddesses, "as if to complete the logic of this type of subjection," often changed their nature and became male gods. Others, patrons of less important villages, were absorbed by powerful neighbors, especially by Ishtar (and her equivalent, Astarte, of the Phoenicians). The weaker goddess, brought into competition with such powerful rivals, also "often suffers the humiliation . . . of serving as the patron of sensuality." However some goddesses, like Nana of Brech, fared much better, transplanted, than they ever had at home. Rome was especially fond of honoring foreign goddesses who represented a currently popular idea.

Goddesses, says Starbuck, are quite capable of doing anything, but usually the male gods are made of sterner stuff and win out where there is need for a ruler, lawgiver, judge, protector, conqueror. Goddesses symbolize "gentler and more heartfelt qualities" (Aurora of Greece, Ushas of India, or Freya, Scandinavian patroness of tender married love). Speaking of Minerva, in many ways the goddess *par excellence*, he mentions Alaghom Naom of Mexico—"she who brings forth the mind." Goddesses, he tells us, seem to have a "pervasive quality" which causes them to "burrow into the depth of things." They, therefore, fix destinies (like the Fates) or may be skilled magicians like Isis of Egypt. Because of their spiritual qualities, goddesses often act as intermediaries between man and the more unapproachable gods. In the Tantric religion of India, quiescent Siva is manifested through his creative female principle, Mahadevi, with a thousand names and a thousand forms.

There is, Starbuck says, "a myth, rather widespread, that the original creative principle is female . . . and another belief that woman alone is embodied with immortality."

Goddesses, though ethereal, are, like most women, practical, concerned with crops and household affairs. The Assyrian Ishtar is probably the most warlike goddess we know, though the intellectual Minerva as Pallas Athene could hurl a really terrifying thunderbolt. Usually, however, the goddess whose constituency became warlike had three choices: she could just "fade away," she could marry a male god of importance, or she could—and some did—change her sex. Contrary to popular belief, goddesses were not at all obsessed with sex, though there was certainly a relation between love and religion. Orgiastic revels were most often in the name of male gods—e.g., Bacchus, Dionysius, or Saturn.

"The large role that priestesses filled in early ritual and worship," Starbuck tells us, "is sufficiently explained on the grounds of the finer nervous organization of women and their capacity for more delicate emotional response and hence their special fitness to act as oracle-givers, witches, sorcerers, mediums, diviners of the will of the god."

There is no reason, he concludes, why women, or goddesses, cannot "hold the highest place" in religion. It depends on the social organization and the place of women in the social structure.

Chapter 2

THE OLD TESTAMENT

Modern Biblical scholarship, which during the past few decades has been adding so much to our understanding and appreciation of the Scriptures, has not as yet given us a soundly documented study of women's contribution to the Hebrew-Christian tradition. Otherwise reliable scholars traditionally neglect Biblical women, and what meaning their stories have for their time or ours. Lacking a reasonably complete and objective survey of women's contribution to the Hebrew-Christian tradition, we keep drawing our illustrative material from the same few female characters and the stylized concept of them as "very, very good" or "very, very horrid."[1] But the women we read about in the Bible were *people* (even as you and I). They had their virtues, their faults, their conflicts, their disappointments, their aspirations, their love, their faith. It is as *people* that we should like to know them, and though many interesting details of their lives have been lost in the telling and retelling (usually by male priests and editors) over a good many centuries, much remains to be revealed by an objective survey based on the disciplines of Biblical scholarship. Beyond this, however, the basic attitude of any culture (such as the Hebrew culture) toward its women is significant for an understanding of that culture.

For our present purposes we shall confine our inquiry to the women of the Bible who appear in the books which purport to be "historic," including the Pentateuch, which comes to us in the historic context of having been attributed to Moses, and such literary accounts as Ruth and Esther. It is difficult to know just where the border line lies between history and historic fiction, but we shall try to deal with this matter as specific instances arise, using all historic or semi-historic references which, taken together, seem to shed valid light on the "Biblical doctrine of women."

The lists of references in the notes may be skipped by readers willing to accept the author's summary evaluations, but we hope will entice some Biblical scholars, as well as laymen seriously interested in the role of women in religion, to further research.

Archaeology must always be a working partner of Biblical records, and, in the case of Palestinian women, archaeology offers us valuable material. The small clay female figures (commonly four to six inches in height) found in many Palestine sites, with their elaborate decorations and hair-dos in the changing styles of the times, the colorful gold and carnelian necklaces, the intricately fashioned bracelets and ornamental pins, the cosmetic jars and implements for applying the fragrant ointments, as well as novel household decorations and implements, seem to speak of a very comfortable place for Hebrew women over the centuries. How responsible and creative the women's lives were is a different question. This varied, apparently, from place to place and century to century, just as it would in our world today. We learn very little about women of any era by generalizing. Let us see if between the layers of pious editorializing, and a desert-inherited cultural mind-set on the part of male editors, we can discover something about the changing role of women as revealed in the early Scriptures.

There is little doubt that those years of desert life and generations of almost constant warfare developed a sense of male superiority among the Hebrews. Nomadic life does not afford woman the chance to make her valued contributions to home life, agriculture, education, and culture. When matters are dependent on strength or are being settled by force, woman's place in society is always at a disadvantage. We shall first try to sketch, in a somewhat orderly fashion, the rather favored place of women in patriarchal days, then the events which, by the time of the exile, brought men into a position of almost complete domination in Hebrew life and religion. Finally, during the exile and post-exilic period, we shall see some signs of revival that look ahead to a completely new attitude toward women in the teachings of Jesus. In studying our materials, we shall try always to keep in mind that the historic sections of the Old Testament, as finally edited, embody material from legendary days to the final contributions and redactions of the third century B.C. Our task is to see through the enthusiasms and prejudices of the male editors (often writing several centuries after the events they are discussing occurred), past their preoccupation with events and institutions of the moment, and try to construct a picture of how women fared in Palestine at the different stages of the country's culture, and what their relation to the Hebrew religion was, from the time Father Abraham and Mother Sarah arrived from Ur of Chaldea, to the time the prophet Nehemiah and the prophetess Noadiah hurled invectives at each other over the new wall of Jerusalem.

The Bible itself makes no claim for documentary records before the time of Moses (c. 1400 B.C.), and by that time the creation and antediluvian and even the patriarchal stories had had a long history. Few scholars would claim written historic sources earlier than 900 B.C. From then on, myths, traditions, legends, temple and court records, legal and ethical codes and manuals were collected, edited, and rewritten with emendations by the scholars and priests of the temple. The main "strands" of Biblical sources we find intertwined in the Old Testament are usually designated as *J, E, D,* and *P. J* represents the traditions of the southern kingdom, often recognizable by their use of the name YAHWEH or *Jehovah; E* represents the northern tradition, referring to God as Elohim; *D* is for the Deuteronomic editor of the seventh century B.C., and redactions made by the Deuteronomic school; *P* is for the priestly school of editors (sixth century B.C.). To these basic materials, compilers of the Old Testament eventually added prophetic writings, temple songs, historic tales, and the practical philosophy of the School of Wisdom. Chronicles (a rewrite to bring Hebrew history up to date), Ezra, and Nehemiah (essentially historic rather than prophetic) were added before 250 B.C. In other words, Old Testament history was writen, edited, and re-edited by many persons and represents many theological schools of thought prevalent during a period between 900 and 250 B.C. and relates (if we just go back to Abraham) to events covering more than our whole Christian era.

We must emphasize, and remind ourselves from time to time, that to simplify our presentation we are focusing our survey on those books which are generally referred to as "historic."

We must also remember that during much of the time this history was being produced the Hebrews were under great pressure of migration, invasion, captivity, and almost continuous war or threat of war. They were also under pressure from religious and political rivalry between the northern and southern kingdoms and religious quarrels with surrounding neighbors. We can only be amazed and awed that the Hebrew faith was able to emerge from these chaotic beginnings as the great world religion it became.

It is easy to see that there might be a considerable overlay of interpretation in the history produced under such circumstances. This is not to challenge the validity of the Scriptures, but rather to accept the challenge to search diligently for the *essential* truth. This interpretive overlay is at least as apparent in materials relating to the place of

women in religion as it is in the Scriptures as a whole. When we look
at any Biblical passage for what valid enlightenment it has to offer
about women, we will ask (1) just when the events are supposed to
have occurred, (2) who wrote the specific stories and when and why,
and (3) what events or circumstances might have influenced what
the writer had to say. We will also remember that it was very likely a
male priest who did the editing![2]

At the present time, moreover, a great amount of new material is
constantly coming to light, upon which there has not yet been time
for competent critical work. We can do little more than touch on the
existence of some of these new archaeological finds, leaving it to coming
scholars to correct, or verify and expand.[3]

Creation Stories

When the priestly leaders of the Hebrew people, during their exile
in Babylon, sought to keep the religion of their forefathers intact, in
spite of political oppression and hardships, by codifying their laws and
assembling their religious literature, the familiar Adam and Eve story
(now Genesis 2) was too persistent and popular to be ignored—and by
this time perhaps too theologically significant to be omitted. One can,
however, imagine the dilemma of the compilation committee. The
story of the garden, and the Lord who planted a tempting and forbidden fruit tree apparently just to test mankind's obedience, the conversations between Eve and the snake, the Lord's making clothing for
the pair out of fig leaves before sending them out into the cruel cold
world—surely this story, beloved as it was, was not the proper framework with which to open a dignified ecclesiastical manifesto whose
purpose it was to set forth forcibly and convincingly the great monotheistic basis of Hebrew beliefs, and to preserve for all generations the
religious insights of God's chosen people! Our compilers' committee
must have had many discussions on the pros and cons of the didactic
value of theological myth.

Yet the compromise solution was probably not too difficult, for the
Jewish people never hesitated to include apparently conflicting accounts
if both had some validity[4]; they were not obsessed, as we are today,
with consistency. The introduction, Genesis 1, was written—one of the
world's greatest literary and theological masterpieces of any day—as a
worthy framework for the materials which would be selected from the
Hebrew archives to represent the growth and meaning of the Hebrew

religion: the covenant with God and his care for his chosen people.

We can surmise with considerable assurance that Genesis 1:27 (P) does represent an official theological view accepted by the ranking theologians of the exile: "God created man in his own image . . . male and female he created them"—co-relative, equally responsible, equally manifestations of the one Creator-God. This God was not just one of a pantheon of gods, each representing a certain human quality. He combined *all* attributes, and in his own image created man and woman, who together reflected their Creator. To both and together he delegated his dominion over the earth.

The Eden story (Genesis, ch. 2—J), on the other hand, like many fragmentary accounts embedded in Genesis, represents legendary material, passed down through the centuries by word of mouth, treasured and loved for its symbolic meaning.[5] It had and still has the validity of true myth which, as Reinhold Niebuhr pointed out, may often be "more true than truth." Yet we can feel reasonably sure that it was not handed down to us through the centuries with any idea that we would regard it as historical or biological information.

We must, at this point, at least mention one novel recent interpretation of the second Genesis story, representing a really radical school of modern thought. Theodor Reik goes to great length to point out, in *The Creation of Woman*,[6] that the real *creation* story is the one in which God created mankind in his own image (Genesis 1), whereas the story in Genesis 2, he suggests, is really the story of Adam's initiation into manhood according to primitive rites. Into this story, he contends, elements of another creation myth have been intermingled, purposely to confuse the uninitiated (a device well known in primitive religion). Reik presses hard the analogy between this story and the rite of initiation of the adult male in many primitive societies—after which the young man is permitted to take his mate. Reik contends that the sequence was: the creation of man and woman—companion and co-equal—by God who is both male and female; then at the time of Adam's initiation into adulthood, he is given Eve as a *wife*. The rib story, he says, is a very clever device. In an era when the mother-goddess under various names pervaded much of the world, and in several instances, as primeval deity, was supposed to have given birth to a son who became her spouse, the male-minded desert tribes needed a comparable story which gave the male rather than the female precedence in the order of creation. For many highly symbolic reasons, the creation of Eve out of Adam's rib was acceptable. It is, according to Reik, a reflection of subincision which is practiced in many primitive rites, in which the boy (allowed for the first time to enter the "men's house" of the village) is drugged into a deep sleep during which he is supposed to "give birth" to the man he is to be. The Genesis 2 story, says Reik, relieves a male sense of inferiority because only Eve, the "Mother of all Living," can bear children. If Eve herself was taken from man's body, they start their careers more nearly even. If this was the idea, it was certainly effective, for it seems to have kept the Eves of the world more or less in their place for some 3000 years.

In justice to Reik, he is quick to disclaim infallibility. He hopes, he says, only to open the door for a more profitable study of the material under survey.

Without turning to Reik, however, we may note from the Scriptures that when we stop looking at texts and words, and search for ideas, the over-all impression we gain is that the theologians of the sixth century B.C. perceived that it was when man and woman forgot their essential unity in God, and began dwelling on their differences and envying each other, that trouble began.

It is interesting to note that the antediluvian stories of Genesis 4 (J—perhaps written down in the ninth or the eighth century B.C.) give the names of women as well as men without prejudice, and it is thought worthy of note that Lemech (v. 19–24) had *two* wives, Adah and Zillah, and made what may have been the first public proclamation of male superiority. However, in the generations of Adam as recorded in Genesis 5 (P), to which Biblical scholars assign a date several centuries later, only men, not women, have names and personalities. Sons are listed by names, but the genealogical notes mention only the fact that "daughters" also were born.

The Women of the Patriarchs

The so-called patriarchal period stories show women with all the normal rights of "persons" and as loved and cherished members of the family. We give credence to this picture because "nothing special" is made of it. It is obviously *not* propaganda: the way women are treated just shows through the rest of the story. This is the most reliable kind of witness in ancient documents. Edith Deen counts 125 "named women" in her book *All the Women of the Bible*.[7] Thirty are named in Genesis, if we count Lot's and Potiphar's wives.[8]

Sarah, Rebecca, and Rachel are as well known and honored as their husbands, Abraham, Isaac, and Jacob. Sarah has no hesitancy about talking with strangers who come to their tent (Genesis 18) (she had no idea at the time they were angels), nor about having her own dealings (though the account is very confused) with King Abimelech (Genesis 20). The story of Hagar, Sarah's Egyptian maid, being given to Abraham first at Sarah's own suggestion, because Sarah considered herself unable to bear children, then later being sent away because of her mistress' jealousy (though Hagar's rights were protected, too), and other passages seem to indicate a society in which women controlled the marriage situation. Both Hagar and Keturah, Abraham's "other wife" (ch. 25), become, like Sarah, mothers of many peoples.

Rebecca of Nahor was certainly in control of the marriage situation when *she* married. She makes arrangements for a strange visitor (though he does bring family credentials), met casually at the community well, to come to her parents' home to spend the night, then runs back to her *"mother's"* household to tell her what she is arranging (24:28). Beuthel, her father, hardly makes a suggestion during the whirlwind courtship.

With her sister, some girl friends, and the aging nurse Deborah, Rebecca sets off with the stranger, to go to a prospective husband in a far country (24:61). And there is not a breath of scandal! The choice of whether to go or not had, moreover, been left specifically to her (24:58).

There does not seem to have been a radical division of labor as between men and women in the household. Either could be a shepherd, and Rebecca and Laban, her brother, share farm chores and hospitality. Later, Rebecca seems to have taught both her sons to cook (25:29; 27:31)! Rebecca turned out to be quite a manager—she managed to get the blessing (and inheritance) of Isaac for her favorite son, Jacob, though it was certainly a tricky thing to do, and having, like her husband's parents, no liking for the Canaanite women, she sent her son back to her own home town for a wife, from the family of her mother's brother.

The story of how Jacob served his prospective father-in-law, Laban, for fourteen years to win Rachel and Leah (and their two maids Zilpah and Bilhah, by whom he also had children) is well known. Just what these stories mean in terms of migrations and cultural history over a period of several centuries, we may never quite untangle. But in the telling, as it comes down to us, through the earliest (J) materials, the women have key parts, and we are led once more to suspect that the Eastern culture from which the early Hebrew migrations originated did not share the later Jewish ideas of male dominance. Certainly

Rachel's manipulation of her father's household gods, for possession of which she outwitted her father (to report the matter in the kindest terms possible), does not represent the way we would expect a dutiful daughter in a patriarchal family to act.

In these early stories women are buried with honor. A great deal is made of Sarah's death (ch. 23) and the negotiations for her burial cave at Machpelah. Later we shall find a too brief but poignant vignette of the beloved family nurse, Deborah, being buried at Bethel, under the "Oak of Weeping" (35:8).

The last of the so-called patriarchal stories involving a woman is the story of Dinah, only daughter of Jacob and Leah (30:21, ch. 34). The family is now living at the ancient city of Shechem—a city on the main east-west Canaan highway. Here Abraham had long ago set up an altar outside the city gates—as was apparently a custom with visitors to this tolerant city—to the God whom he worshiped.

Now Dinah, setting out one day to get acquainted with the women of the district, met the young son of the ruler of the city. The young people apparently fell in love: the report was that Dinah had been "defiled." The young man insisted that he was truly in love and wanted to marry Dinah, and with her apparent consent a marriage was arranged. Jacob made the condition, however, that the men of Shechem all accept the rite of circumcision. This rite was performed, and it was agreed that in the future intermarriage would be permitted. However, before Dinah's marriage can be consummated, her brash brothers return from the fields where they have been working and take matters into their own hands. In a fine rage of piety, they kill the prospective bridegroom and his companions. Jacob, disgraced by his sons' bad faith, leaves the area and goes to live at Bethel. His name is changed to Israel.

We hear no more of Dinah, nor do we meet any more of these comfortable, self-confident patriarchal women. We get the idea that we have somehow reached the end of an era—or at least a crossroads. However, the interpretation which would tell us whether the big problem was intermarriage, circumcision, precedence as between the northern sanctuaries of Shechem and Bethel, or some more political matter, is lost in confused sources and much editing.

Dinah, Jacob's only daughter, might be the key to considerable history, if we only understood all about her.

With her brother Joseph's arrival in Egypt, we meet women of a very different culture from the Hebrew wives and daughters, though of course we must remember that we are seeing both kinds of women through Hebrew eyes, which may make a difference.

The story of Jacob's unfortunate acquaintance with Potiphar's wife (39:7-20), which nearly wrecked his future, is generally considered to be fictitious, since it is an almost exact counterpart of a thirteenth century B.C. Egyptian "Tale of Two Brothers"; scholars say it was probably added to the Joseph story for "local color" and a plausible explanation of why we find Joseph in jail. But the picture of women as women—as persons—still shows through. In Egypt, also, it seems that women had considerable freedom of action, but perhaps not the same standards of moral ethics as the Hebrews had.

In Egypt Joseph married Asenath, and by her had two sons: Manasseh (forgetfulness), so named because now Joseph claimed to have forgotten all his former troubles and even his father's home; and Ephraim (fruitfulness), since God had made Joseph fruitful in the land of his misfortune. Asenath was a very important Egyptian woman. Her father was Potiphera, priest of On, or Heliopolis (Genesis 41:45-50; 46:20). The temple of Heliopolis, the City of the Sun, was the center of worship of the powerful sun-god Re (later the all-powerful Amon-Re), whose priesthood was very rich and influential. Joseph's marriage to Asenath was an excellent match for the young man, probably the social event of the season, and we are told that his fame spread throughout Egypt.

(See special note A on additional Biblical texts, p. 303.)

The Days of Moses

The debts of gratitude which Moses owed to the women of his early life are amazing. There was his mother, Jochebed, stanchly refusing to obey any ruler's edict that imperiled her child's life. There were those unsung Hebrew midwives, Shiphrah and Puah, who were under orders to report all births in the Hebrew colony, so the male babies could be destroyed; but Shiphrah and Puah were not above a bit of civil disobedience in the name of humanity. It seems that when a Hebrew child was about to be born, they never could get there in time to witness the birth and make a report. Hebrew women, they told their government supervisor, had such quick and easy births! And so the baby Moses lived (Exodus 1:19).

There was Moses' sister Miriam who, as a child, guarding her brother and using her wits to negotiate with the Egyptian princess for his royal upbringing, seems to have shown some of the sagacity that later made her a prophet in her own right, Moses' confidante, and an active participant in the religious worship of the Hebrews (Exodus 15:20).

There was the Egyptian princess who raised and educated Moses and made him a prince.

There were the seven shepherdess daughters of Jethro, to whom Moses was so gallant, and one of whom, Zipporah, he married but later divorced.

There was his brother Aaron's wife Elisheba.

There were the Hebrew women who took up the door-to-door offering to finance the Exodus (Exodus 11:2, 12:35).

It was a much later generation (700 to 800 years later, as a matter of fact) which attributed to Moses the codes of law dealing with regulations in regard to selling one's daughter as a slave (Exodus 21:7), ritual uncleanliness (Numbers 19), parental compensation for a virgin seduced (Exodus 22:16, 17), death for a sorceress (Exodus 22:18). Issuing codes and prophecies or even poems under the name of a venerated predecessor, to give authenticity to the material, was a custom of the time not unlike our literary device of ghostwriting. However, whatever authenticity Moses' name may have given to the later legislation, the legislation does *not* reflect conditions, or the community's attitude toward women in Moses' own time. This same priestly edited material from the later days also gives a tremendous build-up to Aaron and his sons as a priestly line and indicates the "unblemished male" sacrifice as the only one acceptable to YAHWEH (Jehovah). To ascribe laws and customs to earlier periods gave them more status than recent innovations would have had.

There is no mention of any service women can perform in the tent of meeting in the codes and regulations of the P (priestly edited) material. The editor seems to have had little doubt that the Hebrew religion of the desert days had already become formal, legalistic, male dominated, with the full approval and personal authority of Moses himself. Certainly, however, the laws which Moses deemed suitable for the wandering horde who came out of Egypt must have been changed, expanded, and adapted to many new conditions through the centuries before they were all fully codified. Any student of English common law and its relation to modern codes of American states, for instance, can understand how this would be so. It is impossible to say at what point male domination became an indisputable fact—as it most assuredly did—during and following the Exodus. Such cultural changes are usually recognized only at a later date, in the light of history.[9]

In one of the early traditions about the Exodus (Numbers 12—E?), Aaron and Miriam make common cause against Moses. They accuse him of getting to be too dictatorial. Whether, like Adam, Aaron put the blame on the lady, we do not know, but, as the story was later told, it was certainly the prophetess Miriam whose position was downgraded by the incident, and who found herself suddenly threatened with leprosy, presumably as a punishment for her impertinence. Neither Aaron nor Moses, it seems, had bargained for anything so drastic, and on their appeal to the Lord she was just temporarily ostracized. Aaron goes scot free without even a rebuke, and the question of whether there was any justification for the charges against Moses is not even discussed.

As a matter of fact, we gather that there was more than one revolt of the laity during the wilderness journey (Numbers 16, 17). In times of migration and invasion, when physical strength is at a premium, a combination of supreme leader and priest (or a combination of military might and priestly sanction) is hard to withstand. The Lord does, however, always seem to have a minority at hand to make a witness at the proper moment, and that minority *can* be female!

When the Promised Land was being parceled out to the tribes, such a protest was heard from the five daughters of Zelophehad, great grandchildren of Gilead. Perhaps they felt strength in numbers. At any rate, Mahlah, Noah, Hoglah, Milcah, and Tirzah were not about to be deprived of their portion of land (and set a precedent for other women who would be expected to accept such treatment without protest). Their father was dead and they had no brother to speak up for the family's share, so the girls themselves made their protest before Moses, Eleazer (Aaron's successor), and the chieftains of the tribes, establishing (after Moses had consulted the Lord) the female right to participate in property inheritance (Numbers 27:1–7), a right that was to stand women in good stead for all time.

It is interesting that in the Deuteronomic account of the Exodus, which was probably written in Shechem, capital of the northern kingdom, shortly before 621 B.C., no women are mentioned except in the statutes (ch. 21–25), but whether this is because women are taken for granted, ignored, or edited out of the report by some priestly redactor is a question to intrigue Biblical scholars for a long time to come.

Pioneer Days

With the possible exception of the Persians, the Hebrews developed
what may have been the most pervasively male culture in the ancient
world. YAHWEH (Jehovah) had no female counterpart; he became a
definitely masculine god served by a male priesthood and continually
at war with the Baal-Anath fertility concept of the Canaanites in the
land he had helped his followers to conquer. It is easy to see how
the result might be a continuous downgrading, by the priests of
YAHWEH, as the Hebrew religion developed, of any active place for
women. At the same time, the strong sense of family solidarity born
from years as a minority group in Egypt, and the hardships of the
desert, as well as from a vestige of the earlier religion in which
women had an honored place, kept the wife and daughters in the
home protected and appreciated and assured them always some semblance of independence.

We are not sure exactly what the religion of the Hebrews in Egypt
was just prior to the Exodus. The patriarchs, the Canaanites, and the
more orthodox priests, as well as Ikhnaton of Egypt, had probably
all contributed; yet perhaps in the end it had become for most of the
people a rather primitive religion of nature and magic. The ethical
(and footloose—never attached to just one place or city) YAHWEH was
presumably not known to them till he revealed himself to Moses in
the Midian desert. There is evidence that even the Semitic rite of
circumcision, important in patriarchal days if we can judge from the
story of Dinah, had been forgotten in Egypt, to be re-revealed with
other aspects of the Hebrew faith by Jethro, priest of Midian, and
his daughter Zipporah, at the proper time (Exodus 4:24-26).[10] The
whole question of circumcision is one on which we need much light.
What was the original meaning to the primitive societies which practiced it? How did it become the mark of a good Jew in full standing, which of course no woman could hope to attain? It seems likely
that the practice of circumcision and its ritual importance in Hebrew
life made it possible for the Hebrew male to keep his women, on
religious grounds, "in their place" through the centuries. It represented
male exclusivism at an even more fundamental level than it represented
Semitic exclusivism. The Gentile male could submit to the rite. But
for the woman the die had been cast at conception. Given circumcision as the basis for participation in the covenant of a theocratic

community, it is rather easy to prophesy what trend women's destiny would take in the Promised Land.

The books of Joshua and Judges tell about life in early Palestine after the arrival of the Hebrews. Actually Joshua has almost nothing to add to our study of women. Caleb gives his daughter Achsah to Othniel for winning a war (15:16) and Joshua confirms Moses' decision as to the property rights of women (17:4). Otherwise, it is a book of, by, and about men.

The book of Judges is another matter. Most Biblical scholars agree that, except for the introduction (1:1–2:5), this is not so much formal history as a collection of folk tales about pioneer days in Palestine, and as such a mine of information about how people lived and thought. One suggestion is that these tales were compiled in the sixth century by an editor of the Deuteronomic school, but the humorous— at times shockingly so—content of some of the legends surely cannot be Deuteronomic! Also, Deuteronomy ignores women, whereas many of these tales make them either the heroes or at least the people who have the last word in the argument. Where the woman does not win out, the terrible treatment she receives, or the pomposity of the male, suggests that these stories just might have been compiled by a woman, writing in the Deuteronomic style, and could even be a satirical protest against the growing subjugation of women.

There are only twenty-one chapters in the little book—a most interesting short evening's reading, and more instructive than most modern rewrites. For the women's point of view begin with chapter 4.

Deborah, Delilah, and Micah's Mother

First there is the story of Deborah (ch. 4–5), wife of the otherwise uncelebrated Lappidoth. Deborah, we are told, was governing Israel at the time of the story. She is probably reasonably historic. From her home in Tomer-Deborah (apparently named for her) near Bethel in Ephraim, she decided that it was high time that the Hebrews pulled themselves together and made a stand against the militarist, Sisera, who was dominating the country to no good ends. She sent for Barak from neighboring Naphtali. He is willing, he says, to fight Sisera, but only if Deborah comes along. She says naturally she will; she warns him that it is by the hands of a woman that Sisera is going down. Either Deborah has foresight, as well as being a judge, warrior, statesman, prophet, and poet, or she and Jael, wife of Heber the

Canaanite, have made some plans of their own. At any rate, Sisera, hard pressed in battle, retires to Jael's tent for a rest, and, while he sleeps, she drives a tent peg through his head.

After that the king of Canaan is pressed harder and harder by the Hebrews, till his forces are at last destroyed. It is interesting to note from the lists of Hebrews by tribes which is given in the first chapters of Chronicles that it is the tribes of Israel, Ephraim, Benjamin, and Naphtali (who participated in Deborah's undertaking) who are most conscientious about reporting the women in their genealogies. Were women in these tribes appreciated, and so amounted to something? or was it because they amounted to something that they were appreciated? (See note B, p. 303.)

The next story of women in our little book is about the woman of Thebes (Judges 9). Helping to defend a tower in which the people had taken refuge during a siege of their city, she tosses a millstone on the head of the ambitious Abimelech (bent on setting up a kingdom). Disgraced that he has been bested by a woman, Abimelech gets a servant to run a sword through his body before he dies.

There is Jephthah's daughter (ch. 11). Her father has made a rash vow that if he is successful in battle against the Ammonites, he will, upon his triumphant return home, give to the Lord, as a burnt offering, the first person to come out of his home to meet him. The slaughter on the battlefield is prolonged and bloody. Jephthah carries it on into twenty cities; the Ammonites are roundly defeated. However, when Jephthah, weary at last of fighting, returns home, there coming out of the house to meet him is his little daughter, shaking her tambourine and dancing a welcome to him. Sorrowfully he explains to her his vow, and she comforts him, fully understanding that such a vow must be kept. She requests only a short reprieve to "roam the mountains and bewail her maidenhood" after which she returns to her destiny—to become a burnt offering to the Lord. It is a terrible story. Did Jephthah's god really demand *this* kind of loyalty? Why didn't he save this virgin *daughter* of a loyal devotee, as he had Isaac when Abraham was confronted with a similar problem?

Women seem to dominate the life of Samson (ch. 13–16); yet with his tremendous physical strength, his insatiable fondness for telling silly riddles, and his impetuous temper, we would hardly describe him as a ladies' man. His mother took particular pains to bring him up (in accord with an angel's instructions) to be a Nazirite, who never shaved, who let his hair grow long, was extra careful about dietary laws, and drank no alcoholic beverages. To prepare her son for his career, his mother was also admonished to observe the same dietary laws during her pregnancy, "for the boy is to be a Nazirite to God from conception to the day of his death." There is no doubt of Samson's physical strength. He uses it freely to overcome the Philistines. And his wit seems to have had appeal for the people of his day. His downfall was in the hands of women. His first wife, a young lady of Timnah, gave away his very best riddle, causing Samson to lose a bet and, to put it mildly, his temper. Before the episode was over, he had lost his wife to a rival, and finally to death in a fire started in his father-in-law's home by the Philistines. Samson did not fall in with his father-in-law's idea that he interest himself in a younger sister of the family. An affair with a harlot of Gaza is simply incidental to his career as a strong man able to pull up the city gates and carry them up the nearest hill on his back. Then he falls in love with Delilah, only to be tricked again—this time into revealing the source of his strength—his hair—and to have Delilah betray him by having it cut off as he sleeps with his head in her lap. Who knows what the meaning and moral (if any) of the Samson cycle of stories is? Never trust a woman? Never underestimate the resources of a woman? Is it a travesty on the idea that women and religion (even the strict religion of the Nazirites) simply don't mix? Or is the author suggesting that these women Samson knew represent the only types of women recognized by narrow-minded religionists, who seek to exclude all women from any active participation in religious services? Are the roles of the mother, the wife, the harlot, the faithless temptress, the only alternatives open to women? Are these the destinies among which God gives her the freedom of choice—and only these?

Micah's mother, in Ephraim, has raised a very spoiled boy (ch. 17, 18). He steals from her—1100 shekels of silver. However, when she utters a curse on the money, he becomes frightened and confesses, returning it to her. "Blessed," says his mother, "is my son in the Lord." Since the money he has stolen is still under her curse, she cannot use it for him or for herself. To remove the curse, or circumvent it, she decides the silver should be melted down and made into a molten image, to supplement the one Micah himself has carved for a shrine in his house. Then they adopt a migratory Levite to act as their priest. However, some wandering people from the tribe of Dan carry off both the images; moreover, they persuade the priest himself that it will be to his advantage to go along with them. It is indeed shocking to learn that this idol-tolerating priest is the purported grandson of Moses. When the Danites and the priest finally settle, they install the image which Micah has carved in their sanctuary at Shiloh, a sanctuary against which the author of the story seems to reveal more than a normal prejudice. We do not hear what happened to the molten image—perhaps it was melted down into coinage again.

A thing that interests us is the degree of local autonomy, probably especially in rural areas, during these pioneer days before centralized government and worship were established and when "everybody did as he pleased." In Ephraim, at least—for better or for worse—women might still apparently act and express themselves in religious matters.

The Crime of Gibeah

The crime of Gibeah (ch. 19, 20) is one of the most revolting stories of Biblical literature. Perverted Benjaminites, living at Gibeah, demand that a man of that city turn over to them a chance male guest. To quiet them, the host offers instead the guest's consort who is accompanying him, or the resident's own virgin daughter. He cannot, he explains, violate hospitality to his chance male guest! But the perverted Benjaminites scorn the offer of the women. Finally the guest literally throws his consort to them, and in the morning he finds her dead at the door. In dramatic indignation, he cuts her body into twelve segments and sends the pieces to the tribes of Israel, to enlist their help in eradicating such crime from the land. The tribes rally to the call, but the tribe of Benjamin stands by its kinsmen, and bitter fighting ensues before the Benjaminites are overcome. The other tribes swear not to give any of their daughters in marriage to Benjaminites. However, they cannot long endure this break in the fellowship of the Hebrew tribes, and they realize the Benjaminites must have wives. The tribe of Jabesh-gilead (the only one which did not respond to the call to arms) is raided, and their daughters captured and given to the Benjaminites, who are also given permission to capture others at the wine festival of Shiloh.

Two short paragraphs inserted among these stories tell of Ibzan of Bethlehem who brought in thirty wives from outside his clan for his thirty sons and married thirty daughters to men outside the family (12:8, 9) and Abdon, who had forty sons and thirty grandsons, who rode seventy saddle asses (12:14).

Much of this material from Israel's pioneer days, even as later edited, seems primitive and crude. So undoubtedly was life for these early settlers. How important to establish law and order! and develop standards of personal morality! Moses, Joshua, Caleb, Gilead, and other great leaders of the migration period had provided inspiration and given a vision of a great theocracy. Later the priests and jurists and the scribes and historians would develop these ideas into a system of law and government and establish formal religious practices, attributing much of what they did (for instance the priestly codes) back to the founding fathers.

During these centuries in-between, however, the job of the pioneers was to keep alive, perpetuate the family, find ways of getting along with their new neighbors, subdue violence, and hold fast to a few basic principles such as monotheism and human integrity, under the terrific pressures and temptations and hardships. People had to learn to make do with what they had, establish new communities, and implant solidly in these new communities the values they themselves had not yet learned to express or explore with clarity—the ideas back of the whole idea of setting out for the Promised Land in the first place.

The Story of Ruth

For such a time and task, we know from our own pioneer days that women are indispensable. We are grateful for this glimpse of their activities in Palestine (whatever the literary framework in which it has come down to us) before institutional patterns colored the picture almost beyond recognition and cast women in an increasingly insignificant role.

The story of Ruth, from this same period, is undoubtedly one of the most beloved, in our own day at least, of any that we have in the Scriptures. This, too, is laid in the time of Judges (Ruth 1:1), but it is in a very different manner from the reckless folk tales we have just been reading. It is a lovely literary idyl about Naomi and her two daughters-in-law, Orpah and Ruth. All had lived and been widowed, in the land of Moab, Ruth's native land. We find Naomi, the two younger women accompanying her, returning to her home in Bethlehem. Naomi urges them to leave her and return, each to her own people, to find husbands and establish new homes. Orpah follows her advice, but Ruth clings to her mother-in-law and, in words that have become symbolic of loyalty and devotion, cries, "Entreat me not to leave you . . . for whither thou goest I will go . . . thy people shall be my people, and thy God my God." We all know the story of how Ruth, shyly gleaming in the fields of the great

Boaz, found favor with this distant relative of Naomi's husband, and how, with Naomi's advice, she found protection and love and eventually marriage to Boaz. Involved in the story is a sort of "test case" of the levirate marriage law when a "next of kin" does not take up the option to buy the land and marry the widow of a deceased relative. Boaz, whom by now we have certainly learned to trust as an upright man, is very meticulous about establishing the correct procedure. There is also suggestion of a sort of adoption rite in relation to Naomi, which would make her officially part of the new family. As to just what is involved here, we can only speculate, but some such arrangement in the pioneer community would seem probable and desirable.

The son of Ruth and Boaz is, according to this account, Obed, father of Jesse, father of David.

Scholars usually agree that the story of Ruth is historical fiction, written around 400 B.C., but laid in Israel's pioneer days. Probably it does not give us a very authoritative picture of pioneer Palestine, many centuries earlier, any more than some of our twentieth-century epic movies re-create an authentic history of the early Christian era. One thing the story of Ruth has proved to be through the ages— propaganda of a most effective sort for the kind of woman approved and admired by the generations of priests and scribes of the Jewish religion in the centuries just prior to the Christian era—loyal, submissive, agreeably dependent, relying almost entirely on marriage and children to fulfill their destiny and give them status in life; never bothering about such concerns as human dignity, community welfare, politics, and least of all about either the formal manifestations or the theological aspects of religion. Ruth seems strangely foreign to her near-contemporary Deborah. Deborah was the more exciting, and probably the stronger character. But it is Ruth, not Deborah, who through the ages has dominated a good deal of churchly thinking as to what nice women should be like.

Under the Rule of Kings

The records we have from the days of the kingdoms give very little information about women. The available documents are either temple or court records or biographical notes about important people long since deceased. Neither the Deuteronomic or priestly editors were much interested in women, and apparently the women didn't do much to interest them. Women were wives, concubines, harlots, or mothers of famous or wicked men. And except for the literary frame-work of Samuel and Kings—a sort of verbal libation to YAHWEH —these books contain only an occasional incident which is of primarily religious significance. The records are non-ethical, and so are many of the main characters. The most celebrated kings display personal morality that is alarming, and any sense of community responsibility is a rarity. The ruler is judged not so much by his ethics as by the number of Baal altars he tears down and the number and splendor of YAHWEH sanctuaries he erects.

If these records from the days of the kingdoms have little to say about women, it is equally true that they have very little to say about the common people and their problems. The Elijah-Elisha stories come from an independent source that somehow got edited into this historic material of Kings, and these Elijah-Elisha traditions offer one of our few opportunities to meet some live and interesting women and get some insight into the everyday life of the times.

Only the introduction of Nathan gives recognition to the school of the prophets who at this time were demanding a moral social order. It is surprising to realize that Amos, Hosea, Isaiah of Jerusalem, and Micah had all made their protest before 700 B.C. There is, indeed, a magic-working prophet Isaiah (II Kings 20:7) who prescribes a cure for Hezekiah's boils: *can* this be the prophet we know by that name? II Kings gives us no hint that Jeremiah had any part in Josiah's temple reforms; Hilkiah the high priest seems to be in entire control. The official Hebrew religion, state, and military are one. At such times there is little room for prophets or women.

Yet at the very beginning of the story of the kingdoms there is Hannah (I Samuel 1:2). Hannah, the wife of Elkanah of Ephraim, is snubbed by Peninnah, his "other wife" (polygamy is now an ac-cepted practice), because Hannah is childless. In spite of her husband's protestations that he should be dearer to her than ten sons, Hannah is inconsolable and takes her grief to the Lord at the temple. Was she overbold? Eli, the priest, seeing her lips move in silent prayer, accuses her of being drunk! But finally he seconds her petition. The child, whom she has vowed to the Lord, is born, dedicated, and raised in the temple, to become the directive force in establishing the king-dom. But at the same time Eli's daughter-in-law, near death in child-birth, may have had a prophetic insight when, hearing that the ark of God has been captured by the Philistines, and that Eli and her husband are dead, names her newborn son Ichabod—"the glory has departed from Israel" (I Samuel 4:22).

Polygamy

With King David's tangled domestic affairs, polygamy no longer calls for any rationalization, such as a childless first wife. There are Merab and Michal—Saul's daughters, Ahinoam and Abigail, Maacah, Haggith, Abital, Eglah, to say nothing of Bath-sheba and Abishag, and others (I Chronicles 14:3).

Michal, who seems to have been married to him first, had apparently loved him and hoped that as king he would be more dignified and reliable. Perhaps it was the adulation of the women, greeting him wherever he went with songs about his conquests and how he was mightier than Saul (I Samuel 18:7) that added to his conceit and turned his head, and that irritated Michal past endurance. When David felt moved to dance, naked, before the ark, she "despised him at heart" (I Chronicles 15:29) and reproached him (II Samuel 6:20) for stripping himself before the servants "like a common rake." David at white heat assures her that in the future he will be even more abandoned in disporting himself before the Lord, and that, as for the maidservants, he will be held in honor by them. Michal dies childless, and a causal relationship seems implied because of her disrespect for her husband (II Samuel 6:22).

Abigail, too, seems to have had a mind of her own. At considerable risk to her own safety, she intervened in a quarrel between Nabal, her husband, and David, smoothing things over by personally supplying David with the food his men needed. A few days later, her husband dies of a stroke, and Abigail, too, marries David (I Samuel 25).

Probably the most famous of David's wives, however, was Bath-sheba. This is not a pretty romance, in spite of movie versions. David saw this beautiful woman, wanted her, and took her for himself. He deceived her husband Uriah and finally schemed to have him sent into the front line of battle (needlessly endangering other lives in the process), where Uriah was killed. Then David added Bath-sheba to his harem. Our present task is not to pass judgment one way or another on David, nor on those who whitewash Biblical materials in order to achieve more obvious and palatable moral interpretations. We are here interested in Biblical women, and the truth is that this is entirely David's story—it is only through him that we know Bath-sheba at all. Moreover, this seems to be increasingly true of women throughout the reign of David—and the other kings that followed him.

Tamar, David's daughter, enters the picture only because she is violated by her half-brother and so stirs up considerable family trouble (II Samuel 13). The wise woman of Tekoa, eventually called in to help settle the dispute (ch. 14), says just the words Joab, David's officer, puts in her mouth. And when Bath-sheba manages to get her son Solomon on the throne to succeed David (I Kings 1), none other than the prophet Nathan puts the proper words in *her* mouth. At least that is as it was reported some centuries later.

We must not leave David without one more consort. Abishag was young and warm and beautiful, and she became his nurse in his old age. Adonijah offered to exchange his claims to the kingdom for her (I Kings 2:15-22).

Solomon reaches some sort of a climax with 700 wives and 300 concubines. He seems to have been particularly interested in foreign women. Perhaps, like Mohammed at a later date, he used the harem to build up foreign relations, beginning with his marriage to the daughter of Egypt's Pharaoh (I Kings 3:1; 9:24). However, it was with his royal visitor, the Queen of Sheba, that he seems to have enjoyed mutual respect, stimulating conversation, and good fellowship, as well as a rather ostentatious exchange of gifts, symbolic of each one's wealth and power (I Kings 10:1-13; II Chronicles 9:1-12).

However, the Queen of Sheba was a foreigner and a powerful monarch. It is doubtful if any of her glory transmitted itself to improve the descending status of the average woman in Jerusalem. On the other hand, the Elijah and Elisha stories, which have been incorporated into these official records, seem to show this average woman going about her business and keeping house, trying to make ends meet, worrying over a sick child, and apparently putting her faith in prophets who are outside the orthodox religious institution of the day, but who are strong in their devotion to the Lord (I Kings 14, 17; II Kings 4, 8).

The status of women has not yet quite reached its nadir. Soon it is not enough that women simply are nothing: our accounts begin to blame the wife or queen mother whenever there is a bad king. The woman in Hebrew history who became the symbol of all evil was Jezebel, who, it was claimed, lured her husband Ahab to worship Baal and build altars to Baal in the northern kingdom. It was said that she slew almost all the prophets of YAHWEH, except, it would seem, Elijah, who was constantly at war with her.

Now Ahab petulantly coveted a vineyard owned by his neighbor, Naboth. Since Ahab was able to build an ivory palace for himself, he certainly did not actually need his poor neighbor's land; he just *wanted* it and was making himself sick about the matter. Jezebel catered to her husband's whim. She arranged for false witnesses to accuse Naboth of blasphemy, so that he was stoned to death. Then Ahab took over the vineyard. Elijah prophesies the horrible war and destruction with which the Lord will end Ahab's days and adds, "The dogs shall eat Jezebel in the district of Jezreel" (I Kings 21:23). The narrator comments, "There was none who sold himself to do what was evil in the sight of the Lord, like Ahab, whom Jezebel, his wife, incited" (I Kings 21:25).

Were women getting worse and worse, or were they getting a worse and worse press both from the contemporary narrators and those who, as the centuries passed, retold the stories with more and more gusto? We suspect it was a vicious circle. Even if a woman wanted to reform, she must certainly have felt that the pattern of society was against her. And of course we have no evidence that Jezebel ever had any intention or desire to reform. Jezebel and King Ahaziah's mother, Athaliah, a "counsellor of wickedness" who slays the royal family and tries to make herself "king" (like Hatshepsut of Egypt) (II Kings 11; II Chronicles 22, 23), vie with each other as symbols of women at their worst. The perpetuation of the memory of the worst rather than the best about women in the official temple and court records did nothing to raise women's own opinion of themselves from generation to generation.

But there is always another side to such a dismal picture. Seeds of recovery are sprouting.

Huldah, the Prophetess

In the time of Jeremiah, there is a decision to make major repairs on the temple, and during these renovations an apparently long-lost document is discovered. If authenic, it is of great significance for the Hebrew religion. Hilkiah the priest shows it to Shaphan the scribe, describing it as a "book of the law." Shaphan refers it to the king, who is also impressed. If this book is authentic, it calls for many drastic reforms in current temple practice. A committee is appointed by the king to examine the document's authenticity. "Inquire," he orders, "for me and for the people and for all Judah, concerning the words of this book that has been found, for great is the wrath of the Lord that is kindled against us because our fathers have not obeyed the words of the book, to do according to all that is written concerning us."

The committee apparently feel that they need an expert opinion, and, surprisingly enough, it is to Huldah, the prophetess, wife of Shallum, living not at the temple but in the Second Quarter (a suburb?) of Jerusalem, that they turn. They show her the document, which she apparently finds authentic, and in response to which she gives them a message from the Lord, which they most certainly take seriously. The document deals with the original covenant between YAHWEH and all the Hebrew people; the people's apostasy has carried them far from the provisions this document stipulates for governing their lives. Immediate and drastic changes are called for.

The message from the Lord which Huldah gives to the committee is: "I will bring evil upon this place and upon its inhabitants, all the words of the book which the king of Judah has read. Because they have forsaken me and have burned incense to other gods, that they might provoke me to anger with all the work of their hands, therefore my wrath will be kindled against this place, and it will not be quenched." But to the king the Lord sends the message, "Regarding the words which you have heard, because your heart was penitent and you humbled yourself before the Lord, when you heard how I spoke against this place, and against its inhabitants . . . I also have heard you . . . I will gather you to your fathers and you shall be gathered to your grave in peace; and your eyes shall not see all the evil which I will bring upon this place" (II Kings 22; cf. II Chronicles 34:14–28). The king proceeds with haste to his famous temple reforms, and it would seem from the account of the foreign gods and their followers who were banished from the temple that those reforms were indeed overdue.

How we wish we knew more about Huldah's story! We know that she was an older contemporary of Jeremiah; at the time she was consulted he would have been a very young man. What a remarkable person she must have been to command, during such times as we have been describing, the evidence of respect accorded her in this instance! Yet that is the only word we have about her! We can be glad, at any rate, that Huldah did not become discouraged and give up her work as a prophetess just because the field of religion in her day seemed to offer almost no opportunities for the services of a competent woman.

A few other women's names appear here and there through the books of Samuel and Kings, but for the most part they are simply genealogical notes. (See note C, p. 304.) We have noted these references for the sake of those who want them.

In Chronicles any suggestion that women might be interesting in themselves is completely abandoned—they are a vehicle between one generation of men and the next. However, one pertinent bit of information shows clearly through the records: the listings by tribes affirm what the stories of Joshua and Judges suggested—that the tribes of the northern kingdom of Israel had much more time and space for their women than was accorded women in the southern kingdom of Judah. Of course Deborah of the north had set a record not easily forgotten—probably the most outstanding record of early Israel. But while this helped to make women more respected in the north, it undoubtedly made them even more obnoxious in the south, for there was persistent rivalry between the two kingdoms, and this rivalry continued through the years. There may also have been a vestige of woman appreciation in the Shechem-Bethel area from patriarchal days, when the position of women had been so much better than it was under the kingdoms. For a list of references to women in the tribal genealogies, see I Chronicles 1-8.

The Captivity

In the days before the Captivity, the "business" of religion was increasingly in the hands of a powerful and exclusive priesthood. YAHWEH had become a battle cry, but his ethical imperatives, as pronounced by the prophets, usually got little attention in high places. Women and laymen had no participating part in organized religion.[11] Even Jecoliah's son, good King Uzziah, is forbidden the right to make his own offering at the temple (II Chronicles 26); persisting, he is reported to have been smitten with leprosy.

But priestly rule does not seem to have been effective in government. First the northern kingdom of Israel and then Judah had become captive nations. The rich, the politically influential, the highly educated families were deported to the land of their captors, but many of the common people were left on the land, and this difference, in later days, became of itself a cause of contention. Moreover, for all the oppression and hardships which the deported people suffered, their horizons were inevitably broadened. Babylon, for instance, in spite of the polemics against her worldliness, was a cultured, literate, and sophisticated city; that her women were held in a position of respect was witnessed by the famous Hammurabi Code.

In this atmosphere—in captivity—the priestly school, deprived of its temple and its temporal power, made its great contribution to Hebrew religion—the organization and editing of the Hebrew records and documents into a co-ordinated presentation of the life and laws of the Hebrews.

During the Captivity there were other exiles, however, who were interested not so much in preserving and interpreting all that had gone before as in finding and interpreting the meaning of God's relationship to his people in the present.

What was God really like? What was his will for mankind? Why did he permit his people to be taken captive?

Prophets as well as priests were among the exiles. Some of them may have said far more drastic things than ever got into the priestly-edited books that we know.[12]

The Second Isaiah: Man or Woman?

One prophet from the days of the Exile stands out above all the others—the one we call Second Isaiah. This prophet, as was customary in those days, wrote in the name of an admired predecessor. In this case the predecessor was Isaiah of Jerusalem, who nearly 200 years before had pleaded in vain with his countrymen to understand the true nature of their religious heritage, and to begin, before it was too late, to live by its precepts.

Isaiah's own wife had been a prophetess (Isaiah 8:3) and must have shared his convictions, for she allowed her whole life to be drawn into the prophetic orbit. There are some persons who make a case for Second Isaiah, the author of Isaiah chapters 40–55 (and possibly Isaiah 40–66), having been written by a woman prophetess writing in the tradition of Isaiah of Jerusalem. The Biblical scholars of that day, they speculate with some assurance, would not accept her—the thought of women's work being included in official religious writings was quite as unthinkable as it would be in many churches today.

We simply do not know who wrote this material that became attached to the Isaiah prophecies, and which some persons have called the "Holy of Holies of the Old Testament." Second Isaiah, the prophet of the Exile, outstanding among the poets of this period, and of all time, certainly *could* have been a woman; it could account for her anonymity. Or the material could have been written by a man with imagination, devotion, and sensibilities for things other than the military prowess, wealth, harems, and religious particularism that had dominated the thinking of Hebrew officialdom during the days of the kingdoms. Whether II Isaiah was a man, or a woman writing of necessity (if she was to have acceptance) in the name of a man, makes little if any difference. As the priests and scribes and the descendants of the kings of Judah—their kingdoms gone, their temple destroyed, themselves in captivity far from their homeland—sought to preserve their religious heritage by rewriting and editing their official religious codes, a voice, probably quite outside the official circles, was raised which cried, "O my fellow countrymen, not by codes and regulations, not by continually dwelling on the glory of our forefathers, will we find the answer to our problems. Our salvation, like the salvation of any people, is with God himself. It is the nature of God himself, just, loving, universal, that we must seek to know, for only as he is understood, and as men act in accord with his will (not just give him military service or temple sacrifices) will they find salvation."

> Have you not known? Have you not heard?
> The Lord is a God everlasting,
> The Creator of the ends of the earth.
> He does not faint nor grow weary;
> His insight is unfathomable.
> He gives power to the fainting,
> And to him that has no might he increases strength.
>   (40:28–29, Amer. trans.)

Are His servants the self-important kings with their international harems?

Or the Priests who seek in the name of Aaron to control the kings?

No, on the contrary, the Servant of the Lord can be a very lowly person, by popular standards.

> He was despised and avoided by men,
> A man of sorrows, and acquainted with pain. . . .
> He was despised and we esteemed him not. . . .
> He was wounded for our transgressions,
> He was crushed for our iniquities . . . [yet]
> Through his affliction shall my servant, the Righteous One,
> Bring righteousness to many,
> And he shall bear their guilt.
> Therefore will I divide him a portion with the great.
> (from the "Servant Song" of Isaiah 52:13–53:12, Amer. trans.)

Some people think that the Servant Songs of II Isaiah were actually written about Isaiah of Jerusalem, who tried so hard to show the kings and priests of his day that they were turning down a road which could only bring disaster to the people. Tradition tells us that Isaiah of Jerusalem, far from being heard at the time, was "sawn asunder" by the king he antagonized. Certainly we will only understand the *prophetic* religion of Israel as we learn to hear the message of the prophets as over against the specific perversions of true religion of the time when they were uttered: a speaking out *against* the pomp and importance of the kings, who were strengthening their pretenses of being mighty men by making war and building up their harems; against the ambitions of the priesthood, with its tradition of being king *makers*, its growing retinue of retainers, the all importance of the temple and temple ritual; or against the apostasy and indifference of the common people, turning to magic and necromancy and the utility religion of Baal and his consort, which promised plenty to eat and a life relatively unhampered by moral imperatives. Prophets spoke out, too, concerning the jealous enmity between the northern and southern kingdoms, and against quarrels between different schools of religious interpretation or scriptural redaction.[13]

It was a remnant indeed who tried to remind the people of the God who called Abraham and Sarah away from past ties to seek, in a new land, an understanding of deity not dependent on one place or the cultural milieu of one people. It was the remnant who remembered Moses, stirred first by a sense of social justice for his fellow man, who led his people out of Egypt and gave them the law for their guidance; the remnant remembered, too, the prophetess Miriam, his confidante and co-worker. And the remnant remembered Deborah, who, impatient to desperation at the indolence and procrastination of her fellow Hebrews, finally stirred them to action. There were Amos and Hosea; Isaiah and his wife; Micah, Huldah, and Jeremiah, and surely many more prophets and prophetesses whose names have not come down to us. By this time there was little place for women in the services of the temple except where its corrupt practices sanctioned sacred prostitution or service to "foreign gods." Huldah, though consulted by priests and rulers to expertize a most important document and give answers on questions of policy, was probably, like many prophets, strictly "free lance." Nor was there any legitimate place for women in the government of the country, except through harem politics.

A favorite allegory with the prophets was that of Israel as the faithless wife of YAHWEH (Jeremiah 2:1–4:4; 11:15, 16; Ezekiel 16; Hosea 4:15; *et al*). Eventually, however (eschatologically perhaps in the time beyond time), the barren one, or the shamed one, will return, and God will forgive (see, e.g., Isaiah 54).

The prophets often have very harsh words for the women whose desire for material wealth and splendor, especially in the royal courts, was certainly contributing to the general apostasy of the land (Isaiah 32:9ff.). It seems very unlikely that, as some scholars have indicated, the protest against Baalism was largely because of the degrading effect the Baalistic religion had on the role of women. Baalism involved far more than just a lowering of sexual standards. It was a way of magic and coercion, whereas the Hebrew religion had been in the beginning a religion of personal responsibility and individual and social integrity—a religion of covenant between the people and God. Insofar as women were subjugated and deprived of their status as persons, those people responsible—however much they proclaimed YAHWEH in the place of worship—were following the way of Baal just as surely as were those who made offerings to fertility gods or patronized religious prostitutes in either Baal's or YAHWEH's places of worship.

As Second Isaiah said, it was to know and understand God, and be faithful to Him, that was important; or, as Micah put it, do justice, love mercy, and walk humbly. It is unfortunate that the prophets' favorite figure of speech about the apostate Israel's promiscuity has been taken so literally and permeated religious thinking through the centuries to the point where the word "sin" became altogether too synonymous with sexual liberties—an idea that has been a problem for both religion and more recently for psychiatry.

It is interesting how often the prophet, in his attempt to emphasize the most profound relationships which Israel should have with her God, brings his wife into the picture: Isaiah of Jerusalem, and the strange names he and "the prophetess" gave their children, the almost unbelievable relationship between Hosea and Gomer, the death of Ezekiel's wife (Ezekiel 24:15-24).

(See additional references from the Prophets and from the Law, notes D and E, p. 304.)

After the Exile

We wish we had more light on the difference, if any, which the years of exile and exposure to world powers made in the way the Hebrew people thought about their women. Certainly there seems to have been some improvement. For instance, by the time of Christ polygamy was

practically extinct. Herod, of course, considered himself above regulations and had nine wives (Josephus 17.1.3).

One cannot read Jeremiah without the impression that he felt women
were people, and although his letters to the exiles in Egypt, for instance, do not spare the ladies for their shortcomings, more than his
predecessors he uses the term "daughter of Zion" in a friendly tone.
He speaks frequently of "sons and daughters" as though they might be
equally important. (See note D, p. 304.)

We like to think about the return of the exiles from Babylon to
Jerusalem, and the rebuilding of the walls and the temple, in terms of
joy and triumph and reunion. This is a rather idealized picture. Not all
the people, by any means, but primarily persons and families of power,
wealth, and learning were transported to Babylon, where in time their
ability and their sense of Hebrew solidarity led to their forming a by no
means uninfluential clique. When they returned, they were still an influential clique, with the added advantage of having made powerful
friends in the land of their captivity. They had also acquired a degree
of spiritual prestige by having suffered captivity for the sake of the
Jewish people. Their Social Register was the list of families whose
members had been in captivity (see Ezra 2). The men who had married foreign women were under heavy pressure to "put them away
with their children" (Ezra 10). Not to do so was "subversive." One
would expect that the Exile might have improved the status of women,
in that it would surely have had a leveling influence on everybody, but
Ezra and Nehemiah, interpreted by the Chronicler (c. 350–250 B.C.),
give the impression that the Exile only tended to make the returnees
more exclusive. On the other hand, women do attend Nehemiah's great
assembly (Nehemiah 8:2).

During the Exile years, the common people of Palestine who had
been left behind on the land got along as best they could and discovered that making common cause with their neighbors was not
nearly as difficult as they had been led to believe. When they heard
that the returnees were going to build a temple, they asked, with apparently the best of motives, if they might help, for, said they, "We
worship the same God, and have been sacrificing to him all along."

The builders, however, were incensed and imputed the worst motives
to the offer. They were very positive that they preferred to do the job
alone, with the backing of their friend, King Cyrus. Hurt and angry at
the rejection, the "people of the land" began to annoy and terrorize
the builders. Some of the resident people had for prestige reasons been
anxious to ally themselves with the returnees and the Nehemiah party.

Some had met them on their own terms and taken advantage of them, loaning them money at such exorbitant rates that the returnees register a protest that interest is so high they have to sell their sons and daughters into slavery. Some of their daughters, they add, have already become slaves.

Increasingly, however, the people of the land had been discovering that the "pious poor" had mutual concerns and a basic ethical religious outlook which held them together. They are identified by Chester C. McCown in his *Genesis of the Social Gospel* as the "humble," "those who wait upon the Lord," or those of "a broken and contrite heart."[14] Their most comprehending spokesman (whether from Palestine or Babylon) was the poet we know as Second Isaiah. It has been suggested that there may have been a religious-cultural agreement or organization involving these more humble worshipers of YAHWEH in northern and southern Palestine, during the years when their former leaders were in captivity. Nothing would be more natural. And naturally these people of the land would have been incensed at being ignored and excluded from the temple-building activities.

They had no arms or resources, and, besides, they had learned to be patient and peaceable. However, now it would seem the time for protest, and perhaps a little civil disobedience, was at hand. Those years when low economic status did not attract warring invaders, together with the absence of the official anti-female pressures of court and temple leaders, had undoubtedly been, for the people of the land, a leveling force as between the sexes—to the women's advantage. When the time for a demonstration came, the ladies were ready and had a woman leader, the prophetess Noadiah, ready to spark the protest. Noadiah seems to have had a whole band of women prophets working with her, though exactly what a prophet was in this context we do not know. Moreover, to get anything like a coherent story, we must gather bits from Ezekiel (ch. 13), Ezra (ch. 4–6), and Nehemiah (ch. 4–6).

These women working with Noadiah apparently had things well organized. Their company wore identifying veils and wristbands. They called for "peace," whereas Nehemiah and his followers thought they *knew* that Hebrew exclusivism was the only hope for the future. When a wall was built, the protesters—men and women—immediately smeared it with whitewash, though whether they covered it with slogans or used the paint to call attention to slipshod workmanship is not quite clear.

The prophets on the builders' side prophesied hailstorms and cloudbursts that would knock down the wall, suggesting the pious hope that the daubers would be under it. The wristbands (the current form of

THE OLD TESTAMENT 43

badge), which must have been an innovation, indicated to them that the protesters were using magic. They said the prophetesses were buying souls with a handful of barley or a piece of bread! (Lunch for the demonstrators?) Men as well as women were active in the protest group, but it was certainly the women's activities which generated the greatest amount of ire among the builders. Sanballat and Tobiah you could talk to—but that Noadiah! And calling herself a prophet! The builders were simply not used to this sort of thing and had no intention of being subjected to such humiliation! She is indeed the thorn in Nehemiah's flesh.

Ezekiel calls on the men to set their faces against the daughters of the people who "prophesy out of their own imagination." The Lord has a message for the women: "You shall no more see delusive visions nor practice divinations. I will deliver my people out of your hands. Then you will know that I am the Lord." We do wish we had a statement from Noadiah—it seems as if she should have been given equal time to tell her side of the story (see Ezekiel 13:17–23).

Nehemiah, somewhat frantically, at last takes to prayer about the prophetesses and the way they deliberately taunt him, concluding with a request that the Lord will remember how he, himself—Nehemiah—was tormented by Noadiah "and the rest of the prophets who wanted to make me afraid" (Nehemiah 6:14).

We wish we knew just what these women were up to. However, one does not need to wonder why they may have thought it was high time the woman took a hand in history.

Shallum's daughters, on the other hand, were helping on Nehemiah's side, but we do not even know their names (Nehemiah 3:12).

The Story of Esther

We must, of course, speak of Esther, who has been a popular character among Jewish and Christian women for some 2000 years.

Most Biblical scholars agree that the author of the book of Esther never expected it to be taken as "real history"; it is a short historical novel, written in the second century B.C. with all the literary liberties and exaggerations the historical novel seems to permit even Biblical subjects. The real reason for the writing seems to have been to popularize the Jewish festival of Purim, which had only recently been established when the tale was written. It is easy to understand that the story might have been popular at that time, when the exclusive and institutional side of Judaism threatened to outweigh the universal and prophetic school. Intentionally or not, the story may also have something to say about the role of women and their proper place in the scheme of things, as the author understood it.

Bible story books and quarterlies have welcomed—to liven up male predominance in most of the older Scriptures—the illustrative possibilities of two beautiful queens in one lesson, but, as well known as the picture and the name of Esther is, it is possible that not all our readers have read the whole Biblical account, so let us review its main outlines.

The setting is in the fifth century B.C. King Xerxes (otherwise known as Ahasuerus), as the climax to the seventh day of a great feast, commands his seven attending eunuchs to fetch Queen Vashti from the feast she is giving for the women, so that all his well-wined male guests may view her beauty. The queen refuses to come. Xerxes, far from being pleased with her modesty, is furious and consults his seven wise men about what should be done to such a defiant woman. The wise men tell him that she has not only wronged Xerxes, but all his princes and people, for if this report gets around the kingdom, as it surely will, it is likely to arouse a rebellion of wives, all thinking they can do as they please. This must be averted. Xerxes must make an example of her. He should send an irrevocable decree (as all Persian decrees are) translated into the languages of the various provinces, and well publicized in every region of the kingdom (India to Ethiopia), that Vashti is deposed for her insubordination, "so that all women shall give honor to their husbands, both high and low." The decree stipulates, moreover, that "every man shall be master in his own home and shall speak whatever seems proper to him."

Then Hegai, the king's eunuch in charge of women, is told to bring in the most beautiful girls he can find, supply them with attendants and whatever cosmetics they require, and have them appear before the king so he can make a choice.

Mordecai, a Benjaminite, now in the Jewish dispersion, is one of Xerxes' minor officers. He arranges to have Esther, his orphaned cousin, whom he has raised, enrolled in the group, and naturally Xerxes chooses her, not knowing she is Jewish. Now Xerxes' chief officer, Haman, has everything else a man could wish, but can find no peace of mind as long as Mordecai, being Jewish, refuses to bow to him. However, Mordecai and Esther, together, have been instrumental in warding off assassination of the king, so Haman does not dare attack Mordecai directly. Instead he gets the king to make an irrevocable decree permitting Haman to destroy all these Jewish people who "are different and have different laws," and to confiscate their property. Mordecai asks Esther to intervene. He tells her that eventually even she, inside the castle walls, will not escape destruction under this edict. Besides, he says, "Who knows whether you have not come to the kingdom for such a time as this?"

Though like everyone else Esther risks death by approaching Xerxes without being summoned, she goes to him, and he holds out to her the golden scepter which gives her permission to speak. She invites Xerxes and Haman to a feast. Meanwhile, the king discovers that it was Mordecai who had saved his life much earlier in the story, and that Mordecai has never been suitably rewarded. Haman arrives at the feast breathless and infuriated at having to do Mordecai public honor, at the king's command. Esther reveals to Xerxes that she is Jewish, Mordecai's kinswoman, and that both of them will fall under his irrevocable edict to destroy all the Jews in the kingdom. The king leaves the room and when he returns finds Haman, who is really pleading for his life, in what seems like a compromising position with the queen. Haman is hung on the gallows he had prepared with considerable relish for Mordecai. Mordecai is raised to a position of high honor. The decree to exterminate the Jews is irrevocable, but Mordecai is authorized to prepare another decree in the king's name, giving them permission to defend themselves. At Esther's request, Haman's ten sons are also hung. To commemorate these events, Mordecai and Esther establish the feast of Purim as a Jewish holiday.

Many scholars, including Jerome, Luther, and in our own generation Robert Pfeiffer, have had their troubles with the book. Luther is reported to have said he was so hostile to the book and to Esther as to "wish they did not exist at all." But we feel that further study of the book itself, as distinct from Esther herself, would be interesting. How did this story with a woman as main character and heroine, at a time when woman's status was still so very low in Palestine, ever get added to the Jewish canon?

Esther's desire for revenge and her Jewish particularism are much easier to understand when we remember that she is a fictional character. For those with whom the book sought popularity, particularism and extremism were admirable characteristics. And who can deny that Esther did have a lot of spunk which was rather lacking in her historic women contemporaries? Though we deplore her vindictiveness, it is good to see even a fictional character reversing the female trend to apathy.

Women in the Apocrypha

It often happens that trends show up in literature before they are
noticeable in history. In the years between the Old and New Testament
writings, we meet quite a few women in literature. We have spoken of
the Adam and Eve stories; a whole cycle of these appeared and were
apparently widely circulated (see note 5). Two books, in this intertestamental period, were, like Esther, named for their heroines. They
showed the women getting the best of the situation and were found in
the Apocrypha, which became attached to the older Scriptures.

The story of Judith is laid during the reign of Nebuchadnezzar.
Judith is a young Jewish widow whose husband died from a sunstroke
during the last barley harvest. She observed rigid mourning, living in a
tent on the rooftop of her home in the city of Bethulia, fasting con-
tinuously except for Sabbaths and holy days. She was beautiful,
wealthy, and very religious.

Now King Nebuchadnezzar was provoked at the coastlands, and the
men of Judah, recently back from captivity, had no desire to provoke
him further. They moved to the hilltops, where they could command
the roads through Judah, and waited. Bethulia is besieged by General
Holofernes, and the elder statesmen, not knowing what to do, decide
that if YAHWEH does not answer their prayers and help them within
five days, they will hand over the city.

"And who are you," Judith demands of them, "that you have
tempted God this day, and stand instead of God among the children
of men? . . . You cannot find the depth and heart of man, neither
can you perceive the things that he thinketh; then how can you search
out God, that hath made all things, and know his mind, or comprehend his purpose? . . . Provoke not the Lord our God to anger.
For if he will not help us within these five days, he hath power to defend us when he will, even every day, or to destroy us before our
enemies. Do not bind the counsels of the Lord our God, for God is
not a man that he may be threatened. . . . Call upon him to help
us and he will hear our voice if it please him. . . . Moreover let us
give thanks to the Lord our God which trieth us, even as he did our
fathers."

Judith then lays aside her mourning, braids her hair attractively, and
dresses in "garments of gladness." She takes bags of parched corn and
dried figs, flasks of oil and wine, and sets off for the enemy camp, pray-

ing God to use her intended speech and deceit to "make every nation and tribe to acknowledge that thou art the God of all power and might and that there is none other that protected the people of Israel but thee." Using her charm and wiles, as well as her "speech and deceit," she works her way into the very tent of Holofernes. When he is sufficiently drunk with wine, she beheads him and carries his head back to the Israelites, who, shamed and inspired by her bravery, rout the enemy.

Judith never remarries, but lives to a ripe and respected old age.

Susanna is the story of a young wife of the Babylonian Joacim. Her father's home in Babylon seems to have been a gathering place for well-to-do Jews during the Captivity. Two old judges were both enamored of Susanna—judges, we are told, of the sort who made popular the saying that "wickedness came to Babylon from ancient judges." The two old men discover each other's secret, and together spy upon her as she bathes in the fountain of her courtyard. Deciding to share the prize they both covet, they tell her that unless she agrees, they will swear that there was a young man there with her. Susanna, cornered, cries, "If I do this thing it is death unto me, and if I do it not, I cannot escape your hands. It is better for me to fall into your hands and not do it, than sin in the sight of the Lord." Thereupon she screams and the servants come running.

The elders, thwarted, tell the lie with which they threatened her, insisting that she uncover, in the courtroom, so they can stand there with their hands piously on her head as they accuse her. The assembly condemns her to death, but a smart young lawyer named Daniel attacks their casual court proceedings. By examining the two elders separately, he catches them in lies which prove the falsity of their testimony and Susanna's innocence.

The book of Tobit should also be mentioned, as a sort of family chronicle from this period. Tobit and his wife Anna send their son Tobias on a long journey to pay a debt they owe. With him they send a guide, who turns out to be the angel Raphael. On the trip they stop at the home of Raquel, a cousin, and his wife Edna. They have a daughter Sara, who has been on the verge of marriage seven times, only to have the bridegroom die before the marriage can be consummated. The parents are anxious to have Tobias for a son-in-law, but they cannot believe that their luck will be any better this time than it has been in the past. Raquel goes so far as to dig a grave, in order to have it ready. But they reckon without the knowledge of magic which

Raphael has learned in Egypt, which (using the heart and liver of a fish) saves the day and the bridegroom.

At the ceremony Tobias says, "Blessed art Thou O God of our fathers, and blessed is thy holy and glorious name forever; let the heavens bless thee and all thy creatures. Thou madest Adam and gavest him Eve his wife for helper and stay; of them came mankind. Thou hast said that it is not good that man should be alone, let us make unto him an aid like unto himself. And now, O Lord, I take not this, my sister, for lust, but uprightly; therefore mercifully ordain that we may become aged together." (And she, Sara, said with him, Amen. So they slept both that night.)

Raquel (the bride's father) said to Sara, "Honor thy father and thy mother-in-law, which are now thy parents, that I may hear good report of thee." (And he kissed her.)

Edna (the bride's mother) said to Tobias, "The Lord of heaven restore thee, my dear brother, and grant that I may see thy children of my daughter Sara before I die, that I may rejoice before the Lord; behold, I commit my daughter unto thee of special trust; wherefore do not entreat her evil."

And Tobit (her father-in-law) welcomes Sara when they return to his home: "Thou art welcome, daughter. God be blessed which has brought thee unto us. And blessed be thy father and thy mother."

Then Tobit (who thinks he is about to die, but who is miraculously healed) says to his son Tobias, "My son, when I am dead, bury me and despise not thy mother, but honor her all the days of thy life, and do that which shall please her and grieve her not. Remember my son, that she saw many dangers for thee, when thou wast in her womb, and when she is dead bury her by me in one grave."

There are many other stories from this period; it was a literary era. And in some ways the literary tales give us a more satisfactory picture of how the people lived and acted and thought than the "history" which has so often been colored by propaganda. Women often have a normative place in the plots which extol some commonly admired virtue such as bravery, justice, human kindness, or reliance on prayer.

Chapter 3

WOMEN IN THE NEW TESTAMENT

Jesus' ministry cuts straight across all that has gone before. In no area is this more evident than as we study the history of women in religion. Certainly the old taboos and arguments which had developed out of a long history of Hebrew prejudice in this field had no place in his thinking. Women were people—friends to be visited, chance acquaintances with whom to discuss theology by the village well, a mother whose child was sick. He would, we believe, have found real humor in the fact that Matthew traces Jesus' genealogy entirely through the male line, mentioning only four women in the forty-two generations from Abraham to *Joseph*, while the genealogist of Luke goes through the line from Adam to Joseph without benefit of any female names.

Since most of our readers will be familiar with the general content of the Gospels, it seemed that the most useful service this book might render would be to give a synthesis of the references to women in the Gospel narratives. We have combined the three "synoptic Gospels" (presumably historic accounts) into such continuity as is possible, giving separately the references from the Gospel of John, which is generally considered "theological" rather than "historical" in character.

Synoptic References Concerning Women[1]

Luke 1:5–24	Elizabeth of the daughters of Aaron, promised birth of a son (John the Baptist).
Luke 1:26–38 Matt. 1:18	Annunciation to Mary of Jesus' forthcoming birth.
Luke 19:56	Mary visits Elizabeth; Mary's Magnificat.
Luke 1:57–66	Elizabeth bears John.
Luke 2 Matt. 1:25	Mary bears Jesus.
Luke 2:36	Anna, the prophetess, living in the temple, acknowledges Jesus.

Matt. 2	The wise men visit the Holy Family.
Luke 2:41–52	Jesus as a child at Nazareth—the visit to Jerusalem—"and his mother kept all these things in her heart."
Mark 6:17, 18	Herodias persuades Herod to arrest John, who opposed Herod's polygamy.
Matt. 8:14 Mark 1:30 Luke 4:38	Simon's wife's mother healed—starts Jesus' fame as a healer.
Matt. 5:27–32	Woman taken in adultery.
Luke 7:11–17	Raising of the widow's son at Nain. "He had compassion on her."
Luke 7:36ff.	Jesus anointed by the sinful woman—he rebukes Simon for protesting.
Luke 8:1–3	Preaching tour in Galilee. The Twelve plus Mary Magdalene; Joanna, wife of Chuza, Herod's steward; Susanna; and "many others."
Luke 11:31	Mention of Queen of the South (Sheba) who "will arise at the judgment with the men of this generation."
Mark 4:10ff. Cf. Luke 8:1 (includes women)	"And when he was alone, those who were about him with the Twelve asked him concerning the parables . . . 'To you has been given the secret of the Kingdom of God. . . .'"
Matt. 13:13 Luke 13:20–21	The Kingdom of Heaven is like the leaven which a woman hid in the meal—a parable.
Matt. 9:18–26 Mark 5:21–43 Luke 8:40–56	Jairus' twelve-year-old daughter raised from death: "Talitha cumi."
Matt. 13:55 Mark 6:3 Luke 4:22	"Is not this the carpenter, the son of Mary?" (Mary not mentioned in Luke.)
Matt. 12:46–50 Mark 3:31 Luke 8:19–21	His family visit Jesus. "Who is my mother?"
Matt. 19:9 Mark 10:11 Luke 16:18	Question of divorce.
Matt. 9:23 Mark 5:34 Luke 8:48	The woman with cancer (?) who touched Jesus' garment. "Thy faith hath made thee whole. Go in peace."
Matt. 14:12–14 Mark 6:12–14	Salome brings about John the Baptist's death.
Matt. 15 Mark 7:25	Healing of the Canaanite woman's daughter, who was possessed of a demon. (Extension of ministry to non-Jews.)
Matt. 15:38	Feeding the 4000 men, besides women and children.

Luke 10:38–42	Mary and Martha as friends of Jesus.
Luke 11:27	Woman in the crowd: "Blessed is the womb that bore thee!" Jesus: "Blessed rather are those who hear the Word of God and keep it."
Matt. 24:49 Luke 12:45	Parable of the unprofitable servant who beat his fellow-man and maidservants.
Luke 15:8ff.	Parable of the woman and the lost coin.
Luke 17:32	Reference to Lot's wife.
Luke 17:35	Two women grinding corn—one will be taken, one left on the "last day."
Luke 18:1–8	Parable of the judge and the persistent widow who got her way (in relation to prayer without ceasing).
Matt. 19:3–12 Mark 10:1–16 Luke 16:18 Cf. Matt. 5 Luke 16 above	The Pharisees discuss divorce—Jesus quotes Genesis 1. Divorce is given men because of their "hardness of heart" but "from the beginning it was not so." The question of eunuchs.
Luke 18:29	Leaving wife and children for the sake of the Kingdom.
Mark 20:20	Mother of James and John asks preferment for her sons in the Kingdom.
Matt. 22:29 Mark 12:18–27 Luke 20:34–38	"In heaven they are neither married or given in marriage." (The Sadducees question about the woman who married seven brothers in succession.)
Mark 12:40	Condemnation of "those who devour widows' houses" and make long prayers.
Mark 12:41–44 Luke 21:1–4	The story of the widow's mite.
Matt. 25:1–13	Ten virgins attend the marriage feast.
Matt. 26:6–13 Mark 14:3–9 Cf. Luke 7:36–38	Anointing of Jesus by a woman.
Luke 22	Multitude of people and of women who bewailed and lamented.
Luke 23:27	Women follow Jesus to Calvary.
Matt. 26 Mark 14	Two maids recognize Peter.
Luke 23:49ff. Cf. 8:1–3 Matt. 27:55ff. Mark 15:40ff.	Jesus' friends, including "the women who had followed him from Galilee," at the Crucifixion. Included Mary Magdalene, Mary the mother of James and Joseph, Salome, mother of James and John, and many others who had been with him in Jerusalem.
Mark 15:47	Mary Magdalene and Mary the mother of Joses see him placed in tomb.

Matt. 28
Mark 16
Luke 24

Three Marys at the tomb on Easter morning. Sent to tell disciples. The women from Galilee found the Eleven and told them. None of the men actually believed—but Peter looked in the tomb and wondered. Cleopas on road to Emmaus tells Jesus about the women finding the empty tomb, and how Jesus had spoken to some of them, and perhaps also to Simon. Jesus rebukes the disciples for lack of faith. It was the women who stood by him at the Crucifixion and who believed in the Resurrection. (See discussion of last verses of Mark in RSV.)

References to Women in the Gospel of John

John 2:3

At request of his mother, Jesus turns the water into wedding wine.

2:12

Visits Capernaum with mother, brothers, disciples.

4

He talks with the woman of Samaria at Jacob's well and reveals that he is the Messiah.

8:3–11

Adultery.

11

Mary and Martha of Bethany send for Jesus—their brother Lazarus is ill. Jesus, at their request, raises him from the dead.

12

Mary Magdalene (?) anoints Jesus; Judas is provoked at this extravagance.

19:25

At the foot of the cross: his mother, her sister, Mary, wife of Clopas, and Mary Magdalene.

19:28

Jesus to John: "Behold your mother. . . ."

20

Easter! Mary Magdalene finds the empty tomb and runs to tell Simon Peter and John. Peter gets there first, but only John goes in. Mary Magdalene talks to the two angels, then to Jesus himself. She tells the disciples, "I have seen the Lord." That night he appears briefly to the disciples and again eight days later he reveals himself at the Sea of Tiberias.

That is the record, from the four sources at our disposal. No amount of homiletical comment can add or detract. While the four Gospel writers differ in some respects, there is no evidence of any difference of opinion on the matter of Jesus' complete acceptance and appreciation of women, in full equality with men. As further evidence, this attitude was fully reflected in the organization of the primitive church in Jerusalem. Women as well as men were at that first celebration of

Pentecost, and it apparently surprised no one that the Holy Spirit came to all of them.

Women had not been, it is true, part of the Twelve, but this was a matter of normal conformance to the culture of the day. We would probably be critical today of a young woman who attached herself to a migrant preacher, following him around the countryside. Jesus did not attack or urge his disciples to attack such normative culture. He had more important things to do than to stir up strife and resentment. He simply accepted women as *people,* and it is interesting to note how many of his healing miracles are performed at the request of some woman, and how often his most profound conversations were not with the learned doctors of the temple but with, for instance, a woman drawing water from a well in Shechem, or two hospitable maiden sisters at their home in Bethany.[2]

Mary and Martha

Because Mary and Martha are so often held up as prototypes of the different approaches women take to life, and more especially to religious work, let us pause for a moment to discuss them. Jesus' conversation with them is about the closest we can come to an expression by him about his concept of women's role in religion or society.

Both sisters were equally devoted to Jesus. Their difference in sense of vocation might have existed between two brothers without becoming such a *cause célèbre.*

Jesus did not berate Mary because she was "different." He almost never berated or belittled people for what they were. He did not tell Mary to leave the company of those who were discussing matters upon which she could speak competently. Born of a woman, he apparently did not have any idea that women were unfit to talk about God, or to God.

Yet neither did he belittle Martha for not being like her sister. He accepted each as she was—with her own special function to fulfill.

We should note in passing that it was Martha, not the men, who was most vocal in resenting Mary's role. It is often the women in the churches who resent one of their number stepping out of line—especially into the pulpit!

Mary and Martha are prototypes: actually there is much of each in almost all Christian women. In the individual as in society, cultural pressures intrude to keep Mary from making her contribution, and the family, the Church, and society are the poorer for it. Increasingly, however, women are coming to believe that when men—or other women —try to keep them from using the talents with which God has endowed them (and which they have conscientiously developed to maximum efficiency), then they must find ways to "obey the dictates of God rather than man."

There are many non-theological reasons, as we shall see, why established churches have frowned upon women cultivating the "Mary" side of their natures. Anyone who reads first-century church history is impressed by the fact that women are to have a new chance. This is often cited by the Church today as one of the great advantages for which we can be thankful to Christianity. We have made a special point of this in the mission fields, where Christianity has often meant a great deal to women, and where they sometimes have a larger share in the work of the Church itself than is allowed their denominational sisters at home.

Women in the Book of Acts and the Pauline Epistles

But let us pass on to the book of Acts.

Pentecost, or the Feast of Weeks, was a Jewish celebration in which the women had for centuries had an active role. It is altogether probable that it was the women followers of Jesus who, as this important Jewish holy day approached, fifty days after the first Easter, sent out the word that brought his followers together—still shocked and frightened—to the festival that afterward became known as the "birthday of the Church." Somehow, as sometimes happens, the little meeting turned into a big meeting, and at the close of the day some 3000 people, from all over the Roman empire, had become Christians.[3]

There were many people, from the far borders of the empire, in Jerusalem for the holiday. When they returned home, these people's homes often became focal points for the spread of the new belief. The first meetings were small. There was no church "organization," and the women must have had considerable part in such arrangements as were necessary. Mary and Martha of Bethany, Mary the mother of John Mark, Lydia, Priscilla, Nympha, Damaris, and "the honorable women of Berea" are some of those whose homes provided a place for the "love feasts," the reading of letters from the group in Jerusalem or Christians traveling to other parts of the world, or a chance to meet and hear such evangelists as Barnabas or Paul. These same homes became places where the sick or the orphaned of the Christian community could be cared for, and new recruits could be taught the principles of the faith. The "ruling widows" became a directive force in the church. Phoebe and other women devoted themselves to what became the traditional work of the deaconess. The tract, *Acts of Paul and Thekla*, accepted as authoritative for the first two centuries of the Christian era, makes Thekla Paul's assistant. As such she would have been the first woman missionary. It has been suggested that she might even have been the unknown author of the books of Luke and Acts—the first Christian journalist.

Priscilla, whom Paul calls by the pet name of Prisca, seems to have had his complete approval as a teacher and theologian. The four unmarried daughters of Philip were accepted as prophets, and their home may well have been the center of a group of Christians especially interested in certain phases of prophecy (Acts 21:8, 9).

Paul's supposed opposition to women was rationalized into church tradition at a date far later than that accorded the book of Acts (70–90 A.D.), for this book leaves little doubt that Paul was one of the best friends women had. One would, indeed, find any fundamental antagonism toward women, as such, completely incomprehensible in so stanch a defender of human rights and personal freedom. Paul encouraged women and depended upon them. In Jerusalem and those communities where support came primarily from the Jewish synagogue, the new Church inclined to retain the pattern of rule by the "elders"; also some of the synagogue customs, including non-participation of women. In the freer thought of Greece, women expected to participate in philosophical and theological discussions, and the ideas of the newly developing Church appealed to their sense of ethics and service, as these same aspects have appealed to women ever since throughout the Christian era.

They participated freely (Paul thought too freely for their own good at times) in the worship service. Examples of early Christian art show women speaking in mixed assemblies, their head coverings pulled back and fastened with the ornament which was the style of the times.[4]

It is difficult for many persons to bring to bear on the New Testament the same critical faculties which they are willing enough to use in relation to the older Scriptures. Yet the component parts of the New Testament, the historic sequence, problems of locale and authorship, are buried under far fewer layers of editing and redaction and can therefore be more easily determined.[5] Moreover, the New Testament speaks in what is psychologically more nearly our own language, which should make our critical judgments far more reliable. Surely we cannot with integrity, in this day of scholarship, continue to take isolated texts, out of context, to keep women in a place of subjugation in the Church, which is quite the contrary of what Jesus himself taught, Paul wrote, and the early Church practiced.

What Paul Really Thought about Women

Let us see then if we can find out what Paul really thought about women.[6] We must base our study on the life and writings of Paul primarily because that is what we have. How normative his acts and his thinking were we do not know. We wish we had parallel accounts from Thomas in India, Philip in North Africa, and most especially from Barnabas, who covered much the same territory as Paul himself, and who, as long as they were together, seems to have taken much of the initiative. We wish we had documents from Mary of Bethany, or Mary Magdalene, or some of the other women friends of Jesus. But it is Paul that we have. And it was Paul's letters, written long before the Gospel accounts were written down, that the earliest churches had. It was his letters, circulated and read in the house churches of the first century, that established what we usually consider a normative understanding of Christian doctrine. Not the organization of the Church, but the teaching of Christ was of supreme importance to Paul, and very often it was the women he met on his missionary journeys who best understood what he was trying to say, and helped him in his work.

In the first place, Paul in his youthful days apparently dragged off to prison Christian men and women alike (Acts 8:3; 22:4; cf. Galatians 1:13, 23). This may have been a left-handed compliment, worth noting. He was always impartial as between men and women.

His first relations with women after his conversion to Christianity were not the best. He took John Mark along on his first missionary journey, possibly at the instigation of the young man's mother, and from Perga sent him back to Jerusalem. Then at Antioch in Pisidia, where he had been speaking for two weeks with much success in the synagogue, the Jews stirred up some of the city's leading women to persecute him (Acts 13:50). But two years later, in Lystra (50 A.D.), he made the acquaintance of Eunice, a Jewish "believer," her mother, Lois, and her son Timothy, who were to be lifelong friends (Acts 16:1–5).

Shortly thereafter he met Lydia of Thyatira, who had come down to the river with her "woman's club" to hear the stranger preach (Acts

16:14). Lydia is described as a "worshiper of God," though just what that meant in this time and place we do not know. We do know that she was a businesswoman, probably well off, and quite a manager. She had her whole household baptized (we wonder what Paul thought of such a "mass baptism"), and she apparently planned to set up a church in her house. She "importuned" Paul to go to her house and undoubtedly entertained him with considerable "to-do." Meanwhile, a local slave girl, possessed of a spirit, kept following him around, embarrassing him. When Paul purged her of the spirit, her masters, who had been exploiting her for profit, were furious, and Paul landed in jail. When he got out, he paid Lydia a brief visit, exhorted the brethren, and departed. We hear no more of Lydia. She is not mentioned in Paul's later letter to the Philippians. We suspect the whole adventure at Philippi was quite an experience.

At Thessalonica and Beroea (Acts 17) Paul's popularity with the Greek women seems to have been matched by the opposition he aroused in the Jewish men. Demaris is mentioned among the converts at Athens (17:34).

Then at Corinth, in 51 A.D., Paul met two fellow Jewish-Christians, Priscilla and Aquila (Acts 18:2). Priscilla was a Roman—with influential relatives in the capital.[7] She and Aquila seem to have been escapees from the Christian persecution in Rome under Claudius, 49–50 A.D. Paul lived with them, working at the trade of tentmaking, and from this time on their fortunes were intertwined. Priscilla, from the capital city of the world, seems to have been educated, sophisticated, and well instructed in Christianity. She was probably one of the most stimulating colleagues Paul ever had. For Paul, this year and a half with Priscilla and Aquila in Corinth, working with his hands at a useful trade, and preaching at the synagogue to a mixed company of Jews and Greeks every Sabbath, may have been one of the happiest times of his life.

But please note especially: it was from Corinth, at this period, that Paul's first epistles—at least the first of which we have any record—went out: I and II Thessalonians. Someone may have been sending out apocalyptic leaflets in his name (II Thessalonians 2:2), and Paul may have thought it was high time to do something about it, since the letters were obviously contrary to his convictions (note II Thessalonians 3:17). On the other hand, how many times has a man of action like Paul first had the urge to write when there was a good editorial secretary at his elbow? Let this question ride for the moment—we shall come back to it.

Probably in 52 A.D. Priscilla and Aquila and Paul move to Ephesus.

While Paul is temporarily away on a missionary trip, Priscilla and Aquila are visited by Apollos of Alexandria, and they are shocked at his lax theology. They instruct him in Christian doctrine.

The Pauline letters of Philippians, Philemon, and Colossians are generally dated from Ephesus, 52–55 A.D., revised in Rome, 59–61 A.D. (remember this for a moment!). In general the mood is one of reconciliation and love: "I entreat Euodia and I entreat Syntyche to agree in the Lord, and I ask you, true yoke-fellows, to help these women, for they have labored side by side with me in the gospel, together with Clement and the rest of my fellow-workers whose names are in the book of life" (Philippians 4:2). The book of Philemon is addressed by Paul from prison in Ephesus to "Philemon, our beloved fellow-worker and Apphia our sister and Archippus, our fellow soldier, and the church in your house." Colossians was to be read to the church which held its meetings "at Nympha's house."

Galatians also was probably written from Ephesus, in the spring of 54. Priscilla and Aquila had established a church in their house in this city (I Corinthians 16:19). But Paul and other Christians are feeling increasing pressure, particularly from the Jews. Paul is grappling with the problem of freedom and law (see Galatians 4:21ff.). Priscilla, a Jewish woman converted to Christianity and actively working in its program, must have been especially aware of this tension, and if she was Paul's amanuensis or secretary, she must have recorded with some satisfaction his statement (Galatians 3:26ff.): "In Christ Jesus you are all sons of God, through faith. . . . There is neither Jew nor Greek, there is neither slave nor free, there is neither male nor female; for you are all one in Christ Jesus."

Corinthians, written at about the same time, also shows Paul conscious of increasing pressures. The church at Corinth was growing up and felt the need of organization and policy decisions as well as theological discussions. Paul, the pioneer evangelist, had little taste for such matters. Still, there were the letters perhaps brought by Chloe (I Corinthians 1:11), with their questions to be answered, and he labored over them conscientiously. One of these practical questions seems to have been about marriage and personal morality (I Corinthians 7): marriage counseling for the citizens of Corinth 53 A.D. The first half of verse 4 is too frequently quoted without the second half, giving a completely wrong impression; in full it reads: "For the wife does not rule over her own body, but the husband does; likewise the husband does not rule over his own body, but the wife does." And that is good marriage counseling in any day and age. As for the current tonsorial matters discussed in Chapter 11, surely it would be well to read a little further and discover the more basic opinion that "in the Lord woman is not independent of man nor man of woman; for as woman was made for man, so man is now born of woman. And all things are from God" (I Corinthians 11:11–12).[8]

As for the church service, Paul has some good points summed up in the statement, "For God is not a God of confusion but of peace," or, "Do all things decently and in order." The women, in their new-found freedom, were undoubtedly becoming loud and obstreperous. The author of the letter from Corinth wanted to know what could be done. And Paul, of all the people, surely in exasperation at having such trivial questions referred to him, replies, of all things, "Tell them to keep quiet—there's a *law* about women speaking in public!" He was undoubtedly referring to the meetings in the synagogue at Corinth (Acts 18:8) where both Greeks and Hebrews attended. Certainly the unrestrained manner of the Greek women would have brought considerable criticism on them from the Jews, and as long as they were accepting synagogue hospitality, they should have the courtesy to abide by the synagogue rules. They could talk things over with their husbands when they got home. Note a similar appeal to the Hebrew law in I Corinthians 9:8 and in regard to Timothy (Acts 16:3). A. C. McGiffert says that Paul's remarks about women not speaking in church "must have sounded strange to the Corinthians" and that Paul himself must have found his arguments weak and inconsistent with his general principles, so he clinches his point with an appeal to the general custom in the churches. Since the group were probably still meeting in the Jewish synagogue, it is probable that his argument was really of a piece with his "if meat maketh my brother to offend, I will eat no meat. . . ." statement. The women of Corinth were really being offensive and it was doing the Christian cause no good.

Aquila and Prisca are still in Ephesus, and greetings from them are added to I Corinthians. (Since part of II Corinthians as we now have it seems to precede I Corinthians, and since one document to Corinth apparently is lost, there is no reason to believe that there is any particular significance in the omission of similar greetings at the end of II Corinthians. I and II Corinthians were written within a short time of each other. Moreover, II Corinthians does not end on a note in which friendly felicitations are particularly in place.) Paul promises to pay them what sounds like a very official visit shortly.

As every student of Paul's career knows, the sources and chronology at this point become confused. Paul's life became increasingly difficult, and it is probable that he was rather seriously injured in the Ephesus riots. He tells (Romans 16:3–4) that Priscilla and Aquila risked their lives for him, and it was probably at this time. There must have been considerable talk about going to Rome (Paul's "vow" of Acts 18:18?) among the three friends, and perhaps when the trouble at Ephesus cooled down Priscilla and Aquila decided to return to the capital city, where her family lived and where the Nero persecutions had not yet gotten under way—for the moment things were quiet. Paul also had announced that he wanted to make one more trip to Jerusalem, "and after I have been there, I must also see Rome" (Acts 19:21). The reason for this chronology is that when Paul's ship for Jerusalem leaves Troas, Paul has decided to sail right past Ephesus, to avoid spending the night in Asia, and so, perhaps, get to Jerusalem for Pentecost. We suspect he would have stayed over in Ephesus if Priscilla and Aquila had still been there. However, at the last moment, he still cannot quite just sail by. He has the ship stop at Miletus and sends for the elders of the church at Ephesus to come down to the seaport town for a conference (Acts 20:17)—and hopefully with news for a lonely man?

The letter of Paul to the Romans, the commentaries tell us, was written from Corinth (55 A.D.) during Paul's promised visit to that city. It was directed to Rome, but was apparently somewhat of a circular letter. A number of copies were found in Ephesus and other cities where Paul was known. It is probably the most polished as well as the most profound of the Pauline letters. It seems altogether probable that he sent the draft to Priscilla in Rome, where she did the kind of editorial work she had done on all his letters and sent out copies to all the churches on the list. We have already noted that the Pauline letters of Philippians, Philemon, and Colossians (52–55 A.D. from Ephesus) are generally believed to have been revised *from Rome*, 59–61 A.D.

In other words, *Prisca was definitely with Paul at the time when every genuine Pauline letter is independently dated, with the exception of Romans, and the sending out of this final letter from Rome, via Priscilla, may well have been agreed upon before they parted in Ephesus.* Moreover, Prisca was in Rome at the time Biblical scholars say Philippians, Philemon, and Colossians were sent out in revised form from that city. We suspect, in fact, that it was Prisca who had the responsibility for sending copies of the various Pauline letters to the house churches of those early years, when their reading was one of the most important parts of the Christian gatherings: "To [Prisca]

not only I [Paul] but all the churches of the Gentiles give thanks"
(Romans 16:3ff.). We have *no* authentic Pauline letters with which
we cannot establish a definite relation to Priscilla.

Quite aside from this, might it not be more profitable for us to try to
reinterpret such a passage as Romans 8:33 to 15:7 in terms of meaning
for the man-woman relationship in our present society, instead of investing so much of our time and thought arguing over how Paul tried to
keep the Greek women attending the meetings held at the Jewish
synagogue in Corinth in the first century from behaving in what their
hosts would consider an unseemly fashion?

In this superb passage from Romans, Paul pointedly raises the question of why people cannot with grace abide the fact that people are
different. He is speaking specifically to the question which is rocking the
Church at the time—the Jewish-Gentile controversy. That was the thing
that was bedeviling Christian life and provoking controversy in both
Rome and Jerusalem. Paul still carried the physical and emotional
wounds he received during the riots at Ephesus. He speaks, as usual, to
a specific point, but he is not really talking at the level of local custom
and expediency, but on a question that is at the very heart of the
Christian faith—the Christian's acceptance of our oneness in Christ,
and our individual responsibility to him.

No Christian (Jew or Gentile, slave or free, male or female) has the
right on these grounds to feel or act superior or inferior. Arguments in
the three categories (which Paul had already established) are parallel.
In another century—perhaps in the twentieth century—we believe Paul
might well have put it this way:

Who shall presume to try to separate *women* from the love of Christ?
If God is for them, who can be against them? Not just *males*, but all
children of his creation are children of God; moreover, God has mercy
on whoever he wills (and it seems often to be a woman). And who
are you, man or woman, to answer back to God? Didn't the potter know
what he was about when he made mankind in two complementary
patterns? If one part of the dough is holy, so is the whole lump; if the
root of a vine is holy, so are the branches. Since we have individual
gifts according to the grace given us, let us use them. Let men and
women both hold fast to that which is good, loving one another with
kindred affection, outdoing one another in showing each other honor,
blessing not cursing, never being haughty or conceited, overcoming evil
with good, never putting a hindrance or stumbling block in each other's
way, but living in such harmony one with another, in accord with
Christ Jesus, that together you may with one voice glorify God.

(We do not believe we have taken any liberties with this paraphrase of the much longer passage, of which Paul would not approve.)

Romans 16:1-16 gives us a long list of people, many of them women, to whom greetings are sent: deaconess Phoebe (bearer of the letter to Rome); Prisca, of course; Mary—we do not know which one; Julia, "the beloved"; Persis; Rufus' mother' Junia, referred to by Chrysostom as a woman apostle; Nereus' sister, and Olympas are among the women singled out for special greeting.

In regard to Paul's correspondence as a whole, the question is bound to arise whether Paul's approval of women's full participation in the Church was normative for the time. The best answer is that Paul, accepting women, never bothered to argue about it. If there had been any question, we would have expected somewhere a justification of his attitude of acceptance.

Considering how many administrative questions come up in the churches today, with 2000 years of tradition behind us, it should not surprise us that many arose in the churches of the first century.

For instance, the ability to "speak with tongues" was at first highly prized in the young churches and considered a "gift of the Spirit," but the women became so apt at it (I Corinthians 11:5) that something had to be done about it. Then, as now, when women "got started" they did not always know when to stop (I Corinthians 14:34). The young church at Corinth was probably feeling the lack of the wise guidance of Aquila and Priscilla, who had been with them in their earliest days, and their successors in that city may have been trying to outdo them and each other, instead of doing everything "decently and in order," as Paul advised.

A side of Paul's genius which is seldom sufficiently emphasized is the extent to which he respected people as *individuals*—male and female, old and young, Jew and Gentile. He expected them, as Christians, to have faith and love, and to use discretion and self-control. He offered no blueprints, and so far as we know suggested no organizational patterns. But he was intensely interested in people who displayed ability for genuine Christian leadership. He preached a gospel of freedom and responsibility for both men and women.

Chapter 4

THE EARLY CHURCH

The Roman Empire, with its geographic unity of vast territory, a good system of roads and communications, and a *lingua franca*, still lacked the unifying force of a common religion. The state religion which the emperor sought to establish (without interfering too radically with the many existing ones), like most state religions, fell short in the all-important area of ethical motivation. There were still some moments of glory for the empire—still some emperors of conscience and dignity. And eventually the persecutions ceased, and there was even patronage for the Christian Church: a sort of belated attempt to bargain with the Lord.

Violence was brooding, however, at least from the second century on, not only in Roman officialdom, but in the satiated hearts of the common people, who had traded in the artistic glory that had once been the hallmark of classic culture for the bloody spectaculars of the arena; and the stimulation of great philosophy for non-ethical loyalty to the military defense of the state.

It is not the shouts of the invading barbarians that chill one's blood as we read the history of the first centuries of the Christian era. The barbarians are at least going somewhere. What really chills us is the sight of opulent emperors sitting there on their decadent thrones, waiting; and the military strategists, busily engaged in battle, the results of which they honestly believe will determine the world's destiny. It is not the blood of the martyrs, as they are tossed about by savage animals for the amusement of the perverted populace, that makes the picture too terrible to contemplate, but the fact that at a time like this the great ecclesiastical debates could center on organizational structure, including the importance of the bishops and the unimportance of women, upon personalities, and upon the niceties of competitive theological schemes.

Haggling over theological wordage, the empire was divided, while from the distance the screams of Alaric and his fast-approaching hordes almost drowned out the churchmen's vitriolic polemics against women heard at some of the great church councils.[1]

These are not the sort of days and conditions to produce a Nefertiti, a Helen of Troy, a Semiramis, a Queen of Sheba, a Dido, or a Sappho. Still, women continued to be born and to bear children and find avenues of communal service. With Christian women especially, religion continued to be a motivating force in their lives. Not all religions and not all women are equally admirable, but most women whose achievements we know from the past have admitted some sort of religious motivation. Perhaps never in history was that motivation more urgent and compelling than in the first centuries of the Christian era.

It was Marcus Aurelius, the last of the great Stoics (121–180), who saw in nascent Christianity those forces which state religion lacked, and which made it, therefore, the most potent rival of emperor worship (which he himself scorned, but which, as emperor, he was bound to defend).[2] Christianity was a very real danger to the empire in its already precarious position, so Marcus Aurelius, otherwise one of the best of emperors, permitted, during his reign, one of the worst of persecutions. These were days of confused patterns of life and confused motives. It is little wonder that some who loved the young Church set about to form a strong organization that would assure its survival. And since it was an era when military strength and a power structure might readily be mistaken for the measure of all things, it is little wonder that women found themselves increasingly outside the inner circles of church organization, but certainly not outside the Christian religion.

Many Varied Patterns

Many scholars have pointed out that neither Jesus nor Paul, nor any of the other apostles, apparently thought of the new religion in organizational terms. None of them seem to have made charts of authority or duties to guide their successors. To some eager and admittedly conscientious churchmen of the second century, this may have seemed like something of an oversight—or at least a lack which it was the assignment of their own generation to rectify. The fact that Christianity had already spread so widely and developed such diverse forms made their task that much more difficult! Says Latourette: "Left as it was by its founder without elaborate organization or carefully formulated creed or ritual, but with the powerful impulse of a transforming experience and a gripping enthusiasm, it is not remarkable that, thrown into the Mediterranean world, Christianity should early develop many forms."[3]

He points out various tensions, such as those which developed between Judaistic formalism on one extreme and gnostic liberties on the other. Adherents of each side, like adherents of our own many denominations today, truly believed that they were most fully expressing the mind and will of Christ. If this multiplicity of interpretation was apparent in the faith itself, how much more obvious it must have been in the organizational structures which grew up to support that faith in various parts of the world. No one could blame the devoted churchmen of the day for wishing to bring some norm of worship practices and polity to the growing ecclesiastical pattern. This need was probably particularly evident to the itinerant evangelists who went from church to church and had opportunity to note how disorganized and diverse the organizational patterns were. Those who, like Paul, had founded many churches were probably besieged from time to time by questions from their "spiritual children," to whom it was indeed difficult to give any definite "ruling" that would have more than local application. It was probably true enough that some basis for general guidance was a practical need.

It seems quite possible that the first attempts toward more uniform rule met with little approval from the women, who had been guiding forces in many of the local Christian groups. Many women, we know, had established churches in their own homes and had probably set up patterns of activity according to their own best judgment. When the young reformers launched their program, were there female cries of protest against "regimentation"?

That might account for some perplexing questions about the so-called pastoral epistles.

We know that both Jesus and Paul not only accepted and appreciated women but that Paul worked with Western women and valued them as associates. Toward the end of the first century or somewhat later, however, three short letters were circulated which used the literary device of purporting to be written by Paul, to Timothy and Titus. They have been described by competent scholars as late first-, or quite possibly second-century manuals, using a number of "Paulisms" (not always too cleverly) to create the impression of authentic Pauline origin.[4] These letters make reference, however, to events which took place long after Paul's day—for instance, to persecutions in which martyrs were burned. Nothing of this sort happened during Paul's lifetime. We do not know who wrote these Timothy and Titus epistles, but it surely could *not* have been Paul. This is also confirmed by a reading of I

Timothy, chapters 3 and 5, which refer to details of church organization, questions about which had not even arisen at the time of Paul. Women are actually forbidden to speak in public meetings or to teach. Imagine Paul trying to explain that to his fellow worker Priscilla, or to some of the other women whom he mentions in the salutations of his letters!

In the sophisticated Greek and Roman atmosphere, where women, before conversion to Christianity, had taken part in pagan religious ceremonies, the idea of keeping silent in the churches certainly never had much appeal. They saw no reason why they should. Moreover, they seem to have had special talent for "speaking in tongues," and since this was regarded as "prophesying," even Jewish converts must have felt it was all right—there was, after all, a tradition of women prophets in the Hebrew religion from the time of Miriam.

The book of I Peter, written about the same time as the pastorals, is likewise certainly not written by the Peter we know from the Scriptures. Here the author admonishes wifely submission and objects to the way the ladies braid their hair, which must have been a popular conceit of the time. Quite aside from literary or historical problems which make it impossible to concede that the Apostle wrote this, it would seem that Peter, busy as he was with the Lord's work, probably had something more important to think and write about.

These are the first *general attacks* on women in the Church of which we have record. Paul's oft-quoted (and generalized) critical remarks were always specific suggestions in answer to specific questions. Also, they are far outweighed, as we have seen, by his more frequent words of appreciation.

It was undoubtedly time, however, to give some thought to the organization of the Church, and the various offices in the churches. The Church's spread and growth had been phenomenal, yet, as in Saul's time, everyone "did as he pleased." The founder-evangelists had quite naturally assumed a continuing responsibility for their "spiritual children," visiting them and corresponding with them, encouraging them and answering their questions. Such a man became known as the "overseer" or "guardian" and finally as "bishop." To the position of bishop it was quite proper for an ambitious young clergyman to aspire (I Timothy 3:1), provided of course he had the spiritual qualifications (Titus 1:7). However, just when the office of bishop—and even more the office of Pope—became official, or just what was involved in its becoming official, is not at all certain.[5] It seems natural enough for the bishop of Rome to have assumed pre-eminence. Rome was the capital city, and one estimate of the size of the church there in 250 A.D. is 30,000. This is, however, admittedly a guess. The size and organization of churches in other parts of the empire is even less well documented.[6]

Home Churches, "Widows," and "Virgins"

It is reasonable enough that considering traveling conditions and social customs of the time, the traveling evangelist, and hence the bishop, should be a man. However, when the young churches outgrew (as they soon did) their status as a Jewish sect, meetings began to be held, and centers of activity were set up, in homes of members. Such a group would be known as "the church that meets at the house of Mary Mark," for instance (Acts 12:12). Considering the communal structure of the early Church as described in the first part of the book of Acts, a good deal of activity aside from the worship service must have gone on in these "house churches," and it seems altogether probable that the resident woman may have taken on a good many functions of a local pastor, as distinct from a visiting preaching minister or evangelist.

Latourette points out that the Christian ministry shares the priestly function of Judaism, but that from the first it has also "embraced a purpose which seems to have been derived directly from the example of Jesus himself, that of pastor or shepherd." Included in this pastoral function is "care of individuals, with the ideal of loving, self-forgetful effort, to win them to what the Christian conceives as the highest life and to help them to grow into it."[7] It seems to have been something of this sort of ministry which the women sought to demonstrate at the churches in their houses of the early Christian era.

Men, from the beginning, developed a taste for itineration and were welcomed to the home churches, or neighboring churches, for the stories of their experiences, news of friends in other churches, reading of letters from fellow evangelists, and Christian insights gleaned from their wider fields of contact. They were the preachers. But it was probably the women who took care of the ongoing counseling and teaching functions. It was in the ministry of love and care and consolation that the women made their greatest contribution to the life of the early Church. The "widows" (who in the beginning were probably real widows dependent upon the Church for support) were charged primarily, at this time, with "fasting and prayer." They apparently cut out their own work for themselves and were not dependent on masculine supervision. Later their work would vary from place to place, according to the needs of the Christian group and the competence and special abilities of the women. Ignatius (*Ad Smyrnaeos* XIII) refers to the widows as "intercessors of the Church," and with the bishops, deacons, and presbyters the "altar of God." The woman who was a deacon (not till the third century was there a differentiation between a deacon and deaconess) was at first one of those who served the communal meal (Acts 6), so that the apostles could devote full time to preaching. Soon, however, and as the Church moved out from Jerusalem, they became responsible for the common supplies, and for the distribution of food or funds to those in need, hence, to helping fellow Christians in most any kind of need or trouble. The work of the deaconess, as we shall see, also varied from time to time and place to place, but through the centuries it has kept this basic commitment to be the hands of Christ where help is needed.[8] During this early period they visited the sick, gave consolation to the bereaved, made arrangements for funerals and baptisms, cared for orphans, secured financial aid for those who lost their employment or found themselves in other difficulties because they had joined the Christian group.

A third group of women within the primitive church were the "virgins." These were younger women—probably girls who had been raised in or by the Christian community. They do not seem to have been assigned any specific duties in connection with this title, but were considered general assistants.

As the Church continued to grow and spread, opposition to it became stronger, and it became increasingly obvious to the traveling evangelists that even the unity of faith would be endangered if the churches were to continue each to go its own way, adopting local forms of worship and establishing patterns of activity conforming to local needs and the interests and abilities of local personnel.

It might have been Tertullian (c. 150–230) who first fully perceived the necessity for some normative structure which would be basic for a religion destined by its missionary commitment to become universal. Moreover, people of the second and third centuries (like people today) seemed forever to be going somewhere, and it was highly desirable that they be able to fit into the church life of areas they visited, or where they settled, without a major amount of upheaval and adjustment.

Tertullian was the great theologian of his age. To his orderly mind, the disorder of the Church must have seemed really scandalous. Born in Carthage, son of an army officer, trained as a lawyer, he was con-

verted to Christianity by the "fringe group" Montanists. Devoutly
Christian, he sounded a battle cry against both the pagan world and
worldly Christians, while trying desperately to marshal the Christian
forces into an efficient and effective system.[9] Yet he attacked the growing ecclesiasticism of the Church, demanding, "Are not we laymen
priests also?" Whether he included women in his thinking on this
subject, we have no way of knowing. He seems to have had the all-
inclusive type of mind which is so often labeled by lesser minds as
"inconsistent." It is easy for most any modern churchman to find a
quote from Tertullian to fit the need of his own argument. It would
seem that most writers on early Christianity have done so. It was said
that he thought of church reorganization in military terms. Yet he
finally broke with the church organization he had defended and helped
to build, apparently because he could not bear to see it become a
political organization. His last days were spent as a presbyter in the
Montanist group in Carthage.

We are frankly not quite sure what his attitude about women was.
Some of the "fringe groups" among the Christians, then as now, made
far more room for women than the "main line" churches did. The
Montanists, for instance, had both women bishops and women prophets
in their churches. When the other theologians attacked them, it was a
little hard to tell for sure whether they were being attacked for their
theology, or because of their tolerance for women in the work of the
Church. We are told that Tertullian forbade women to give instruction,
but of course the same accusation—or a similar one—was made against
Paul. Perhaps Tertullian also had been speaking to a specific case—
perhaps to an illiterate woman with big ideas of her own importance!
If he directed some polemics against woman's vanity, so did Jeremiah
in his day—in both cases probably in a deeply concerned effort to get
women to see their responsibilities in wider perspectives.

At any rate, we are not going to blame Tertullian for the fact that
beginning with the third or fourth centuries there seems to have been
a gradual wearing away of women's responsibility in the Church. Probably it was simply that those who recognized that the church organization called for a reform saw its women as the most vulnerable possibility.

During the earliest Christian centuries, there seem to have been no
general lists of responsibilities for the various offices, and no indication
of what was or was not "proper" church work for a man or for a
woman.

Many mature women had been attracted to the new religion, and the
number of widows recruited posed a practical problem, since they often

had no means of personal or community support; their conversion had cut many of them off from their families. The churches had no intention of repudiating their responsibility for these women; yet everyone was supposed to contribute to the general communal funds. It was decided that they could make their best contribution through fasting and prayer. However, some younger women, and some who were by no means needy, saw the devotional life as the channel through which they, also, could make their greatest contribution to the faith. There were instances of unmarried women under twenty being enrolled as "widows" and to some theologians this constituted a "scandal." Whether they received their living free, we do not know. In some areas "widows," no longer necessarily "real widows" but mature women of good character, had been given teaching functions, or responsibilities in regard to preparing women for baptism or communion; some were doorkeepers and ushers in the churches. The fact that the "virgins" had been absorbed by the "widows" undoubtedly lowered the age range of the latter group and made them seem more efficient in an age that had given up the rather total emphasis on fasting and prayer while waiting for the Second Coming, and in which Christians were trying to work out a *modus vivendi*[10] in relation to the Roman Empire. The "presiding widow," who was approximately what her title implies, was often a very powerful woman in her church.

The Deaconesses

The work of the deaconesses had also been increasing. Hospitality to travelers, negotiating on behalf of Christians who were in prison because of their faith, and help to the general community (not just to Christians only) in case of pestilence or disaster were in their department. A deaconess might carry the sacraments to the sick (though as early as the second century Justin Martyr had thought it necessary to make a clear statement that a deaconess was doing this as an assistant to the bishop, and *not* as a "minister of the altar").

Sometimes the work of the widow and the deaconess overlapped, and as the churches became less persecution- and more prestige-conscious, this could become a subject of serious contention.

Actually what we know concerning women's work in the churches during the first few centuries of the Christian era comes not from records of what they are permitted or expected to do, but from some theologian's speculation or some council's decision as to things they are no longer permitted to do. Because these prohibitions (like the "evils" they sought to correct) varied greatly from place to place, we can, from them, form something of a picture of the many diverse things women in the early Church did before they were prohibited (and many of which they undoubtedly kept right on doing for a while at least, prohibition or no prohibition, because these services were needed.[11]

For instance: In the third century the Church fathers speak frequently of the widows, some with great approval, but Tertullian (Monagomis 11) was against their teaching or baptizing. There is a scandal about a Montanus group allowing two women to preach.

Deaconesses are mentioned in various council pronouncements, but Ambrose (c. 340–397), commenting on the I Timothy passage about women, says they are not allowed to hold office in the Church. Jerome (347?–419) assures us they do in the East.

The Council of Laodicea (c. 381) held that no more women presbyters could be appointed, and that no women could "approach the altar," but the Council of Chalcedon (451) allows the consecration of a deaconess on probation at the age of forty.

Olympias (360–408?) was a widow and deaconess at the age of eighteen, and highly appreciated by Chrysostom, who wrote her at least seventeen letters.

The Synod of Orange (441) forbade ordination of women, but the Second Council of Orleans (533) speaks of deaconesses (presumably ordained) in Gaul. Yet presumably the same council denies woman "on account of the weakness of her sex" the right to give the diaconal benediction. However, deaconesses and archdeaconesses aided in a communion service at Constantinople in the twelfth century.

Deaconesses seem to have had a very high degree of resiliency. Or, as one pagan writer put it, "What women there are among the Christians!"

An interesting subject for speculation is why Syrian writings showed high regard for their Christian women for some time after that regard had faded in Rome.[12]

The Syrian Didascalia (300) gives women a definite order of ministry "side by side with the bishops, deacons and priests." Richardson finds it significant that, especially in the East, the Holy Spirit is referred to as feminine and is identified with the work of the deaconesses. The deaconess receives the newly baptized woman as she emerges from the water and instructs her "how the seal of baptism may be unbroken in chastity and holiness."

The Testament of the Lord (Asia Minor) ranks widows above deaconesses, but the deaconess takes the sacrament to sick women.

The Apostolic Constitutions, which *purports to be the voice of the apostles* themselves, speaking at a top-level conference, is a typically confusing document; it was apparently *written in the fourth century* and officially confirmed at an even later date—the Third Council of Constantinople (680). This document indicates that the bishop anoints only the head of a woman; the deaconess anoints the rest. But the deaconess is not to serve at the altar, teach, or baptize. The document seems to provide, however, an ordaining prayer and rules for the imposition of the hands of the bishop in the presence of presbyters, deacons, and other deaconesses. The order of precedence seems to be bishops, presbyters, deacons and deaconesses, widows. The ordination of a deacon or deaconess is the same except for one notable exception: the prayer for the men promises that if they serve faithfully and well, they may aspire to be "appointed eventually to higher office in the Church." For women being consecrated for the same duties, the Church prays that God will "grant unto her the Holy Spirit . . . that she may worthily accomplish the work committed to her."

The attitude of any locality at any time was apt to be more or less the reflection of the power and attitude of the local bishop (or his predecessor). Chrysostom of Antioch (347?–407), in spite of his quarrels with the Empress Eudoxia, had a high regard for women in the Church, and he may well have influenced the Eastern attitude of his century.

Any document from the period of the Church fathers should be related to the context. To generalize either the procedure or theology or chronology of these first centuries, and the doctrines they seem to propound, is quite impossible. Each church was busily working out its own problems and its own contribution to the Church, but there was certainly no unanimity, nor should we try to discover it where it did not exist.

What Latourette has called a "generation of peace for the Church" (260–303) had given the Christians a chance to expand their influence and consolidate their forces. We get a frequent but fleeting glimpse of women of all ranks, throughout the empire, telling the story of Christianity wherever people would listen, from the palace to the wash houses. Origen gives us the story of how "some Christians make it their business to wander, not only from city to city, but even to villages and hamlets, to win fresh converts . . . and the people give hospitality to these messengers of the faith." A non-Christian writer reports how

Christian servants in a home encourage the children and women of the family to come secretly to the women's quarters or the laundry to hear the full story, which they can only mention as they go about their daily tasks. Christianity could not wait to have the organizational structure complete—it was already a missionary movement.[13]

How the Church Organization Became All Male

The way in which the *organization* of the Church became an all-male operation is a mystery, but it was very likely a result, at least in part, of the close alliance which came about between the Church and the Roman Army. Constantine's agreement, if there was a formal one, was not entirely altruistic. He expected a *quid pro quo* in the way of prayers which would outweigh his enemies' reliance on magic formulas. He also expected the priests to accompany the troops and help their military morale. In this capacity women were unacceptable.

One rationalization for exclusion of women from the organization of the Church was that there were altogether too many women in the mystery cults with which Rome was infested. The emperor had many reasons, as a matter of fact, for his attitude of tolerance for Christians: the miraculous "in hoc signo" sign in the sky; the fact that a large proportion of his people held to the new faith, and he needed their support[14]; but also his mother's interest in Christianity and the fact that she reassured him that the libelous statements against the Christians were false. After Constantine made peace with the Church, one of his daughters founded the first women's cloister, and Helena, his mother, built a hospice for pilgrims. Other noble ladies followed their example. In similar activities many women found new outlets for creative religious instincts which were being dangerously curbed in the organized Church itself. At this period, too, women began taking an interest in education and the founding of schools.[15] Fabiola founded the first hospital in Rome, and was called by Jerome "the praise of Christians, the wonder of the Gentiles, the mourning of the poor, and the consolation of the monks."

We do not seem to have any record of the extent to which women were allowed, at this period, to do the actual work in the churches, but under male direction. As long as a slave society supplied manpower, this was probably not necessary.

Because materials about Rome are generally more readily available than those about other parts of the empire, there is always a temptation to treat the Roman story as if it were normative, which of course it was not. Michael Gough[16] points out that even while Rome was trying to hold back the progress of Christianity by periodic persecutions, actually the Roman roads and the various systems of communication and transportation which the empire developed were of tremendous importance to the spread of the young religion. In the West, missionaries traveled the highways which had been built for military purposes. In the East, however, which had a longer history of settled civilization, the missionaries were more apt to get off the highways onto age-old side roads. Because of this difference, the Eastern type of Christianity tended to be less patterned after the highly organized military-minded empire, and to be more indigenous and flexible, and perhaps less practically efficient. It is tempting to follow with Gough the expansion, especially in the East; also all the various military, governmental, and personal elements involved in the institutional success of Christianity, and the ways in which it was adapted and sometimes perverted in important matters by its cultural milieu.

We are less tempted to go into the rampant theological controversies that rocked the inner circles of the Church itself. Unfortunately there do not seem to have been women with an appreciation of the value of organization, which might have led them to make an issue of their own right to continue to serve the Church in a creative capacity. The women appear to have been too busy spreading the Gospel to put up much of a protest against being gradually relegated to an ineffective and unchallenging position within the structure of the Church. In the famous Council of Nicaea (325) they apparently had no part at all, although almost anyone studying the minutes might point out where their counsel would have been of benefit. And the women certainly would have been right in mentioning the precedent of their presence at that even more important meeting in the upper room in Jerusalem at the time of the first Christian Pentecost. McGiffert tells us that self-abnegation rather than self-assertion is the recognized ideal of the Christian of these first centuries.[17] If any woman raised a voice of protest, the story has not come down to us. But then neither have we often heard the women of the twentieth century protesting that there are so few women at the policy level of our great denominations, or in the presidium or central committee of the World Council of Churches. And the longer the negative trend goes on, the more precedent there is, and the harder it is to make the correction which is ultimately inevitable.

It was largely the women's own fault that the message did not get through to the churchmen of the fourth and fifth centuries that the new

Gospel included a new attitude toward women.[18] We can understand the women of the East falling back into submissive attitudes which had been theirs for a matter of centuries. But we can hardly understand why the women of the West failed to make at least a protest. Women's pacifistic attitudes toward life have more than once in history led them to fail to take the responsibility they should, and it seems likely that this was one of those times.

As we read the accounts of the arrogance, and the linguistic and sometimes physical violence, that took place at the Council of Nicaea, presided over by the emperor who was not even a baptized Christian, we cannot help but wonder what some churchwomen would have thought of such a meeting, even if they had been thought worthy to attend.

But whether they were allowed at Church councils or not, women went right on having a most significant part in the growth and formation of the character of the new religion.

Let us pause now to meet just a few of the women of this period who, each in her own way, helped to shape the course Christianity was to take in the years ahead.[19]

The Female Martyrs

It has been pointed out as evidence of the respect which the Christian men held for their women that they never denied them the honor of being martyrs for the Church. One of the earliest martyrs was the little slave girl Blandina. Blandina was one of the forty-eight martyrs of Lyons (177), during the persecutions of Marcus Aurelius. Eusebius tells of this persecution. Christians were first excluded from the baths, the markets, then their homes. They were exposed to all manner of public indignities, and finally to stonings. Persons who feared for their own safety made gross charges against the Christians, and finally the populace and the magistrates fell upon these Christian people and dragged them to their deaths. Blandina's mistress, herself a Christian, was afraid the girl might weaken under such persecution, but her resolute spirit revived for a moment even as her body was being torn asunder, and with her dying breath she raised her voice and cried out: "I am a Christian; no wickedness is carried on by us!" After it was all over, her persecutors were inclined to believe her.

Perpetua and Felicity were another lady and her slave, martyred in Carthage during the persecution under Severus in 202. Perpetua was a young wife and mother, daughter of a Carthaginian pagan. She and Felicity were thrown into prison, where Felicity gave birth to a daughter while they were awaiting the great festival for victorious returning soldiers, at which the two women were exposed to wild beasts, to be tossed about on their horns in a particularly bloodthirsty manner, before being finally stabbed by gladiators. At a later date a yearly festival was instituted in honor of Perpetua and Felicity.

Agnes and Anastasia died in the Diocletian persecution (303). Agnes, a Roman girl in her early teens, was a very popular young lady, and already very much sought after by the young blades of the time because of her wealth and beauty. She was, however, a "virgin" of the Church and felt very strongly the call to a Christian vocation. A disgruntled rejected suitor reported her to the governor. She was arrested and ordered to sacrifice to the Roman gods. When she refused to make the required libation, she was either stabbed to death or (some reports say) beheaded. Her sister Emerentiana was also a Christian martyr.

Anastasia was the daughter of the Roman nobleman, Praetextatus, but her mother was a Christian and had raised her daughter in the Christian faith, a fact that Praetextatus neglected to mention when he was arranging for the girl's marriage. Discovering the truth only after the marriage had taken place, the husband neglected and abused Anastasia and set to work to squander her fortune. Eventually he died, and Anastasia began to devote herself and what fortune was left to Christian charity. She was especially interested in making life more bearable for the Christian prisoners awaiting their fate in the prison at Aquileia. Her efforts to help them aroused suspicion, and she was accused, tried, and burned alive.

Christian women often had what might be called a catalytic effect on society. For a child raised in the pagan culture of Roman society, particularly if he happened to have a pagan father, the anti-Christian social pressures would have been very powerful. Many of the early churchmen were proud to give credit for their conversion, or their particular competence in some chosen field of church work, to some woman—usually a mother, sister, or wife.

Augustine's Mother

Augustine (354–430) pays a heartwarming tribute to what his mother, Monica, meant to him (*Confessions*, passim). Monica was the Christian wife of the "personable but dissolute" (later converted by Monica) pagan Patricius of Tagaste, North Africa. Augustine, their eldest son, was, as a lad, not much credit to her influence; he seemed to be more inclined to follow in his father's footsteps. Monica, sustained it seems by an early vision which persuaded her that her son was destined for a life of Christian service and devotion, continued year after year in her praying and fasting on his behalf. When he was nineteen, he became interested in the Manichaeans. This was a sad time for his more orthodox mother, who had looked forward to his conversion to "main line" Christianity. She tried to get the bishop to talk to him, but the bishop was wise enough to see that Augustine's religious development must take its own course, even if it was a roundabout one. His own development had taken him over the same path. Then, as Augustine reports it, "When [after the bishop had told her this] she would not be satisfied, but urged him more, with entreaties and many tears, that he would see me and discourse with me, he, a little displeased at her importunity, saith, 'Go thy way and God bless thee, for it is not possible that the son of these tears should perish.' Which answer she took (as she often mentioned in her conversations with me) as if it had sounded from heaven." Nine years later, when Augustine, now twenty-eight, joined her own church, she felt that the tears and the fasts had indeed not been in vain. Of course she had no way of knowing that he was to continue in his spiritual growth and become, in due time, the outstanding theologian of the Christian Church.

Because of Augustine's great devotion to his mother, and because he was a "writing saint," we know much more about Monica than we do about almost any woman of this period. But we do not know too much about how she looked, or kept house, or even what offices if any she held in the local church. The things Augustine thought worth telling about his mother related to how she thought, how she interpreted her Christian responsibility, how she talked to her friends and neighbors about life and death, what her strength and her prayers meant to her husband and children. It is only as we read about Augustine's mother in this light, in the words of her son, that we realize how seldom the theologians and historians of any period have bothered to give us this kind of a report as to what Christian women were really like.

Augustine (in his Confessions addressing God) gives us the word picture of Augustine and Monica standing before the garden window, "enquiring between ourselves in the presence of the Truth which Thou art, of what sort the eternal life of the saints was to be, which eye hath not seen nor ear heard. . . . And when our discourse was brought to that point that the very highest delight of the earthly senses, in the very purest material light, was, in respect to the sweetness of that life, not only not worthy of comparison, but not even of mention, we, raising up ourselves with a more glowing affection toward the 'Self-name,' did by degree pass through all things bodily . . . we came to our own minds and went beyond them that we might arrive at the region of never-failing plenty, where Thou feedest Israel forever with the food of truth, and where life is the Wisdom by whom all things are made, and what have been, and what shall be! and she is not made, but is, as she hath been, and so shall she ever be, yea rather to 'have been' and 'hereafter to be' are not in her, but only 'to be' seeing she is eternal."

Augustine is to be read, not quoted piecemeal, and we must apologize to him. But our point is a very simple one: who but Augustine—surely one of the most respected names in theology—would have had the courage and honesty to report that it was in conversation with his mother that he developed many of the most profound insights of his career?

Norma and Arethusa are famous for their influence on their sons Gregory of Nazianzen and Chrysostom. Marcella, sister of Ambrose, raised and educated him in the Christian tradition. Marcina helped raise and teach her three brothers—Basil the eloquent; Gregory of Nyssa, the administrator; and Peter of Sebaste, the humanitarian—all prominent churchmen.

Women of Action

But many Christian women were persons of action in their own right: Paula (347-404), scholar and traveler, was from one of the noblest Roman families and possessed of great wealth (she owned a whole city). But she was interested in religion and education; she was reported to be a fine Hebrew scholar. Jerome was a frequent visitor at her home, and Paula and her daughter, Eustochium, also a Hebrew scholar, helped him translate the Hebrew Bible into Latin (the Vulgate). Paula was a generous patron of education and welfare work, and after her husband's death devoted herself increasingly to charity, saying she hoped to die a pauper and be buried in a borrowed shroud. She interested a group of Roman Christians in making a trip to Palestine under Jerome's leadership. There they established a group of church institutions, including a monastery, nunneries, and a hospital.

Her friend Fabiola established the first hospital in Rome.

Brigid of Kildare (c. 453-523) took an active part in the evangelization of Ireland. The daughter of a prince of Ulster and his bonds-woman, she distinguished herself by piety and charity, founded four monasteries, and became the patron saint of Ireland.

Scholastica (480–547) worked with Benedict as a brother-sister team of evangelists in northern Europe.

Genevieve lived in Paris at the time Attila the Hun attacked the city (451). By prayers to God and appeals to the people, she aroused the populace to defend themselves, and the city was saved.

Olympias was one of the court of Theodosius the Great, the wife, as a matter of fact, of his treasurer. When her husband died, she was besieged by many gentlemen with an eye for her beauty and her wealth. When she refused a relative of the emperor, the emperor became angry, confiscated all her property, and appointed a guardian for her. Olympias, instead of retaliating in some way, thanked him for relieving her of the responsibility involved, for a Christian, in possession of great wealth. He retorted by returning it to her—probably one of the most unusual financial arguments in history. Olympias' great interest was in re-habilitating people; she concerned herself over persons in jail, exiles, beggars. She is said to have purchased hundreds of slaves, for the sole purpose of setting them free. She upheld Chrysostom in some of his more radical moods, to the point where she lost favor with the court and eventually died in poverty. Chrysostom made her his confidante in many letters.

Royal Missionaries

Many women of royal households used their influence to further the spread of Christianity. Bertha (d. 612) was the daughter of the Frankish Charibert, and married King Ethelbert of Kent, stipulating that she might keep her Christian religion and bring with her to England her chaplain, Liudhard. She restored the church of St. Martin's at Canterbury and welcomed St. Augustine and the forty monks who accompanied him on his trip to Britain. The Pope had been impressed, it seems, with the personal popularity which Bertha enjoyed and had thought this was an opportune time to further the cause of Christianity in the country where she was queen. Between the queen and the monks, the king soon asked for public baptism and promulgated a code of laws which he considered in keeping with his new religion.

Ludmilla trained her grandson, later King Wenceslaus of Bohemia, and through him brought that land to Christianity; Dambrowka of

Bohemia married Micislaus of Poland and converted him, and through him his people.

Pulcheria (399–453) was a granddaughter of Theodosius the Great, a daughter of Arcadius. She was a devout Christian and well educated. She had a real taste for scholarship and was especially talented in languages. She and her brother became joint rulers, with Pulcheria carrying the heavier load. When an educated and cultured young woman came to Pulcheria from Athens, complaining that she was being imposed upon by her brothers, Pulcheria was sympathetic and decided that Athanias would be a good wife for her brother, Theodosius II, and would also be a good help in running the government. Pulcheria prepared her for her new role by giving her thorough instruction in Christianity. Perhaps it was as part of this instruction that she paraphrased the first eight books of the Old Testament and the prophecies of Daniel and Zechariah into verse. Pulcheria also gave her the new name Eudocia. Eventually jealousy arose between the sister and the wife as to who was to control Theodosius II and the government. There was conflict also, because Eudocia, in the church quarrels of the day, decided to support the Nestorians. For a while Pulcheria was banished, but in 441 Eudocia was exiled for infidelity and Pulcheria returned. Theodosius II died in 450 and Pulcheria was made empress. She married an army officer by the name of Marcianus and had him proclaimed emperor, but it was Pulcheria who continued in control. Together they sponsored the famous Council of Chalcedon, which denounced monophysitism (the "heresy" that in Jesus Christ the human and divine constituted one composite nature). Pulcheria's interest in religion continued till her death. She built many churches and at her death left all her possessions to the poor.

Radegund (518–587) was the daughter of the pagan king of Thuringia. When the king was murdered by his brother Hermenfrid, Hermenfrid took responsibility for Radegund, but when the Frankish King Clotaire V of Neustria defeated Hermenfrid, Radegund, now twelve, was part of his booty. He had her educated in France as a Christian, and six years later married her. Clotaire was, it seems, both cruel and unfaithful, but his young wife stood for everything till he murdered her brother. At this point she decided to become a nun, but the bishop was not at all sure about accepting her. She told him, "If you refuse to receive me, if you fear man more than God, you will have to answer for it before the shepherd of the flock." Accepted at last, she became a nun at Saix and in 557 built the double monastery at

Poitiers, the first of its kind, and helped to establish it as a famous seat of learning.

Hypatia, the Greek philosopher of Alexandria (d. 415) must be mentioned, though she was the victim rather than the follower of the Church—or at least of certain people connected with it. She is still part of its history, which we know has not always been completely glorious. Hypatia was the daughter of a teacher of philosophy, but she, also a teacher, was recognized as exceeding her parent in brilliance and also in her interest in public affairs. She was consulted by important men and officials of the city of Alexandria, and by the governor, Orestes. The bishop, jealous of her influence and intolerant of her philosophy, allowed his followers to stir up trouble, in the course of which she was dragged from her carriage into a church, stripped naked, beaten to death, and her body finally burned. The presumed instigator, Cyril, afterward himself became bishop and led a mob to drive the Jews from Alexandria, where for many years they had enjoyed freedom.

Theodora (508–548) was the wife of Justinian, whose throne and responsibility she shared as queen consort. She was probably born in Cyprus, where her father had been a bear feeder with a circus. After his death, she and her sisters became pantomime dancers to support the family. To marry her, Justinian, then a senator, had to get a law abrogated which forbade marriage between a senator and a plebeian. Two years later, Justinian became emperor, and for twenty-three years Theodora shared—fully—his responsibilities. During a revolt in 532, she is credited with saving the throne. Remembering her own poverty-stricken youth, she always tried to alleviate the sufferings of the poor. Theodora was perhaps the first influential woman to concern herself over the special problems that confronted her own sex.

Theodelina (580–628) was the daughter of the Duke of Bavaria, and as wife of Auturi was queen of the Lombards. After Auturi's death and that of a second husband, Flavius Agiluphus, she became regent. As a Christian she was mediator between the Lombards and the Roman Catholic Church, placing the Lombard nation under the protection of John the Baptist, to whom she built a church near the royal palace. She was interested in methods of agriculture, in charitable foundations, in the erection of monasteries, and in reducing taxes, especially for low-income groups—something in which few monarchs of that age demonstrated much concern.

We must give at least one instance of a mass conversion due to a Christian woman, which had important results. Clotilda (c. 474–545), a Burgundian princess, born in Lyons, married (493) Clovis, founder of the Frankish monarchy. She talked to him about Christianity, but though he had their children baptized as Christians, he himself hesitated. At the battle of Alemanni, he vowed that if victorious, he would accept the Christian faith. After the battle, he and 3000 followers were baptized by Bishop Remi, who admonished them to "adore what they had burned" (the cross) and "burn what they had adored" (idols). Thereafter, Clovis was a stanch defender of Christianity, passing on this heritage to what was to become the great empire of Charlemagne.

A similar story involves Saba of Madia (d. 487), whose father was an ardent follower of Zoroaster. His mother, however, hired a Christian nurse and had him sent to a Christian school. As a man, he persuaded the whole city and its Zoroastrian priest to become Christian.

A curtain of darkness was lowering over the Mediterranean lands which only a short time before had seemed so vigorous and cultured. We have little enough history of any sort for the next few centuries, and of the life and work of women, almost nothing at all.

Yet in almost every part of the known world—and largely one way or another through the work and faith of women—the Christian belief was established and had followers who would weather the storms and the gloom of the "centuries in-between."[20,21]

Chapter 5

FINDING NEW CHANNELS OF SERVICE

In the centuries following the breakup of the Roman Empire, woman's lot was not a happy one. Survival for self and family and being able to maintain some degree of personal chastity became major concerns in countries which had long been able to take these blessings for granted. Education and culture were at low ebb. The folk religion of the common people was inclined to be vague, superstitious, and not very explicit as to everyday ethics, culture, and general *mores*. The local clergy could be gracious shepherds of their flocks, or they could be corrupt and demanding.

The men were away, trying vainly to protect the frontiers, and too many of them did not come home. The women at first did the best they could to protect their homes and property. However, as conditions worsened, survival and personal safety became paramount. Often the only place to which they could look for help was the Church. There the destitute, the orphaned, and the aged could often hope for some semblance of physical care and spiritual comfort. Many wealthy women also took refuge in the monasteries and gave their property to the Church.

Meanwhile, logically enough at the time, the organized Church was gathering increasing power into the hands of the male hierarchy as the one hope for order in a disrupting world.[1] However, this situation, which put a great premium on men and the kind of protection they could offer, inevitably affected their attitude toward women in the work and worship of the Church.

The new limitations on women's role imposed by the early church councils, or even more often and effectively by local ecclesiastics, must have seemed wrong and insulting to the women who had been doing so much for the spread of Christianity.[2] Deprived of their traditional "orders" (whether or not so-called) in the churches, the more capable women formed lay associations to care for the poor, the sick, the orphaned, the widowed. The most effective channels available to them were the monasteries, which, at their best, also provided whatever educational, cultural, and welfare services the people of the community could hope for.

At the same time, some church leaders were developing a new interest in ascetics, which has always had its devotees in all religions, but seems too abstract to have had a primary appeal to most women. The monastic idea may have started with Anthony of Egypt in the third century, though some say with John the Baptist, or with some of the pre-Christian desert communities in Palestine. Undoubtedly there have always been hermits, but the "movement" as we think of it became important in the third century.

The Monasteries

Marcella, a noble and wealthy widow of Rome, may have been the first woman to join the Christian monastic movement. Since girlhood she had been attracted to the ascetic way of life. When the Egyptian monk Peter visited Rome in 374, she heard him speak and call for recruits. Marcella was the first to make the monastic profession. She continued to live in the ancestral castle and look after her mother, living, however, in the utmost simplicity. Their home became a center for Christian activity and also for a group of women interested in Bible study and church history. When her mother died in 387, Marcella and a friend, Principia, moved to a small house in the country, where she continued to study and write. She was a member of a group, of which Jerome was a key figure, and involved herself in a controversy between him and Origen. Marcella finally got the Pope's ear and persuaded him to condemn Origen's views. She died during the sack of Rome by Alaric.[3]

Martin of Tours, after making his case as a "conscientious objector" in the army that went against the Goths, sought refuge in a wooded retreat near Poitiers, but disciples made a path to his door. John Cassian, a wealthy young man of Gaul, highly educated in the classics, made trips to Syria and Africa and Palestine to study the monasteries. He visited the monks of the salt marshes of Egypt, where he met Chaeremon, a centurion who prayed so much he could not stand upright, but could still preach and lecture on subjugation, obedience, and mortification. Cassian saw, too, the monasteries of the Libyan Desert, with their fortresses, libraries, and personal hiding places (in case of invasion). And he learned the eight faults of monastic life:

gluttony, fornication, covetousness, anger, dejection, vainglory, pride, and, one more, *accidie*—being without care, which could become religious indifference. Later, his notes, it is said, became the basis of St. Benedict's rule.

Jerome tried hard to be a hermit in the wilderness near Antioch, but was glad to get back to Rome and the stimulating company of Paula and her two daughters, Blesilla and Eustochium, and the comfortable house of Marcella. Jerome formed a class in Bible study for the wives and daughters of the Roman aristocracy and apparently was quite the rage. He seems, however, to have been terribly strict, telling poor Eustochium to avoid married women, widows, all men, and especially the perfumed clergy. He found holiness and wedded life incompatible and had a great argument with good-natured Jovinian, to whom marriage, widowhood, or virginity were indifferent, "being alike pleasing to God." Women at this period do not seem to have been overly interested in the ascetic approach to religion. They saw the monastery as a way to bring them closer to—not isolate them from—community life. The future pattern of the monasteries was far from established.[4]

It was Benedict of Nursia who saw that a different type of religious order was needed in the West and who, in 526, founded the Benedictine order on the site of an ancient temple at Monte Cassino. Benedict (480–543) was well educated; he had studied at Rome. It is said that he fled from the slovenliness and disorder of his fellow students. He was a hermit in a cave at Subiaco for three years, building up a monastery of "secluded" monks. His sister, Scholastica (possibly a twin), was very close to him, and when he built the monastery at Monte Cassino, she established one for women at the foot of the mountain. It is variously reported that she "worked under her brother's supervision"; that this was, in effect, a "double monastery"; or that the brother and sister worked quite independently, meeting only once a year for a day of high-level spiritual conversation. After one such meeting, Benedict, standing by a window overlooking the valley, is said to have had a vision in which he saw his sister's soul ascend to heaven; the very next day Benedict himself died, and they were buried side by side, for Scholastica had, indeed, died at the time her brother had seen the vision.

The Benedictine order combined a degree of withdrawal from the distracting interests of worldly life with a deep concern for and service to one's fellow men, especially care for the poor and sick. Benedict also saw from the first that a great need in these troubled times was for a teaching ministry, and for a communal "rule" rather than simply a loosely organized community of like-minded pious individuals. The monasteries became less austere and inclined to be patterned after the devout Christian family, with brothers engaged in a shared pattern of worship and programs of manual labor. Respect for the human person was paramount. In time there were 40,000 Benedictine monasteries. These new-type monasteries proved to be very much in line with the needs of the highest type of woman of the period.

The Great Abbesses

Says Mrs. Houghton: "During the turbulent centuries after the breakup of the Empire, [the monastery] offered women the only place they could work fruitfully and develop and cultivate intellectual tastes. It offered them also an opportunity for social life. . . . Convent life was varied and interesting. . . . Up to the Tenth Century a large number of 'double monasteries' (of both men and women) were ruled by women."[5]

The double monasteries were favored as a matter of protection; there were many in Rome, Gaul, Britain, and later in Belgium, Germany, and especially Ireland. At Whitby, England, Hilda, a grandniece of King Edwin of Northumbria, formed a school for both men and women, which proved very popular with the royalty, and sent out evangelists all over Western Europe. Hilda presided over a synod meeting at Whitby where a vigorous power contest developed between the types of Christianity then prevalent in England and Ireland. Hilda must have presided forcefully enough, for of this synod Toynbee says[6] that until the synod of Whitby in 664 the English might have become converts to the "far western Christianity of the Celtic Fringe." In that case, without the support of papal connections, he suggests that when the Moslems appeared on the Atlantic seaboard, England might have completely lost touch with their co-religionists on the European continent, as the churches of Abyssinia and Central Asia did; England might even have been converted to Islam.

In the tenth century four abbesses were actually peers in England. On the continent some had the right to ban, sent out their own contingent of knights, gave judgment in court, attended the imperial diet (Germany), and minted their own coin. In a world whose business was war, it was not considered a disgrace for even young princes to be illiterate, so long as they were skillful at arms. Culture was, therefore, more and more in the hands of the women and in the monasteries. In the tenth century, Roswitha made the Saxon monastery of Gandersheim famous for its brilliant learning and drama. Those who were politically minded cultivated the art of promoting peace between the warring factions of the land. Matilda of Tuscany (1046–1115), from her castle (certainly not a cloister) at Canossa, was famous in this field. She had entered vigorously into the politics of the Vatican. As one of Italy's most powerful feudatories, she supported the Pope in his conflict with the emperor, and it was outside her castle, where the Pope was a guest, that Henry IV stood for three days, barefoot in the snow, waiting for the opportunity to humble himself before Gregory VII and be absolved from excommunication.

The Benedictine settlement at Fontevrault (3000 persons) was ruled for 600 years by a line of thirty-two distinguished abbesses.

Florentine of Spain became the superior of forty monasteries, and by her "knowledge, her virtues, and even her sacred songs ranks high among nuns." Bertile of Chilles drew large audiences to her lectures on the Scriptures.

The monastery was, in those days, anything but an isolated and strictly meditative community. It was a busy and active unit of society with its own economy and definitely an outward thrust of service to the community.

The number of nuns in Western Europe had been increasing tremendously since the seventh century. Looking ahead to the twelfth century, however, we see that power was to lead to abuses, and to a far too frequent forgetfulness of the sense of religious vocation which had brought the monastic life into existence. Laxness brought about movement for reform. One "reform" was to make the wearing of the habit obligatory for nuns, and along with this the movement to make nuns "cloistered."[7] There was also a definite ruling from the Church: a monastic, though above the laity, was not clergy. It is almost certain that the stricter regulations (especially the habit and cloister) caused many women with a sense of religious vocation which could not be interpreted in these restrictive terms to seek self-expression elsewhere.

The Missionaries

One avenue of service they rediscovered was missions. We have spoken of women's contribution to the missionary outreach of the early Church. We shall speak again of their contribution to missionary work in recent centuries. We are getting too far ahead of our story! This, however, is the place to tell about Boniface and how the women helped in the great movement of Christianizing northern Europe.

Boniface was one of the great churchmen of his day or any day. Latourette calls him one of the most remarkable missionaries in the entire history of Christian expansion. He was born at Wessex, England (c. 675). After studying in a monastery and being ordained, he turned down various high posts offered him, preferring to go as a missionary to northern Germany, which Charles Martel was just beginning to hammer into the Frankish kingdom. It was a difficult and wild territory, from which, during the fifth-century invasions, Roman culture and Christianity had all but disappeared. There had been some renewal of Christian impact from the Franks, but the people were largely uneducated, pagan, given to magic practices. Of the very few clergy, most were poorly trained, disorganized. Boniface seems to have gone directly to the people and baptized many in Thuringia, Saxony, and Hesse.

He found his hands strengthened by the prayers of many English friends and relatives. Abbesses and bishops were among his correspondents. The abbesses found a special way of helping his enterprise by having copies of books made (all, of course, had to be done by hand) and sent to him. They also made and sent vestments. Many missionaries, both men and women, went out from England to serve under Boniface; much of his success has been attributed to his ability to attract and hold colleagues. He depended upon friends at home, and men and women who came from home to help him, but he also recruited men and women helpers from the area in which he worked. Says Latourette: "The one markedly new feature in Boniface's method was the place given to women." To the frontiers only men were assigned, but wherever Christianity was fairly well established, he put women in places of authority. He especially asked to have Leoba, a cousin, who had been trained in an English monastery, sent to assist him, and she became the head of a religious house for women at Bischefsheim near Würzburg. Another woman assistant was Walpurga, also a relative, who came with her two brothers—all highly educated, traveled, and probably of the royal line of Kent. Latourette notes that it was perhaps the world's greatest missionary who gave women missionaries their greatest opportunity in several centuries—and probably up till the nineteenth century—to have such active and significant participation in the Church's program.[8, 9]

Chapter 6

ELEVENTH-CENTURY REVIVAL

Suddenly the eleventh century was upon the world! To step from the tenth to the eleventh century can only be compared to stepping from the middle of the nineteenth to the middle of the twentieth century. Everything was different. We find ourselves in the midst of a vigorous, stimulating, though admittedly confusing civilization for which—even if we know our ancient history—we are quite unprepared. Yet this century holds in its vigorous hands, as we immediately recognize, the seed grain of modern life. The women of the eleventh and twelfth centuries have again reached the top of a curve in cultural development. The great cathedrals of Europe are being built to the Virgin. Heloise and Abelard are casting their amorous and scholarly enchantment over the world.[1] Queen Eleanor and Mary, her daughter, and Blanche, her granddaughter, are sponsoring the "Courts of Courteous Love" and gentling the male population.

The famous Cistercian order, founded in 1098, is laying the foundations of the modern monastic movements. Francis and Clare are setting up what is probably, next to the ministry of the Lord himself, one of the most uniting streams of love and service that has persisted in the Christian Church—Catholic, Protestant, or loyal dissenter—to the present day.

Those who have not yet read Henry Adams' *Mont-Saint-Michel and Chartres*[2] have before them the enticing experience of dipping into this volume for the first time. Do not try, unless you are a professional historian, to follow at first reading all the author has to tell. The pattern is too complex, the author's mind too fertile, the writing too replete with allusions to events in the past and the future. Just open the book and start living the life of amazing activity in this neglected period of the world's history. Moreover, if we were to ask Adams where to begin a survey of this period, he would undoubtedly answer promptly, "With women."

Devotion to the Virgin

Devotion to the Virgin (including St. Anne) became suddenly popular at this time. To the Virgin, with loving hands and hearts, and a tremendous amount of time and labor, the great cathedrals began to be built, especially in France. One of the loveliest, and a favorite, we are told, of the Virgin, was Chartres.[3]

We should rightly spend a great deal of time on this period. However, we have felt that way about other periods, too. Perhaps the truth is that we should long ago have spent a great deal more time on the whole subject of women in religion.

M. Garreau, writing in 1899, seems to feel that the eleventh and twelfth centuries were a time when something like a balance was achieved in the relations between the sexes. "Men," he tells us, "had a right to dissolve in tears, and women that of talking without prudery."[4]

To quote Adams:

The superiority of woman was not a fancy, but a fact. Man's business was to fight or hunt or feast or make love. The man was always the travelling partner in commerce, commonly absent from the home for months together, while the woman carried on the business. The woman ruled the household and workshop, cared for the economy, supplied the intelligence and dictated the taste. Her ascendancy was secured by her alliance with the Church, into which she sent her most intelligent children.[5]

Or again:

The man never cared; he was always getting himself into crusades or feuds, or love, or debt, and depended on the woman to get him out. . . . The woman might be a good or evil spirit, but she was always the stronger force. The twelfth and thirteenth centuries were a period when men were at their strongest; . . . yet these marvels of history—these Plantagenets, these scholastic philosophers, these architects of Rheims and Amiens; these Innocents, and Robin Hoods and Marco Polos; these crusaders . . . all, without apparent exception, bowed down before the woman. Explain it who will![6]

The surprising thing is that there seemed to be no question in anyone's mind—men or women—that all this new energy and culture and courtesy was somehow related to religion, and that somehow, whether you wanted it or not, whether indeed you deserved it or not, religion did dominate, in one way or another, the whole of your life.

Take it if you will simply as a balancing off of the excessive male influence in the organized Church which had been going on for at least six centuries. Take it as a groundswell of theology from the often illiterate but by no means stupid common people, whose common sense told them that somewhere in the concept of God there must be room for feminine as well as masculine traits. Take it as a tribute to the ability of the women who during the "dark ages" had held the line of education, culture, and decency from their often powerful positions in the uncloistered monasteries. Take it as an outcropping of primitive *Mutterrecht*, or of the concept that persisted in many countries and well into the Christian era of the all-pervasive Mother-goddess. Say if you will that male strength had been weakened throughout the West because of the continual fighting that seemed to be men's one preoccupation. Add to all this the subtle influence, in Europe, of a remarkable line of capable queens. Or say that women had once more reached the top of an upswing of the cycle of feminine influence in the cultural pattern of society. We shall probably do best simply to accept the facts, and not try to isolate the causes, which were undoubtedly many and varied.

The Powerful Queens

Perhaps the most remarkable political figure of the time was Eleanor of Aquitaine (1122–1204). She first married Louis VII of France and went with him on a crusade to the Holy Land. Later she married Henry Plantagenet and sponsored this powerful duke against her first husband. However, in 1170 she decided to establish her own court and promoted her two sons, Richard and John, to make them kings of England. Her slightly older contemporary was Margaret of Scotland, wife of Malcolm III. Queen (later Saint) Margaret's chapel still stands on Castle Rock, the oldest building in Edinburgh.

As for the common people in Western Europe, a most peculiar sidelight is the fact that men's fashionable dress and mannerisms became extremely effeminate—probably just before the first Crusade. The monk Orderic is quoted as saying that "at this time effeminacy was the prevailing vice throughout the world. . . . They parted their hair from the crown of the head on each side of the forehead, and let their locks grow long like women, and wore long shirts and tunics, closely tied with points . . . our wanton youths are sunk in effeminacy. . . . They insert their toes in things like serpents' tails. . . . Sweeping the ground with the prodigious trains of their robes and mantles, they cover their hands with gloves. . . ." Even the rules of the game of chess were revised, Adams tells us, to make the queen free to move about the board practically as she pleased. He says: "For a hundred and fifty years, the Virgin and Queens ruled French taste and thought so successfully that the French man has never yet quite decided whether he is proud or ashamed of it." That we have known so little about this period is explained by Adams: one of the chief chroniclers of the period was the monk Orderic, and "monks and historians abhor emancipated women—with good reason, since such women are apt to abhor them."[7]

We have spoken mostly of the queens of France, but we could have made the same case in other countries. Gregory the Great had made a specialty of working through queens to reach their people. Queens of the Franks and Lombards, and Berta of Kent, were among his correspondents. He even wrote a special prayer appropriate for the crowning services of a queen: "that she may be enabled to call barbarous nations to a knowledge of the truth." Other churchmen had followed with considerable success his example of first winning the queen to the Christian belief and then relying on her support and help to convert her people. In Kiev, the widow of the archduke was baptized in 954. Later, her grandson, Archduke Vladimir (c. 956–1015), on his marriage to Anna, sister of Emperor Basil II, accepted Christianity as the official religion of the state that was to become Russia. Halfway around the world, in Peking, the famous Kublai Khan, listening to his mother's advice, was declaring his respect and tolerance for all religions. His mother was a Kerait princess, a Nestorian Christian, and one of many Christians who had been moving eastward into China, where she had married the former Khan. Monasteries had been founded in China in the seventh century; the people had asked for Christian teachers, but only two were sent.

One of the historical sources for this period is Anna Comnena (1083–1148). The daughter of the Greek Emperor Alexius, she wrote her father's life in such an interesting manner that the *Journal des Savants* (1675) is quoted as saying, "The elegance with which Anna Comnena has, in fifteen books, described the life and actions of her father, are so much above the ordinary capacity of women as to excite a doubt whether she were, indeed, the author of the work."[8]

We should speak of the Crusades, the universities, the papacy, each of which took on importance in this period, and in relation to each of which we would find interesting material about women.[9] However, from this time on the general historical background is better known and more readily accessible, so let us even more closely limit our discussions to women's own activity.

One phase of life we must not overlook was going on in the monasteries.

From our vantage point in history, it seems incredible that over a period of several hundred years it was the monasteries, whatever their shortcomings, which were custodians of whatever remained of the Hellenic and Roman cultures, as well as what remained of early Christian art, manuscripts, traditions. They were centers, too, of community life, in which women had an active part. We often read of the dark days of monasticism, when celibacy remained a vow, but was by no means a necessary way of life,[10] and when laxness, gluttony and very crude living often seemed common practice. Other historians write glowingly about the great reformed monastery at Cluny (founded 910), as though it were typical of the Middle Ages.[11] Yet by the thirteenth century, Cluny, with its 10,000 monks and over 300 houses, would become almost scandalously powerful. Two of its monks became Popes, and a third, the great Hildebrand, was also a Cluniac. The abbot was, in the Western world, next in power to the Pope and was even in a position to choose his own successor.

With the development of the feudal system, the monasteries became not only havens of safety but, as we have indicated, community centers of education and culture. Abbots and abbesses were often the equivalent of feudal lords in their areas. Yet the monasteries were also a democratizing force in their way, for here royalty and peasants rubbed elbows. Only here, as a rule, could the woman with a desire for education or a "call" to religion find the opportunity for self-fulfillment and useful service. We have already mentioned how some women responded and proved their ability. We should, moreover, stress the *number* of women who were attracted to this way of life. There are no statistics, and guessing at such figures is futile. However, it is significant that there was a monastery for women founded in 1101 at Fontevrault, run entirely by the women themselves, from which, over a fifty-year period, fifty daughter houses were founded.

St. Clare and St. Francis

For a closer view of one woman—and one order—let us look briefly at the story of Clare and Francis. There is a great deal of material about St. Francis, but St. Clare is apt to be disposed of with the brief statement that Francis also founded the Poor Clares, who have done much good work in the world. Due search finally led us to the more recent research (1933) of Patrick Cowley and a few more modern scholars who share our interest in Clare.[12]

Francis was born in the twelfth century, when Innocent III was bringing reform and dignity to the papacy. (If temporal power was overemphasized, that is another matter.) Francis of Assisi (1182?–1226) was the son of a well-to-do merchant. He seems to have been a ringleader among the young blades of the town where he lived. Becoming somewhat bored with this life, he set out, when he was about twenty, on a military expedition, but the first day he became ill and had to return home. His illness brought on some sort of a spiritual crisis, but for a while he continued his old pattern of life. Then one day after a party, at which his friends had crowned him king of the revelers, they went out to roam the streets and presumably wake up the populace. Presently his friends missed Francis. When he was at last found, he was in a trance and permanently a changed person. From that day on he devoted himself to solitude, prayer, care for the poor and the sick, with a special concern for lepers. He owned all nature as his brothers and spoke of his espousal to Lady Poverty. Before his father could carry out his intention to disinherit him, Francis repudiated all his former life and went to live in the wooded area of Subasio, worshiping at the little ruined chapel of Portinuncula, preaching to the poor, and gradually gathering around him twelve friends who shared his views. In 1209 or 1210 they went to Rome and received from Innocent III the rule for their new preaching order, based on the principles of poverty, chastity, and obedience.

Cowley points out that "the character of Francis was clearly moulded and influenced by three women of very different natures." There was Prassede, an elderly recluse whom he met in Rome, and with whose ascetic life he was so impressed that he made her a member of the Friars Minor. There was Lady Giocoma, a widow with two small sons, whom he knew through the years, and for whom he sent as he lay dying. However, it was Lady Clare in whom he found a truly kindred spirit—a person who apparently understood as no one else the full purport of his message, and who held fast to those principles long after Francis had gone and the Franciscans were in more "practical" hands.

At eighteen, the noble young Lady Clare ran away from home (where her parents were arranging a marriage she could not tolerate) to join the Franciscan community, still a small band who had received their first rule only two years before.

In the woods near Portinuncula, Francis and the other members of the order met her, and in a candle-lit procession they proceeded to a small church. Her hair was cut. She was given the gown of the order. She dedicated herself to the life of poverty, chastity, and the true Gospel. For a while Clare stayed at the Benedictine convent of Saint Paul, refusing all pleas of her parents to return home. Instead, she was soon joined by her sister Agnes, who also became a Franciscan.

Later, in the repaired chapel of St. Damian, which the Benedictines gave to Francis, he established the two girls and founded the Poor Clares, which became, in time, famous as a nursing order.

For years they operated with amazing freedom. When Francis was away in Egypt in 1219, it seemed to the papal legate to be an opportune time to "regularize" the Poor Clares. But he underestimated Clare. She refused to be institutionalized, regardless of material advantages involved. The Ugoline Constitutions were adopted by other women's communities related to the Franciscan monasteries, but not by San Damiano, where Clare held stubbornly to the original vows. She defied the Pope himself when he tried to stop the Portinuncula friars from preaching at San Damiano and won her point. It was under the olive trees of San Damiano that Francis is said to have composed his "Canticle of Brother Sun."

The Franciscan order went through many changes after the death of its founder. Says his biographer Father Cuthbert: "When Clare at length died, twenty-four years after Francis had gone to his rest, she left the community of San Damiano established in the pure observance of Franciscan Poverty and in the essential Franciscan life." Adds Cowley: "When we look for the real Francis, our companion and brother, we see him best and clearest with Clare."[13]

Chapter 7

SEARCH FOR MEANING

Europe in the fourteenth century was restless. The men who had been on the Crusades found it hard to settle down on the old feudal farm. Wandering bands of preachers were raising pointed questions in the minds of the common people about the accepted practices of religion and some of the powers claimed by the priests. People were anxious to pit their critical and analytical faculties (newly discovered in the universities) against the material universe and see what they could make of it. However, there were those who mistrusted the new intellectualism and seemed to feel that it was time people, instead of once more plunging recklessly into some new venture, should take religion seriously and listen for the voice of God to tell them where they should be going. A series of natural disasters—earthquakes, floods, famine, and Black Death—sweeping over Europe and taking a fourth of the population intensified (often in a superstitious way) people's desire to discover—for sure—the will of God for his children.

The Jews became scapegoats: hundreds were burned alive. Flagellants wandered about flaying themselves and each other, and dancing maniacs formed weird processions.

The Beguine Movement

One of the more constructive groups that had recently appeared were the Beguines—groups of women living and worshiping together, devoting themselves to deeds of charity and service, but without monastic vows.[1]

The movement probably officially had its beginning when Lambert le Begue of Liège spent his entire fortune, before he died in 1180, in founding a cloister and church for the widows and orphans of crusaders. It is probably from him that the Beguines took their name, though another theory is that it came from the old Flemish word *beghem,* meaning *pray.* (It could not be related to the English word beg, for they were never a "begging" order.) However, in the twelfth century, there were living in the lowland of Western Europe many single women and widows, devoting themselves to prayer and good works, in a world which they felt was becoming more and more desolate. Unlike hermits, who retired to the forests, they lived on the edge of town, where they could conveniently serve those who needed help. At first they lived singly, in their own homes, later in small groups. Those who lived in their own houses had their own servants if they so desired and could afford them. Each community was complete in itself and fixed its own program. They accepted no charity, but earned what they needed by doing small manual labor—often housework or teaching children in the homes of the community. At the beginning of the thirteenth century, some of these women began to group their cabins into what was called a Beguinage, and to designate one of their number as mistress, whose primary duty it was to train new recruits for the fellowship. The Great Beguinage of Ghent had a thousand members. The women were sometimes referred to as demi-nuns. They did not renounce ownership of property and could withdraw if they wanted to. They took no vows, but as their number increased and they spread into southern France and along the western seaboard, they often lived in a common house and had a common purse. Some adopted the rule of St. Francis' Third Order (laymen). Persons of all classes were admitted —some well-to-do, others very poor.

Ernest Gilliat-Smith, in an article in the *Catholic Encyclopaedia*, emphasizes the essentially religious character of the movement, describing the groups as centers of mysticism. It was, he says, "not the monks who dwelt in the countryside, nor even the secular clergy, but the Beguines, the Beghards, and the sons of St. Francis who moulded the thought of the urban population of the Netherlands." By the end of the thirteenth century there were large beguinages in most major cities, and working groups in every community.

The Beghards were the male counterpart of the Beguines only to a certain point. They were usually older or partially incapacitated artisans, living in small groups and with possessions in common. These *fratres voluntarii pauperes*, being in many cases retired workingmen, were able to be of considerable influence in the religious life of the guilds in the towns and cities, especially of the Netherlands.

Unhampered and unguided by church control, however, both the Beguines and the Beghards tended to become heretical and politically radical, yet at the same time were accused of a theological trend toward the currently much discussed "error" of "quietism," described as an extreme form of mysticism, including the complete passivity of the soul, abandonment of all conscious effort, and belief that the entrance of God into the soul is facilitated when the soul becomes "inert." Quietism suggested that even the interior passivity of the soul—without the necessity to try to control even thought—was the way to perfection. Certainly, then, one would not be bound by human authority, or even the Church. The "good works" program on which the Beguines were founded makes the charge of quietism seem most inappropriate, but it was the popular attack of the day, and Marguerite de Hainault, probably a Beguine, had been burned in Paris (1310) for writing that "the soul that has annihilated itself in the love of the Creator can accord to nature everything it desires."

Neither the commands of the Archbishop of Mainz nor the attacks of the scholar Albertus Magnus (Cologne 1260) had been able to subdue the Beguines. There was a definite effort to suppress them in the sixteenth century, and again in the eighteenth, but in Ghent, for instance, some groups still exist.

Other heretical sects included the apocalyptic Ortlibiens, who identified the Pope and the Roman Church with the anti-Christ, and themselves with the Trinity—the Father was those who had joined the sect, those who were converted were the Son, and those they helped were the Holy Spirit. The Grubenheimers emphasized a concept of becoming "perfected ones." Brothers and sisters of the Free Spirit have been described as "mystic pantheists." They claimed perfect individual and group freedom, held that they were living in the age of the Holy Spirit, that the sacraments were not essential, and that the sins recognized by the Church were not sins if committed in love. They said not even the Jews and Saracens were to be damned, and that all parts of the Scriptures were not of equal value. They were condemned by the Inquisition in 1317.

There were many, many more of these heretical sects, but their records are scarce and modern interpretations of their beliefs differ so widely and are often so obviously prejudiced one way or another as to be quite unreliable.

Women in the Pre-Reformation Sects

Some men and women, particularly conscious of the Christian motivation prompting their desire to be of service to their fellow men, found their way into the pre-Reformation movements such as the

Waldensians and, somewhat later, the Lollards. The influence of the women, who were welcome in many of these pre-Reformation sects, probably helped set the pattern of service which characterized them then and has continued to be a dominant factor in many churches which trace their origins to pre-Reformation sources. We shall mention only the Waldensians now and meet other groups later.

Some people maintain that the Waldensians (still a strong church today) were founded by the Apostle Paul as he went through the valleys of northern Italy on his way to Spain. Another story says they had their origin in a protest against the secular forces entering the Church at the time of Constantine. More probable is the report that they were originally an iconoclastic group led by Claude Turin in the eighth century, and with a claim to be known as the original pre-Reformation movement. Certainly they are older than Peter Waldo (d. 1217?), from whom they took their name and their distinctive character. Since women have, from the first, had an important part in the Waldensian Church, Peter Waldo's story can appropriately be repeated here:

Young Peter Waldo, of Lyons, France, was getting very rich indeed by what he later described as "sinful usury." He had a wife and daughters and a villa and much gold—but not peace of mind.

One day he stopped on the street to listen to an itinerant monk preacher and heard the story of St. Alexis, who had abandoned home and wealth and position to become, unrecognized, the lowliest servant in his father's household. An emphasis on the virtues of poverty dominated much of the preaching of the time, and probably the story would not have struck Peter Waldo so forcibly had it not been that while he was discussing these very matters with a friend—perhaps the person closest to his heart—the friend was suddenly stricken and died.

Another element also entered into the decision which Peter Waldo now made—a decision which was to change his life completely and make its impact on the course of history. Unable to follow the Latin services in the Church, but anxious to know what they were all about, he had hired two priests to translate portions of the Bible for him. Reading and memorizing, Peter Waldo came to identify himself with the "rich young man" of the Gospels. Listening to the Lord's demands as he came to understand them through the Scriptures, he systematically gave away all he had, partly as restitution for the usury he had demanded, partly as pure charity.

Memorizing chapter after chapter of the Scriptures, he set out, clad in coarse clothing and unshod, to repeat the Gospel story to all who would listen, urging listeners, in turn, to memorize those portions of the Scriptures which each man found best spoke to his own heart and then to repeat them to others. He and his followers became known as "The Poor Men of Lyons."

When the local priesthood forbade them to preach, they replied by quoting: "Go ye into all the world and preach the Gospel."

There followed years of injunctions on the part of councils and bishops, and willful disobedience on the part of the lay preachers. Whenever anyone tried to stop them, they repeated the words of St. Paul: "We ought to obey God rather than men."

When "The Poor Men of Lyons" were dispersed, they moved to other parts of Europe and established new bridgeheads. There is little doubt that they spoke to the spiritual need of the culture of the day. Traveling as itinerant peddlers, or maintaining small inns, they gave copies of portions of the Bible in the vernacular to those able to read, and helped others memorize useful passages, always urging them in turn to teach others. They followed as closely as possible Jesus' instructions to the Seventy. Women were included in their brotherhood.

The Church at Rome tried to be reasonable with them, but to all theological arguments they replied by quoting the Scriptures in Italian. In 1184 the Waldensians, along with other "heretical" groups, were put under the ban by the Council of Verona. Peter Waldo continued to preach, however, until the day of his death.

The Waldensians emphasized the symbolic character of the sacrament, refusal to take oaths, opposition to war and to the death penalty for crime. Most of all, they preached the right of the people to have the Bible and to interpret it for themselves.

The Waldensians stressed memorization of large portions of the Bible (at first because many of their members were unable to read the Scriptures); later they stressed education. They developed a remarkable preaching ministry. Women took an active part, even in the itinerant preaching. Efforts of the Pope or bishops either to destroy these groups or bring them back into the fold of the established Church were continuous and futile. We shall have more to say about them as our survey continues.

Innocent III did not underestimate the seriousness of the matter. He sent legates in all directions to suppress the Waldensians, and finally in 1210 launched a crusade. Waldensians were burned and massacred, but through the centuries they have kept their preaching and their witness for religious liberty. And men and women have accepted each other as working partners.

Hildegard and the "Friends of God"

Of a different type were the Friends of God. This was such an informal fellowship that one is surprised at how well the group, their memory, and their influence have lasted. Possibly the fact that they were largely a writing group explains it. They never seem to have been really "founded." Perhaps St. Bernard gave them their name "Friends of God," simply indicating a mystic. Dominic and Francis were of the informal brotherhood; so was the famous German Benedictine nun Hildegard of Bingen (1098–1179), counselor, prophet, missionary, and founder of the convent of Rupertsberg. Weak in body, but with tremendous intellectual power, she wrote many books, and there seemed to be no limit to the scope of her interests: the medical properties of herbs, ecclesiastical laxity and corruption, the politics of the time. She corresponded with the great men who should have been doing something about such politics. She was also a musician and poet; over sixty hymns are attributed to her. She traveled widely in the course of her work, especially in her later years—and she lived to be over eighty! Yet, above all else, Hildegard valued a life of contemplation, and it was the experience of mystical vision which she felt constrained to share with, or pass on to, her sisters in the abbey. The God who spoke to her she liked to refer to as "the Living Light," whose brightness is "not limited to space, and is more brilliant than the radiance around the sun." Her emphasis on the "Light" is probably responsible at least in part for a similar emphasis in the vocabularies of many of the later mystics. Something of the same sort may be said of her quite exact description of her visions—pictures which, she reported, were seen within the mind—neither in sleep, dreams, nor in any frenzy, perceived not with eyes or ears, but according to God's will. She shared her visions and her prophecies with other remarkable women, especially Abbess Elizabeth of Schönau.

There were several Friends of God at the convent of Helfta; especially to be noted is Saint Gertrude the Great (1256–1301). This woman had been raised in a convent from the time she was five. Like Hildegard, she was famous for her mystic visions and writings, becoming known as "the Prophetess of Devotion to the Sacred Heart." Also, at Helfta was Beguine Mechtild (or Matilda) of Magdeburg (1207–1282), famous for her poetry and beautiful voice, and St. Mechtild of Hackeborn (1241–1299), author of *The Book of Special Grace*. The close-knit fellowship of the Friends of God at Helfta was the nucleus of a spiritual revival.

The Friends of God were not a heretical group, though some of them might have been so considered in another age; for the most part they were original thinkers but, especially at first, well within the Roman Catholic Church. Perhaps their most famous member was Meister Eckhart, a Dominican and follower of Thomas Aquinas, though more of a mystic, stressing complete union with God, with whom there is already essential unity. Pope John XXII mistrusted Eckhart's teaching and condemned some of his writings.

The Friends of God probably became a recognizable entity under the leadership of Johannes Tauler (c. 1300–1361), who emphasized "Christ in the Heart." Heinrich Nördlingen, a "secular priest," encouraged the formation of small groups of the Friends of God and also promoted correspondence within the circle. His own correspondence with Margaret Ebner of Bavaria is said to be not only an important contribution to the Friends of God literature, but an important contribution to early German literature.[2]

Women in general—not just a few outstanding personalities—seem to have made important contributions to the Friends of God movement. This is probably partly because of the practice of issuing writings anonymously—not to avoid responsibility but to minimize pride of authorship. The *Theologia Germanica*, the *Imitation of Christ*, and the *Book of the Poor in Spirit* have through the years intrigued literary critics who prefer the non-sanguinary task of discovering authorship to the solution of murder mysteries. Among the women writers mentioned by C. F. Kelly are the Dominican Beguine Mechtild of Magdeburg, as a possible author of the lovely *Book of the Poor in Spirit*, parts of which do seem to have the "woman's touch"; also mentioned in this connection is the Beguine Hedwig II. Other authors were two German nuns, Margaret and Christina Ebner, Elizabeth von Begenhofen, Adelheid Langmann, and Elisabeth Stagel. We know little about most of them except for their writings. The Swiss nun Elisabeth Stagel we know from her extensive correspondence with Suso. After considerable reading of Eckhart and other mystics, she had written Master Suso asking him to advise her on certain points, but suggesting (since she was quite well informed) that he pass over the preliminaries and deal with higher subjects. Suso replied that "true bliss lies not in beautiful words but good deeds," and that since she was apparently a "young unexercised sister" that they begin with "the beginning of spiritual life." She took the rebuke and became his favorite pupil.

Kelly thinks this development of the mystic spirit is due largely to the presence of educated women in the Dominican convents. The continual wars had brought about a general shortage of men, and the task of writing and teaching in the field of religion was not only more definitely in the hands of women but was directed toward women. A more personal tone was introduced into works on religion, but the Friends of God were much too close to scholasticism for the materials to become trite.

Other Female Mystics

Noteworthy among the mystics of the period is Angela of Toligno, called "the Mistress of the Theologians." She had lived a worldly life till she was well into middle age (as middle age was reckoned then). She was married and had a family and was perhaps a nominal Franciscan tertiary, but gives us a very unattractive picture of her early spiritual self. Finally, under guidance she felt she received from St. Francis, she began, step by step, to climb the ladder of spiritual regeneration, giving away her possessions, but not without frequent misgivings and backslidings, between rather dramatic ecstatic experiences. Underhill calls her a "bit by bit mystic," but she seems to have made a great impression on the men of her time. One cannot help but have certain misgivings about Angela, however, since it was only after the death of her husband and children and finally her mother that she found herself completely freed for this spiritual experience. She complained that the biography which her uncle Arnaldo, a friar, wrote concerning her was "inadequate."

Juliana of Norwich (fourteenth century) had a dramatic spiritual experience of a different sort. As a girl she prayed that she might have a severe illness at thirty, together with a deeper understanding of the Passion. It seems the illness did come, with a trance that lasted five hours, and that—perhaps out of subsequent spiritual development— she was able to write a spiritual interpretation. It would be interesting to know how common these "spiritual confessions" were at the time. We are not at all sure that all that have come down to us represent the best of the period or are, perhaps, the type of mysticism appropriate for all persons or for our own day. There can be little doubt that the excesses of mysticism have done it theological harm and robbed Protestantism of much of the value that true mysticism affords. The evidence seems to be that women outside the restraining influence of the Church or some organized group often went off on rather subjective tangents, and have since been held up as examples of "women in religion" and "rampant mysticism" (and by no means uncritically of either).

Other women mystics who must be mentioned are Catherine of Genoa, a Christian Platonist who is said to have established the first modern hospital and was particularly praised for her care of patients during one of the sieges of the plague; Saint Brigid of Sweden, of royal family and a happy mother of eight, who as a widow founded the monastery of Wadstena, instituting the Order of the Most Holy Savior, and entered with considerable vigor into international affairs; Catherine of Cologne, an outstanding Superioress of the Poor Clares; the recluse Saint Colette of Corbie, successively a Beguine, Benedictine, and Poor Clare (with a sort of traveling assignment to reform the convents she visited) and herself the founder of seventeen convents.

If it is true that religion is "caught rather than taught," this is doubly true of that manifestation of religion which is known as mysticism. It was, very frequently, through the day-by-day contacts of women in the market place, or in family gatherings, or as they waited outside the cathedral for the Mass, that the contagious spirit of the Friends of God must have permeated the religious atmosphere and given even those who had never heard tell of mysticism by name something of a different concept of what religion means.

There had been a question in some minds as to whether the Friends of God were close to being a pre-Reformation movement, but to say this would probably be inaccurate. It was a uniting rather than a separating force, and certainly transcended the usual doctrinal differences which plague probably all religions. A study of the activities and writings of the Friends of God—about whose work we seldom hear today—might be one appropriate way of reaching greater understanding between the great Protestant and Roman Catholic branches of the Christian faith.

Latourette refers to the Rhineland movement as "the flowering of lay piety"; but it was part of a larger movement. The mendicant friars (monks were laity, not clergy), the followers of Peter Waldo, Wyclif, and Hus, the Brethren of the Common Life, the newly vocal Anabaptists (whom Luther was to find much too radical for his theological taste)—these and many other independent groups seemed to have little in common except a spiritual unrest and a religious hunger which, as the centuries wore on, spread to more and more people and was manifested in many ways. One strength of many of these groups, especially in their early days, was in the active participation of their women.

It is of definite importance that the mystics, as a rule, wrote and taught in the vernacular, thus helping to break the language barrier to full participation in religion set up by the Latin-speaking churchmen. This also gave women, few of whom were well versed in Latin, a chance to participate on a more even footing in the theological discussions. In the Friends of God movement and among the Franciscan and Dominican tertiaries, women seem to have been regarded in a position of equality with men, and their writings were valued on the basis of their intrinsic spiritual and literary worth. This literary acceptance of women was probably partially responsible for a new appreciation of women as suitable subjects for secular literary works.

In De Claris Mulieribus, Boccaccio (1313-1375) wrote about such women as Eve, Cleopatra, Lucretia, Portia, Semiramis, Sappho, and Giovanna of Naples.

Dante (1265-1321) and Petrarch (1304-1374) started "Beatrice" and "Laura" respectively on their very durable romantic careers in fiction.

Geoffre de la Tour, in the fourteenth century, wrote a book which advised brides how to win power, prestige, and wealth by proper management of their husbands and their families. Some of this interest in women's education may have been due to the new classic learning, for Herodotus and Tacitus had both included women in their histories. On the other hand, there were the apocryphal stories about women, often not at all complimentary, in which some Italian writers of the fourteenth century set a pattern for male colleagues of the future.

The courses which the Friends of God movement took in later times are represented on the one hand by the work of the shoemaker-theologian Jakob Böhme (1575-1624); on the other by Theresa, a Spanish nun and great organizer of the Carmelite order (1515-1582), of whom it was said that her active influence was a powerful check on the quietistic tendencies of French mysticism. She established seventeen convents and worked with John of the Cross to establish comparable reforms of the Spanish friars.

We should also undoubtedly make special mention of such women as, first, Madame Jeanne Guyon (1648-1717), who was imprisoned and finally banished from Paris in 1695 for her writing (forty volumes) on quietist beliefs; and second, of the "Reverend Mother" of the near-by convent, who inspired Brother Lawrence in the late seventeenth century to take time out from his pots and pans in the monastery kitchen to

write (during the last years of life for each of them) his beautiful
letters on how one achieves "the Presence of God." Among those who
led a life of "practical mysticism" firmly within the Catholic fold was St.
Vincent de Paul (1576–1660), described as a genius in the field of
charitable organization, who founded the Sisters of Charity, and through
them gave a tremendous impetus to the whole concept of social work in
the Roman Catholic Church.

Chapter 8

THE RENAISSANCE

Constantinople had fallen to the Turks in 1453, and with this event the old Roman Empire had officially come to an end. Feudalism had seen its best days. The papacy was established and the general outlines of the great European and Asiatic nations were becoming distinguishable. The scholastics were still arguing.

And now, with Queen Isabella's backing, Columbus had discovered a new world. In the year 1492, Leonardo da Vinci, the ecumenical man *par excellence*, symbol of the Renaissance, was painting his famous picture of the Last Supper. In Italy the old classic culture had been rediscovered. The first classes in Greek were offered at Oxford. New ideas, the new spirit exploded all over the continent of Europe, and suddenly we were in a modern age, with a new international culture and a new appreciation of the individual, with an interest not only in his day-by-day needs but in his heritage from the past and what he might hope for the future.

Mankind's time horizons expanded as surely as his geographic horizons during the age of exploration. It did not all happen at once. Perhaps historians of the future will say it is still going on. In the long run, it may have meant more to women than it did to men.

Typical of the new spirit of independence were the guilds, which developed, as the cities developed, after the heyday of feudalism. Guilds were the equivalent of our modern unions and professional societies. Membership was based on occupation, and the object was presumably to control standards, working conditions, competition. Though they were in a way an attempt to regulate the disorganized life of the Middle Ages, they also gave the individual, as a member of the group, a status and a sense of his place in society, which increased his self-respect and self-reliance. It must have been a very different feeling to be a vassal of a liege lord, however decent the fellow might be, and to know oneself to be a member of a trade guild. Some of the fourteenth-century records of eighty-five English guilds—social and craft—have been published by the Early English Text Society. In at least seventy-two of them, women were members on an equal basis with men. In others, widows were admitted if their husbands had been members. Nine guilds for men only were restricted for obvious reasons; they included the guild for preparing young scholars for the priesthood, shipmen of Lynn, smiths at Chester, fullers at Bristol, cordwinders at Exeter. To the religious and benevolent guilds (not apparently church-related), women and men belonged. There were guilds for morals, manners, health, and welfare. Of the twenty-two founders of the Guild of the Blessed Virgin Mary at Kingston-on-Hull, twelve were women. Men and women seem to have had the same rights and responsibilities. Associations were easy and outspoken, and either men or women were fined if they were too obstreperous.

At one time the male bakers decided to get rid of the women in their guild, on the grounds that women "are not strong enough to knead the bread." However, Parliament upheld the women's rights. Women were, however, excluded from the carpetmakers' guild. The work was judged too strenuous for them during pregnancy. Says Renard: "It would be a mistake to imagine that woman in the Middle Ages was confined to her home, and was ignorant of the difficulties of a worker's life. In those days she had economic independence such as is hardly to be met with in our own times."[1]

The churches of this time apparently afforded little opportunity for social relationships. The practical-minded merchants of Florence tried to get the Church interested—not to do something on behalf of the laborers of the city, but to persuade the women to dress more humbly—not for the good of their souls, but so they would not waste for their own clothing good wool which might be exported at a profit.[2] The ordinary women were, if we believe Coulton, "into everything from Church to brawls." Some were inspiring influences, some "consorts of the devil."[3]

The Church accepted new ideas of art and architecture; but it did not find the basically secular spirit of the Renaissance, its emphasis on the autonomy of the individual, and its intense interest in pre-Christian culture of the classic period of Greece and Rome, much to its liking.

Modern Women

Neither, we suspect, was the Church too favorably impressed with the modern woman. There were, of course, still wealthy and pious aristocrats who gave generously to the support of the Church and church work among the indigent and sick. Yet one misses the sense of complete commitment to the religious ideal that had dominated even such worldly queens as Eleanor of Aquitaine, or the devotees of the monastic life. Fewer able young women were attracted to the full-time service of the Church in the cloistered nunneries than had been recruited to the double monasteries in the days when they were centers of community activity. The probability of finding gifted teachers and administrators, let alone religious geniuses, within the ranks of the churchwomen, was proportionately less. Many women who, in an earlier century might have found their way into the convents, were in the present adventuresome atmosphere going into trade or joining one of the guilds, or even studying at one of the universities, which were beginning to open to them. Those of means got much satisfaction out of sponsoring—or at least investing money in—the great overseas trading companies, or, like Isabella of Spain, personally sponsoring explorers. There were few in this day who, like the "Great Countess" Matilda of Tuscany, saw church and state and economic development and people all as essential parts of the over-all—religious—pattern of life.

It was easy enough to look at Henry VIII's progressive harem, and some of the queens who followed him on the English throne, and understand how John Knox (1505–1572) could write a treatise, "The First Blast of the Trumpet against the Monstrous Regiment of Women." Unfortunately, women in high places—good or bad—during the sixteenth and seventeenth centuries were so spectacular as to overshadow their more prosaic sisters.

We mention only two distinguished women who seem to have understood not only the need—each of her own generation and circumstances—but also her personal responsibility to keep alive, to the extent of her own ability, opportunity, and understanding, the true spirit of religion, and so to conduct herself as to strengthen others to do the same. The reader will have his own favorite names from the pages of history to add to the list.[4]

Two Margarets and Anne Boleyn

Margaret Beaufort (1443–1509) was the very gifted and learned mother of Henry VII of England. She arose at five o'clock each morning, so she might have a longer day for prayer, meditation, and good works. She always kept twelve very poor people in her house, caring for them in menial ways and doing what she could to rehabilitate them. She was interested in the Church's responsibility to young people and mothered the university students, especially at Cambridge, where she endowed the colleges of Christ and St. John.

Margaret of Austria (1480–1530), daughter of Emperor Maximilian, had a varied international career, as princesses often did in those days. She was betrothed to the Dauphin of France, was the wife of John of Spain, and later wife of Philbert of Savoy. In 1507 she was made regent of the Netherlands and guardian of her nephew Charles (later Emperor Charles V). She brought about important trade agreements in Western Europe. Charles, as he grew older, felt she was one of his wisest advisers. The Treaty of Cambrai (1529), between Margaret on behalf of Charles and Louise of Savoy, representing her son Francis I of France, was called "the Ladies' Peace." Margaret's interest in international peace may have been fanned by Savonarola, who had preached on the ideal Christian state before he was hanged and burned in 1498.

Let us also say a thank-you to a woman to whom thank-you's are somewhat of a novelty and may be appreciated. It was the unfortunate Anne Boleyn (of whom we shall have more to say later), who persuaded her husband Henry VIII to sponsor the first "official" translation of the Bible into English—the Great Bible of Coverdale. However, before the translation was finished (1539), Anne had been beheaded for infidelity and Henry VIII had married his next wife.[5]

In the excitement of the global expansion of the sixteenth century, it was easy for the Western world more or less to shove religion aside. The Reformation as such was new and official Protestantism just getting on its feet, though we hope we have said enough about the pre-Reformation movements so that no one will tag it as "beginning in 1617." On the other hand, the Roman Catholic Church was very well aware of its own need for reform and revitalization; the papacy was at low ebb. In the East and in Africa the Orthodox churches were subject to Turkish rulers and had become increasingly inward in their religion, as a possible protection of their very existence.

In Western Europe, power and material advancement, rather than religion, seemed uppermost in people's minds. Ethical guidance was up to the local priest. Astronomical instruments were important; so were mechanical clocks and compasses. So were microscopes, telescopes, and, incidentally, eyeglasses. Printing from movable type was acclaimed and put to use. Machiavelli preached a "statecraft which exalted the prince, set forth political principles which were quite opposed to Christianity and either ignored religion or made it the tool of the state."[6]

Even such a pious monarch as Isabella strove for power in her own hands as opposed to those of the Pope. Seldom had individuals felt such power as the monarchs of this period, and most of them—male or female—were duly corrupted by it.

Catherine of Siena

Piety of the period may be represented by the general admiration of Catherine of Siena (1347–1380), renowned, we are told, for ecstatic visions and revelations and supreme devotion to the cause of peace. We know her best as the person who helped Pope Gregory decide to give up his exile in Avignon and return to Rome (1377). In one way she was typical of the period so far as religion was concerned. Almost everyone, it seemed, had come to think of religion not in terms of moral and ethical content, but in terms of political allegiance and the power, or control, of the Pope. Catherine was undoubtedly a personal saint, but though she did much to feed the hungry and clothe the naked, one reads in vain for indication that she was interested in what the average woman of Italy thought—or did not think—about religion in general, or in helping her find ways of making Christianity work in Siena in the second half of the fourteenth century. Perhaps, a generation later, something of the same sort could have been said of Joan of Arc. Neither woman was really part of the picture of "women in religion" of her era. Each was strictly on her own, and in the case of Joan it was a long time before the Church could be sure she was on the Church's side or the Church on hers. Though her burning as a witch was repudiated (1456), it was only in 1920 that she was canonized. (We shall speak more of Joan later.)

Women were interested in the arts; Juliana Berners (c. 1400) is sometimes said to have been the earliest female English writer, turning out a treatise on hunting while prioress of the convent at Hertfordshire. But the evidence is sketchy and only makes us wonder which—religion or horses—was her main interest. Hunting is a long way from either theology or the everyday practice of religion.

It seems sad that the intellectual Renaissance of the West was not at a time when a unified Christianity could accept and interpret it for the world. The Church needed the Renaissance and the Renaissance needed the spirit of religious devotion, as science and religion of any day need each other and should meet in the best minds.

Some writers have indicated that a general lowering of the standard of women's education in the fourteenth and fifteenth centuries was due to the intense interest in the monastic life which tended to narrow her sphere of interest. However, the contrary is probably the truth. When the monasteries became cloistered, the women's opportunity (unless they wanted to become nuns) for classic education was cut off. However, literary development of the vernacular was enriched by their participation in such groups as the Friends of God and some of the pre-Reformation movements. The thing that really hurt women was that leaders of the Protestant Reformation quite ignored the fact that women were of tremendous value to the life and work of the Church and failed to provide for them, in the new structure of either Anglicanism or Protestantism as a whole, any challenging avenue of religious study and service.

Moreover, in a day when the Church itself seemed to be conforming to the standards of an affluent society, it must have been very hard for the average woman to see, for instance, the notorious Agnes Sorel, mistress of King Charles VII of France, or, later, Madame de Pompadour, in all their finery and splendor, and at the same time keep their own souls free from material envy, or their minds free from some rather irreligious speculations as to the possibility of a similar career for themselves or perhaps their daughters. Many of the "finest ladies," they must have told themselves in secret moments, had started no higher than themselves and had risen by a definitely non-religious stairway to their present elegance.

Fiction has given us a number of stories about this period, some of which furnish an insight into the life of the common people, but about the average woman's religion at this time we have very little authentic information. It was probably in most cases pious, personal, semi-magical, and much too casual.

Chapter 9

THE REFORMATION

Margery Backster, charged with heresy in 1428 before the Bishops of Norwich, is said to have denounced the Pope, cardinals, archbishops, and bishops of England as persecutors of the people; she and her husband scorned feasts, fasts, and holy water, but "read together nightly from the Laws of Christ." Margery was certainly not typical of her generation. She was, indeed, quite shocking. But there she was. And there she stood.

Acceptance of women and encouraging them to have the courage of their convictions was a mark of many pre-Reformation movements. The women had actually often shown amazing courage in opposing some of the very abuses which the great reformers themselves attacked. Yet neither Luther nor Calvin set an example of making women feel needed and wanted in the new Protestant faith. Women might be useful around the church, but not as responsible religious colleagues or co-workers. The idea of a woman having anything significant to say, theologically, was apparently unthinkable to the sixteenth-century reformers, as it would be in many churches today.

Luther and Calvin on Women

Luther, in spite of his marriage to the nun Katharina von Bora, and his development of a real affection for her and their children and the comforts of family life, remained at heart a monk. Wealthy women and good cooks had their places, but he shows no inclination to make them intellectual or spiritual companions. It probably never occurred to him —nor perhaps to his wife either—that patronizing humor, even though apparently affectionate, can be degrading.

Women, said Luther, should have nothing to do with "divine service, the priestly office, or God's Word." He did not make it clear how he thought the children were to be instructed. A midwife, he said, *could* baptize, if necessary, but the concession was made in the context of his views on infant baptism, not as any concession to woman's right to act as a priest.

Yet we must admit that Luther's finding a definite place for women, even if it was restricted to the kitchen and nursery, may have kept them attached to the Church instead of sending them, like their sisters in some other countries, into a secular orbit.[1] We can still question whether he might not have offered them more freedom of choice and opportunity for self-expression and personal development, and whether his attitude did not deprive the new Protestantism of a most valuable spiritual resource. Most of all, we should like to know how he rationalized one child of God assuming the responsibility of dictating and delimiting the activity of another child of God. For there was never any question that women were God's children, morally responsible for their own actions and with hope of eternal life. To intervene in this process seems like a staggering responsibility for men to assume.

As for Calvin, it probably never occurred to *him* that a woman could possibly be well enough educated to be worthy of serious conversation; he was wedded to the *Institutes*. As Georgia Harkness points out in *John Calvin, the Man and his Ethics*,[2] Calvin's requirements for a good wife were that she be chaste, patient, solicitous of her husband's health and prosperity. The greatest compliment he had for his own wife was that she never hindered his work. The woman should recognize, he said, that "this is my husband who is my chief; he has authority over me and God compels me" (*Opera* 28:149; see also *Sermon on Deuteronomy* 24:1–4). The husband is to rule but not be a tyrant, and the wife is to "yield modestly to his demands." Dr. Harkness remarks that "the double standard ingrained in the concepts of his time, as in ours, put a certain strain on Calvin's logic." At the same time, she emphasizes the tremendous influence which the expressed attitudes of these two leaders concerning women has had on subsequent developments.

Yet in neither case do the reformers' opinions seem to have been founded on anything more than rather casual acceptance of prevailing cultural patterns, plus their own personal opinions and convenience. There is no evidence of theological or Biblical study on the subject of man-woman relationship in God's scheme of things, or that either Luther or Calvin pretended to have what the Apostle Paul would have called "special knowledge" on the subject. Yet their attitudes in relation to women have been taken with greater seriousness than some of their main-line theology.

With neither Luther nor Calvin did the women have much to say about creeds or forms of service. But even more surprising is the fact that they apparently never so much as opened their mouths with a suggestion. If they did, we have no record of it! Margery Backster and her sisters from all the pre-Reformation movements had been ready and willing to risk their very lives for the kind of religious freedom in which they believed. But when the cause was becoming organized, it never did seem to occur to the women that they should be in there helping create the kind of an organization that would afford them the channels for doing the Lord's work as they understood it, in and through the Church.

It had been the same when the monastery reforms insisted that women should be cloistered and wear habits. Then, too, the women had had a chance to speak up. Perhaps some did and it is not recorded for us. We suspect the same thing—in its modern parallel—could happen again.

The Protestant churches did, indeed, establish channels for the women to serve in the church institutions, but almost invariably under the strong "guidance" of the male; the man's mind, the woman's hands. The work offered the women required great devotion, but little opportunity for personal development. The woman with outstanding education or talents found it wasteful of her time and energy. Most of all, her work—the sort of service she was allowed to perform—was cut out for her. She did not have the stimulus of deciding for herself. Variations of this pattern have been a continuing source of irritation and frustration to women in practically all the Protestant churches during all the intervening centuries and have kept the Church itself from making the witness it should in the world. The vital religious witness of many women has been crowded out, as they have been assigned much too exclusively to the realm of *Kücke und Kinder*. Strangely enough it did not seem to be a cause for much concern at the time that the mother should be prepared to provide much more than good cooking toward the upbringing of her children. We wonder why the women themselves did not make a point of this.

How we wish that the brilliant, powerful, church reform conscious Margaret of Navarre (1492–1549), for instance, might have concerned herself seriously with the role of women in organized religion, and with religious education for the young. The courts this devout Protestant mystic established at Nerac and Pau were said to have been the most intellectually brilliant in Europe, and she realized the power of education and communication, writing considerable prose and poetry. But, like so many women in religion, she does not seem to have been concerned with passing on her light to other women of the Church and the future.

"Ladies of the Reformation" in England and Scotland

Instead of discussing further the Reformation on the continent, let us cross the Channel and see what was going on, as described in *Ladies of the Reformation*, written in 1855 by the Reverend James Anderson.[3] As we dip into the history of women's contribution to religion through the centuries, we find much of our best material in dusty, unquoted volumes, often authored by reputable scholars, whose other works have been acclaimed, though their writings about women have been rather studiously ignored. It is as if a thin substratum of church history—seldom noted—does deal with women and their contribution to religion, and has a tensile strength and resilience which permeates all history. Isolated instances and personalities are in fact simply ground swells of something that is going on all the time. Women's work in the Church is of the essence, after all—the enriching subsoil that feeds and nourishes (and not only with meat loaf and generous checks) the very institutions from which they seem to be excluded from all but menial participation.

Some of the names the Reverend Mr. Anderson mentions are well known, but try this list on your church historian friends:

England: Anne of Bohemia, Anne Boleyn, Anne Askew, Catherine Parr, Lady Jane Grey, Katherine Willoughby, Ann de Tserclas, Katharine Vermilia, Mildred Cook. Scotland: Katharine Hamilton, Helen Stark, Isabel Scrimger, Elizabeth Aske, Marjory Bowes, Elizabeth Campbell, Elizabeth Knox. Netherlands: Wendelmuta Klaas, Lysken Dirks, Mrs. Robert Oguier, Betkyn, Elizabeth Vander Kerk, Charlotte de Bourbon, Louise de Colligny.

Look for these names in histories of the Protestant Reformation. Then, perhaps in some dusty corner of one of the larger theological libraries, find Mr. Anderson's 700-page book and, dipping into the stories, realize that such material has existed at probably every period of the world's history. But where is it now? When the stories of one generation are not preserved, there is neither example nor direction for the next generation. Before long, it is easy to believe that women have *never* had a place in traditional religion, and that, for some unexplained reason, the good Lord has seen fit to endow all his female children with inferior minds, incapable of understanding the intricacies of theology, ecclesiology, or ethics, yet certainly equipped with souls, and to be judged by the same moral precepts as his male children.

Good Queen Anne

The first lady of the Reformation to whom Anderson introduces us is definitely pre-Reformation: Anne of Bohemia, a lady of mighty royal blood, whom we shall identify merely as the sister of King Wenceslaus. She was born in Prague in 1367. In her early youth she became interested in the three reformers, John Melice, Conrad Strickna, and Matthias Janovius, who was confessor to Anne's father, Charles IV, until the latter banished him for trying to reform the Communion.

It seems that Anne's beauty, goodness, and amiable disposition were well publicized in Europe; probably less was said about the fact that she could and did study the Gospels in various languages. One of many marriage proposals she received was on behalf of young King Richard II of England, and when she was fifteen and could make her own choice, this was the proposal she accepted. One of the main attractions in going so far from home was that Anne had heard of an English reformer by the name of Wyclif, with whom she was anxious to have conversation. She took with her, as was proper, quite a train of attendants, most of them, it seems, of the reformed opinions. We can almost hear the king saying, as he gave his gracious consent to the list, "And good riddance!"

Anne and Richard liked each other at once, but before she would consummate the marriage, Anne insisted on a general pardon for the insurgents who had been roused (and jailed) by John Ball's famous couplet:

> When Adam delved and Eve span,
> Who was then the gentleman?

It was not long before the new queen was known as "Good Queen Anne." She does not seem to have troubled herself unduly over the two rival Popes, Urban VI and Clement VII, but was intrigued by the scholar Wyclif, whose activity at first went comparatively unnoticed in the institutional turbulence of the papacy. She had what, in those times, was a priceless possession—the Gospels in three languages, Bohemian, English, and Latin. She also collected commentaries

written by learned scholars and devoted part of each day to study of
these materials. Wyclif held her up as an example.

When Anne first came to England, Wyclif (1328?–1384), sometimes
called "the Morning Star of the Reformation," had not yet reached
his zenith. He had not yet attacked the Church at Rome or the
Pope, but only abuses within the churches as he saw them in England.
Above all, he was convinced that the Bible in the hands of the
people was basic to bringing about the kind of reform that was
needed. He distributed Bibles through many channels. It was his
interest in the Scriptures that had been instrumental in enticing Anne
to England, and this mutual interest made them allies. Involved, too,
was Wyclif's stanch belief in the independence and dignity of the
common man—as Wyclif read this in the Scriptures and as it had
evolved in his days at Oxford. Says W. H. Poole, his perceptive
apologist: "It is this principle of the dependence of the individual
upon God alone and upon none else that distinguishes Wyclif's from
any other system of the Middle Ages." . . . "By this formula all
laymen became priests, and all priests laymen, so far as their religious
position was concerned."

Wyclif was against force, except to put down tyranny. However,
and here he was headed for trouble, he also held that what a man
is within himself, and not his office, is his measure: the Pope himself,
if a bad man, loses his entire right to Lordship. Wyclif admitted that
he could conceive of a Church without a Pope or cardinals—just
laymen! This was indeed strong medicine: really too much for Oxford.
Oxford condemned his views and his associates, though not Wyclif
himself. On the same grounds (although he believed in the "real
presence" at the Lord's table), Wyclif could not admit that the
prayer of the priest brought about transubstantiation.

By the time Anne arrived in London and married the king (1382),
Wyclif had been called before the Convention of London for attacking
the wealth of the Church and the power of excommunication. He
had also espoused the opinion that there should be separation of
Church and state, and that either the Pope or the king should be
answerable to the layman.

Whether or not Wyclif officially considered himself a Lollard is a
question, but at least these "lolling fellows" followed him, theologically.
They gained considerable importance toward the end of the century,
and to be a Lollard became a capital offense in 1401.

But let us get back to Anne, who certainly understood both her
Scriptures and her theology, and who took the extra step of in-

terpreting them in terms of the monarch's obligations of responsible brotherly love for her subjects.

The Archbishop of York, whom Anne took pains to inform about her interest in the Scriptures, could do nothing—but he saw to it that the same books did not fall into the hands of the common people. He could do nothing about Anne because she was the queen, the most amiable of wives, and because she continued to espouse the cause of the poor and unfortunate—at one time it was said that 6000 indigent poor ate at the royal table.

In the showdown between Wyclif and the Archbishop of Canterbury, it was Anne's pleas to Richard that probably saved the reformer's life. But by now Anne had a new ally in her mother-in-law, Joan, who spoke forcefully on Wyclif's behalf and as queen mother issued a mandate forbidding the ecclesiastical court to condemn him. The Pope had just sent word to the king, Archbishop of Canterbury, Bishop of London, and the University of Oxford, requiring his arrest and the suppression of all people tainted with his heresies! John of Gaunt, Duke of Lancaster, leader of the Lollards, and other nobles also supported Anne and Joan, as did many of the common people whom Anne had so impressed with her personal goodness and kindness. This combined influence was sufficient to stave off action against Wyclif until, in 1384, he died a natural death. So long as Anne lived, Richard was also stayed from attack on the Lollards, and none of them were put to death during his reign.

Anne died in June 1394. She was twenty-seven, and had ruled with Richard for twelve years. Richard was deposed in 1399 by Henry IV, who passed a statute authorizing the burning of heretics. Preaching, teaching, and writing in opposition to the Catholic faith were prohibited; heretical books were confiscated. Offenders or those who supported them were to be burned before the people, "to the intent that this kind of punishment may strike a terror on the minds of others."

But there is a sequel: "After the death of Anne, many members of her household, having returned to Bohemia, carried with them the opinions and the writings of the English reformer Wyclif, and were the means of scattering the seed of the reform faith among their countrymen. . . . It was from this source (and some Bohemian students at Oxford) that John Huss and Jerome of Prague, the honored successors of Melice, Strickna, and Janovius, imbued the opinions which they disseminated. . . ." Huss, it might be added, originally received what support *he* had from Queen Sophia of Bohemia.

Betkyn, the Maidservant

The exploits of Henry VIII (1491–1547) have made us more or less familiar with some of the "Ladies of the Reformation"—for instance, Henry's wives Katharine of Aragon, Anne Boleyn, Jane Seymour, Anne of Cleves, Catherine Howard, Catherine Parr. Also we know Lady Jane Grey, Mary Tudor, and especially, of course, Henry's daughter Elizabeth (1533–1603); also Mary Stuart, who, with her husband, William of Orange, assumed the throne in 1689. But while women and religion were both involved in this amazing period of history, the overtones of political power and world domination were such that religion as such seems to have been an afterthought, or at most a tool. And when religion becomes a tool, surely it ceases to be religion. Some of the women were undoubtedly sincere in their religious devotion and certainly some were of great ability, but the facts lead us to wonder whether women, power politics, and religion ever belong in one package.

Instead of looking at royalty, let us consider the story of Betkyn— that is the only name by which we know her. Betkyn was the maidservant of Peter Van Kulen, who was a goldsmith in the town of Breda and held an office which was probably that of elder in the Reformed Church. Members of a free church were not allowed to assemble publicly, so they had been meeting at Van Kulen's home, and Betkyn had become an active member of the group.

Van Kulen was apparently not very discreet about letting his beliefs be known. News that the meetings were being held, and where, reached the authorities. He was imprisoned and put into irons, but, lest he contaminate other prisoners with his views, he was removed to a solitary room in the castle. It was up to such prisoners to provide their own maintenance, and of course those who came to visit them were closely watched. For nine months Betkyn faithfully brought Van Kulen food every day. Then she, too, was arrested. Her only comment was that she was very happy to be called to suffer for righteousness' sake.

Both Betkyn and Van Kulen underwent various forms of torture considered appropriate for the day, to get them to tell who their Christian brothers were. Even on the rack, Van Kulen stood fast and made no revelations. Betkyn apparently trusted herself, but thought the rack was something to avoid if possible. "My masters," she is reported as saying, "wherefore put me to the torture since I have in no way offended you? Is it for my faith's sake? You need not torment me for that, for as I am never ashamed to make a confession thereof, no more will I be so now. When before you, I shall freely disclose to you my mind herein." They were not satisfied. Betkyn added, "My masters, if it be so I must suffer this pain, then give me leave first to call upon God." Thereupon she fell to her knees and prayed so eloquently that one of the commissioners, convinced of her innocence and terrified at having a part in her sufferings, swooned and for a long time could not be revived. Betkyn was not put to the rack.

Shortly, however, Betkyn and Van Kulen were examined together, both professing again their faith, but refusing steadfastly to give the names of the other members of their church or themselves to recant and return to the arms of the Roman Catholic Church. On the morning of May 29, 1563, a "vast multitude" assembled to see them burned. Some of their Christian friends were said to be in the crowd, bent on encouraging them. There seems also to have been considerable display of sympathy and indignation against the execution on the part of the witnesses. Some of the women broke through to the prisoners as they were being taken to the place of execution and embraced them; there were cries of "Fight manfully!" and "The crown is prepared for you."

The prisoners prayed as they went along the way. They asked God to be pleased to perfect the good work which he had mercifully begun in them by the power of the Holy Spirit until they had finished their course. At the place of execution, Betkyn addressed the crowd, exhorting them always to be obedient to the Word of God and not fear those who had no power over the soul. "As for me," she said, "I am now going to meet my glorious spouse, the Lord Jesus Christ." Then they both fell on their knees and prayed with fervor.

Betkyn encouraged Van Kulen to be strong in the Lord, as he was first strangled, then burned. However, Betkyn, Anderson tells us, "being more obnoxious from her greater intrepidity and freedom of owning her sentiments, which was interpreted as proof of her invincible obstinacy, was denied the poor favour of being strangled before the flames seized upon her. But her faith, if it did not literally quench the volume of the fire, gave her fortitude to endure it, without shrinking, and out of the midst of the devouring element she was heard and seen, to the admiration of many of the spectators, to magnify the Lord."

Shortly thereafter, it was ordered that when persons were executed, wooden balls should be placed in their mouths, to keep them from such last-minute witnessing. These wooden balls sometimes fell out, however, so an ingenious iron clamp was devised. The hot iron, placed through the tongue in a designated manner, was said not only to keep the victim from saying anything articulate, but also it caused the loose end of the tongue, as the heat increased, to wiggle in what was described as a most amusing manner.

Lysken Dirks and Janet Montgomery

Then there was Lysken Dirks, the Anabaptist—a group repudiated even by many of their fellow reformers. Married in 1549, she and her young husband had lived in Antwerp for two years and were expecting their first child, when they were suddenly seized and thrown into prison. They never saw each other again, but were permitted to correspond. The story is told that visiting monks, anxious to get her to recant, once said, "Why should you meddle with the Scriptures; you had better mind your sewing." To this she replied, "Christ commands us to search the Scriptures, and God is to be obeyed rather than man." So effective was her witness, even from her prison cell, that the authorities decided against rousing the people by burning her. She was, instead, placed in a sack and quietly drowned in the river Scheldt one morning before daybreak.

Anderson would not forgive us if we did not include mention of at least one Scotswoman. For some reason not entirely clear, but which suggests a most intriguing avenue of study, Scottish families seem, from a very early period, to have had a high regard for education and looked upon it as a right of their daughters as well as their sons. It is told that at one time John Campbell of Cesnock and his wife, Janet Montgomery, were on trial for their liberal opinions. It seems they kept their own priest, who read from the Scriptures and instructed the family daily; the priest also was accused. Campbell, with no desire to mince matters, appealed directly to King James IV, making a cautious and reasonable presentation of his position. The king then asked Janet if she had anything to add, whereupon she "pled the cause of them all with such ability and boldness, readily and appropriately quoting from the Scriptures in support of her statement, as to astonish the sovereign, who not only acquitted all the defendants—Campbell, his wife, and the priest—but rising up shook Mrs. Campbell by the hand and highly commended her acquaintance with the Christian doctrine." He reproved the accusers, threatened them with severe punishment if they ever again so harassed such honorable and innocent persons, and made the Campbells a present of several villages.

Their granddaughter, Elizabeth Campbell, married a distant relative, Robert Campbell, likewise of the reformed faith. Both were well educated and religiously informed. In their house ministers met, and the lines which the Church of Scotland should follow were worked out. Many meetings were held in the Campbell home. Mrs. Campbell seems to have participated fully in the discussions. At the same time, Robert Campbell covered much of Scotland on horseback, stimulating the cause of liberty and "Christ's kirk and the gospel."

One of the women of the Reformation least known and best worth knowing is Katharina Schutz Zell (1497–1562). She was the wife of Matthaus Zell, first Protestant preacher of Strassburg, who was a rather ardent follower of Zwingli. Matthaus celebrated Mass in the vernacular and broke with the ecclesiastical structure in 1523. The Zell house was a place of refuge for persecuted brethren from many cities—including the Anabaptists, who were having a particularly bad time. Katharina helped in all the work, and it is said that she built in Strassburg a spirit of intellectual Christian tolerance which persists in the Alsatian city to this day. Matthaus Zell died in 1548, but Katharina lived till 1562. She was particularly interested in working with and writing for women.[4]

The overdue reform movement came also to the Roman Catholic Church, especially through the efforts of Ignatius of Loyola (1491–1556) and Francis de Sales (1567–1622). In 1535 the Ursuline order for the teaching of young girls—the first with this as a special responsibility—was founded by Angela Merici of Brescia.[5]

Latourette points out that it was a reformed type of Christianity —Protestant or Catholic—which went out from Europe to the New World. It was the monks of the Roman Catholic Church who were by far the most numerous missionaries in the first years. However, it was with the North American colonists, whose families often had a long history, one way or another, of protesting attitudes, that a different type of missionary endeavor was sent around the world.[6]

The idea of woman missionaries was by no means new. We have pointed out how they had a hand in Christianizing much of Europe. Pierre Dubois, in the thirteenth century, had suggested that since it seemed impossible for the Crusaders to conquer the infidel by violence, thought should be given to training girls in theology and medicine, to win them by spirit and service. He was about six centuries ahead of his time.[7]

In Europe the situation was made no more bearable for the women of Reformation countries by the fact that in France, which had, for the time being, chosen the way of rampant secularism, women were having somewhat of a heyday. In 1608 the Marquise de Rambouillet started her famous salon in Paris, and the idea was taken up by many Frenchwomen. One woman's home was a gathering place for the skeptics; Voltaire was her special "lion." In another home there were two literary and philosophic assemblies each week—one for beginners, one for celebrities. Julie de Lespinasse was partial to English and American guests, including Franklin, Jefferson, and Paine. Since the Estates General was out after 1614, with no machinery for reform till the Revolution started in 1789, the importance of these salons was obvious. Inevitably they were reproduced at all levels of society. Inevitably they gave their women organizers—whether in palace or coffee shop—a sense of doing something significant—for which the Church offered no counterpart.

Chapter 10

WITCHES

Joan of Arc (1412–1431) was apparently just another nice girl—the fourth child of a peasant family of the village of Domrémy, France. Her father was the "head man," or mayor of the community, where people were undoubtedly far more worried about the weather and crops than over the continuing struggles between the French and the English rulers. There was, however, a legend, told by the fireside of an evening, about a young woman who would come in the fullness of time to save France and restore her rightful line of sovereigns. . . . Joan undoubtedly heard the story, and as she grew older it seems she heard voices—voices of no earthly origin, telling her that she was this maid of destiny. She was undoubtedly persuaded that somehow it was she—Joan—who must put the Dauphin on the throne of her country. And the strange part of the story is that, somehow, she did just that, and no one knew quite what to think about it, except the Dauphin, who of course was pleased.

Somehow—no one knew quite how—she had gained access to his court, persuaded him with her help to raise the siege of Orléans, and had seen him ride triumphantly into Rheims, where kings of France were traditionally crowned, and where, with holy oil, he was consecrated Charles VII. It was Joan's hour of triumph, as well as that of the new king.

Shortly thereafter, however, she was captured in battle by John of Luxemburg, and for due consideration in each case turned over first to the Duke of Burgundy and then to John of Lancaster, Duke of Bedford. Bedford, with the help of the Cardinal of Winchester, arranged to have her tried under the rules of the University of Paris, which was then under the domination of England. She was charged with witchcraft and heresy, prosecuted by French ecclesiastics, condemned, and burned at the stake in 1431.

Joan had been accused of "devil worship by trees and fountains."

She admitted she had sung with others by the "Fairy Tree" and near-by spring, which was a legendary spot near her home. At festival time she had—like everyone else—even hung garlands on the tree. It must have seemed foolish to everyone to refer to this as devil worship. The questioning by the ecclesiastics was primarily about her "voices." The first thing the voices told her, she said, was to be good and go to church. But the judges wanted to know more—much more. Had she *seen* them? Had they touched her? If so, were they warm or cold? The judges did not seem to be trying to find out whether or not Joan believed in witchcraft, so much as to find out, from her, about a subject in which they quite firmly believed and about which they wanted concrete information. Joan, as it seems any honest and re-ligiously sensitive person must have done, refused to discuss in open court the matter of what her voices meant to her. As a test of whether she owed allegiance to Christ and the Church, or to some devils of the magic world, the judges insisted that she recite the Lord's Prayer. Again she refused—she would say it in the confessional, but not recite it in public. She appealed to the Pope, but would not promise un-conditionally to submit to his decision. The ecclesiastical judges felt they had no choice. They found her guilty and burned her. Yet Joan won.

In 1456 Charles VII, belatedly, ordered another trial and the de-cision was reversed. Joan was innocent, after all, but she had long since been consumed by the flames. And it was not until 1920 that the Roman Catholic Church declared her a saint; two years later, in 1922, she was declared the patroness of France. Meanwhile—and since —the greatest writers—English writers especially—have made her one of the most popular heroines of historic fiction and the stage. Her case was one of the most controversial and one of the most highly publicized trials in history. Certainly it was *the* great witch trial of all time, and more or less set the stage for the scandalous involvement of the Church in such procedures during the next two centuries. It set the stage also for the legacy of anti-feminine sentiment which has so often, and in times and places which have prided themselves on their modern and scientific outlook on life, made women the very embodiment of evil.

The Witch and the Scapegoat

Witches are common to most primitive societies and may be either male or female. Like the priest and the medicine man, the witch has unexplainable powers, usually believed to be derived from some supernatural source. These powers may be used to harm others, to the witch's direct personal advantage, or to pay a grudge for some real or imagined offense. Or for a due consideration the witch (acting as a sort of evil priest) may gain for some other person desired wealth, the embraces of an otherwise reluctant mate, or even the death of a real or imagined enemy. A witch could also cause damage to the other person's crops or flocks, his house or family.

Roughly speaking, the primitive priest is in charge of contact with benevolent forces (though they may sometimes be stern for one's own good); the witch deals with malevolence, and the malevolent forces upon which the witch depends for power demand a tremendous price— ultimately the witch's very soul.

Closely akin to the belief in primitive witchcraft is recourse to the scapegoat, an idea which, in theological categories, is quite as ingenious as the invention of the wheel—and perhaps from almost as early a date.

In the Middle Ages the idea of the witch and the scapegoat came together, and their paths crossed with dramatic results.

It is amazing how common the idea of the scapegoat is in primitive communities—and very often a real goat is the animal chosen for the role. What goats as a race have done to deserve this fate and designation—who knows? The sixteenth chapter of Leviticus gives an early Hebrew version of the scapegoat ceremony in relation to the ancient yearly ritual of atonement. Two live goats are to be taken by the priest to the tent of meeting, and lots are cast—one for the Lord, one for Azazel. The goat who falls to the Lord's lot is then to be sacrificed, but upon the head of the live goat the priest is to lay his hands, confessing all the sins and iniquities of the people of Israel, after which it is to be turned out into the wilderness, "carrying all their iniquities out into a desolate region." It does not seem to be quite clear whether the goat himself is Azazel, or whether he carries the sins of all the people out to a "fallen angel" (or devil) known as Azazel, waiting in the desert.[1]

Many primitive people have counterparts of this ceremony even in recent times. In one community in the South Pacific, at the time of the spring festival, a hapless goat is led from one hut to another. He is fastened inside each hut in turn, while all the villagers beat on the walls from the outside, thus driving into the goat all the evil spirits that may have accumulated there during the past year. After he has been taken to all the huts, and accumulated all the sins of all the people, he is indeed ready to make his escape and never be seen again.

The kindred institution of the "whipping boy" has survived down to modern times. In southern plantations, the little Negro slave used to take the blows for the "young master" who had been a bad boy. Hitler put the "whipping boy" principle to work against the Jews as a race. It was partially at least out of this same type of Azazel reasoning that the case against witches became so popular.

The Code Hammurabi (2000 B.C.) provides for trial of witches by plunging them into a sacred river. If the accused sinks, he is indeed a witch and the accuser gets his house.

The Hebrew Scriptures command the execution of witches. However, Saul, though determined to enforce the law against witches, could not resist, personally, going to consult the Witch of Endor, a rather kindly old soul who was blessed, or cursed, with extra-sensory perception. Duke University would undoubtedly have appreciated her for their ESP research—she is not really the kind of witch we are talking about. Or is she? Through the ages the kindly old souls with ESP are often exactly the ones the self-righteous bigots of the community have chosen (on the basis of their being witches) as whipping girls, through whom the community sins could somehow be exorcised by fire and water.

How did it come about that, as time went on, women were especially singled out for the role of witch? It is not hard to guess. Could anything have been more alarming to the primitive mind than a woman's menstrual periods—especially when one noticed that they were somehow related to the moon? Woman certainly had unseen and unexplainable allies of some sort! To say nothing of the mystery of childbearing! All such things made the Hebrew woman ritually "unclean" for a specified time.

As the Hebrew religion developed, with YAHWEH surrounded by the rivalry of many fertility goddesses—some of whom certainly approved sex excesses—and later as Christianity met the opposition of the mystery cults, again often tolerating sex excesses, women began to be symbols of temptation. Eve, of course, had a reputation as a temptress. And then there was the rabbinical story of Lilith, supposedly Adam's first wife, who was cast out of Eden and took up harming little children as a career. Surely Lilith was a witch!

In New Testament times, the strong belief that the Day of Judgment was at hand led to a widespread advocacy of celibacy: why marry and start to raise a family if the world was coming to an end in your own generation? This thinking got somewhat confused with asceticism and carried over into the early monastic way of life. Again, women were temptation, hence evil.

During the years of the barbaric invasions, and the Dark Ages, it must have been almost impossible for most women to keep themselves physically chaste, except, perhaps, under the protection of the Church. It was at this time that the exaltation of the Virgin Mary, as opposed to the degradation of her everyday sisters, became apparent to most churchmen.

Latourette mentions that while the Church upheld better marriage and family relationships, and forbade polygamy and pre-marital experimentation, or sexual intercourse outside the marital bond, it also stressed asceticism as the highest standard of Christian living. Thus woman continued to be a temptation and an evil and, by making her relatively unattainable, the Church, he suggests, actually encouraged irregular sex connections and certainly immoderate sex interest.

"A crass attitude toward women and toward marriage was widespread," says Latourette. "Romance and wedlock were probably more frequently divorced than united. On the other hand, the cult of the Virgin Mary, which was so prominent in both Greek East and Latin West and which owed so much to the ascetic ideal, exalted womanhood and chastity."[2]

We feel sure, also, that the very active part assumed by women in the growing number of pre-Reformation "cults" did nothing at all to endear women to the ecclesiastics; they were certainly appropriate whipping girls.

So now we have women, witches, and whipping girls in one package. The main characteristics of the modern witch and witchery and witch trials were becoming distinguishable.

In general the Church was (to start with) historically against witch trials. (You couldn't logically be against *witches themselves* unless you believed in them, could you? And such belief was heresy.) In the ninth century the Archbishop of Lyons had found it necessary officially to argue against trying presumed witches by fire and water, but another archbishop had put forth his profound arguments in favor of *judicum aquae frigidae*.[3]

Brews and Spells

But then, there is no such thing as a witch—is there? A witch is (with notable exceptions) just a poor, unfortunate old woman, often a bit queer in the head, or at least believing something quite different from what "we" and other sound and sensible people recognize as the right thing to believe. Perhaps she really does have a bit of ESP— whatever that is—or maybe she has just lived alone and has watched what was going on in the community till she has a pretty good idea what is going to happen next. She may know something about herbs, or sense that by mixing up some sort of a harmless placebo she can make the person who comes to her for help feel a lot better, even without drugs. Living alone, she probably has a cat, or maybe even an owl or a toad (they all earn their own living) for company. They often have the run of the house; the cat, especially, often exchanges conversation with her, which they both more or less understand and can supplement for each other. Being "queer," she has not felt too much at home at the church's social affairs, and not being too bright, she may have rashly turned against the church as she knows it, because of the way some Christians have treated her. One thing is almost sure: she has been called a witch so often that she is, herself, convinced that she really is one, and in a sense is proud of it. Since this is probably the only distinction the poor soul will ever have, she makes the most of it. To her native equipment she adds, bit by bit, the embellishments which, she has heard the gossips say, other witches are known to have. If she can read, she may even have looked the matter up in religious books. A broomstick is certainly easy to come by—there is probably a worn-out broom on the wood pile. And as she sits outside her hut, some night when the full moon is high, rubbing grease into the smooth wood with a calloused forefinger, how is she to tell whether it is a witch's dream or reality that sends her soaring aloft into the blue-black sky to come, presently, to the great clearing where, she has often heard, witches from miles around gather on a night like this to taste—in celebration of the witches' Sabbath—the joys of good food and danc- ing, companionship, sex, and even the ecstasy of the "witches' mass" in lieu of the church service from which they have felt excluded, but which they have always subconsciously missed. In their witch world they are important as they never can be in real life. Once they have been accused, and have broken down, they often confess with much gusto and show a great understanding of what is expected of a first-class witch. If there is to be a fire for burning, let it not be a dim and smoldering one! Today we would have the TV cameras! Besides, it is a fact that burning almost never follows lurid confessions—does it?

Brews and spells, broom and cat, and the celebration of the witches' Sabbath are the simple elements of witchhood, which vary to some extent with place and time. Strangely enough, since we do not believe in witches, questions about these matters occur again and again in witch trials. However, Herbert Thurston, writing in the *Catholic Encyclopaedia*,[4] mentions two points which gave the churches of the Middle Ages a basis for involvement. The first of these is the existence or non-existence of a "diabolical pact"[5] or at least evidence that the witch has appealed, in her work, for the intervention of the spirits of evil, for instance, in causing the death of an obnoxious person, awakening passion in a client's desired partner, calling up the dead for consultation, or punishing enemies, rivals, or economic oppressors. To obtain such help, it was presumed that the witch would make a compact to abjure Christian Scripture, observe the witches' Sabbath, worship the devil. Often they were given an "imp," known as a "familiar," perhaps in the form of an animal, to help carry out the plans agreed upon.

The other matter that became important as the witch trials became more sophisticated was that the witch should actually have caused harm to some person or his property. As early as the third century, the Romans had introduced laws demanding the burning of a witch alive for causing the death of another person. More theologically, the Councils of Elvira (306) and Ancyra (314) had passed rulings against witches and *those who consult them*, on the grounds that this was the way of idolatry or devil worship. This seems to have been the norm of church attitudes for several centuries. Probably it was only the wisest people who recognized the fact that while it might be foolish to "believe in witches" or in one's own prowess as a witch, the real danger was in the way such a belief could involve and contaminate others, making it the duty of priests at every level to emphasize that stories of witches were "absolutely untrue" and "implanted in human minds by the spirit of evil." Thus, "doing and believing" witchcraft became a sin requiring penance. Hence, it fell into the hands of the Inquisition.

The Inquisition

In 1275 at Toulouse a witch was burned after judicial sentence of
the Inquisition. She had confessed to intercourse with a demon monster
she had fed with human flesh. Thomas Aquinas is said to have upheld
the idea that human intercourse with demons was indeed possible.
Again at Toulouse, in 1335, sixty-three persons were accused, eight
burned, the rest imprisoned for life or long terms. Imprisonment was
really an irrational sentence. If one believed in witchcraft at all, burning
was supposed to be a process for purging the devil out of the afflicted
one even if it destroyed his life; hence, it was theologically more
sensible. Would being behind prison bars stop the demonic power of
the accused? In England supposed witches were usually hung, on the
grounds of simply purging society of their influence.

Interest in witchcraft spread in all directions. In 1324 two old women
were tried for witchcraft in Ireland, confessed under pressure, and were
burned. In the fifteenth century there were literally hundreds of
executions by fire and drowning in Switzerland, ordered by secular
courts.

Belief in witches as something to be eradicated as a menace to mankind spread throughout Europe. Fear of the devil, and his use of
witches and witchery as malevolent instruments, was one obsession
uniting cleric, statesman, and peasant. The terror of being harmed by
or accused of being a witch haunted every city and hamlet. In Ireland
the bishop brought charges of the whole gamut of witchery practices
against Lady Alice Kyteler, claiming she used magic conveniently to
rid herself of successive husbands. In such high rank cases important property rights were often involved, frequently as a motivation for the accusation. In England Henry V accused his stepmother,
Joan of Navarre, of magic attempts on his life. No one seemed exempt
from either belief in witches or being accused of being a witch. And to
all these evils was added another which in some ways was worst of all:
pre-burning torture, apparently for the sole purpose of providing a
spectacle for the populace. For instance, in 1462 four men and four
women were accused in rural France and burned. However, one of
the women, who was supposed to have given herself to an incubus and
eaten children, was forced, as a preliminary to her burning, to sit
naked on a red-hot iron for three minutes. Something, indeed, about
which spectators could look forward to telling their grandchildren!

Joan of Arc's burning seems only to have whetted the appetite for executions and the perverted interest in witchery, and reversal of the ecclesiastical court's decision did nothing to slow down the madness. What seems most incredible is that such a mania could last as long as it did. At the end of the fifteenth century, it was, indeed, just cutting its fangs.

In 1485 (Luther was just a toddler that year) Pope Innocent VIII issued a famous papal bull. It had come to the Pope's ears, said the document, that certain people were abandoning themselves to devils, incubi, and succubi, and by their incantations, spells, conjurations, and other accursed charms and crafts, enormities and horrid offenses, slaying unborn infants, men and women, various kinds of animals, ruining fields and vineyards, meadows and orchards. By their spells they were also torturing people, preventing men from being able to perform the sexual act or women from conceiving. He went into considerable detail and gave no hint at all that he thought all this was just unfortunate rumor. He appointed inquisitors to track down all such harmful individuals and bring them to speedy trial. Those with information to help the inquisitors were duty bound to reveal all they knew. This was no scholarly attack on the heretical aspects of witchery. It was a shocking attack on witchery as a very real thing and a dangerous social evil, and against all its traditional manifestations and apparatus. It seemed to give substance to all the alleged phenomena which good church people were supposed to know—or at least pretend to know—did not exist.

The Textbook on Witchcraft

Shortly thereafter, Jakob Sprenger, Inquisitor of Cologne, with Heinrick Kraemer, published one of the best-sellers of literary history—the *Malleus Maleficarum*, often called the standard textbook of witchcraft. It purported to give the Biblical basis of witchery, its horrors, and tell how to deal with them in secular and ecclesiastical courts. It was reproduced in quantity on a printing press. Fraudulent claims were made that it was "approved" by the University of Cologne. Rumor said that its preparation had high ecclesiastical sponsorship. Its popularity is hard to imagine. It was said that every judge had a copy beside him as he presided in court. Those who did not believe a word of it still obviously had to read it to be "informed." Fourteen editions were printed 1487–1530; sixteen editions 1574–1669.

Witchcraft is represented as worse than heresy. The female sex of the witch is presumed, and the judge is given a variety of suggestions as to how he may, with clear conscience, trap her into a confession and get her to name other women she knows to be witches. The judge may, for instance, promise she will not be burned if she will name other witches. Thinking he means she will go free, she may name several. Ah, but he did not say she would go free; she may still be imprisoned for life on bread and water. Or he may actually keep his promise and release her—but presumably such a promise is only for a given time; she may be tried again and this time burned! A third very clever trick for getting a confession or accusation is for one judge to promise immunity, but then turn the case over to another judge for sentencing; of course the second judge has promised nothing and may "with honor" pass a sentence of execution. The vileness with which contact with witchery could contaminate otherwise apparently honorable men is unbelievable. And who can calculate the extent of the mind set it induced against women, as possible or probable witches, or the length of time such a mind set could contaminate society!

Publication of the *Malleus* unloosed a flood of sermons and criticisms, which Thurston says were mostly on the side of sense but nevertheless inflamed the popular imagination. In 1532 a penal code declared sorcery a penal offense throughout Germany, and in 1572 Saxony decreed burning for any kind of witchcraft, even simple fortunetelling, if it resulted in injury.

In 1583, at Wolfenbuttel, 121 witches were burned in three months; in 1593 they were burning ten witches a day.

Some of the doings of royalty and high clergy, in various countries, made it apparent that not all witches were poor and old, but did little to contradict the opinion that almost all witches were women, and quite probably vice versa. There were innumerable witch trials in England during the reign of Elizabeth. James I wrote a book on *Daemonology* and personally presided over several witch trials, though he expressed the opinion that most of the witnesses were "extreme liars."

Emphasis on sin and the devil in early Protestant theology, as well as the tendency not to give women a responsible place in the organization of the main-line Protestant churches, may very well be one indirect effect of Pope Innocent VIII's papal bull and Jakob Sprenger's *Malleus* (among other causes).

We have indicated that there were many exceptions to the rule which pictured the typical witch as a poor, half-witted old woman. Charles Williams, in his book *Witchcraft*, devotes one chapter to "The Centuries of Noble Trials" and presents a really shocking picture of the way this interest in witchcraft reached not only into the palaces of the continent but even into the Vatican. These were rumors of the use of magic arts against members of the papal court.

The witchcraft craze might have died down much sooner except for the *Malleus Maleficarum*, which became for centuries "the great formulation of the Catholic attack on sorcery." From it all manner of witchery could be documented, and so could witchcraft's relation to sex.

The Link between Magic and Sex

Starting with the rather simple proposition that "the most prolific source of witchcraft is quarrelling between unmarried women and their lovers," the book went on to emphasize the link between magic and sex and to become an encyclopedia of witchery excesses of every sort. It told, as plain as you could ask for, all about the witches' Sabbaths, the novice's first intercourse with Satan himself, and thereafter with his friends. It told also of the satanic Mass, and the ways witches killed children—sometimes their own, often those for which they were midwives—and ate them, or used their bodies to make the ointment necessary to grease their broomsticks. It was a vile book, but it undoubtedly gave the people of that day (some of the people, that is) exactly what they wanted. This was the sort of thing they had been hoping to hear and trying to draw out from the accused at the trials, before the witches were burned, and about which the accused people often obstinately claimed to have no knowledge at all.

It has been said that during the sixteenth and seventeenth centuries "contrition for sin had largely vanished from Christendom; conflict *about* sin took its place." And the sin of sins was witchcraft. Instead of theological discussions, there was speculation as to what happened if a sorcerer (or the devil himself), perhaps masquerading as a priest, got control of the elements and took over the Communion. This gave rise to the frequently quoted question, "If a mouse eats the Host [Communion bread], does he receive God?"

Tales of witchery on the continent became more and more repulsive; repetition of details has no value. Williams finds that only in England and Spain was there much of an effort to keep trials unbiased.[6] In Spain the *Malleus* as a final authority was questioned, and confessions of witchery were not accepted at face value. On the continent, informing and witch hunting became profitable business, and in Essex Matthew Hopkins boasted of having been responsible for the death of 200 witches between 1645 and 1647. Blackmail was one of the very profitable sidelines. Of course the informer always ran the risk of being, himself, accused of being in cahoots with the devil and pretending to find one witch in order to protect another.

Children were often taken to see executions and were discovered to be very effective witnesses against their parents. A child whose mother had been burned might be whipped three times around the stake, when the actual burning was over, to exorcise the devil's influence with which he might be tainted.

In Paris, Louis XIV decided to have a very thorough investigation of all the ramifications of a sort of witchery gang, working under the direction of the notorious woman called Catherine La Voisin. But the scope of this investigation put the king in a most embarrassing position. La Voisin's activities reached into every level of society, and amorous Louis discovered that his current favorite had paid very well indeed to ensnare him by means of a witches' mass performed by La Voisin and associates. Such masses, it seems, also accounted for this favorite's three children, of whom the king was very fond, though they had been born at a time when his affection for their mother had been noticeably cooling. The witchery investigations continued, but in a highly secret and confidential manner. Participants were rounded up and chained for life, four to a room, to the prison wall, "but with a chain long enough so they could lie down." The last of these "witches of Paris" is reported to have died in 1724.

English witchery never seems to have developed the taste for torture that characterized executions on the continent. Much of the testimony reported at the trials has the elements of a naïvely unimaginative version of Alice in Wonderland, full of shaggy dogs that turn into toads, cats that can provide a lonely lady with a succession of husbands or bags of gold, as circumstances require, rabbits that keep rendezvous in the forest, to give instructions for the sacraments required for the witches' mass. It is interesting that royalty and charwomen seemed to meet on somewhat of a common ground at the witch trials, and smug little girl witnesses related their evidence against the accused, ending up with an appeal for the Lord's care and guidance. The slightly sanctimonious attitude of the common people of England did not offer the most fertile seedbed for a virulent type of witchery. From reading a number of (usually quite dull) cases, one gets the impression that power and profit motives played a larger part than sadism or simple vindictiveness, though these were not lacking.

Witches in America

Witches came to America with the first settlers from Europe, and it was in America that, before long, they were (more or less) laid to rest; not, however, before they had ruined many reputations, cost innocent lives, and perilously undermined the self-esteem and self-confidence of some otherwise fine men of the Church. Cotton Mather, in his *Wonders of the Invisible World* (1693), gives an account of nineteen executions in New England. One person was pressed to death—something of a novelty. So we have firsthand reporting from a not too antagonistic observer.

The Salem trials, as witch trials go, were not very unusual as to evidence, but certainly showed up the network of associations which could from a simple beginning involve hundreds of innocent, and not so innocent, persons; also the extent to which ordinary people's gullibility could contribute to the horrible picture. They disclosed, also, the extent of the harm to, as well as by, otherwise innocent children, whose imaginations and desire for attention had made them accusers and star witnesses in trials of whose significance—at least at the beginning—they could not be aware.

There had been very few witch trials in the New World. The trouble at Salem started when Elizabeth Parris, nine-year-old daughter of a Salem minister, with Abigail Williams, her eleven-year-old cousin, and Anne Putnam, the twelve-year-old daughter of the parish clerk, made up a sort of game—quite possibly in line with an illustrated book they might have seen in Mr. Parris' library. They began crawling under chairs, peering out from dark corners, striking weird poses, letting out queer noises and shrieks. Naturally the older people were alarmed, and quite naturally the word bewitched came into the conversation. Prayed over and questioned, they supplied the names of three people they all knew—Tituba, an old West Indian servant in the minister's home, Sarah Good, and Sarah Osburn, old women of the community who probably corresponded with what the children thought a witch should look like, though they apparently had no reason for disliking any of the three they accused. Tituba, fearful lest she be accused of putting such ideas into the children's heads with the stories they were always begging her to tell them, confessed and put the blame on the other two. She told of a tall man and four women, with their familiars like shaggy dogs, hogs, or little birds, of weird human forms who had told her to harm the children as directed, or expect worse for herself. Now that Tituba mentioned it, the children also remembered similar details.

The women were imprisoned and the trials began. Sarah Osburn died in prison. Sarah Good and Tituba were put to death. However, Tituba had mentioned *five* persons. Who were the other two? They were at large somewhere in the community and must be found. What harm might these malevolent forces not do next! Every woman in Salem was under suspicion and the children continued to think up ingenious ways to attract attention to their bewitchment, at the same time attracting other, and considerably older, children as new recruits.

Little Sarah Carrier, nearly eight years old, testified in court against her accused mother that she (Sarah) had been a witch since she was six, having been taught by her mother, "who made her set her hand on a book." She had been set to serve her apprenticeship by pinching people, under the supervision of a black cat, who identified herself to Sarah as her mother. The mother, it seems, had been promised by the devil that she should be Queen of Hell. She was executed. So also was the Reverend George Burroughs, a former minister of Salem, now serving another parish, against whom twelve-year-old Anne Putnam said she had been warned by the shrouded figures of his first two wives, who revealed that he had murdered them. The children's lurid revelations continued, but when the accused made a prayer and an address on his own behalf, it was Cotton Mather, one of the "pillars of the community," who maintained that Mr. Burroughs was not a genuine ordained minister and that, besides, "The devil has often been transformed into an angel of light," in order to perform his nefarious deeds. All the traditional manifestations of witchery became part of the trials, including the official informer, Joseph Ring, who seems to have been an inside agent who had, himself, seen the witches at their meetings and hence could recognize a number of their brotherhood (or more properly sisterhood) on sight. Husbands and wives, parents and children suspected each other. At one time fifty persons were under indictment. A magistrate who was reluctant to grant more indictments had to flee, with his wife, to avoid being accused. Rebecca Nurse, a woman of seventy, and of excellent reputation, was actually found not guilty by a jury; but then there was such an outcry in the courtroom, and the "afflicted children" screamed in such agony, that the jury tried again and found her guilty. In spite of the governor's attempt to issue a reprieve, the jury now understood its duty. Rebecca Nurse was executed. If she had dishonestly "confessed," she might likely have been saved.

If some Protestant ministers in New England looked askance at the witch-hunt trials, it only made them the more susceptible to accusation. However, when the wife of the Reverend John Hale of Beverly was accused, this one minister, at least, had had enough. The governor was glad to join him. The governor refused to allow witnesses in the court to say that there were people or creatures in the court which only they could see (or feel pinch them and make them cry out!), and he did away with the court which was specializing in witchcraft trials. Although the power of witchcraft persecutions as a form of public mania had been so long and so widespread in its development, enthusiasm for it stopped almost suddenly. Within about six months from the time Mrs. Hale was accused, the witchery prisoners (about 150) were released. About 200 more had been accused, but nothing came of their cases. During the previous year, twenty had been executed and two died in prison. Eight of those now released were awaiting execution.

Eight men of Mr. Parris' church drew up a paper which was presented to the minister. It accused him of credulity, lack of charity, and explained the fear they felt when they saw better persons than themselves condemned. It said Mr. Parris' continued emphasis on the iniquity dwelling among them was not profitable but offensive. Mr. Parris found himself on the accused rather than the accusing side and was quickly repentant, but he left the church and the community.

In 1706 Anne Putnam, being received into the church and desiring to "put herself right with God," confessed her part in the whole affair. Shortly thereafter, Judge Sewall read a paper in church confessing his own blame and praying forgiveness. We have the document of the confession presented shortly thereafter by the twelve jurors. Along with her heritage of guilt from the early witch trials, America has also a great heritage of individual courage represented by these confessions.

No one would, we suppose, be brash enough to contend that this series of events and documents would lay to rest once for all the long addiction of the West to witches and witchery. The jurors' confession is, perhaps, a literary monument to the fact that man had at least outgrown and shed—more nearly all at once than anyone would have believed possible—one particular type of theological perversion.

Though there were very few witch trials after 1700,[7] many religious folks still have an uneasy feeling that the devil is not dead by any means, but just wandering here and there on the face of the earth, wondering,

"What next?" Commercialization of sex, drugs, gambling, materialism, the dark side of daemonology (as a mental exercise), an undue obsession with conquering the physical universe for "our side," the price in freedom that man seems increasingly willing to pay for "security"—before each door the devil cocks an eyebrow and wonders, "What could I make of that if I really set my mind to it!"

Hellish as it was, witchery was essentially "kid stuff." The devil and all of us are more sophisticated now; we have more space, and tools, and means of communication; we know a lot better how to manipulate both our physical and mental environment. And the world is still young.

The Fruits of the Trials

For our purposes here, the important thing is to consider the degree to which women bore the brunt of the witch hunts and trials, and the degree to which the official sanction of the *Malleus* made this practically the official attitude of the ecclesiastical courts, and unofficially of secular courts as well.

Would the whole story of the centuries of witchery trials have been the same if it had not been possible to use the women as whipping girls? Certainly the tendency to use them in this way increased as the years went by and interest in witchery reached its fenzied climax. Certainly the Protestant churches born in this era still bear the scars of its anti-feminine sentiments. Undoubtedly the Victorian culture, over-emphasizing the natural taboos of sex, was to some extent predicated on the stories of the witch and her incubus and the revelries of the witches' Sabbath. (These stories may, in turn, have been invented largely by men subconsciously to outweigh the long-existent code of double standards in sex matters which weighed on their consciences!) And in the Victorian code of sex, to which we are the heirs, so psychologists tell us, lay the roots of many of the problems which are driving us to the psychoanalyst—or to the perverted sex novel or TV serial.

It has only been a short breathing spell, as time goes, since the devil and the witches finished a rather protracted inning in the world's history.

Now if the Church will just help mankind find ground for strengthening his confidence in himself, his fellow man, and his God, perhaps the angels will have a better chance for the next 500 years. But if we have any such hopes as that, we shall need the women, and the women will need to have increased support from the churches—and we do mean theologically as well as in their practical undertakings. The church woman needs very much to know that the Church actually does accept her as a whole person, and that it values her for what she is, as well as for what she does.

Chapter 11

PURITANS AND PIETISTS, METHODISTS, TOO

Women have always known that convictions really matter, and that there is small profit in reaching the right theological dogma, or the top ecclesiastical status, unless you put your religious convictions to work —in the family, the community, the world. It has always seemed ridiculous to most women, for instance, to preach and sing about the Prince of Peace and make war on one's neighbors. In the seventeenth century we see, among the churches in which women had a voice, something of a concentration of will too bring Christian thinking and doing into focus. It was rather an abortive movement, but it left its mark, as such attempts always do. Future attempts would accomplish more—and still more. The Kingdom itself might only come eschatologically, but it would come!

It might not come on a date that you could predict and mark on a calendar. It might not even come on a day in history—if you can conceive of a day beyond history. On the other hand, it might be today— this very day—that the Lord would choose to act. One must always be ready, and always hopeful, whether for today or for "that day in the fullness of God's time."

In the first days of Christianity, many Christians had expected Jesus to return almost immediately in power and glory to establish his Kingdom and bring judgment on this earth. As time passed and it became apparent that they might have misunderstood the time element in his promise, it was the eschatological faith and hope that sustained— and still sustains—the Church. Someday God's will is to prevail; we do our part from day to day and trust in his promise. And women, as we were saying, always seemed to know how to keep working—in ultimate faith—without demanding immediate proof of results.

But to get back into history——

The Days of Cromwell

The years of Oliver Cromwell's rule in England were more than just an interesting change of pace between Charles I and Charles II. Perhaps Cromwell (1599-1658) understood eschatology, too. During the years of his control we see the interplay between church and state when the champion of Protestantism and democracy becomes, however unwillingly, a dictator. The situation is especially interesting when we realize that the dictator is a champion of religious liberty, a Puritan, and a friend of women; yet his years had to be dedicated to war, and he was guilty of regicide. And all the while he kept repeating, in varying phraseology, "That which you have by force, I look upon it as nothing."[1] He never got around to many of the causes which were in his heart, but he probably did bolster the courage of radical religious thinkers of his day, and his appreciation of women must have been very good indeed for their self-confidence.

England in Cromwell's time was alive with splinter religious groups. The exact origin of many of them was early and uncertain. Latourette points out how strongly the leadership of these groups impressed their views and personalities upon the particular organizations with which they were associated. Since there were few high theological fences between the groups, and their programs often overlapped, it does not seem surprising that membership also often overlapped, and persons moved rather easily from one group to another. Yet differences were often pointed up sharply.

Independent groups of Christians had sprung up in different places and at different times, and had a strong tendency to move west. Their uniting force was largely the negative one of being in opposition to "established" practices wherever they found them. Since to a certain extent they showed a willingness to accept each other's viewpoints—or at least respect each other's points of view—they could communicate without agreeing. Conversely, there was the tendency to dissent from their own leaders and set up a new brand of "heretics." Most of the groups had a long history of persecution; also of women's active participation in the full program of the church.

Most numerous perhaps were the Anabaptists, though this general name included several varieties. Hubmeyer, one of their leaders, had broken with Zwingli to become head of the Swiss Anabaptists. He was hanged in Austria, and his wife was drowned in the Danube. In 1539 a group of Anabaptists—sixteen men and fifteen women—fled from England to Holland; but the men were beheaded, the women drowned. Yet now there were a great many of them in all these countries. Their special opposition was to infant baptism. The Lollards we have met as followers of Wyclif. They emphasized separation of church and state, and, like many other of these protest groups, objected to bearing arms. The Seekers claimed that they belonged only to the Invisible Church, but found considerable satisfaction with the Quakers, about whom we shall say more in a moment. There were the ecumenical-minded Philadelphia Constitutions, the Family of Love, the Ranters, and many more.

There were perhaps 20,000 Puritans in England at the end of the seventeenth century, a tremendous growth since the Pilgrims set sail for America in 1620, but the picture of protest was still confused. The Puritans did not consider themselves in the same class with the Anabaptists or the Lollards, for instance. The Puritans wanted to stay within the established church and purify it. But some of them gave up this hope and were then very likely recruits for one of the other protest groups. The people of Lincolnshire, though Separatists, refused to be counted as Puritans, because, they said, the Church of England simply couldn't be purified.

Things were just as confused in America, where Congregationalists would have scorned the idea of being "established," but countenanced the hanging of Quakeress Mary Dyer on Boston Common (where there is now a beautiful statue to her memory), Roger Williams and Anne Hutchinson (Baptists of a sort) exiled from the original colonies because of their divergent beliefs, founded the new settlement of Providence, where freedom of religion was basic. It is important to admit that the objection to Anne and Mary was technically not on the basis of sex, though they undoubtedly found it harder to defend themselves than men would. Anne was accused of propounding antinomianism doctrines; but it was also said that more people were coming to her for counsel on "matters of conscience" than came to any minister in the county.

Lines from a popular journal said that "When women preach and cobblers pray, the fiends of hell make holiday." And it is sad to report that a Presbyterian minister (1644) puts "women's preaching" at the forefront of the Baptists' "horrible disorders, strange practices, not only against the light of Scripture, but Nature."

On the other hand, the congregations of a free church in Holland (1641) offered a prayer for "our she-fellow laborers, our holy and good blessed women, who are not only able to talk on any text, but search into the deep sense of the Scriptures, and preach both in their families and elsewhere."

Most of the preachers in the free churches in those days were part-time ministers who worked at some other occupation to pay expenses. Women sometimes took in washing and were ridiculed as "tub preachers." Making the most of the term, when the day's work was done, they would turn the wooden tub upside down and use it for a platform.

Rufus Jones sees mysticism, humanism, pantheism, and puritanism, also the new availability of the Bible, combining to give the religious life of the era an intensity which "together with the creation of the self-governing type of church, had a powerful influence in bringing Democracy to birth in the state."[2]

The Spiritual Mother of the Quakers

The growth of the Quaker movement in England is worth our very special attention—especially the career of Margaret Fell, known as the "spiritual mother" of the movement. George Fox, the Quaker leader, whom she later married, was said to consider with complete impartiality the ministry of men and women. The Spirit, he said, asks no one where to go, and men and women are equally likely to be endowed with the "inner light," and with the religious compulsion to share it.[3] The Quaker women proved themselves worthy of his confidence in them.

If George Fox (1625–1691) appreciated women, it was for good reason. Women from the very start seemed to know what he was saying and understood not only why he was attacking the established or other main-line churches, with such vehemence, but also why the Quaker movement he headed was different from, and must be kept distinct from, other protest movements of the day.

Early in his career, Fox met Elizabeth Hooton, a middle-aged woman, and probably a Baptist, in Nottinghamshire. He describes himself as, at that time, a "man of sorrows" and just beginning to realize that the Lord was speaking to him. He described Elizabeth as a "very tender woman," and she became one of his first converts. Though married, she became the first woman Quaker preacher. Through the years she was often imprisoned for her faith—or rather for preaching about it—and made two missionary trips to America and the West Indies. It was in America, at age sixty, that she was subjected to the whipping post and cart-tail treatment to improve her theology. She died in Jamaica at the age of seventy.

At Leicester, a year after he met Elizabeth Hooton, Fox seems to have started his long history of public protests against accepted church practices of the day. He had been attending a meeting in a church and, at the end of it, the speaker asked if there were any questions. A woman got to her feet and put a question. We do not know what the question was. However, the priest protested: "I permit no woman to speak in the Church!" And Fox, before he knew it, and although there is no indication that he knew the woman who had been so bold, jumped to his feet, demanding, "Why?"

Then, preaching in Westmorland, Fox really set the area afire with his message. The Seekers, of whom there were many present, decided that Fox's message was something they had been seeking. So did Margaret Fell, wife of a distinguished judge, Thomas Fell, and mother of seven (apparently precocious) children. The judge was out of town, but Margaret was not going to let a person like Fox escape—perhaps into oblivion—without hearing more about his views. She invited him home with her. (After all, she was ten years his senior, and there were seven children to chaperone them.) On Sunday he went to church with the family, and, as was to become a habit with him, he spoke up, uninvited, during the service. Margaret found herself defending him. The children, too, were charmed, and in no time at all he had converted Margaret, her daughters, and a servant, Ann Clayton (who later distinguished herself by marrying, successively, two Quaker governors of Rhode Island).

The judge was due home, and Margaret Fell understandably had some misgivings as to what he would think of all this, but she timed the news to follow immediately after a very good dinner, and also after the judge had had a chance to meet and be very pleased with young Fox.

The next Sunday the church was more or less deserted—there was a Quaker meeting at the Fells' home. Though the judge never did quite become a Quaker, the meetings continued to be held at Swarthmoor for the next forty years, and it is said that the judge left his door open, so he could hear.

Margaret Fell became the financial secretary for the movement. Swarthmoor Hall, her home, became the nerve center of the organization. From here, somewhat later, missionaries went out to various parts of the world, and Margaret often helped finance their undertakings.

By 1645, Fox had managed to build up a band of about sixty.

Besides Margaret Fell, there were Elizabeth Hooton and five other married women—twelve women altogether. Isobel Buttery and one of the other women took the Quaker message to London. It was in answer to criticisms of these women preachers that Margaret Fell wrote the pamphlet "Women Speaking Justified, Proved, and Allowed by the Scriptures." She cited Mary's "Magnificat" as a precedent. It was an age of pamphlets in England, and they were a recognized means of self-correction among the free movements.

That women's interest in Quakerism was the opportunity to work in the field of religion—not just hero worship of Fox—is testified by the fact that in a clash between Fox and James Nayler for leadership, it was four women (known only as Mildred, Judy, Martha, and Hannah) who were leaders on Nayler's side.

Margaret Fell was always enthusiastically loyal to Fox. Her home housed the movement, she supplied or raised funds, kept in touch with members, and could, when occasion demanded, assemble a petition signed by 7000 Quaker women, with her own and her daughters' names heading the list. She wrote innumerable letters. When Fox was held what she considered too long in jail, she went to London personally to call on the king and get him released. In 1662, George Fox and Margaret Fell were both arrested. Though he was soon free, for some reason she was held for four years and threatened with life imprisonment and forfeiture of all her property. But eventually she was freed.

In the meantime, Judge Fell had died, and in 1669, after consulting all Margaret's children (Margaret's devotion, especially to her daughters, was most important in her life) and various Quaker friends, George Fox and Margaret Fell were married.

Before the first year of married life was over, Margaret was back in jail again, and she apparently understood perfectly well that with all he had to do—getting the organization firmly established—Fox just couldn't devote all his time to trying to get her out. Her daughters could take care of that, but only he, personally, and with tremendous devotion and physical effort, could give Quakerism itself the necessary attention. A woman like Margaret Fell certainly deserved to be called the "Spiritual Mother of Quakerism."

However, there were other Quaker women, too.

Elizabeth Fletcher and Elizabeth Leavens were both of the original "Sixty." They decided to go to Oxford to convert the students. Elizabeth Fletcher is described as a gentlewoman and a dainty girl of seventeen. Following the prophetic pattern as she understood it, she

walked naked through the streets, as a sign that God would strip
man of his hypocrisy. The girls were beaten by the populace, but it
seems that George Fox had no word of reproach for them. How
people felt about their witness was their own affair. He never seems
to have cautioned women that what they were undertaking was "too
much for them" physically, mentally, or emotionally.

If couples wanted to leave their farms or businesses, or if individuals
decided to leave their families and homes, to become Quaker preachers
and perhaps land in prison for expressing their beliefs, Fox would
be sympathetic, but such decisions were up to them. People with no
sense of geography or linguistics started off to preach in far places
like America or Adrianople, and, to no one's great surprise, usually
did get there, preach, and get home again.

Calling on the Sultan of Turkey

Mary Fisher was one of these. She was also of the first "Sixty" and
had already done a good deal of preaching when she felt the call
to go to Turkey and tell the sultan about Quakerism. With her went,
at the beginning, Mary Price (who had been to America), Beatrice
Beckley, John Perrott, John Luffe, and John Buckley. At Zanta, Perrott
and Buckley left them to stop at Greece, while the others went on
to Smyrna (a favorite Quaker destination). The group began to split
up. Mary Price returned home. But Mary Fisher had started out
specifically to speak to the sultan. She kept on—now quite alone.
Somehow she got word that the sultan was encamped at Adrianople;
she kept on going until she found him. She sent in word that she
was an Englishwoman with a message from God for him. The sultan,
a young man of seventeen, was impressed with this introduction. He
received her as he would an ambassador, sitting on his throne in a
tent, amid Oriental luxury and surrounded by his ministers and generals.
He provided an interpreter and invited Mary Fisher to speak. Mary
Fisher preached at length and he listened courteously, then offered
her an escort back to Constantinople, which she gratefully refused,
feeling quite competent to get there by herself. When the Turks asked
her what she thought of their prophet Mohammed, she "answered
warily that she knew him not, but that Christ, the true prophet,
who . . . enlightened every man coming into the world, Him she
knew. And concerning Mohammed she said that they might judge
of him to be true or false according to the words and prophecies

he spoke."⁴ The Mohammedans admitted this to be true. Mary bade the young Sultan goodbye and returned to London, ready to undertake another preaching mission.

Much less fortunate were Katherine Evans and Sarah Chevers, two married women who in 1659 set out for Jerusalem. Going ashore at Malta, against the advice of the English consul, they ran squarely into the Inquisition. They were lodged first in the consul's house, then taken to the Inquisition headquarters, and constantly questioned. They refused to swear by either the crucifix or the Bible and, when called heretics, said their accusers were the unbelievers, "since they lived in sin and wickedness, and such were heathen, who knew not God." After that, they were confined in a small, hot room, with two holes for windows, (through which food was passed in) and a door that was not opened during the five weeks they were confined there. Both were very ill. One of the girls developed a high fever. Their hair fell out, and their skin became leathery. The keeper threatened to beat them with a crucifix and told them both were to be quartered and burned that very night. They wrote later, "We desired to die, but death fled from us." Finally they were separated and allowed to write home. Their release was offered if someone would post a bond for the equivalent of $4000 that they would never again come to Malta. Quaker Daniel Baker, on his way to Smyrna, broke his journey at Malta and, discovering their predicament, offered to exchange his freedom for theirs, but he could not get the bargain accepted. Now, however, the news of their detainment had reached London, and Fox, going to the high Roman Catholic official there, was able to negotiate the women's release and their return to England. Later they said that, even though they thought each breath might be their last, they never regretted having gone.⁵

The German Pietists

On the continent, similarly motivated protest against overinstitutionalized religion had taken quite a different road.

Who can say where the pietism of northern Germany had its roots? Philipp Jakob Spener (1635–1705) made it a movement within the Lutheran Church, but it was in the hearts of the people before that. Says one authoritative work:

A forerunner of Pietism is the Separatism of Jean de Labadie (1610–1674) who, in his own life's journey from the Jesuit Order in France, by way of the Huguenot churches in France and Geneva, to the "Precisionist" theology of the Netherlands, from there to German Lutheranism in Herford in Westphalia, and finally to Mennonite Altona, set forth symbolically his conviction that the true Church can be found in any existing Church, but cannot be identified with any of them.[6]

This much traveled gentleman also undoubtedly had friends among the Moravians and the Brethren, or their predecessors. Early in the eighteenth century the Dunkards, a sect of German Baptist Brethren, were organized, but emigrated to America because of opposition. A number of smaller church groups in America seem to have been influenced by the people of this area who put "doing" Christianity ahead of creeds and brought down upon themselves the accusation of depending upon "works" instead of "faith." Perhaps because of the Lutheran background, the acceptance of women was nowhere near as obvious in these freethinking groups as it was in England. Yet at the theological level many women made a very real contribution to the pietistic emphasis in religion. By the very nature of pietism, it is natural that some of their most perceptive thinking should be the thinking of individuals not necessarily relating to a specific group.

One such individual was Jane Leade (1623–1704), who had been greatly influenced by the writing of Jakob Böhme. A man whose name has not come down to us was traveling in Europe and looked up Jane Leade as the author of a book entitled *The Heavenly Cloud Now Breaking,* which had greatly impressed him. He urged her to translate and publish all her books. Out of this contact came others, and the formation of a society known as the Philadelphia Constitutions, which had considerable influence in both Germany and England. It emphasized personal illumination of individual members and exchange of experience with each other. Its final goal was the reunion of the separated brethren of Christendom, restoration of peace, and the abolition of the type of separatism which leads one group to declare itself the exclusive way of salvation. It looked, however, to the *conversion* of the Turks and Jews. Some scholars find a root of the modern ecumenical movement in Jane Leade's writings. The "Cloud Now Breaking" apparently referred to the desired spiritual rebirth which should restore the love and unity of the primitive church.[7]

Anna Maria von Schurman was an outstanding member of the British "spiritual society" who probably came to Germany via Holland. She has been called the most learned and accomplished woman of her age.

At the beginning of our survey, we were glad to find the records of a single person who could represent her generation or her country.

Now we have an embarrassment of material, and each person mentioned suggests a dozen or a hundred, equally important. The time has come to discuss movements rather than individuals. Still, there are some individuals who simply must be mentioned, and one of these is Susanah Annesley Wesley.

John Wesley's Mother

Susanah was the twenty-fifth (sic!) child of a minister of the Church of the Dissenters in England. Besides the subjects usual for a girl's schooling in the England of those days, she learned Greek, Latin, French, and studied theology. Perhaps her father thought the theological education was a mistake after all, for when she was thirteen she felt compelled to leave her father's congregation and join the Church of England.

She, too, married a clergyman and presented him with nineteen children.[8] It was almost too much for one poor minister to support. The seventeenth was named John Benjamin, probably a hint to the Lord that he might appropriately be the last. But then came Charles, who was to be the great hymn writer.

In 1709, while Susanah was carrying her nineteenth (and last) child, the rectory caught on fire. Susanah, too heavy with child to climb out of a window, felt her way through the smoke-filled rooms, with, she reported, no damage beyond a little scorching of her hands and face.

One can imagine the hasty roll call of the children—all safe and accounted for till they got to John. His father rushed into the house to rescue him, but the staircase had collapsed, and there was no way to reach the upstairs bedroom where John Benjamin had been sleeping. However, at that moment, the little boy appeared at a window, and the neighbors, forming a human pyramid, were able to reach him and pull him to safety. His mother referred to him as "a brand plucked from the burning," and this phrase became a favorite with John Wesley; recalling it reminded him that God must surely have saved him for some good reason.

Susanah was a firm believer in orderliness and method. She worked out a plan of education for the children, and for the first five years of each one's schooling he was under his mother's supervision. The boys and girls were taught exactly alike—for the edification of their souls, minds, and bodies. She was strict and methodical. They were taught to "fear the rod and cry softly." She believed that the reason and piety of the parents should govern the child until his own reason and piety had a chance to take root and mature.

Girls had to learn to read before they were taught to sew, and to speak up so they could be heard.

The day a child was five was his special day. His mother spent the whole day with him—and at the end of the day he knew his alphabet perfectly. The next day they started on Genesis and "were all good readers by the time they were six." When they were ten, the boys started prep school, and the girls helped with housework and teaching the younger children.

Susanah tried to treat all the children with equal concern, but she perceived that there was something different about John. Once she wrote his father concerning the boy: "I do intend to be more particularly careful of the soul of this child."

It still took the learning of Oxford, the companionship of his brother Charles, a trip to America, exposure to the piety of the Moravians, the Biblical exegesis of Martin Luther, and the vigorous preaching of George Whitefield—among many other influences—to produce John Wesley and the Methodist Church. But Susanah had laid a sound foundation.

Thirty years after the brand was snatched from the fire, John Wesley had overcome his problems and uncertainties and had mastered the technique of speaking—indoors or out. He had a band of young preachers working with him, and brother Charles' "hymns of salvation" were sung at every meeting. Their father had died, and his great work on the *Book of Job* had been published (1735) posthumously and dedicated to the queen.

In 1739, John Wesley, who had been holding meetings in rented buildings, decided that it was time for Methodism to have a home of its own. He leased an old foundry at Moorfields, rebuilt much of it, and held the first great meeting, with 5000 attending, at the Foundry Preaching House. Part of the building had been made over into a suitable apartment for his mother, and her influence continued as the Methodist movement grew and the Foundry became the headquarters of Methodism.

Barbara Heck is credited with starting the first Methodist group in America. She and her cousin Philip Embury were en route from Germany to America in 1760. They stopped over in Ireland and heard Wesley preach. Brother Embury had become a lay preacher, but apparently did not as yet give a great deal of time and attention to the matter.

In New York they met some other immigrant Methodists, but no services were held and their interest in religion was not much in evidence. One day Barbara came into the room where they were all playing cards. She suddenly swooped up the cards, threw them in the fire, and is reported to have said, "Brother Embury, you must preach to us or we shall all go to hell, and God will require our blood at your hands." Barbara Heck recruited their fellow Methodists and a few other friends. They met in her house, with the lay preacher giving the message. And that was the beginning of Methodism in America.

During the following century it was often the pioneer woman who welcomed the itinerant minister, as the nation and Methodism, with its constant emphasis on social concerns, moved westward across the continent.

Chapter 12

MISSIONS

From the day St. Paul started out toward Europe and St. Thomas toward India, Christianity was a missionary movement. In the Christianization of Europe, women played a very important part: we have mentioned some of their undertakings. When it came to establishing monasteries in such distant places as China, however, this was considered work for teams of men. During the Middle Ages there was very little real missionary work, and in what there was, women did not, as a rule, have much part.

In the sixteenth and seventeenth centuries, the intense interest in geographical exploration aroused a new interest in missions. It was said that the missionaries went along with the conquerers. However, missionary work in the New World was considered much too rugged and dangerous for women. Roman Catholic missions were put under the direction of the Congregation for the Propagation of the Faith, at Rome, working through the various orders, and the Franciscans and the newly founded Jesuits sent many members to establish the Christian faith in the Americas. A group of Catholic women went to Mexico at the end of the sixteenth century, especially to teach young girls.[1]

The colonization of North America gave an immediate impetus to British missions. In 1607 Robert Hunt read sentences from the Book of Common Prayer to the Jamestown colonists and served them Communion on their first Sunday in Virginia, and the story of this, told in London, helped to make graphic to the people of England their responsibility for the spiritual life of America. A number of British missionary societies were founded in the seventeenth and early eighteenth centuries, including the Society for the Propagation of the Gospel in New England (1649), Society for Promoting Christian Knowledge (1698), and the Society for the Propagation of the Gospel in Foreign Parts (1701). Scotland sent missionaries to American Indians in 1742. Denmark sent Lutheran missionaries—mostly German pietists—to the East and West Indies. Before 1670 Moravians had gone to every continent but Australia.

The Quakers had been aware, from the start, of the urgency of missions. With no restrictions to hold them back, the women went quite frequently on long and difficult trips. They were very interested in the New World. As early as 1655, Quakers in London were contributing to the expenses of their fellows who were going to New England, Barbados, and, by 1661, to Jamaica. We have already told about Mary Fisher and the missionary journey which she made to preach to the Sultan of Turkey.

The idea of a resident missionary in a foreign country—let alone a missionary family overseas—dependent upon home support, was not common until the end of the eighteenth century.

William Carey went to India as representative of the English Baptists in 1792 and, as a resident missionary, established a school, church, and press; he taught Sanskrit in a college and issued translations of the Scriptures in nearly forty languages and dialects, besides compiling dictionaries and grammars and getting out an edition of the Ramayana. Here was certainly a new pattern for missions.

In 1812 Adoniram Judson[2] and his brand-new wife Ann Hasseltine Judson started on their history-making missionary career. With four other men, and another brand-new wife, Harriett Newell, they made up the "Immortal Seven," commissioned by the American Board of Commissioners for Foreign Missions, an organization with $500 in the treasury and $1200 "in sight," as their first missionaries to "the heathen of Asia." They called themselves the "five loaves and two fishes." The ship on which they sailed from Salem was the *Caravan*, ninety feet long and twenty-six feet broad, and it seems that the War of 1812 was suspended for the day to let the missionaries safely out of the harbor. It took them seventeen weeks to get to India. There must have been some Baptist literature aboard the ship, for by the time they reached India, the Judsons had decided they were Baptists. This was easily taken care of, however. The American Baptists had wanted a missionary to go to Burma and were glad to accept the Judsons and transfer them to that country. For this special purpose in 1814 they established the American Baptist Mission Union. Judson's was the sort of missionary career often referred to as "fabulous." He not only founded churches and schools, compiled a Burmese-English dictionary, and translated the Bible into Burmese. He set the pattern which was to become accepted for Protestant missions, of the missionary family living and working and worshiping in the community and becoming part of it—and hopefully starting a missionary dynasty. Ann, besides working in partnership with her husband, founded a girls' school in Rangoon. She died in 1826. He then married Sarah Hall Boardman, whose contribution to Christianity in Burma was the translation of *Pilgrim's Progress* into Burmese. One son became a famous surgeon; one was the founder of the Judson Memorial Church in New York. Judson's third wife was Emily Chubbuck, a successful novelist who wrote under the pseudonym of Fanny Forester.

The London Missionary Society was formed in 1795 and the Church Missionary Society (Anglican) for Africa and the East in 1799; the Wesleyan Methodist Missionary Society in 1813. In the United States the American Board of Commissioners for Foreign Missions (combining the interests of the Congregational and Presbyterian Churches) was founded in 1810, the Methodist Board in 1819, Protestant Episcopal Board in 1820. Missionary societies sprang up in Holland, Germany, Switzerland, France. Missionaries went to China, Japan, the South Sea Islands, preaching and establishing educational and medical work. There had never been such an opportunity and challenge to the women in the Protestant churches.

"The King and I": Fiction and Reality

The Thai people will laughingly tell you today that the movie *The King and I* was the first indication a lot of people ever had that there was anything in Siam but cats and twins. The story of the play is, of course, a highly fictionalized picture of the life of an early woman missionary, but it did, undoubtedly, give many people their first notion of the amazing importance and independence that the female missionary could have in the life and culture of the land to which she was assigned—quite apart from her abilities more specifically in the field of religion.

A bit of real history relating to Thailand concerns the careers of Mabel and Carl Cort—Presbyterian missionaries from the United States. Mabel Gibson was already a missionary teaching at the girls' school in Chiengmai, when Dr. Edwin Charles (for some reason called Carl) Cort arrived, fresh from the Johns Hopkins Medical School, to begin his service, on behalf of the Presbyterian Board, at Lampang, and later at Chiengmai. Here, in what was a very gay social event for the Western missionary contingent, the two young people were married. Here in northern Thailand, Dr. Cort became one of the great physicians of his era—whether in the hospital he built at Chiengmai, or, many years later, after his retirement, as consultant on tropical diseases in the government hospital at Washington, D.C. He was a fellow of the American College of Physicians, the American College of Surgeons, and of the Royal Society of Tropical Medicine (England). He built a hospital and a nursing school and raised funds for the Chiengmai Medical School affiliated with the government university. Mrs. Cort "stood in" for non-existent nurses in the early days, managed to get a nursing school started, and even a nurses' dormitory. She supervised the planning and serving of meals. She taught the nurses and the doctors about the importance of diet. She studied books on nutrition and took courses in the subject at Johns Hopkins during her furlough. In this Thailand area, where the standard of nutrition was very low, she became an expert on possible uses and the nutritive value of the soybean and encouraged people to plant and use it.

When they took over in 1915, the hospital was a makeshift clinic in one section of a barracks, where the missionaries did what they could for outbreaks of plague, cholera, smallpox, and famine, against a background of malaria and dysentery. No one could tell Mabel Cort that the problem of nutrition was not basic to that sort of picture. She instituted demonstrations to show the women of the area how to make dishes palatable to the Siamese taste, from soybeans they themselves could grow.

During the Japanese occupation of Thailand during World War II, the Corts were forced to evacuate to India. The Thai people suffered greatly, but, they told the Corts upon their return, it really could have been much worse—if they had not known how to plant and use soybeans as a supplementary diet. Also, the Corts were bringing as a gift from the American churches enough atabrine to put 350,000 victims of malaria on their feet in time to save the harvest.

The day the Corts returned home to Chiengmai, there was a great party to welcome them. There is a custom in Thailand—when you wish to honor certain persons, pour water from a silver bowl over their wrists. Ten thousand Thai people came that day to pour the ceremonial water from their small silver bowls over the wrists of their two friends.

As a feature of the occasion, one of their colleagues, Margaretta Burr Wells, wrote a little play, *Journey Among Friends*, which was supposed to depict, with some accuracy, episodes in the lives of the Corts. Many persons "played themselves in younger years." A scene that delighted everyone depicted the cutting of the wedding cake when Carl and Mabel were married:

FIRST LADY: A lovely wedding!

SECOND LADY: Mr. Eakin says he took the stethoscope out of Carl's pocket *just* as they went into the church.

FIRST LADY: A lovely wedding! Now the bride must cut the cake.

SECOND LADY: Carl, don't you dare suggest using a scalpel!

DR. CORT: I've never been so forehanded in my life. I have a house all furnished, and a year's supply of food in the storehouse. What's this, another telegram? I thought we'd been congratulated by everyone— Oh, NO. There's been a fire. Our house! Everything's gone up in smoke. The house is burned to the ground, but (much more cheerfully) NOT THE HOSPITAL.

MABEL CORT: A year's supply of food—all that butter melting and sizzling. Oh, I'm going to cry. I can't bear to think of it.

DR. YAI (a prince of the royal house): My brother and I have not yet sent our wedding gift. In view of what has happened, we'd like to have something made for you that you could use—some kind of furniture perhaps—to remind you of us every time you look at it, you know.

DR. CORT: Why, Dr. Yai, that's wonderful. Doesn't that cheer you up, Mabel? I'd like—that is, I think my wife and I would like—a table —an operating table!

Later one of the royal family—impossible as it may seem, a descendant of the king in *The King and I*—was to study medicine in America and intern with the Corts in Thailand. One scene in Mrs. Wells' play depicts his tremendous enthusiasm over bringing into the world a pair of twins for a peasant woman, who just a few generations before would not have dared to stand upright in the presence of a member of his family. One of the main hospital buildings was a gift of the royal family.[3]

Not all missionaries—not even all women missionaries—had the full vision of what their work meant, but many did. And the women's male colleagues were forced to recognize that women's talents in the fields of personal relations, on the one hand, and linguistics, on the other, and their ability to approach the native women (remember how women have always proved their worth as "carriers" of religion) made the woman missionary invaluable.

The Outstanding Teachers

Nowhere has the woman missionary's ability, and the value of the work she has been able to accomplish, been more evident than in the field of women's education. Governments are now increasingly accepting the necessity for the same education for boys and girls at the primary and secondary levels, but for a long time girls' education was handicapped by the lack of qualified teachers. Also there was always the exceptional girl who wanted exceptional training of some sort; until recently the one place she was likely to find it available in many countries was in one of the Christian colleges for women. Often, at first, that college was headed by a Western woman, but often, too, she was thinking in terms of training a younger native woman to be her replacement. Some of these women have been powerful Christian leaders, not only in their own countries but on the world scene. One thinks immediately of Sarah Chakko, the brilliant president of Isabella Thoburn College in India, who became the first lay president of the World Council of Churches. (They elected a presidium of six at the Constituting Assembly in Amsterdam, 1948; the other five were all prominent church men—clerical.) One thinks of Helen Kim, for forty-four years associated with Ewah University, Seoul, and involved in every sort of Christian work and movement in Korea, as well as many world movements. There was Wu I-fang, president of the famous Ginling College in China and prominent in the work of the International Missionary Council; and Ivy Chou, president of the Methodist Theological Seminary in Sarawak.

Many Western women were outstanding teachers in the colleges they served. There was Isabel MacCausland, who taught sociology at Kobe College, Japan; E. Lolita Wood, professor of Old Testament at Poona, India; and Alma Locke Cook, who, when she was forced to leave China, went at her own expense to Southern Rhodesia, where, at one time, she was financially responsible for the medical education of ten African students. There was Charlotte B. DeForest, who served many years as president of Kobe College and was called back after her retirement to receive a medal of honor and appreciation from the emperor. And these are just a few—part of a much longer list—mentioned casually by one authority on missions, Dr. Hugh Vernon White, when asked for the names of some of the missionary women who had distinguished themselves for educational work in his denomination. He admitted that there is almost nothing in print that gives anything like adequate recognition to the service women have rendered in the mission field; his only explanation was that there is just so much to say that no one would know where to begin.

Stories of those earlier mission days must be picked up here and there through the denominations. What a mosaic of Christian service they would make, if they could all be worked into a full picture! Many who could help clarify the design are still alive, living in retirement.

The missionary women, especially in the earliest days, undoubtedly underwent impossible hardships. They grew very lonesome for someone of their own land to talk to. James Michener gives a heart-tugging story of this in his book *Hawaii*. Many died—or saw their children die—of strange maladies. Not a few were martyred by the people they were trying to help. Along with love and respect they knew ridicule and hatred. There was always more work than one pair of hands could do. Yet probably never did women have such an opportunity to work creatively for the cause of religion—and they made the most of it.

Ida Scudder

Each church has its own missionary heroines; but some missionaries were born or grew up in the country they wished to serve and were impressed by that country's great need, which crossed all denominational dividing lines. To choose one such missionary—not quite at random—there was Ida Scudder. Ida was the daughter of a pioneer missionary doctor in India. One night, when she was in her teens, her sleep was interrupted three times by the voices of men who had come to consult her father. Each one had the same problem. "Tell me," each one begged, "what I can do and I will try to do it. My wife is in labor and needs help. No, it is quite impossible for any other man than myself to be with her—even a doctor. Just tell me how to help her, and I will do my best." But the help so given was not enough; each woman needed an attending physician. The next day young Ida watched three funeral processions wind their way down the village road to the burning area by the river. And that day Ida Scudder knew what her career was to be.

She came to America, applied herself to the best medical training available, and returned to India, not only to practice medicine (and especially to go where the male physicians of that day could not go) but to found a hospital and nurses' training school and a medical college. The little eight-by-ten room where she first set up her practice was one corner of the mission bungalow, and the guest room was equipped with two beds to become an infirmary. Then she moved to a larger bungalow where there was room for six beds, and from there to the newly built Mary Taber Schell Hospital, where there were at first forty, then sixty beds, and that somehow managed to take care of about a hundred patients at a time. One by one came the Medical School for Women, the Radium and X-ray Therapy Building, the Student Hostels, the

Gynaecological Block, and the Women's Medical Ward, the students' quarters, the child welfare center, the mobile leprosy unit.

Three men were admitted for postgraduate work in 1945, and two years later the first men students were admitted to the medical course, with a great number of applicants of excellent scholarship from which to choose. Today the great interdenominational, coeducational Vellore Medical Center is a worthy monument to a very great person. Ida Scudder herself claimed that she could never tell exactly how it happened. She was apt to say that she just kept doing what needed doing from day to day.[4]

But the women in the field were only half the story. In the "sending" countries, the women of the local congregations formed their missionary societies to study about the country to which their own particular missionary was being sent, or to which they were sending supplies. They made supplies for medical work, collected books and pictures for Sunday school use, held bazaars, gave church suppers, and counted birthday pennies, to raise funds for their missionary family. They sent letters to the children born overseas, prayed without ceasing, and listened avidly when the missionaries returned home on furlough and spoke in the church. They bought stereoscope views and learned about the lands where their missionaries were serving. The women worked so hard, and they themselves often had so little, that surely they can be excused if their judgment was not always perfect as to what was appropriate to go into the missionary barrel.

There were women on the receiving end of missions, too. They were still good "carriers" of religion. Again we choose one not quite at random.

When Adolphus C. Good, founder of a great missionary family in western Africa, arrived as the first missionary in the Cameroun, he was at a loss to know how to start. Also, he was hot and tired. But when he tried to approach a group of people, they all ran away—that is, all but one woman. She explained later that she was too pregnant to run, but actually she saw that this stranger was lonely and thirsty. She stayed and offered him a cup of water. That was the beginning of the missionary work in the Cameroun.

The other people were afraid and doubted whether, because she had talked to the stranger, her child would be properly born. So when the time came, Madame Abu'u named her son Biso, which means "doubt." He lived, grew, received his education through the mission school, studied theology, and became Pastor Biso, of what was the largest Presbyterian church on the continent. The Presbyterian Church of the

Cameroun, with some 73,000 membership, and since 1961 a full member of the World Council of Churches, is a monument to her courage and faith in her fellow man.

Male and Female Missionaries

Although the missionary work in most countries was done largely by women, and women raised much of the money to keep it going, it is notable that the top direction was almost always in the hands of men. By this time this might be regarded as just an ecclesiastical habit.

Any sort of accurate over-all statistic concerning the work in the mission field is very hard to come by. This is particularly true in this day when "missions" are being recognized as part of the ecumenical church and are being rapidly transferred to the jurisdiction of their own national leaders. In 1947 there were about 20,000,000 persons affiliated with Protestant churches in non-Christian lands. The Roman Catholic figures were not readily available, but in general it is said that they would be just about the same for the world picture. Of the Protestants there were about 6000 mission centers in about 100 countries. There were an estimated 55,000 churches; more than 55,000 schools and colleges, 62,000 Sunday schools, 3500 hospitals and dispensaries.[5]

One denominational representative said that his board's policy was to send couples for the top personnel in the mission field—both man and wife commissioned missionaries. Only for some very specific and special assignment would they be likely to send a single man. However, they sent many single women as teachers, doctors, nurses, technicians. He believed the proportion in their denomination would be something like 500 married men, 500 married women, 300 single women, and that in general this proportion would be good for the mission field as a whole, so far as the main-line denominations were concerned. The smaller, independent groups, which send missionaries direct from the local church, rather than through a national board, would show a higher percentage of women.[6]

Was the interest in foreign missions in part a result of the awakening of Christian conscience which seemed to take place in the Western world during the eighteenth and first half of the nineteenth centuries? Or was the more general awakening to the ethical implications of Christianity due in part to awareness aroused by the missionary program? Who can say?

The so-called Great Awakening, sparked by Jonathan Edwards (1703–

1758), had resulted in a serious concern within the churches over the problems of slavery, prison reform, American Indians; and interest in these problems led into concern over child labor, prohibition, mental institutions, regulation of wages and working conditions for women, and the social gospel in general. The generation of a thousand years from now will undoubtedly see the nineteenth century as a period when the social implications of the Christian religion became paramount in Christian thinking. Moreover, again and again the historian who reads his history with care will discover that it was Christian women who nursed the movements from unpopular causes into major concerns of the great denominational and interdenominational bodies.

One effect of the "awakening" was that it led to a western thrust of evangelism, as state after state was added to the United States. The home missions program as it developed in America was the child of both the missionary and the social gospel concerns of the churches.

The First White Woman to Cross the Rockies

By no means all missions were overseas, and that brings us to the story of Oregon—and Narcissa Whitman. Narcissa Prentiss Whitman and Eliza Harmon Spalding, both ordained missionaries of the American Board of Commissioners for Foreign Missions (Congregational and Presbyterian) were the first white women to cross the Rockies via the Overland Route (1836).[7]

Narcissa (1808–1847) had been a religious child from her very early youth, and it seems she was fond of reading aloud from theological works for the edification of her mother and four younger sisters. She also had a good singing voice, and an old man of her church said that when she prayed "she could offer up the finest petition to the throne of grace" of any person he had heard in his life. Her father was Judge Prentiss, founder of the Franklin Academy, and in 1827 (perhaps with Narcissa's needs in mind) he persuaded the school to become coeducational and helped build the boarding quarters for women. Narcissa also had the advantage of attending the now famous "Female Seminary" in Troy, which had been sponsored with considerable determination by Emma Willard.

Marcus Whitman, whom Narcissa married, had studied medicine and practiced for eight years before he felt the call to give up his private practice and go west to work with the American Indians under the ABCFM. He and Samuel Parker made a first exploratory trip. Then the Whitmans, the Spaldings, and Mr. W. H. Gray started the long trek. The story of the crossing of the continent was not too different from the stories that have since been told by pioneers, except that this was the *first time* white women had been seen on the western part of the uncertain trail. The rolling wagon, the skittish riding horses, the swollen rivers, and the bitter cold, the tiresome grub and the misgivings of persons met along the way all show through Narcissa's diary, but she seems always to have been cheerful and to have looked forward to their new home in the West. So they made the trip and in 1836 arrived at their destination and set up two stations—one on the Walla Walla River, the other near Lewiston, Idaho. They built their homes and built their furniture, and started raising their families, holding religious services, trying to teach the Indians English (though they gave this up). In 1838 welcome reinforcements arrived and they established two more stations.

Mrs. Mary Walker came at this time and kept a meticulous diary, which is a first-rate source book for early Western history. It includes such matters as the ever-present necessity to *wash* (including the matter of starch for the ladies dresses!), diet substitutes recommended by the Indians to replace scarce items, the indifference of the Cayuse Indians to an educational program, and the utter inefficiency of the Indian adults to perform, without constant supervision, what seemed to the missionaries the simplest farm and home chores. Dialect dictionaries were compiled instead of trying to get the Indians to speak English. A woman who could draw began experimenting with visual aids for Indian education. A man learned to cut leather and make shoes, but he was stingy with the skins, and they were always a bit too small where they should be ample. One of the little girls—daughter of a missionary, too—insisted on going for a pleasure walk on a Sunday afternoon without her bonnet. She lost a good side comb, which should teach her to be more religious and more obedient. Mary, who had come along with Elkanah Walker after a forty-eight-hour courtship, kept her diary for ten years.

In 1842 there was considerable talk about the possibility of the English taking over Oregon. There was also news of tension between the northern and southern states. But news was scarce, and no one really knew what was coming. The American Board of Commissioners for Foreign Missions ordered the abandonment of two centers, and the rumor persisted that all work in Oregon might be abandoned. At this point Marcus Whitman, leaving Narcissa in Walla Walla, made his famous 3000-mile horseback ride to Washington, D.C. Exactly what he had in mind no one can say for certain—to save the mission, or to save Oregon from the British. Probably both. He was gone a longer time than they expected. The winter was cold, a certain amount of dissension arose among the mission personnel; everyone was worried. And then one morning in the spring of 1843, Narcissa looked down the road and there was Marcus, riding along on his horse, and behind him a whole caravan of new settlers. He had joined up to guide them through the mountains, and that was what had delayed him.

It is not plain just what went wrong with the spirit of the mission during the next three years. Some said that personal friction between some of the missionaries developed. Narcissa thought some of the neighboring Jesuits were alienating friendly Indians. Another theory was that more recent settlers had brought in measles, which soon developed into epidemic proportions among the Indians, who had never had a chance to build up any resistance to this strange disease. Many of the Indians were loyal to their friendship with the missionaries, but with increasing deaths, especially among the Indians, it was easy for enemies to say that Dr. Whitman, who had never approved of the witch doctor, was using black magic. There were accusations by the Indians that the food distributed by the missionaries had been poisoned. Trouble—serious trouble—seemed inevitable. Yet when it came, it was too shocking to believe. Mrs. Walker had company and was expecting Marcus Whitman to join them. However, he was late, and they were just about to sit down to dinner without him when a letter came by messenger—Narcissa, Marcus, and eleven others had been attacked by the Cayuse Indians— massacred.

The mission closed—for the time being—but Narcissa Whitman had demonstrated that women could cross the Rockies, make a home, and carry on mission work in the Northwest. Biographers speak in glowing terms of her fine faith as well as her practical contributions to the foundations laid for Christian work.

Women's Missionary Societies

Dr. Joseph B. Clark, writing the story of American home missions, pays tribute to women's part in the western expansion of Christianity.[8] "The Kingdom of Heaven is like the leaven which a *woman* took (Matthew 13:33)," he says, gallantly underlining the right word. Just at the turn of the nineteenth century, he tells us, before the official work of the church mission societies was under way, a group of fourteen women of Boston—some Baptist, some Congregational—met to organize the "Boston Female Society for Missionary Purposes." By the end of the year they had raised $150 for home missions, and Female Mite and Cent Societies were springing up in other communities throughout the state. "It was," says Dr. Clark, "a missionary decade. The atmosphere of New England was charged with evangelistic ozone."

In 1877 Women's Baptist Home Missionary Societies were formed in both Boston and Chicago, with the avowed purpose of helping people on their own doorsteps—Negroes, American Indians, immigrant populations; also to set up a training school in Chicago and give Christian education to young Negro women of the South.

In 1878 the Women's Executive Committee of Home Missions was founded as an auxiliary of the Presbyterian Board, to co-operate with it on behalf of "exceptional populations." The Presbyterian Home Board itself was constitutionally restricted to preaching the Gospel and establishing churches. The women, working with them, aimed at the "diffusion of missionary intelligence, the unification of women's work for home missions, the raising of money for teachers' salaries, the preparation and distribution of missionary boxes, and the furnishing of aid and comfort in special cases of affliction and need."

In the 1870s the Congregational Missionary Societies began to form into state unions and to tell the story of home missions whenever they got a chance at their denominational meetings. The Congregational Women's Home Missionary Association was founded in 1880 as a national organization. Says Dr. Clark: "No sudden crisis . . . made a vain appeal to these organized women. Emergency funds, Jubilee funds, Rolls of Honor, and whatever other distress or need befell . . . received from them an instant and generous response."

The Reformed Church Board of Domestic Missions, organized 1882, added to the growing pattern the erection of parsonages for mission churches and a "Paper Mission" for supplying good literature to mission families.

The Women's Home Missionary Society of the Methodist Church (1880) became interested in building mission schools, also in a training school for deaconesses.

The Episcopal Auxiliary (1871) made a great point of raising funds for the ongoing home mission work of the denomination, and within a little over thirty years these women collected $5,000,000.

That's the way it went; women were always seeing something that needed doing, and finding a way of doing it, even if it seemed impossible; and then, one way or another, bringing it within the structure of the church organization. And then, more often than not, they found to their own bewilderment that they were not considered to have the religious understanding or the organizational experience to sit on the board of directors that decided future policy.[9]

Well, the thing still needed doing, and the women still kept on working. And it seemed as if there were more and more things to which they felt the Church should give its attention. They seemed, in fact, to have the idea that the whole world and all the people in it were the Church's concern!

Amanda Smith

The women were just too busy—and perhaps also too shortsighted—however, to worry over organizational matters. Thus the program of church work, the denominational structure, and the interdenominational movements all moved ahead, with the women staying pretty strictly at the service level and more and more relinquishing any right to help determine policy. And the more firmly entrenched became the theory that women had "always" been subordinate to men and that you could prove this was the Lord's will by citing Genesis 2.

But sometimes a lady just didn't believe it. Take, for example, Amanda Smith.

Amanda was born in Maryland in 1837, the daughter of Miriam Matthews and Darby Insor, slaves on adjoining farms. Darby's mistress helped him work out a scheme for doing extra work, or sometimes working for other people, so he could buy his freedom. But to buy his wife's freedom was another matter, for the five children were the property of her "family." The young daughter of the master's family "got religion" and, since the family did not approve, she used to run away to the servants' quarters and sing and pray with Amanda and Amanda's mother. It was the oft-repeated request of the young mistress that Amanda and her family should be given their freedom, and when at last the young girl lay dying of typhoid, her wish was granted. Then Amanda and her mother, father, and the other children, all free at last, went to live in Pennsylvania, and Amanda had a chance for just a little schooling. She also, through the church, had a chance to work for a woman in Strausburg. Here, as a girl of thirteen, she went to a Methodist revival—a poor, forlorn child, and the only Negro, it turned out, in the hall. But when it came time for the helpers to go through the congregation and invite people to the altar, a Miss Mary Bloser, who was "a power for good everywhere she went," came, just as she had to the others, to "a poor colored girl sitting way back by the door." She put her arm around that little girl and, with tears in her eyes, pleaded with her to come forward. And Amanda did.

Amanda Smith's autobiography, written when she was an old lady, is one of the most amazing odysseys of faith and courage you will ever read. Amanda never stopped serving the Lord long enough to accumulate any worldly goods, but she learned not to worry, that he would always provide, one way or another, for her needs. We see her earning her living as a housemaid at six dollars per month, rescuing a relative by the underground railway, hearing for the first time about India and giving the woman missionary her very last two dollars, and crying impetuously, "Can't I go to India? If only I could go and sing and pray with them!"

Eventually, the Lord always providing, she *did* go, to preach, not only in India but in Scotland, England, Italy, and Egypt, and several countries of Africa. She attended the great national camp meeting at Knoxville, Queen Victoria's jubilee in London, and the great "ecumenical" meeting in Bangalore. She argued, personally, with the devil and praised the Lord vociferously. She hobnobbed with sinners and bishops, spoke in pulpits or out when she was invited, and once, asked to lead the devotions at a Washington, D.C. conference, walked around the city for two days looking for a restaurant that would serve her.

But Amanda Smith would tell us that if we left the story at that point we would have missed the whole purpose of her autobiography. She concludes:

> My whole object and wish is that God will make [the book] a blessing to all who may read it, and with this desire and prayer I send it forth into the world. And especially do I pray that many of my own people will be led to a more full consecration and that the Spirit of the Lord may come upon some of the younger women who have talent, and who had better opportunities than I ever had, and so must do better work for the Master; so that when I have fallen in the battle, and can do no more, they may take up the standard and bear it on, with the inscription deeply engraved on heart and life, "Without holiness, no man shall see the Lord."[10]

Chapter 13

WOMEN AND CAUSES

The American colonies inherited a sort of distillation of liberal thinking about women in the Church; this liberal viewpoint had appeared here and there on the continent of Europe, traveled westward, and seemed to come to a focus in the "free churches" of England. From there it moved across the Atlantic to New England.[1]

The civil law which the colonies inherited was, however, far from kindly to women, and when the close bonds of the original religiously rooted groups gave way to legislation for a wider community, the women found themselves with very little legal protection.

Moreover, it was not long before the colonists became aware of the tremendous potential wealth of the new continent, and at about the same time of a responsibility to protect not religious freedom so much as sound orthodoxy, New England style. Mary Dyer, the Quaker, was hanged in 1660 on Boston Common. Anne Hutchinson was exiled; gathering women to discuss the Sunday sermon was one of her shocking ideas. Such acts were rationalized as attempts to maintain the purity of belief. However, it seems likely that these free-speaking and -thinking women were also a goading reminder to the colonists of their more pious days, when they, too, had been willing to speak out, at all cost, for the sort of religion in which they believed. Now, in this surprisingly rich new land, they may have tried to persuade themselves that their previous attitudes were a little naïve. With their growing sophistication, American patriots were anxious to be accepted—especially by the mother country—as first-class citizens and theologians. Pious aristocrats could advocate the social philosophy of democracy and constitutional forms and safeguards; but as a way of life such philosophy stopped short of solving—or fully considering—the problems of slaves or of women.

The free-thinking women in the churches may have seemed like a throwback to much less promising days in England. Such women could be convenient "whipping girls" for a people feeling their new impor-

tance, and at the same time pricked by an uneasy sense of falling somewhat short of former high convictions. Actually, when you got around
to fully considering the matter, some of the things women were doing
and saying these days might be downright *dangerous* to the status quo!

Stories of women's participation in either the church or community at
the time of the Revolution are infrequent. Molly Pitcher and Deborah
Gannett, though undoubtedly very brave persons, became famous not
for acting like women but for fighting like men. Mercy Warren, sometimes called the "first lady of the Revolution," was known as a friend
of patriots and as a writer.

It was apparently only that blessed and perceptive pamphleteer,
Thomas Paine, who saw what was happening to the women and tried,
at different times, to call the matter to their attention. Didn't the
women, he asked, have inalienable rights as well as the men? Maybe
Abigail Adams (1744–1818) was the only one who really heard him.
Moreover, Abigail Adams (a minister's daughter) had already understood that women really must have a chance to make use of their
talents with which the Lord had endowed them. She wrote to her
husband—only half in jest, we feel sure—in 1777:

> In the new code of laws which I suppose it will be necessary for you
> to make, I desire you would remember the ladies and be more gener-
> ous and favorable to them than your ancestors. Do not put such un-
> limited power into the hands of husbands. Remember, all men would
> be tyrants if they could. If particular care and attention is not paid to
> the ladies, we are determined to foment a rebellion, and will not hold
> ourselves bound by any laws in which we have no voice or representa-
> tion.[2]

The Women's Rights Movement

At the same time Judith Murray was sounding a pioneer cry for
better education for girls and pointing out that the so-called mental
superiority of the male was due to the fact that his sister from the age
of two on was being "wholly domesticated," while he was being led by
the hand through "all the flowery paths of science." She asked:

> Is it reasonable that a candidate for immortality, for the joys of
> heaven, an intelligent being, who is to spend an eternity contemplat-
> ing the works of Deity . . . should be . . . allowed no other ideas,
> than those which are suggested by the mechanism of a pudding?[3]

Eleanor Flexner, in her very informative book about women's activity from 1800 to 1900, which she calls *Century of Struggle*, speaks avowedly in the context of the women's rights movement. She thinks the great day for women was when, early in the nineteenth century, spinning and weaving moved from the home to the factory, using equipment run by water power.[4] Yet perhaps the really important thing for women during the first decades of the new century was the evidence that the tradition of educated womanhood had followed the earliest settlers from the free churches of England to this country. In spite of hardships, revolutions, and the temptation of high rewards for industrial work, there were, from the very first days in America, those who had insisted that their daughters, like their sons, should be educated persons.[5] There was always a "dame" who could make time to teach the village children; or a man, like Louise Seymour Houghton's father, at a later date, who would see to it that, although there were no theological seminaries open to a gifted daughter, she was not denied the opportunity for sound Biblical study and linguistics. This made Mrs. Houghton one of the few competent authorities on the over-all history of women in the Church to whom we were able to refer in this study. The Reverend Lyman Beecher and the Reverend Joseph Emerson and other churchmen also often did all they could on behalf of women's education.

One woman educated by her father was Emma Hart Willard, who in 1821 opened the Troy Female Seminary, where a number of the rising group of women interested in working for women's rights were educated. To open the school, she had to persuade the New York Legislature to give her a charter, and the town of Troy to furnish a modest endowment. But it would have been "improper" for her to address such groups directly. She had either to present her proposition in a document (without being able to support it in person when it came up for discussion) or talk to small groups of men, who could in turn present her ideas to the proper bodies. Still, she did get the charter and the endowment, and American women got the school.[6]

Frances Wright of Scotland, visiting America in 1828, had no inhibitions as to what was "seemly," so far as speaking in public on behalf of education for women was concerned. She told audiences who came to *see her* to please use their minds about education for their daughters. The "elegant" of the land, who considered themselves *avant-garde* when they approved of china painting or harp lessons for their daughters, attacked her with the one sure weapon against such liberal women —they accused her of free love and atheism. But the people of the growing working class in the cities heard her gladly and apparently pondered what she said.[7]

Lucy Stone and Antoinette Brown

The real breakthrough in women's education did not come until 1833, when Congregational-oriented Oberlin opened its doors to all comers without regard to race, color, or sex. Interestingly enough, Oberlin did not by any means feel it was embarking on the championship of "feminism," but just female education. It aimed to elevate the female character by "bringing within the reach of the misjudged and neglected sex all the instructive privileges which hitherto unreasonably distinguished the leading sex from theirs." It provided a shortened "literary" course which it was correctly presumed most of the women would take. However, the directors had not even suspected that two such young ladies as Lucy Stone and Antoinette Brown would be among the first registrants, eager to take the full course, and knowing exactly what they hoped to get out of such an education. By the time the faculty learned, there was not much Oberlin could do about it. Lucy's avowed ambition was to "prepare herself as a public speaker on behalf of the oppressed." Antoinette had set her goal to become an ordained minister.

Lucy Stone had been raised on a dairy farm. Just before she was born, her mother had had to go out and milk eight cows. All the men had left that job to her, because they had to go out and get in the hay before it rained. When Lucy was born, her mother said she was sorry the baby was a girl, because girls had such a hard life. There were seven children in the family, and when Lucy was twelve, she decided that along with her schoolwork she would save her mother what work she could by taking over responsibility for the family laundry. At sixteen she began to teach school and, besides helping the family, saved what money she could in hopes of getting some higher education. Oberlin was her opportunity. She said: "I expect to plead not for the slave only but for suffering humanity everywhere. Especially do I mean to labor for the elevation of my sex." By the time she graduated in 1841, she was already in the middle of the women's rights movement. Her brother had become a minister at Gardner, Massachusetts, and she gave her first lecture from his pulpit. Shortly thereafter she became an agent and lecturer for the Anti-Slavery Society. She had a bad time keeping the two subjects in which she was so interested separated in her lectures. The abolitionist people thought it did their cause no good to be forcibly bound up with women's rights. Eventually all concerned reached a compromise. Lucy Stone would speak on abolition on Saturdays and Sundays, and for women's rights on the other days of the week. As a matter of fact, she usually gave a series of lectures when she spoke on women's rights: (1) social and industrial rights; (2) legal and political rights; (3) moral and religious discrimination.

When, in 1855, Lucy let it be known that she was about to be married, a wit published a jingle in the *Boston Post*, hailing the man who with a wedding kiss could shut up Lucy Stone's mouth. But it didn't work out that way. Henry Blackwell was almost as ardent an advocate of women's rights as Lucy herself, and in the years ahead, their daughter, Alice Stone Blackwell, carried the movement forward till 1920.

Moreover, Lucy did not pass by the chance to make even her own wedding a sounding board for one phase of the movement in which she and her new husband were so involved. During the ceremony the two participants joined hands and publicly declared that, "While we acknowledge our mutual affection by publicly assuming the relationship of husband and wife . . . we deem it a duty to declare that this act on our part implies no sanction of, or promise of voluntary obedience to such of the present laws of marriage as refuse to recognize the wife as an independent, rational being, while they confer upon the husband an injurious and unnatural superiority."

They enumerated specifically their repudiation of laws which gave the husband custody over the wife's person, exclusive control of the children, sole ownership of her personal property and use of her real property, right to her wages; they likewise rejected inequality in inheritance settlements, and in fact "the whole system by which legal existence of the wife is suspended during marriage," so that in most states she had no part in the choice of residence, might not make a will, be sued in her own name, or inherit property.[8]

Antoinette Brown married Henry's brother. Her ministerial standing did not exempt her from rude and contemptuous remarks. One editorial gave a graphic picture of a possible scene in the pulpit when Antoinette might have to stop her sermon to give birth to a boy or girl—or even twins. Far from understanding that a woman minister might feel she had a special call to work for some of the "causes" that so obviously needed attention in the mid-nineteenth century in America, many men —and often the very vocal ones—seemed to feel that the combination of church vocation and social involvement was reason for special resentment against the female.

Antoinette had six daughters and continued to preach (in the Unitarian Church which she served for fifteen years) till she was ninety. In 1908 Oberlin conferred upon her a B.D. degree.

In the meantime, the sister of the Blackwell family, Elizabeth, was devoting her energies to hammering down the doors that kept women from entering the field of medicine. The Blackwells were, indeed, quite a lively clan.

A Century of Causes

It was a century of causes. The men, however, were very busy opening up new territory, developing the huge fortunes and businesses that were the marvel and scandal of the New World, finding gold, and fighting a major war. So to nourish and further the "causes" became largely the responsibility—and the obsession—of the women. Those who started with the modest demand that surely their daughters needed *some* education to raise their families properly found themselves running underground railroads to rescue runaway slaves. Those who felt quite bold when they wrote to the governor's wife commending her for not serving liquor at official parties somehow got involved in the women's movement and found themselves elbowing their way through groups of highly inebriated senators, trying to round up that extra half vote that was needed to assure the passage of the woman's suffrage act.

Women never dreamed that they could or would do the things they did—speaking in open-air meetings, demanding the opportunity to talk to a recalcitrant official, subjecting themselves to ridicule and insults when they appeared in the bloomer dress as a symbol of freedom, writing and publishing women's rights papers and magazines. The women moved easily from one organization to another—or founded a new one. Perhaps it was at this time that someone first said, "If you want to get something done, ask a busy woman."

The thing that surprised the women most—more even than their ability to work this way for causes in which they believed—was the fact that their husbands stood for it and at times even seemed proud of them.

The press was hostile at first, but, finding the women's movement particularly good copy, was frequently won over to genuine friendliness. Some churchmen were among the best friends the women had. Some supported one cause, some another. As a whole, however, the Church refused to associate itself with the women's movement as such and gave little support to the suffrage campaign. Of course it couldn't, logically, without rethinking its own attitude toward the role of women in the Church, and, to do this, most churches were not yet ready.

It is a fact, however, that many women got their very first experience with the modern idea of working through an organization from their church experience—usually participation in one of the missionary societies or the "literary and sewing societies" at which, while the women worked with their hands, one of their number read a book or a paper prepared on a serious subject by one of the members. This was followed by discussion; and this was as near as most of the women had ever come to speaking in public.

We should be wary, however, of thinking that the churches or their pastors approved of everything the women said or did at their meetings. The churches were, as a matter of fact, in somewhat of a quandary. To what extent did making their buildings available for meetings imply to the community that they fully endorsed what was said and done at those meetings? Yet many pastors had an uncomfortable feeling that they must not close the door to the prophetic voice. But how did you tell the difference between a female prophet and just a plain troublemaker? When a New York minister auctioned off a beautiful young slave girl from his pulpit—buying her freedom—he was pointedly asked why she had to be beautiful, young, and female, and whether the whole thing was not a rather cheap publicity idea. Was that a prophetic voice?

Somewhat later, awareness that they needed clearer insights into the nature of religion itself, and the relevance of the Scriptures to the present day, often came to the women through some young woman who participated in the World Student Christian Federation (founded 1895 through the concern, in part, of the great churchman John R. Mott). It was largely, also, women raised in this movement—or in the national movements on the college campuses—who held the door ajar for a larger degree of female participation, at a still later date, in the whole ecumenical movement than would otherwise have been probable for women.

Woman had suspected all along that the Lord knew what he was doing when he created her with a brain and with various creative and directive capacities. Now woman could no longer, with any degree of honesty, accept the concept of herself as having been created an inferior being. The time had come to be *herself*. She felt the Church needed her and she knew she needed the Church. But all these causes on her doorstep were so urgent! They just couldn't wait.

The Grimke Sisters

There are many women of this period whose stories should be better known. Somehow we can't remember hearing about many of them, either in our history classes or in Sunday school.

There were, for instance the Grimke sisters—Sarah and Angelina. These girls were the cultured and well-educated daughters of a southern slave-owner. Their father held a very high judicial office in South Carolina; brother Frederick was a Supreme Court Justice in Ohio, and brother Thomas, also a lawyer, was an organizer of the American Temperance Society and American Peace Society. Thomas, it seems, was dissatisfied with the lack of activity in the South Carolina Episcopal Church and communicated this to Sarah. On a visit to Philadelphia, Sarah joined the Friends, and her sister Angelina followed her lead, but, as seems to have been the family pattern, went further. She became an abolitionist, and in turn brought Sarah into that movement. They were said to have been the first women to speak publicly for abolition. A point they stressed was that slavery meant degradation not only for the Negroes but for every white woman in the South. The girls were smart enough to realize the great advantage of their aristocratic southern background in their attacks upon the institution of slavery.

Angelina, in 1836, wrote "An Appeal to the Christian Women of the South," and Sarah, not to be outdone by her sister, wrote "An Epistle to the Clergy of the Southern States." The girls persuaded their mother to give them slaves as their share of the family estate; all these they promptly freed. They lectured in New York and Massachusetts. Angelina, who had developed into quite an orator, was invited to speak at the Massachusetts Legislative Committee on Anti-Slavery Petitions. She spoke at three successive sessions (1838) and was a sensation. For a while there was a tussle for the first loyalty of the sister—both the abolitionists and the women's rights people saw their abilities as prime assets to either movement. Theodore Weld, who had been more or less sponsoring their activities, was afraid their interest in women's rights would divide the abolitionists. John Greenleaf Whittier agreed with Weld, but William Lloyd Garrison tempted them into his circle by proclaiming both causes. Weld helped them settle the question by marrying Angelina and persuading the sisters that, however important any other cause might be, their background gave them a very special value to the abolitionist movement.

But Weld had also been right that involvement in the women's cause

would bring them grief. At first they had often spoken (about abolition) in the churches; now, to Angelina's great distress, Christian ministers of Massachusetts denounced her activities. A pastoral letter from the
Council of Congregational Ministers, the largest denomination in the
state, did not call the Grimke sisters by name, but invited the attention
of its members to "the dangers which at present seem to threaten the
female character with widespread and permanent injury." Appealing
to the New Testament, the ministers found that "the power of woman
is her dependence, flowing from the consciousness of that weakness
which God has given her for her protection." Expressing appreciation
for the unostentatious prayers of women in advancing the cause of
religion at home and abroad; in the Sabbath schools; in leading religious
inquirers to the pastor for instruction; and "in all such associated efforts
as become the modesty of her sex," they held that when she "assumes
the place and tone of a man as a public reformer, she yields her claim
for protection and her character becomes unnatural."

Sarah, who had somewhere in her career acquired what for that day
was a remarkable grasp of Biblical criticism, wrote a series of articles
for the *New England Spectator* on "The Province of Women," which
were later reprinted in a pamphlet entitled "The Equality of the Sexes
and the Condition of Women." Repudiating the fundamentalist interpretation of Scripture upon which the superiority of the male was predicated, she suggested that even accepting Eve's responsibility for original sin, surely Adam's ready acquiescence in his wife's proposal does
not savor much of the boasted superior strength of the male mind. She
says: "I ask no favors for my sex. I surrender not our claim to equality.
All I ask of our brethren is that they take their feet off our necks, and
permit us to stand upright on the ground which God has designated us
to occupy."[9]

Angelina, however, to whom the opinion of her fellow Christians was
very important, broke down under the strain. One week in Boston she
had spoken for six nights in a row, filling the uppermost tiers of the hall
with her splendid voice and electrifying message. Now she found herself
unable to speak at all, and it was several years before she regained her
voice and composure sufficiently to speak again in public.

The Seneca Falls Convention

Lucy Stone came to the problem of women's rights from working in
her church, but, as anyone knowing Lucy would suspect, not exactly
from the orthodox angle. She was, it seems, busy in her sewing and

literary society, stitching a shirt for a theological student, when it suddenly occurred to her that the young man who would get that shirt could earn more in a week than she, or almost any other woman, could make in a month. She tossed the shirt aside, saying she hoped no one would ever complete it. From then on she put her time and energies into working for women's rights. That was shortly before the movement was officially launched at the Seneca Falls Convention in 1848. Her literary and sewing society marked the occasion by officially endorsing the idea of women going into politics.[10]

Lucretia Coffin Mott, an ordained Quaker minister, and Elizabeth Cady Stanton, the daughter of a judge, were the guiding spirits of the Seneca Falls meeting. Both of them had been working with their husbands in the abolitionist movements for several years. In 1840 they met at a world anti-slavery convention in London. But at that meeting women delegates were not allowed to be seated, so Mrs. Stanton and Mrs. Mott fumed it out together in the balcony. The Motts, Nantucket Quakers, were especially incensed. She had taught school, been ordained in the Quaker meeting, used their home for an underground railway station, and founded the first anti-slavery society. But in London all her experience had to be wasted and useless—because she happened to be a woman. Elizabeth Cady Stanton had not only attended Miss Willard's school at Troy, but had received an even better education, so far as the problems of women's rights were concerned, by listening to the tales of many persons who came to her father for advice about domestic problems. Many of these problems had to do with the wife's inheritance, which the husband was squandering or investing foolishly against her wishes; or about the wages (his or hers) spent by him for drink instead of for the children and home. Divorce would mean that he might have complete custody and control of the children. And all the judge could tell these poor souls was that they had *no legal redress*. It was abundantly clear to the young woman listening to such conversations day after day, year after year, that legislative action to change the laws was the one program above all others worth fighting for. In 1840 she married Henry Stanton, an abolitionist leader, and met the Grimke sisters and others prominent in the various reform movements of the day. Then the Stantons moved to Seneca Falls, and her education was completed by the discovery of what the average married woman's program was like—filled with babies and housekeeping and no opportunity for cultural pursuits or even "causes" which were dear to her heart. The causes she would not give up—something had to give way to make room for them. She and three other women got permission to use the Wesleyan chapel for a two-day meeting, July 19 and 20. They got out a handbill inviting women only for the first day, but men and women both for July 20, to hear Mrs. Lucretia Coffin Mott of New York address a women's rights convention dealing with all aspects of women's social, civil, and religious restrictions.

For a platform to present, the women used a paraphrase of the Declaration of Independence: "When in the course of human events, one portion of the family of man assumes——" There was only money enough to run the ad once in the Seneca Falls newspaper inviting people to the meeting. Imagine the women's surprise when 300 people (including forty men, who were not even invited for the first day) were on hand for the opening session. The chapel had been promised, but either someone thought better of the promise or forgot. A small boy had to be boosted in a window to unlock the church from the inside.

High point of the meeting was the passage of a resolution: Resolved that it is the sacred duty of the women of this country to secure to themselves their sacred right to the elective franchise. A third of those present (sixty-eight women and thirty-two men) signed the Declaration of Principles, though a few of these thought better of it later and withdrew their names. One of the younger persons enthusiastically supporting the ideas of the convention was Charlotte Woodward, who lived to vote for the President of the United States in 1920.

Susan B. Anthony

That convention was the real beginning of the women's rights movement, the organization which Susan B. Anthony took as her special project. With a genius for organization, she had vacillated between schoolteaching and farming, neither of which had any special appeal for her. She had worked briefly for the abolitionists and for the temperance societies. But the women's rights movement was her real challenge. The state was divided and subdivided under captains; everyone was given a petition on which to get signatures, and the huge rolls of petitions were duly assembled and presented to the proper legislative bodies. It is often said that as the women's movement gained momentum it was Susan Anthony who was the organizer, Lucy Stone who was the eloquent voice, Elizabeth Stanton who supplied the philosophical background, and Lucretia Mott who always remained the moral force of the movement. The Motts, incidentally, were instrumental in founding Swarthmore College in 1864. But that is "another part of the forest."

The unprecedented influx of European immigrants to the United States during the 1840s to meet the needs of industrialization and expansion presented new problems for the city dwellers and sparked, especially among educated women, a concern for the problems of child labor and the wider fields of social welfare. Also the interest of many women was aroused by the large number of families being disrupted by the extremely heavy drinking of the period.

Temperance and Other Causes

Frances Willard, a graduate of Northwestern Female College in 1859, gave up a promising career in education because she saw the possibilities of harnessing women's concerns for temperance, purity, and peace, along with the women's rights movement. She joined the temperance crusade, which had started in Ohio and was spreading rapidly. Women, singing and praying, held meetings in churches, saloons, and on street corners. In 1874 rather scattered groups organized into the Women's Christian Temperance Union, with Frances Willard first as its secretary and before long as its president.

From the beginning she seems to have advocated women's suffrage as the one permanent way to achieve some of the other objectives women were demanding. Frances Willard was actually a born politician. She had some cause for everybody and a way of getting support without making enemies. There were departments in the WCTU for every phase of life that touched the American home, from kindergartens to prisons, physical culture to prostitution. The movement spread to every state in the union and claimed 200,000 women. Again conflicts of interest developed between various phases of the movement. The liquor interests were against the WCTU and (identifying the two) were therefore opposed to votes for women. And liquor interest had considerable weight in some legislative circles. But who was going to stand up and be counted against purity in the American home? Many churches which had not been able to embrace the cause of women's rights with any enthusiasm (their inconsistency in doing so while debarring women from participation in church government would have been all too evident) could nevertheless give unqualified support to the WCTU, as a crusade against drunkenness. The Ministerial Alliance, the Sunday School Association, the Grange, and Knights of Labor were all to be counted on the side of the WCTU. The small bow of white ribbon on one's lapel became one of the most prevalent symbols the country has known. When Frances Willard died in 1898 (while McKinley was President) the U. S. Congress put her statue in its rotunda and voted her the "first woman of the nineteenth century and best-loved character of her time."

Carry Nation (1846–1911), with similar motivation so far as liquor was concerned, put her faith in direct action and elicited far less male admiration. The saloonkeepers, especially, dreaded and certainly disapproved of her direct-action methods—coming in and smashing their stock. She often posed for pictures with a Bible in one hand, a hatchet in the other. Both, she said, were divinely inspired. She was arrested over thirty times for wrecking saloons and sold souvenir hatchets to get funds to establish a home for drunkards' wives.

Everywhere women looked they saw so much that needed doing. Often they wished the churches would take more initiative, but the women were certainly not going to wait till they did. The religious conviction which was the heritage of the church woman told her that the welfare of her fellow men was her concern and responsibility, and that she must respond to that need.

Hundreds of names might be mentioned, each with its own interesting story.

Dorothea Dix became interested in prison and hospital reform, and especially in the humane care of the insane. She worked in several countries of Europe, as well as in America. Her investigations and reports brought many needed legislative reforms.

Harriet Tubman, an escaped slave, brought 300 men, women, and children through the underground railroad. There was a price of $40,000 on her head, but she said that when you were a Negro and a woman, surely you had nothing to lose.

Elizabeth Blackwell was finally accepted as a medical student at Syracuse—the twenty-ninth medical school to which she had applied for training. She and her friend Florence Nightingale and her sister Emily, who also became an M.D., and Dr. Zakrzewska, a Polish midwife, who came to study in the United States and founded the New England Hospital for Women and Children, were the vanguard of women's work in medicine. Florence Nightingale had hoped, rather desperately, to work in the framework of her church, but found no opportunity.

The nineteenth century was an important era for women writers both in America and Europe. While by no means all the literature produced by women during this period was avowedly "religious" in nature, it was almost always characterized by a high moral tone and often, as in the work of Harriet Beecher Stowe, by an impassioned devotion to one or the other of the causes of the day. Mrs. Stowe's *Uncle Tom's Cabin* was based upon stories told her by guests at the underground station in her home.

Margaret Fuller was the leading spirit in the transcendentalist group and co-editor with Ralph Waldo Emerson of *The Dial.*

Mrs. Sarah Hale, editor of the much read *Godey's Lady's Book,* never entered into the campaign for women's rights as such, but seems to have campaigned in her own way for one cause after another—for higher education for women, including nursing, for physical education, and against corsets.

Actually, with denominationalism as rampant as it was at this time, and without any of the ecumenical machinery of the present day, it may well be regarded as providential that the women had the sudden courage to go ahead and act, when necessary, without church support. Even more is it providential that they were always conscious of a truly religious motivation and kept close enough to the Church so that when the term "social gospel" became a sort of slogan for many churches in the early twentieth century, the women knew exactly what they were talking about and could move with some ease into the church programs and through the Church out again into the community.

History may tell us that as the women lost themselves in Christian causes—whether or not so designated—they found themselves and made a good start toward rediscovering their right and necessary role in the Church.

Meanwhile, the great women's colleges were being established, most of them reflecting, to a greater or lesser degree, Christian concern and backing: Mount Holyoke opened 1837; Vassar, 1865; Wellesley, 1875; Smith, 1875; Bryn Mawr, 1885.[11]

On September 6, 1870, women voted for the first time in Wyoming, and no major catastrophe befell Wyoming, the nation, or American motherhood. In 1878, an amendment to the Constitution of the United States was proposed by Susan B. Anthony and submitted to Congress: "The right of citizens of the United States to vote shall not be denied or abridged by the United States or by any state on account of sex."

However, it was 1920 before the Nineteenth Amendment was ratified.

The causes which challenged women in the nineteenth century are by no means all settled. The Emancipation Proclamation was signed in 1863, but, a hundred years later, Negroes were demanding, "Freedom NOW!" Prohibition came—and went; alcoholism, social drinking, sales of liquor near schools and colleges and public buildings has increased. Housing, birth control, use of narcotics, aging, automation, problems of peace and war—there will be enough causes to keep women busy for some time to come. And the Church and women will continue to need each other in their search for the right solutions.

Chapter 14

THE "PROSPECTOR" GROUPS

Many women have made a contribution to the American religious scene by their association with one of the small groups that we commonly refer to as the cults or sects.[1] Christianity was originally a Jewish sect; it was very small; and without the women it is hard to see how it would have survived. So when we speak of cults and sects there is no disparagement in our voice.

There was a real blossoming of cults and sects in the late nineteenth and early twentieth centuries. Most of the people who frequented and supported them were originally members of the main-line churches. Also, it was very often a woman who, lacking authority to explore her ideas under the auspices of her church, set up an independent group which functioned, with varying degrees of popularity, for longer or shorter periods of time. To what extent these peripheral groups, indirectly or through some personal relationships, influenced the theological climate of America is impossible to evaluate. There are many well-documented stories of how outstanding ministers, theologians, and theological professors were touched by some such cult in their youth; many testify privately that it broadened and deepened their outlook and understanding. Yet it is not always wise (from a practical consideration) to pay too much tribute to such a rootage, after one becomes famous.

It was something more than what has been referred to as the "hospital complex" (modern man's tendency just to sit there and let somebody come and do something for him) that made him welcome healing, prosperity, personality, and perpetuity cults. It was, perhaps, quite the reverse. Women had demonstrated to their own satisfaction that they could become involved with worthy causes of all kinds and accomplish a great deal without in the least jeopardizing their relation to the churches. In fact, more often than not, the churches did, eventually, decide that the causes for which women had been working were, after all, basically religious, and that church support for those causes fell under the heading of Christian imperative. Women's concern in the field of social welfare had certainly almost always been based on religious conviction as acquired through a church; but the same women were unwilling to wait for the churches to establish the practical programs they felt were urgently needed; when they went ahead on their own, any blessing from their churches was usually delayed, but did come, eventually. So now women sensed an inherent relationship between religion and the developing science of psychology and, with the self-confidence born of their new freedom and demonstrated abilities, rushed in where no sensible angel would have thought of treading. The results, as in any new and untried field, were mixed, sometimes deplorable, sometimes emerging into useful new patterns, or old patterns of church life of the gospel days rediscovered and revitalized. A perfect example is the way in which the well-publicized "speaking in tongues" of the early churches (which Paul felt the women overdid) was taken up by some cults, and has in recent years been hailed in some highly respectable and privileged churches of major denominations as a release technique from the inhibiting pressures of modern culture. We are not passing judgment on this or any other technique any church chooses to adopt—just reporting history.

A curious convergence of forces in the latter nineteenth century seems to have brought about the unprecedented number of cults and sects which Donald Meyer, in his book *The Positive Thinkers*,[2] describes as mind-cure movements "moving swiftly into the vacuums left by medical, political, economic and social dilemmas."

First, there was the great need. Things had been moving very fast in the eighteenth century (at least by eighteenth-century standards). They were perhaps moving fastest of all in the mental realm. People— a great many people—needed help in straightening out their own concepts. They needed help which the leadership of the rural churches of America were seldom equipped to give them at that time. Perhaps it was worse in the growing cities. It was one thing to "know oneself" when you could get yourself occasionally at least into some degree of isolation and commune with your Maker. In the swarming busyness of modern city life, man was forced also to see himself as reflected in a myriad of other persons—good, bad, indifferent, responsible, irresponsible, sick, and well—all part in one way or another of his own life and consciousness and relation to God. The integrity of the individual needed all the support religion could offer; but too often the churches felt themselves caught in the same cultural trap.

Certainly there was a mental restlessness abroad in the world. There was a wealth of new scientific knowledge, which the minds of the common people had not yet had time to assimilate. What about evolution, for instance? Charles Darwin had studied for the ministry at Edinburgh and Cambridge; yet in 1859 he could write *Origin of Species.* And what had happened to the family picture on which you were yourself brought up—the *pater familias,* about whose authority in the home there was absolutely no question? What about God the Father? It made you wonder. What about the Bible? A traveling lecturer had suggested that maybe it wasn't written by Moses. But at church the minister had just nothing to say about these questions. He could preach real well about church attendance, sin and forgiveness, about accepting your lot, the Streets of Gold and foreign missions. But not, well, for instance, about sex. How could marriage be so good, and sex something you never even talked about, even to the minister? But if you didn't talk about it, you thought about it all the more. And wasn't that wicked? But how in the world could you help it?

Or maybe you were a man and wanted to write poetry instead of going into business to make a lot of money, as everyone thought you should. Or maybe you were a woman with a conviction about suffrage for females, but your family kept laughing you out of it. If you only had the strength of mind to stand up to the rest of the world and be *yourself.* You were sure you would feel a lot better and things in general would be a lot better, if you could. But women had *always* been so dependent on men! Was it possible to learn to think for yourself? Act for yourself? Could you possibly be a *person* quite on your own?

While women may have asked the question more often, men, too, in the breakdown of the familiar economic, social, and cultural patterns, were beginning to wonder if they did not need the kind of help the "mind cure" cults offered.

Second: Into these troubled waters the early psychologists had long since tossed the fomenting question. There is an old, old story about the man who was exceedingly fond of his long, white beard. Then, one day, someone asked, "Do you sleep with it inside or outside the blankets?" Of course the poor old fellow had no way of telling for sure, and it preyed on his mind till at last he had to have the beloved beard shaved off, so he could get some sleep. In a somewhat similar manner, Sigmund Freud (1856–1939), whether or not you agreed with some of his theories (or the theories of those who purported to interpret his theories), shook people's minds in a devastating manner that neither religion nor psychology could ignore. William

James had also made his contribution to the atmosphere that made the rash of cults possible, with his "general philosophy seeming to justify any philosophy 'that worked,'" along with his conviction that what the popular mind needs most is that "their faiths should be broken up and ventilated, that the northwest wind of science should get into them and blow their sickness and barbarism away."[3] The cults were often equally *non grata* to both science and religion, but for the popular mind they did help to bridge the gap between the two.

Third: The women were ready. A nucleus of women had been trying their hands at some of the causes we discussed in the last chapter. They were ready to take on something where their leadership ability would give them a chance to be of service more clearly and definitely in the name of religion. Other more timid women had been watching, with some admiration and even envy. They would not be bold enough to make any abrupt break with the *status quo*, but many of these new groups did not expect exclusive allegiance. The women could visit and see what they decided—meetings were seldom scheduled to conflict with regular church hours. And there was no harm in buying and reading their literature—just to be informed. It was like eating your cake and having it, too.

Spiritual Healing

The beginning of the modern interest specifically in spiritual healing probably started with Melinda Cramer. Two sisters, Althea Brook Small and Fanny Brook Jones, worked with her and brought their sister-in-law, Nana Lovell Brook, into the fellowship. It was probably through Nana Brook that Mary Baker Eddy became interested in spiritual healing as a forgotten New Testament ministry.[4]

Mary Baker Eddy (1821–1910) and the Christian Science Church which she founded are known around the world, but it is very difficult to get an authentic story of her and her work. Most of the biographies and autobiographies are carefully edited, copyrighted, and controlled, as is all official Christian Science literature, by the definitely monolithic Mother Church in Boston. On the other hand, many persons have sought to discredit the doctrine of Christian Science by personal attacks on the founder. Actually the uniqueness of Mary Baker Eddy's inspiration makes very little difference to us.

She was a rather sickly child, and at a very early age she seems to have become interested in Biblical stories of miraculous healing. She wrote in later years that from the time she was a child she was "impelled by a hunger and thirst after divine things." Not strong enough for regular schooling, she was coached by her brother and promised him that she would someday write a book. She reported hearing voices calling her, as they did Joan of Arc. When she was twenty-two, she married, but after six months her husband died of yellow fever. Her son, and only child, was born posthumously, and, after much soul-searching, his mother allowed him to be placed with a nurse, while she lived with relatives and worked when she was strong enough. In 1853 she married again, but this unhappy period of her life ended in her obtaining a divorce (1873) on grounds of adultery and desertion. The people who had been caring for her son had moved away and told him his mother was dead; she did not see him again till he was thirty-five, and then the relationship was not a happy one.

When she was forty-five, she had a bad fall and experienced a miraculous recovery. At this time she claimed the principles of Christian Science were revealed to her. She began to practice healing and to write the first edition of *Science and Health,* published in 1875. To one of her classes came Asa Gilbert Eddy, a "hopeless invalid" who was healed and whom she married. But he died five years later, and from then on Mary Baker Eddy's one preoccupation was with healing, teaching, and, most of all, perhaps, with publishing. The Church of Christ, Scientist, was chartered in 1879, the Christian Science Publishing Society in 1898. The first issue of the *Christian Science Monitor* appeared in 1908. She gave every detail of the prescribed procedure for the practice of Christian Science, and its many business ramifications, the strictest personal attention and was pastor emeritus of the home church till her death in 1910. She had, it would seem, discovered not only the laws of health, but that those same laws were applicable to material prosperity, for the estate she left was estimated at over $2,000,000, and there were churches, Christian Science practitioners, and publications around the world.

The Unity School

Interestingly enough, the seed bed of many of the specifically "mind care" movements was in New England. Many local groups whose main bond was their willingness to engage in more or less radical mental experimentation formed, in 1892, the International Divine Science Association. Not long afterward, the International Metaphysical League came into existence, and finally (1906) the National (later International) New Thought Alliance, which is still extant. These were not, nor did their constituent groups represent them as, new churches. Most members continued as members of their former churches, with one brand or another of New Thought as a sort of experimental supplement. Moreover, there was always a flood of books and pamphlets to explain and amplify each point of view. A great many of the publications were written by women. "Best-sellers" were Julia Anderson Root's *Healing Power of Mind* (1884), Helen Bigelow Merriam's *What Shall Make Us Whole?* (1888), and Elizabeth Towne's magazine *The Nautilus* (first edition 1898).

One organization which has kept the original concept of "mind care" more or less in its pristine form started as the Unity School of Christianity in Kansas City. It was founded late in the nineteenth century by Charles and Myrtle Filmore, with Myrtle carrying the major load. Both had studied with Mary Baker Eddy and later with Emma Curtis Hopkins of Chicago, whom Meyer describes as one of the many talented women who broke with Mrs. Eddy to teach on their own. The Filmores conceived of their work as a school, not a church. Several times they broke—finally for good—with the New Thought Alliance. Through their concept of Silent Unity and their constantly expanding publications program, they claimed, in 1954, to reach a million homes a month with eight magazines and hundreds of low-priced publications. Unity still works through members of other churches or isolated individuals, but has its own channels as well, including the generous use of radio. When they started the work and brought out their first magazine, *Modern Thought* in 1889, both Mr. and Mrs. Filmore had long been semi-invalids and had just lost a small fortune in Kansas City real estate. Mrs. Filmore lived to the age of eighty-six, and Mr. Filmore died in 1948 at the age of ninety-four. Their son carries on the movement. Out of their organization came Alice Bailey, founder of the Arcane School of Unity.[5]

Women do not seem to have given so much leadership to the confessedly success cults, but they avidly bought the books that have appeared, often without sponsorship of any specific group but as a private matter between the author and publisher, on various aspects of "mind over matter," "thought control," "positive thinking," and even more admittedly material-success slanted offerings. It is often hard to tell when a cult becomes a cult and when it ceases to be one.

The Spiritualists

Aside from the promises of health and success of which we have been speaking, there was one more type of promise which, in the depth of the need which it sought to meet, on the one hand, and on the other, its opportunities for victimizing of adherents by unscrupulous promoters, led all the rest. Most of all in this hectic and disheveled world, when war seemed to be constantly with us, many people wanted some assurance of continuing life for dear ones who had gone on to another world. They wanted to commune with them—on a physical (or astral) plane; to be reassured about them; and through them to be reassured about their own immortality.

The Fox sisters—Katherine and Margaretta—seem to have been responsible for the popularization of spiritualism in the United States about 1848. It was "theosophist and occultist" Helena Petrovna Blavatsky of Russia, however, who actually founded the Theosophical Society in New York City in 1875. In 1877 she wrote Isis Unveiled, which was used as a text by her followers, of whom, at her death in 1891, there were purported to be 100,000. In 1879 she moved to India and set up her headquarters in Madras. Here she was joined by her disciple Annie Wood Besant of England. Mrs. Besant became very active in Indian affairs and was president of the Indian National Congress in 1917. Probably no one would want to guess how many "good church members" in both England and the United States were making side trips to seances and occult meetings in the early twentieth century. It took Duke University's ESP[6] investigations to make the subject "respectable," and about the same time spiritualism lost much of its popular appeal.

Women Evangelists

There were many women evangelists about the turn of the century, and many cults came and went. One of the most permanent was the Four Square Gospel, which is the outgrowth of the work of its often storm-tossed but always effective Aimee Semple McPherson.

Of a completely different character, but still to be mentioned in the category of new movements inaugurated by women in this period, are the Seventh-Day Adventists, founded by Ellen G. White and her husband, James White. Ellen (1827–1915) and her twin sister were the youngest of eight children of a hatter living in Gorham, Maine. Her father conducted his business in the family home, and they all helped. When Ellen was about thirteen, her Methodist parents began to attend Adventist meetings led by a Baptist layman. When she was nineteen, she married James White, a minister, and they had four sons. The health of her family got Ellen White interested in foods, and her first speaking was on health through food and temperance. She and her husband started a small publishing business to give their ideas wider circulation. They are said to have been the inspiration behind the Battle Creek food manufacturing concern, and to have encouraged John Harvey Kellogg (one of sixteen children of a Michigan Adventist family) to study medicine. He, in turn, began the manufacture of cornflakes and promoted Ellen White's ideas of health through fresh air, sun, and simple diet. In 1866 the Adventists opened the Western Health Reform Institute at Battle Creek, with Mr. Kellogg as a director. In 1876 this became the Battle Creek Sanitarium.

Ellen White liked to point out that "God is truly the author of physical laws as well as moral law." She did not begin to preach till she was in her forties. She did it then because she wanted to testify to the miraculous in her own life. She was, in her earlier years, accounted as "frail" and with a weak voice. Now she spoke to crowds of up to 20,000. She was very active in establishing schools and colleges. When her husband suffered four successive strokes, she took over his work and carried on two heavy loads instead of one, besides caring for his comfort until his death, fourteen years after the first attack.

When Ellen White herself died in 1915, the Seventh-Day Adventists claimed 140,000 members, 2500 clergy, eighty medical centers, a mission on every continent. Forty publishing houses had printed seventy books, and twenty-five were published posthumously. And everything was left in capable hands that would carry on effectively. One can hardly doubt why, when Ellen White preached about the miraculous, folks said that she spoke with conviction.

To end on a real family note, let us mention the Salvation Army, founded in England by General William Booth and his wife Catherine in 1865, and introduced into America in 1880. The sons and daughters of this prolific family, and the people they married, entered vigorously into the Army's evangelistic pattern, and the movement rapidly spread around the world. A daughter, Evangeline, was commander in the United States (1904–1934), and the following five years was commander of the International Salvation Army.

The Salvation Army not only tolerates women; it emphasizes their place in the organization. There has always been division of labor, but with mutual appreciation. When a member marries, it must be with a member of the same rank, so there can be no professional rivalry. If the couple are of different ranks, the one of lower rank is given special training to raise him or her to a matching rank, so they can always work as partners.

Chapter 15

THE CAUSE OF YOUTH

Grace Dodge, a young woman of education, culture, and wealth, and also with amazing initiative and religious conviction, was ready about 1880 to be presented to New York society. Instead of a "coming out" party which might well have been the envy of other society girls and their mothers, Grace Dodge asked her father to present her at a series of luncheons to which he would invite "persons who had accomplished something." She was especially interested in meeting people who were active in the various social movements of the time, and while her contemporaries danced their way through one of New York's most glittering eras, she familiarized herself with the problems of the girls in the silk factories or helped develop the "Kitchen Garden Association," which she persuaded the ladies to rename "the Industrial Education Association." The purpose of this organization was to promote "special training of both sexes in any of those industries which affect the house or home directly or indirectly and which will enable those receiving it to become self-supporting."

Grace Dodge organized a children's industrial exhibition, in which they exhibited their work to arouse interest in industrial training for young people. From George W. Vanderbilt she got the money for training leadership for her activities—an enterprise that developed into the New York College for the Training of Teachers (now Teachers College), with Dr. Nicholas Murray Butler as president. She was appointed to a Commission on Education for New York City—the first time a woman had been a member of the Board of Education of that city.

The YWCA

However, most of all, perhaps, Grace Dodge is remembered as the guiding spirit of the formative years of the Young Women's Christian Association.

If the Church at this time was "rediscovering the human race," as W. E. Garrison suggests,[1] women were, after their concentration on economic and political causes for the better part of a century, beginning to rediscover youth as a very special concern for which they felt a very special responsibility. Women had, of course, always had a large share in the care of the children of the Church, though in a church of any size their religious education was usually under the direction of a young male assistant pastor working his way up to appointment to a full preaching ministry, and interested only temporarily and out of necessity, in the field of religious education.

Horace Bushnell had written *Christian Nurture* to challenge the revivalism which called for dramatic "conversion" of little children on much the same basis as aged sinners, but for the most part society still tried to raise children as little ladies and gentlemen, who should, however, be seen and not heard. They grew, hopefully, by natural means, into adults, but that youth itself was a period of life with special requirements and responsibilities was, strange as it may seem today, a rather revolutionary idea. "Teen-agers" had not been heard of. During the latter decades of the century, various youth groups were formed within the denominations, often under the guidance of a volunteer woman of the congregation, but the idea of united youth work among young people of various churches, or of the potential of young people for carrying the message of the Church into the community, was still far in the future. Realization of these ideas came about through many diverse causes and movements, but the development of the Young Women's Christian Association is one which is particularly typical and significant for our consideration.

The YWCA had its beginning in London in 1855. That year Emma Roberts asked her friends to come together to pray for the young ladies who were coming to London to enter such genteel occupations as millinery and dressmaking. The same year, Lady Arthur Kinnaird, aware that housing for young ladies in the city was a problem, interested her friends in establishing the General Female Training Institute and in opening a home for nurses returning from the Crimean War. The two movements joined in 1877.

The first such movement in America was the Ladies' Christian Association, organized in New York in 1858. An attempt at something of the sort was turned down in Boston in 1859. The group of women sponsoring the project were told by the ministers of that city that it would be "hazardous" for the ladies to undertake such a scheme. The men stressed that in advising against it they were "kindly preventing them from making a failure." But by 1866 the women had established the Boston Young Women's Christian Association (the first time the YW name was used in America). It included a boardinghouse and had as its objective "the temporal, moral and religious welfare of young women who are dependent on their own exertion for support." Out of the needs of the young women themselves developed programs of housing, employment counseling, recreation, temporary loan service. And at the heart of the YW in those early programs was not only Christian motivation but religious services and study groups.

It was the need for Christian study, conversation, and fellowship that led to the first university YWCA group at the Illinois State Normal University in 1873; this group seems to have had a particularly evangelistic approach. It sent a committee to call on the pastors of the churches to "see if they will not enter heartily into union with us and have meetings for the promotion of Christ's kingdom." This movement, too, spread rapidly and joined with the YMCA in 1895 to form the World's Student Christian Federation. Some confusing years—organizationally—followed, with different groups trying to define their basis of membership, motivating philosophy, relation to the churches, and practical programs to which they could most effectively address themselves.

It was largely through the conciliatory efforts of Grace Dodge that the early organizational rivalries between various facets of the YW were successfully brought into harmony, and the Young Women's Christian Association formed in 1906. Grace Dodge became the president of the National Board.

Born in an era of profound changes in cultural environment, the YWCA came into existence and grew to maturity among many conflicting ideologies. Its basic membership was, at the beginning, an evangelical Christology which today would be described as definitely conservative. Independent in most matters, the YW accepted a statement of faith adopted from the YM. However, the YW was born of a deep concern for women as *people* and an interest in the "social gospel" which, while certainly not new to the Christian religion, was receiving greatly increased emphasis in the preaching of the churches during the first decades of the twentieth century.

The missionary spirit abroad among the churches of America early in the century was undoubtedly one of the channels through which the YW also became increasingly an international organization. In some countries the YW became part of the church organization itself. But the spirit of fellowship between all young women in these countries was also precious, even when it cut across lines of church allegiance. YW members were unwilling to exclude their friends from an organization which they themselves (quite apart from religion) found most desirable, and the idea of the Y as a sort of halfway house—an open door— frequently meant that non-Christians often became not only members but board members and officers. In the countries where the Y was definitely a part of the evangelical church (not yet "infected" with the social gospel), such an idea was little short of a scandal. There was a wide variation, to say the least, in YW patterns around the world.

In the United States the local YW usually depended primarily upon the support and leadership of devoted church-related women. Sometimes this included the enthusiasm of the local churches, but at times these same churches could not help but feel somewhat resentful over the generous funds that found their way into the YW exchequer. They approved of the work the YW was doing and its free-wheeling activity, most of the time, but not without a tinge of envy.

The Ecumenical Spirit

The YW, being from the first interdenominational, had no denominational brakes—for better or for worse.

With the Federal Council of Churches, forerunner of the National Council of Churches, the YW had a working affinity almost from the first, and in 1920 the YW adopted the council's liberal statement on "Social Ideals for the Churches." As the movement to organize church councils in local communities throughout the United States gained momentum, one of the problems was leadership effectively to carry out programs. Ministers were the employees of their local churches and, however interested, could conscientiously give only a small percentage of their time to building up interdenominational work, the full significance and economy of which were not yet apparent to their churches. In many places the councils found YW women, available and capable, willing to work in interdenominational activities. In the long decades during which the ecumenical pioneers (sometimes referred to as "ecumaniacs") were traveling through the land explaining the idea of the embryonic World Council of Churches, it was often the women trained in YW work who heard most gladly and gave most generously.

In recent years an odd situation has developed. The YW, anxious to demonstrate its genuine solidarity with the Church, has been placing a value on sound theological training for staff workers, which goes beyond that which most women receive from their denominations. Also, the YW has always emphasized that in an all-woman organization it is easier for a capable girl to get the leadership training that will be valuable to her in any kind of organization than it would be in a mixed situation, where the men expect to "carry the ball" and the women are reluctant to evoke masculine hostility by putting themselves forward. (This has also been one of the most valid reasons advanced for women's colleges.) When it became somewhat disgraceful that there were so few women on the national staffs of the great denominations or in the ecumenical councils, and that more responsible female personnel was imperative, what more natural than to turn to the YW for new appointees? Here were religiously oriented and extremely well-trained women who could do the required work (and more!) and serve as evidence (or at least as a gesture) of women being acceptable in the Church; yet since they had not come up vocationally through their own denominations, and most did not have theological degrees (though they might well have the equivalent), they established no precedent nor did they offer a real threat that women might be invading the sanctum sanctorum of the upper ecclesiastical realms. The B.D. staff head of a denominational or interdenominational department did not have to worry over being "crowded" by his assistant; he did not in the least mind a capable Ph.D. woman in the department—even as an associate. She could never be the threat that an equally capable fellow B.D. (male or female) could be. Or could she? For that matter, some seemed quite capable of going off and getting a theological degree while holding down the job.

One thing which should surely be emphasized about the YW is the ecumenical spirit. Drop in at the YW anywhere around the world for a cup of tea, a hearty welcome, and good conversation about significant matters. At least that is the YW ideal.

Cornelia van Asch van Wijck, who almost singlehanded (by the carefully documented research she did in her home during the Nazi occupation of her native Holland) broke down the Biblical-theological barriers to women's ordination in the churches of her country; Suzanne de Deitrich, long a teacher at the Ecumenical Institute at Bossey, Switzerland; and Ruth Woodsmall, well known in ecumenical circles of both England and the United States, are among many women worthy of mention who came up through the YW. Ruth Rouse, co-author of A History of the Ecumenical Movement 1517–1948 (Westminster, 1948), calls the YW one of the "major allies" (with the YM and WSCF) of the World Council of Churches. She also pays tribute to the YW as a training ground for leadership of such persons as Sarah

Chakko, one of the first presidents of the World Council, and Madeleine Barot, director of the World Council's Department on Cooperation of Men and Women in Church, Family and Society.

Regarding the spread of the YW, Ruth Rouse says: "No officer or merchant's wife abroad, if she had been a member of the YWCA at home, was content till she had brought into existence a YWCA in the land where her lot was cast."[2]

Chapter 16

AT THE HEART OF THE MATTER:
WOMAN IN HER CHURCH

Many things—but not usually denominational policy—determine whether the women in a given local church are treated as expendable, pampered pets, wheel horses, or full working partners.

A church's attitude toward its women may, for instance, reflect the open or subconscious attitude of the pastor, often reflecting, in turn, the mind set of the theological seminary where he had his training. Some seminaries—again it is not nearly always a denominational matter—have a fine appreciation of women, and what, in various capacities, they can contribute to the religious life of the Church and the world. In other seminaries they have no standing at all, or perhaps a negative one, and it may be quite a shock to a young pastor when he finds women cluttering up his congregation, and himself and the church he serves largely dependent on them.

The attitude of the local church toward its women will also depend—let us face it—largely on the women themselves—on both their ability and amiability.

The history and tradition of the particular local church are also factors. So, too, are community attitudes, and, where one ethnic group dominates, old world customs may enter into the picture of how the church thinks its women should behave.

It is, moreover, hard to get an objective appraisal of how women *do* fare in any local church; the account often sounds quite different according to who is telling the story.

Much will depend on how the women think of themselves, whether they take a responsible part in planning the church program, and whether the program as developed leaves them challenged, frenzied, or frustrated. Often the woman takes a pragmatic attitude, deciding she can get along more comfortably and maybe even accomplish more—at least for the present—by not raising a fuss. Especially if a woman is in a position of some comparative importance, she may decide to make the most of her own existing opportunities rather than "sound the siren" on behalf of women in general. She is, in fact, never quite sure whether the rank and file of the women in the church will stand by her if, on their behalf, she forces the general issue of women's responsible participation in the whole program of the church. Far from being appreciative and responsive, they may only find ways to demonstrate that they consider her forward.

The Subtle Power of Usage

Theoretically most denominations as such have seldom put any real restrictions on *laywomen's* participation in the *work* of the churches. Heads of denominations which do are apt to tell you that the restrictions reflect an understanding through the centuries, in which the women have had their own special roles, with which they are quite satisfied. Possibly not all the women of these denominations agree, but probably they lack channels of protest. For the most part, too, the restrictions on women have been based not in definite rulings, but in the subtle power of usage.

It is also true that many women might choose the very roles to which they find themselves assigned, but they seldom like, in the least, being assigned and restricted to any role by the men of the church. Freedom of choice is a cherished right. Most women feel, moreover, that when a woman has any proved ability, and wants to use it in the service of the Church, the doors must not be arbitrarily closed against her simply on the basis of sex. This, she may well contend, is giving sex too dominant a place in religion.

There is little doubt that the strong determination to keep women out of the priesthood and the pulpit has downgraded the position of all women throughout the Church (and even in denominations which theoretically "accept" women in the ministry).

It has been difficult until very recently to have significant discussions of the whole subject of women's role in the churches at denominational meetings. Many men as well as women believe that more open discussion of the man-woman relationship would clear the air and, without necessarily precipitating any major changes, would make for far more harmonious working and worshiping conditions. Women's place in the organizational structure of the Church, the appointment of women representatives or committee members, and the relative unimportance (as shown by the budget) of the Christian education program are, women say, subjects to be discussed with time and dignity, not settled by the men, in advance, at washroom conferences, or by the arbitrary whim of the minister or denominational representative. Nor are they, as the hour of the meeting approaches dinnertime, to be wiped off the agenda with a facetious comment or a funny story.

The kinds of discrimination which bar women from the opportunity to serve to their fullest capacity are, moreover, no easier for the well-trained and devoted woman to accept in the denominations where women have, theoretically, all rights and privileges, but where they can be completely and effectively ignored, than they are in those churches which in age-old rites and rituals find irrevocable barriers to women entering into significant church ministries. (In one recent survey of women's religious responsibilities, a report from one denomination stated that it was the task of the women in their churches to keep the whole building clean—except, of course, the altar, which they were not permitted to approach.)

A great many women serve on committees and commissions within their denominations, at state and national levels. This is often a very significant opportunity, where competence may be recognized rather than thwarted. However, the mechanism of appointment is very frequently such that these women are chosen by and may reflect the thinking of the top staff and board members (usually predominantly male) rather than reflecting the viewpoint and concerns of the women of the denomination. Democratic representation of the woman's viewpoint at any level is seldom fully achieved, unless it is in the denominational women's societies, and sometimes the head of the women's work in the denomination is "appointed" (of course by the men).

It is heartening, nevertheless, to note the number of capable and forceful women heading such societies, for these women can be a leavening force in the over-all denominational picture. If sensitive to the voice of the women who are her constituency, such a person can be a most effective channel through which the women of the churches can make their voices heard. If they are wise, they will help her in every way possible to do a creditable job and to exemplify the ability and creativity of which women are capable at the executive level.

A survey of the *Yearbook of the American Churches*[1] published by the National Council of Churches, indicates that practically all the major Protestant denominations have some sort of national women's organization, and in almost every case it is headed by a woman. Names of organizations vary: Women's Fellowship, Women's Council, Women's Auxiliary, Board (or Convention) of Women's Work, (the denomination's) Council of Women, Women's Missionary Union (League or Society), Division (or Department) of Women's Service (or Work), to mention a few. Usually names are historic rather than descriptive of present function. In some denominational headquarters, there is a women's associate board in each major department.

At present there seems to be a trend toward combining men's and women's work into a "Department of the Laity"; the United Church of Christ pioneered this pattern among the denominations, following the lead of the World Council of Churches. As of 1965, the National Council of Churches has also adopted this pattern.

So far as could be determined, no major U.S. denomination has a woman bishop, and none has a woman in the top executive post, though Baptists, Congregationalists, Friends, some united churches, and probably others have sometimes elected women presidents, moderators, and presiding clerks. The Friends have recently re-elected Blanche W. Shaffer as their top *international* executive. The American Baptist Convention, the Methodist Church, the Protestant Episcopal Church, the United Presbyterian Church, United Church of Christ indicate women heading some general division of the denomination's work, and there are quite a few "associate" executives, mostly in the fields of religious education, Christian social service, or missions. Several top-level boards have women secretaries. So varied and so in flux are the patterns of life at the various denominational headquarters that any attempt at descriptive comparison would be worse than futile. For the reader to give attention to the lists of personnel in the current *Yearbook of the American Churches* will be far more enlightening.

Even the denominations which ordain women seldom welcome competent ones too cordially when theology *per se* is being discussed. It is important, however, that women understand the theology of their denominations, and also that they have the opportunity to discuss it and to contribute their insights. For a woman does have a theology, and it is nonetheless valid and authentic because it may be different from that which the men have evolved. The woman working (voluntary or staff) in almost any field of religion often feels quite cut off from theological roots and denominational relationships. She has comparatively little opportunity for any depth discussion of Biblical interpretation or the philosophy of religion or ethics. Even if she is admittedly competent in such fields, and schools herself not to be hypersensitive to unwarranted criticism, it is hard for her to speak freely and spontaneously and without consciousness that a large percentage of those who hear her, listen with the mental reservation that, being a woman, she should not speak at all.

Such respected professors as Dr. Mary Lyman of Union Seminary (N.Y.C.) and Dr. Georgia Harkness of Pacific School of Religion (Berkeley, California) have done much to raise the popular respect for women theologians. The situation seems to call for more pioneer women of high ability and willingness to take this long, difficult, but rewarding road.

The Women's Own Fault

If the male members of the Church—both clergy and laity—have rather consistently seemed to feel that they alone are capable of reflecting the wholeness of the Creator, woman has been equally culpable in not assuming her rightful and necessary responsibility to the Church. She has accepted responsibility to her husband, her children, her community, and to the housekeeping and social functions of church life. She has, however, seemed to regard church activity as an extension of home interests, rather than trying to make the home a valid reflection, in terms comprehensible to the family, of her religious convictions.

Often she has cluttered her life with minor responsibilities in a truly disorderly fashion, leaving no time to help the Church achieve its full destiny in the community or the world. In spite of her demonstrated ability through the centuries with language skills and communications, she has repeated creeds, apparently not even caring what they were all about, and has apparently never made much if any attempt to formulate them—or to repudiate them. She has sung hymns, and taught them to children in home and Sunday school, without question or explanation of just what the words mean, or what effect repeated singing of them might have on impressionable young minds. Until quite recently her Bible study at the age of sixty was probably only slightly more sophisticated in tone than when she was twelve.

But of course the same, or similar, things are also true about the men.

Unless woman herself takes the initiative in insisting, in and out of meeting, and without blame or sarcasm or bitterness toward the other half of the human race, that the time has come for a theological and practical definition—which she herself must have a recognized part in formulating—of the joint responsibility of men and women in the Church, probably nothing can, or perhaps rightly should, come of such discussions as this. That women themselves become concerned, not over any affront to their dignity, but over obstacles in the way of their rendering the greatest possible service to all religion stands for in the world, is the crux of the whole matter.

Roman Catholic Women

Roman Catholic interest in the role of the lay woman in religion is especially evident—and most attractively presented—by the Grailville publication (1960) *Woman, Some Aspects of Her Role in the Modern World*, by Dr. Lydwine Van Kersbergen.[2] The Grail movement is an "international lay apostolic movement at work today in twenty countries, on all continents, under the direction of the Hierarchy." It defines its aim as "to call women, whatever their walk of life, to a dedication to the Christ—a dedication which ripens into a conscious apostolic readyness to participate in his Redeeming Work. . . ." Its motivation— or vision—is described as "a recognition of God's plan for the conversion of the world and a positive and profound concept of women's specific role. . . ." The movement's headquarters are at Grailville, Loveland, Ohio.

Dr. Van Kersbergen looks at her subject "Woman" from the point of view of both sociology and psychology, and especially theology. She is definitely on the side of "being true to woman's nature," but fears that those who urge modern woman to be true to herself often base their counsel on an incomplete and highly inadequate view of human nature. She urges Catholic scholars to "enlarge and deepen the current concept of woman."

Rosemary Lauer, writing on "Women in the Church,"[3] can speak for both Catholic and Protestant laywomen when she says that discrimination against the female sex has not even been rationalized by the "separate but equal" theory. Women, she says, are separate because they are held to be *inferior*. She quotes (not with approval) Robert Bellamine in the sixteenth century as saying that three classes of people can grasp no more theology than the sound of words—country folk, idiots, and women. However, the real trouble, she finds, stems from Thomas Aquinas, who entered a monastery at the age of five and got most of his ideas about women from Aristotle, who characterized them as "misbegotten men."

Dr. Gertrude Heinzelmann of Zurich, it seems, dispatched a memorandum along these general lines to the General Preparatory Commission of Vatican Council. Genesis, the Apostle Paul, and other "authorities" are usually interpreted, the ladies say, not with objective scholarship, but in the light of what "everyone knows" and what we "have always done."

The press, always inclined to the side of the ladies on this as well as other discussions, seems to be quietly keeping its eyes open for interesting incidents to report, such as that of a woman journalist who was prevented from receiving Communion at a Council Mass—frankly on the grounds that she was a woman[4]; or the story of how Italy's high court upheld a law imposing a greater punishment for a woman than a man in a trial for adultery, justifying its decree on the grounds that infidelity is "of greater gravity in a woman."

Chapter 17

THE COMING OF THE COUNCILS

Women who did not fit into the social pattern that was somehow "part and parcel" of women's work in their local churches have sometimes found a fellowship that seemed a more challenging use of their time in some phase of church council work—local, state, national, or world. When councils were new, there often seemed to be less competition for responsible creative jobs than was evident in some of the member churches. Women found themselves working effectively and congenially in the ecumenical atmosphere. Employed, or formerly employed women—used to working with men—felt especially at home in the councils and often gave liberally of their time and talents. However, the women engaging in council work had no more official standing than they brought with them from their local churches, and the *official* delegates were almost sure to be men. Very often, however, women found places to work on council committees or special programs with a great deal of freedom and a chance for initiative.

At the local level when councils were young (and even yet), there was a great variety of relationships between councils of churches and councils of churchwomen. The local councils of churches frequently liked to emphasize that they were councils of *local congregations*, and as such deeply rooted in the community, with strong ties and responsibilities to local affairs. Some of these local councils have taken the lead in promoting very broad-based programs—civil liberties, international peace, interfaith theological discussions, for instance. They were and are likely to look to the National Council of Churches for materials and speakers acceptable to the largest possible number of local churches.

In some places a women's council started as a sort of auxiliary to the council of churches, though organizationally separate. Such a women's council really had freedom of action—beholden to neither the council nor the churches. Such groups might develop a very wide base of membership, including women from religious groups who neither would nor logically could (on theological grounds) join the council of churches.

All sorts of relationships between the councils of churches and the women's councils developed—according largely to the patterns of the community. Sometimes the councils of churches and the women's councils were "separate but equal," even holding meetings—presumably for the convenience of husband and wife—at the same hour. Sometimes the women supplemented the general program and became in effect a shadow council. Sometimes there was a sort of husband-and-wife division of labor. Sometimes the women's council was an integral part of the council of churches, which could mean either that the women had a busy and interesting part in council activities, or that they were called upon to drill the children for the community pageant or to serve the annual church dinner. The women were always good fund raisers. Sometimes they raised their own funds and spent them as they pleased, while in other circumstances they made raising the council budget one of their major concerns and developed no separate program of their own. Almost always there was some sort of liaison, and usually increasingly cordial relationships between the council of churches and the council of churchwomen, with some women finding great satisfaction in working for both.

The United Church Women

A somewhat similar trial-and-adjustment program in man-woman relationships had been going on at the national level, which brings our attention specifically to the organization of United Church Women in 1941, "to unite churchwomen in allegiance to their Lord and Savior, Jesus Christ, through a program looking to their integration in the total life and work of the church and the building of the Christian community."

At first the organization and program, under the inspired guidance of such persons as Amy Welcher, Georgiana Sibley and Ruth Worrell, were very informal, the money scarce, and convictions strong. One conviction was that all local groups should be integrated. It is a good memory to recall the day when the writer participated with a Negro and white group in a large southern city in the formation of their local UCW. We were told that many of the group had never before had an opportunity to sit down socially and visit with members of the other race. Later we had dinner in a basement room which the liberal-minded proprietor of the hotel had set up especially for us, since we could not eat together legally in the same public dining room.

In 1945 it was again the writer's privilege to have a part in the UCW program, taking to France, as a staff member of Church World Service, the first token shipment of material aid—a large box of household linens and bedding for Mrs. Marc Boegner, wife of the head of the French Protestant Church. We placed the big box in the center of her living-room floor and knelt on either side as she opened it. The first article she lifted out was a lovely lemon-colored wool blanket. It was new and fleecy and warm. She held it against her cheek, and tears filled her eyes. The women of France, at the end of the war, had almost forgotten such things existed. She hugged the blanket in her arms, while she heard that a box like this one was being readied for every parsonage in France, from churchwomen friends in the United States. That was the beginning of a tremendous flow of goods from the American women to the people of the devastated countries of Europe and Asia—layettes, children's kits, dress material ("pieces for peace")—it went on and on.

World peace and brotherhood were motivating forces of UCW from the beginning, one project after another demonstrating that, given sufficient motivation, women could do almost anything.

United Church Women became part of the National Council of Churches in 1950. There were some misgivings that, as part of the National Council, UCW might lose its autonomy, and with it some of its prophetic spirit. Instead it became, with Dorothy McLeod as executive director, one of the National Council's strongest departments, and often a spark of inspiration for various council programs such as those dealing with world affairs, race, refugees, migrant workers, the laity, missions, the ecumenical movement, peace. It kept a good balance between ecumenical relations and independence and made wide use of women of ability—sometimes of women to whom it had never occurred to their own denominations or local church leaders to give appropriate responsible assignments. UCW built a strong program and capable staff, as well as a nation-wide network of responsible and enthusiastic leadership among the churchwomen of the various denominations. As of January 1966, Dr. Margaret Shannon, an outstanding member of the United Presbyterian national staff, succeeded Mrs. McLeod as executive director.

UCW in 1965 claimed a constituency of 12,000,000 churchwomen served and serving through 2300 state and local councils of churchwomen in the United States. In one typical year—1962—the offering for the World Day of Prayer—to mention one project—accounted for $553,300, distributed $50,000 to help establish a radio station in North Africa; $50,000 for home missions work in Alaska; $15,000 for one-year vocational scholarships (through the United Nations) for thirty Palestinian refugee girls; sizable gifts to twelve women's colleges in Asia and Africa; Christian literature for women and girls around the world; a gift to help promote friendly relations with foreign students; support for migrant ministries; American Indian work.

From the beginning UCW felt a special kinship with the ecumenical movement on one hand, and the United Nations on the other. The churchwomen's active support of the United Nations is easy to understand. When the U.N. charter was signed in 1945, the women of only forty nations had political rights; by March 1963, women of a hundred nations had the vote. A new political role for women around the world seemed to be an idea whose time had come in this century.

One U.N. item in which the churchwomen were particularly interested was the signing (December 10, 1962) of the Convention on Consent to Marriage, Minimum Age for Marriage, and Registration of Marriage. Simple as it sounds, this was the culmination of years of work and negotiation by the Commission on the Status of Women. Gladys Tillett signed the Convention for the United States—the first time we have deigned, since 1949, to sign a Human Rights Convention—though our representatives have worked hard at drafting them. Another major interest was demonstrated by the providing of scholarships by UCW for key women throughout the country to go to New York for leadership training seminars at the new Church Center at the United Nations "so they can develop more effective international affairs programs in their church organizations, in their communions, and communities."

However, busy as they were, and effective as they were, within the ranks of the UCW a new line of thinking was developing. There had been within the Church in recent years—and particularly within the ecumenical movement—a powerful and persistent emphasis on the role of the laity. This was no mere movement for better industrial movies and higher-ranking political speakers for the men's club; it was a new understanding of the laity as the very center of the Church's ministry to the world. It involved a study of today's automation and cybernation problems, and of the Christian layperson's responsibility in the world today, along with a study of the spread of the Gospel in the first centuries of the Christian era, and the part the laity had in building the very foundations of the Christian Church. There was, moreover, in this new lay movement, little doubt but that "laity" involved both men and women working together.

Dr. Cynthia Wedel, an Episcopal woman, writing in *Church Woman*, November 1962, challenged the women of the churches, including those of UCW, to concern themselves with providing more opportunities for women to serve significantly *in the churches themselves and in church councils*. One way she hoped this could be done was through added emphasis on the "ministry of the laity" which, she indicated, may well be "*the* great forward thrust of the churches in the next ten years, involving a new look at the task of the Church." This new look at the laity, she predicted, would "involve men and women working together more than before; it will see us moving *out* of the churches to work in the name of Christ in the community, the nation and the world; and it will require us—laymen and -women —to know and understand far more than we do now about the Bible and theology."

As the National Council was reorganized, January 1965, under the executive leadership of Dr. Edwin Espe, himself deeply committed to both the ministry of the laity and women's participation in the life of the Church, United Church Women and United Church Men have come together in the Department of the Laity, Division of Christian Unity, with Cynthia Wedel as top executive. Developments of this new plan will be historic and most interesting to watch.[1]

Strategy at Amsterdam

Just before the Constituting Assembly of the World Council of Churches met at Amsterdam, Holland, in 1948, Protestant and Orthodox women church leaders held a preliminary meeting at Baarn, Holland. A stimulating three-day discussion culminated in a statement that might have been called a women's religious bill of rights. The women hoped to present this statement to the forthcoming assembly at Amsterdam. However, they were warned by an "ecumenical statesman" that to present their document at this meeting would not be wise and might lead to the elimination of the proposed "Commission on the Place of Women in the Church," which it was hoped the assembly would authorize. The women were not pleased; they had worked hard on that statement and felt they had constructive ideas to suggest. However, they knew the advice offered was friendly and undoubtedly sound.

The women from the churches most rigidly opposed to women's participation were the most disappointed; yet they realized that their own churches were the very ones which, it was feared, would reject the whole proposal for a "woman's commission" and might even shy away from the idea of the council itself, if confronted with the evidence of how the women really felt about their "traditional role."

Instead, an official Assembly Committee was appointed and drew up a less bombastic report. While this report did actually speak out for ordination being open to women, the only action it asked the assembly to take was to authorize a commission to study "Life and Work of Women in the Church." This the assembly graciously did. The assembly also elected Sarah Chakko, president of Isabella Thoburn College for Women, at Lucknow, India, one of the six presidents of the council, the first layman and only woman ever so honored.

The council idea was relatively new at the time, and it was hard for some women to realize that no delegated council can proceed faster than its member churches. This, of course, still needs to be remembered. Among the delegates sent to Amsterdam from churches around the world were undoubtedly a majority who at that time would have opposed any statement that seemed to endorse women's right to participate in the preaching or business of the churches. The entry of the Eastern Orthodox into the fellowship of the World Council at the New Delhi assembly may well have accentuated this particular problem, and it may have reinforced the conservatism, in this particular respect, of some of the original member churches. Any ecumenical rapprochement between the Roman Catholics and Protestants will probably find this a serious matter. One Roman Catholic churchman in West Germany finds the recent decisions of several Protestant denominations to ordain women "a grave obstacle to Christian unity" and asks that the Protestants "think well what they are doing."[2] Yet Protestant women engaging in interfaith discussions are frequently amazed at the freedom with which their Catholic counterparts work, and the responsible positions which they hold.

The change of title under which the World Council's Commission has operated is somewhat indicative of what is expected of it. At first it was the Commission on the Life and Work of Women in the Church—authorized only to study the status of women in the council's member churches. After the Evanston assembly (1954), the commission became a department, to explore "Cooperation of Men and Women in Church and Society." At New Delhi this title was changed to "Cooperation of Men and Women in Church, Family and Society," and discussion seemed to focus on problems of responsible parenthood, family planning, world populations—questions which were major concerns of the World Council's Study Department.

It has been suggested that some people might prefer a commission of men and women to deal with specific problems, such as population as a concern of the Church, instead of a department to discuss problems of women in the churches, which the male-centered Church is overlooking and does not particularly care to have called to its attention. But if this is to be how it is, then there should surely be a goodly representation of women on, let us say, the Commission of the Churches on International Affairs, a subject upon which women demonstrate real competence. In fact, from this viewpoint, women should be well represented on every one of the Council's departments and commissions, for women are surely interested in every phase of religion.

Actually the department, with Dr. Madeleine Barot as executive director for most of its history, has done a remarkable piece of work. It has analyzed with perception and from differing viewpoints the basic question of women's status in the churches[3]; it has offered, through consultations on every continent, an opportunity for exchange of views and ecumenical fellowship; it has given courage and new vision to women of nations in which the position of women, politically, was non-existent. It has called attention to the fact that in some countries woman is still little more than a chattel, and that until her position is raised more nearly to the world norm, there is little hope of these women being received as equal persons even in their religious groups. It has tried to help women of various areas pinpoint the particular problems that beset women in their own areas and, so far as possible, to work out their own solutions.

Dr. W. A. Visser 't Hooft, present as General Secretary of the World Council of Churches at one of these conferences, closed it with these words:

> In this age of emancipation of races, of women, by a natural historic process, Christians have not to argue about rights, but about opportunities for people to make their spiritual contributions. The whole Church cannot afford to deprive itself of the gifts God is trying to administer. The reason for the emancipation of women in the Church is not the barren fight for the rights of women, but the fruitful discovery of their spiritual gifts, of their full creative contributions. . . .

See Appendix III for world results of a survey of women's status in regard to ordination, conducted by the W.C.C. department.

Chapter 18

PREACHING, TEACHING,
AND OTHER OCCUPATIONS

It was the first day of the semester in the theological seminary, and the professor was trying to draw the class, mostly first-year men, into meaningful dialogue. "What," he asked, "do you think God is like?"

Silence.

"Doesn't someone care to venture an opinion?" he prodded.

From the back row came a strong but pleasant feminine voice: "The astronauts say she's black." The dialogue was launched.

In most churches during the first half of the twentieth century the parallel conversation concerning the person in the pulpit of most Protestant and all Anglican, Roman Catholic, and Eastern Orthodox churches, or any Jewish synagogue, would have been no less shocking.

Yet women's ordination to the preaching ministry has never been a really closed question in America. From the beginning, the Congregationalists and Baptists, bringing with them certain dissenter traditions from Europe, disclaimed any formal prejudice against women in the pulpit; the Quakers and Salvation Army took women's participation in all phases of church work for granted. For the Congregational churches it was probably, in the early days, lack of facilities for women's training for an educated ministry, more than religious prejudice against women, that kept the women from making the contribution of which they were capable in the New World. By the time colleges and schools of theology were open to women—by the time Antoinette Brown had taken her theological degree at Oberlin and the Grimke sisters had been cruelly repudiated because of their sex (though they were carrying the anti-slavery message to packed audiences of thousands), and by the time Olympia Brown had overcome the objections to her studying at St. Lawrence College and being ordained (1864),[1] the theological scene in the United States had been complicated by a degree of worldly sophistication which repudiated "woman ministers" and set up obstacles of prejudice where no doctrinal ones existed.

The new waves of immigration from Europe in the mid-nineteenth century vastly increased the ratio of Anglican, Lutheran, Presbyterian, and Roman Catholic in relation to the early Congregational-type churches, and these more structured churches brought with them various forms of the male hierarchy inherited from European antecedents. Methodism softened but did not overcome the obstacles which stood in the way of women's preaching.

In the great Western migrations, the church was a center of decency and order—a most important force in the community, and the pioneer women undoubtedly performed one of their greatest possible services in recognizing and catering to this need for a gentling influence on the new towns.

However, about this time, too, women began to discover "causes" and their own strength and effectiveness in dealing with them. Male preachers, and women, too, often from the most unprejudiced pre-Reformation backgrounds, had no intention of letting their pulpits be invaded by bloomer-clad suffragettes, bent once more, in this generation, on turning the world upside down. And wouldn't that be the very kind, they asked, who would invade the pulpit? To be honest, it was always fairly evident that only a very few women showed much desire to undertake a preaching ministry. However, how can one be sure that the camel won't follow the camel's nose?

Actually in the pioneer churches the women were apt to be very much in charge, for there were far too few ministers being trained for each church to have a competent resident pastor. The church in a new community welcomed the itinerant evangelist, but it was most often the women who related the life of the church to the community and to the world. They sewed for the expectant mother, cared for the sick, comforted the bereaved, taught Sunday school, packed missionary boxes. The circuit-riding minister was welcome and presumably raised the spiritual sights of the community, but it was around the devoted women of the church that religion took root as a normative and integral part of American culture.[2]

Yet the first woman to enroll for a theological degree in the United States did so under a *nom de plume*, so not to disgrace her family.

The First Female Theologian in America

Theoretically, Boston University had always welcomed women to both its student body and faculty; the first woman to enroll in the School of Theology did so without much fanfare under the name of

Anna Oliver. Actually that was not her real name; her distinguished and scholarly family, and especially her brother, who was rector of an Episcopal church in Brooklyn, were so upset over her determination to study and work in the field of religion that she decided not to embarrass them with any possible notoriety. So she dropped the family name of Snowden and used, instead, the name of an aunt—Oliver. She had first enrolled at Oberlin, but found that, in spite of its faculty policy of welcoming all educationally qualified students, there was still much discrimination against women in the theological department. So she transferred to Boston, graduating in 1876. Among the number of distinguished scholars in the class, Anna Oliver was chosen to give the final oration on "Christian Enterprise: Its Field and Reward."

Problems related to Anna Oliver's ordination kept the Methodist General Conference busy for some time thereafter. The church where she began her preaching career seems to have been so heavily in debt that it had to be put up for sale. Anna Oliver bought it and continued to preach. However, technical difficulties developed. The church was no longer on the conference books, so she was not a conference member, and there was no one to plead her case for status as a Methodist minister. Again she was called to a Methodist church, this time in Passaic, New Jersey. This church had just acquired a handsome building and also, unfortunately, a handsome debt, creating a situation so embarrassing that something drastic had to be done. They called Anna Oliver, quite possibly with a view to saving money on the minister's salary. It is not clear what she did about the conference problem, but in the church she got along splendidly. She even brought in Amanda Smith, an outstanding Negro evangelist, as an assistant. This time the opposition came from the other churches in the city. How could you arrange for union services on special occasions with a church like that? Said one report: "Passaic is having a lively time; what with stirring up sinners and Christians on the one hand, and on the other two women in the pulpit, and one black, the buzzing grows apace." Anna Oliver lived and preached till 1893.[3]

Boston University, which likes to boast more than a little about its theological women, also tells the story of Miss Betsy Dow, first theological instructor at Newbury Biblical Institute. Newbury Seminary in Vermont had registered some female students as early as 1834. Betsy Dow was preceptress and teacher in the seminary in 1837 and 1838, while her father, John G. Dow, was the Methodist pastor in the area. Several young men from the seminary petitioned the faculty to form a class in "Mental Philosophy." The class was formed, but none of the men on the seminary staff had time to teach it. So the class was given to Miss Betsy Dow. At the end of the year, both the class and the teacher received special commendation from the Board of Visitors for the curriculum undertaken and the work accomplished. Miss Dow continued to teach the course as long as she was at the school. Newbury Seminary later became associated with Boston University School of Theology, the oldest and one of the most honored Methodist theological schools in America. They like to point to Betsy Dow as their first teacher of theology.[4]

The Methodist Church really had no objection to ordaining women for either a preaching or teaching ministry. However, they were always very realistic about the practical problems of placing women ministers, in light of an organizational structure in which married ministers were favored, ministers were assigned to their parishes, the family lived in a church parsonage and usually did not stay too long in one place. On practical grounds, women who studied theology could be ordained, but they could not be members of the annual conference; and appointments to the pulpit ministry came through the conference. One man explained that it might be all right for a church to decide that a woman preacher was all they could afford, but to have one appointed to serve them was another matter. So most theologically trained Methodist women went into teaching or missionary work.

C. G. Finney was quoted as saying that, "bringing out women as preachers and desiring to hear them preach is an aberration of amativeness."[5]

Women have traditionally had good treatment and fairly good status in the Presbyterian churches of America. This may well reflect the high status of the laity—men and women—in these churches. It seems difficult to believe that as late as 1877, however, a Mr. See was brought to trial in the New York presbytery for allowing two women to speak in his church. The charge was sustained and the preaching of women was forbidden in that presbytery. However, it was a period of controversy and trials in the Presbyterian churches, and few Presbyterian women will hold the incident against their denomination. It was some eighty years later that the two main branches of the Presbyterian Church gave full ordination to women. Meanwhile, the Presbyterian Church in the U.S.A. (now part of the United Presbyterian Church) made unusually good use of their women's abilities in boards and committees and commissions—from the local to the national level. Since 1930, women could be ordained as deacons or elders, in which capacity they might serve Communion. They kept working on the question of ordination to full ministerial standing.

The Disciples Church, which during the nineteenth century was gaining considerable strength in the Midwest, not only gave women full access to the pulpit but, more than most of the main-line churches, offered them places of real responsibility in the organizational staff structure of the church.

Until well into the twentieth century, persistent discussions about the place of women in the life and work of the Church could be hushed in most circles with the simple comment that, after all, very few women wanted to be ministers. This begged the question quite effectively because it was probably quite true. Moreover, among the persons most interested in having women assume their responsible position in the Church, there was some fear that the broader subject of women in religion might bog down in the opposition to ordination. Yet, to others, denial of ordination was symbolic of women's subordinate status in the Church. No man, these people said, had the right to stand in the way of a woman who felt a clear call to serve God— and such a call could be to the pulpit ministry. With the growing one-world consciousness of people everywhere, moreover, the whole question took on a new significance. Women were part of God's world-wide family, and as such should be acknowledged as first-class citizens of the Christian community.[6]

At the New Delhi meeting of the World Council of Churches in 1961, there was an attempt to get the Faith and Order Commission to make a full-scale study of women's ordination. However, at the Montreal World Conference on Faith and Order in 1963—to which only one woman was a delegate (she was from England)—this question of ordination was tossed back to the churches for "real ecumenical dialogue." A survey of the "present status" was attached to the report and is reproduced (updated to 1966) as Appendix III of this volume.

The Big Breakthrough in Ordination

Meanwhile, the pressure for full ordination of women within the main-line churches of the United States was increasing. In 1950 the United States census had undertaken to ascertain just how many women were in the country's pulpits. These figures, the last official ones available, showed 6777 women in the United States listed as clergymen; of these, 5791 were ordained or licensed. It was admittedly impossible to tell what these figures meant, since most of these clergymen were in the smallest churches. Less than 2900 were pastors of local churches.

Only ten per cent of these were in churches affiliated with the National Council of Churches, which includes almost all the larger denominations. Some sixty-three religious bodies said they ordained women; seventy-seven ordained or licensed.

Benson Landis, in *Religion in the United States*,[7] says that approximately eighty Protestant bodies now ordain women, but that not over four per cent of all ordained ministers are women. Most of these are working in the field of religious education or other teaching assignments, or in mission work. *Very* few are senior pastors.

The big breakthrough in ordination came in 1956, when the Methodist Church, which had formerly ordained women on a restricted basis as to placement, granted them full clergy rights, and the United Presbyterian Church authorized the ordination of women to the full ministry of the Church.

The conservative faction of the Methodists had held out to the very last. When it became obvious at their 1956 General Conference that the resolution was going to pass, the conservatives tried first to get it restricted to unmarried women and widows. This lost, and so did a minority motion to keep the *status quo*. The question was put, there was a vote by a show of hands, and suddenly the long campaign was history. The goodly number of Methodist women already ordained now automatically had full clergy rights; so would all women ordained in the future by the Methodist Church.

Since 1953 the Presbyterian Church, U.S.A., urged on by Dr. Robert Speer, had been "studying" the matter of ordination. One woman remarked at the 1955 assembly that the ladies had been "studied" quite long enough and called for action. When put to a vote, the "overture" on ordination was approved and sent to the presbyteries, who approved it by far more than the required two thirds. In 1956, the General Assembly incorporated it in the constitution as an appropriate way of celebrating the denomination's 250th anniversary. The Southern Presbyterians followed their lead in 1964; the first person they ordained was a grandmother, who had put in almost a lifetime of service to her church.

Controversy among Episcopalians and Lutherans

Meanwhile, the competent women of the Episcopal Church could look on, and perhaps in private grind their teeth a bit in frustration. Strangely enough, it was not the clergy, but the laity, and not the men, but the women themselves who apparently defeated every effort to give them a vote at least in their own vestries. They could find comfort, however, in the fact that the cream of appointments in the interdenominational offices so often went to Episcopal women. Leila Anderson and Cynthia Wedel, both very competent Episcopalians, were successive appointees to the top-rank staff positions opened up to women at the National Council of Churches.

In California much attention centered during 1965 on the proposed ordination of Sister Phyllis Edwards to the position of "perpetual deacon." Bishop James Pike's decision to ordain the forty-eight-year-old widow and grandmother, with good theological training and many years of church experience, to this position caused what one newspaper described as a "semantic tempest in a theological teapot." A recent ruling of the Episcopal Church permits ordination to the office of perpetual deacon, a position ranking as "clergy." However, after the ordination of Deaconess Edwards was scheduled, it was suddenly postponed, presumably to clear up some technical questions which would be discussed at a later date by the House of Bishops, due to meet in September 1965 at Glacier National Park. At that time it was suggested that Bishop Pike should *not* ordain Sister Phyllis at this time. About the same time, the appointment of Sister Phyllis to begin work as deaconess in charge of the Church House for Deaconesses at Evanston, Illinois, was canceled, reportedly on the grounds that she had become "controversial." Said Bishop Pike, in a heated official statement on the whole matter, "This [the fact that she is 'controversial'] should add to her qualifications to be grafted into the Apostolic Succession; so were the Apostles and their—and our—Lord." Sister Phyllis had recently taken part in anti-segregation demonstrations, but this was not mentioned specifically as a cause for canceling her appointment to the Evanston position. After much controversy, she was finally ordained to the "fourth order of the ministry." *Pacific Churchman* quoted Bishop Pike as saying that this recognition represented "but a little step forward" in the recognition of women "as persons" by the Church.

Lutheran women in the United States have for a long time had their eyes on Scandinavia, where the women are at long last, with state approval, winning the struggle for ordination. The Lutheran Church in most Scandinavian countries is the state church, and the state feels it needs to use theologically trained women to fill the need for new pastors. Not all the bishops agree, but it seems the antagonism to women in the pulpit of Sweden lessened considerably when it was proposed that any pastor who would refuse to ordain a woman might not be appointed as a bishop. In April 1960, three women were solemnly ordained as ministers in Sweden's Lutheran Church. One of the most colorful ceremonies was the ordination of Dr. Margit Sahlin, forty-six, theological graduate of Uppsala University and already, without benefit of her church's ordination, a member of the Central Committee of the World Council of Churches, a high ecclesiastical honor attained by very few women of any denomination. The ordination ceremony was performed by Archbishop Hultgren, assisted by four priests. But some Swedish Lutheran pastors went so far as to suggest that ordained women should be put under a sort of boycott, on the grounds that their acceptance would constitute a serious threat to mutual acceptance of each other's priests by the Church of Sweden and the Church of England. In Norway, when some of the parishioners objected to the appointment of Mrs. Ingrid Bjerkas as the first Lutheran pastor of that country, she was given a retired male pastor as an assistant, to take care of any parishioners who felt that only a man could be a "proper" priest.

One Lutheran objection to women's ordination heard in certain branches of the Lutheran Church in the United States is that, if ordained as pastors, women would have authority over men. This, it seems, must not be.

Meanwhile, though the Baptist and Congregational (now United Church of Christ) churches of the United States have never denied ordination to women, only in New England are there many women serving in parishes. Some of these are serving multiple parishes with considerable distinction. The Reverend Margaret Henrichsen's book, *Seven Steeples*, gives an authentic picture of one woman minister's experience.[8]

Missionaries, Social Workers, Teachers

In 1948, main-line Protestant churches in the United States had some 600 women representing them as foreign missionaries. Changing patterns in the missionary field make more recent figures very hard to get. Among the 600, medical and nursing degrees were far more common than B.D.'s.

In religious education the churches have seemed to find women indispensable, but they work mostly on a volunteer basis. Most of the top-level executive and planning positions—denominational and interdenominational—are in the hands of ordained men. Larger churches do often employ a woman with the degree of M.R.E.—Master of Religious Education. Too often they keep her very busy with chores, to which the relation to religion is purely incidental.

Social service work attracts many religion-minded women, but they tend to take their professional training and placement through secular channels. The Methodists, Mennonites, and Episcopalians have made serious efforts to revive deaconess work as a genuine religious calling, but professionally the trained women seem to find that government service offers more opportunity for accomplishment and more enriching contacts with professional colleagues.

In 1963 the *Christian Century*[9] asked readers to send them names of women theologians who deserved to be heard on college campuses. The list of sixty which they published showed a wide range of church-related occupations, but very few were "theologians" in the traditional sense of the word. A good many women, like Margaret Frakes, one of the *Christian Century* editors, are finding ways to serve the Church through a writing rather than a speaking ministry, and some have been ordained specifically for such a ministry.

Seminary teaching or the pulpit ministry are, however, the two doors which most often lead to denominational or interdenominational appointments, and hence to the important policy-making positions in the Church at national or world levels. Women, however competent, seldom travel this road.

The Important Role of Nuns

Within the Roman Catholic Church the idea of a female bishop or Pope is unthinkable. However, the restrictions under which women within the institutions of the Catholic Church carry on their work have certainly been vastly overestimated by most Protestants. The various women's orders are still very important, and within these orders the women have unusually good opportunity to develop special talents for religion, administration, the arts and professions, though they may not have the temporal power some did in earlier ages. A career in religion is a definite possibility for the Roman Catholic girl.[10]

The *National Catholic Almanac* (Doubleday, 1966, p. 383) gives the world figure of 1,049,060 for the number of Roman Catholic "Women Religious," not including those in Communist-dominated countries from which statistics are not available. It has been estimated by Catholic authorities that there are probably some 1,200,000 "Women Religious" in the world. The *Catholic Almanac* (p. 526) indicates 3,137 U. S. Catholic "sisters" working in overseas mission programs. Latourette says a hundred new Catholic orders for women were founded in the nineteenth century.

The late Pope Pius XII was apparently very interested in the question of women's role in the Church. Available from Catholic bookstores or the National Catholic Welfare Conference are his addresses on "The Greatness of Widowhood," and "Counsel to Teaching Sisters"; also the Encyclical Letter (1954) "On Holy Virginity." We quote from his address (1945) on "Women's Duties in Social and Political Life":

> The problem regarding women, both in its entirety as a whole and in all its many details, resolves itself into preserving and augmenting that dignity which woman has from God. For us, accordingly, it is not a problem that is merely juridical or economic, educational or biological, political or demographic—it is rather one which, in spite of its complexity, hinges entirely on the question of how to maintain and strengthen that dignity of women, especially today, in circumstances in which Providence has placed us. . . . In their personal dignity as children of God a man and woman are absolutely equal, as they are in relation to the happiness of heaven. . . . The two sexes, by the very qualities that distinguish them are mutually complementary to such an extent that their coordination makes itself felt in every phase of man's social life. . . . But where the two sexes, forgetful of that intimate harmony willed and established by God, give themselves up to perverted individualism where their mutual relations are governed by selfishness and covetousness, when they do not collaborate by mutual accord for the service of mankind . . . then the common good of human society, in the temporal as well as the spiritual order, is gravely compromised.

Though the Roman Catholic women have undoubtedly been giving considerable thought, all the while, to their responsible place in their Church and in the field of religion generally, the concrete evidence of increasing concern began to "make the news" somewhat precipitously.

St. Jean's International Alliance in the Catholic Church, meeting in 1963, officially requested that if the diaconate was to be restored, as proposed, as an official office of the Roman Catholic Church, that it be organized for women as well as for men (*Commonweal*, 12–20–63). Another issue of *Commonweal* (11–15–65) carried articles by two Roman Catholic laywomen, insisting that tradition is not insuperable and that discussion of women's ordination is inevitable.

It was a real milestone when room was found for a few women observers at the Vatican Council—three from the United States.

In the long run, more important may have been the invitations to the male Protestant observers, representing as it did a new spirit of rapprochement which quickly spread to the local communities. Springs of will to mutual understanding between the various faiths represented in the American culture began to bubble, at the local level, and strangely enough many of these were both coeducational and interfaith. Moreover, they often went deep into the heart of previous understandings and misunderstandings.

For a three-day regional conference on faith and order in San Francisco (March 1965), the Eastern Orthodox, Protestant, and Roman Catholic churches took joint responsibility. Catholic sisters had charge of the opening service of worship, which was the only session to which the general public was invited. It was in the nature of a hymn-sing. For it one of the sisters had selected hymns which appeared in the hymnals of various families of the Protestant faith and were also well known to many Roman Catholics. Singing was directed jointly by a Roman Catholic sister and a Presbyterian preacher, and someone remarked that as the voices of the men and women, laity and clergy, shook the rafters of the great auditorium, St. Paul's concept of oneness in Christ came a step nearer to comprehension. After that, the conference delegates moved on into depth discussion of "tradition" and "scripture" as sources of authority for the Church, with one of the liveliest study groups (mostly male Protestant pastors or seminary professors) challengingly led by a woman Roman Catholic Biblical professor. When a seminarian member of the group graduated in the spring from the fundamentalist seminary he was attending, Sister Mary Joseph was pleased to receive an invitation to his ordination.

The Conference of Major Religious Superiors of Women, representing 180,000 Roman Catholic nuns in the United States, met in Denver in the summer of 1965 and unanimously supported a resolution proposing that sisters have a voice in the Vatican Council deliberations that affect their lives. This proposal must go to the bishops of the United States, then to the Sacred Congregation of the Religious at Rome, then to the Vatican Council. Sister Mary Luke, the conference chairman, and a Vatican Council "auditor," speaking on behalf of 400 major superiors from forty-four states, said there is a serious concern on the part of the women religious that "women should have something to do with the regulations that bind them."[11]

Some time ago, apparently in an effort to demonstrate to the public that not all sisters are "sanctimonious," some Catholic public relations officers apparently decided that it was advisable to furnish newspapers with pictures of sisters umpiring baseball games, participating in folk-dance classes, or assisting the carpenter on church repairs. Undoubtedly the sisters can and on occasion must do all these things, but the "new image" was at least startling, and apparently not too well received, for it was of short duration. There is of course, a great difference between different orders, and even more difference between individuals within the orders. Women just never do fit well into stereotypes.

St. Jean's International Alliance of Catholic Women in 1964 and again in 1965 (this time with only one dissenting vote) affirmed a conviction that "should the Church in her wisdom and in her good time decide to extend to women the dignity of the priesthood, women would be eager and willing to respond." (*National Catholic Almanac,* 1966, p. 87.)

The Suffragan Bishop of Cologne has told Roman Catholic women that it is no longer sufficient just to affirm their equality with men. Better ways must be found, he said, for women to use their talents in the service of the Church and community—including even the teaching of theology at university level.

Cardinal Suenens, Archbishop of Malines-Brussels and Primate of Belgium, in *The Nun in the Modern World,*[12] has come out as a most effective champion of women's place in the Roman Catholic Church—undoubtedly both religious and laywomen will bless him for his understanding friendliness.

The Catholic editor, social worker, nurse, or teacher is very apt to have had at least some of her training under religious auspices and usually attends conferences from time to time and reads professional-religious publications, which keep her aware of the current Catholic viewpoint.

In 1956 the Catholic International Union for Social Service, meeting in Switzerland, addressed a plea to the U. N. Commission on the Status of Women, calling for more consideration of the problems of women in the underdeveloped countries, including more training in domestic science and more attention to supplying labor-saving devices to make women's household chores less burdensome. They asked for attention to proper drainage, electricity for household use, communal wash houses with modern equipment, and basic education for women in nutrition, community organization, and other areas. "There is no need," the conference said, "to stress the moral, social, cultural and economic value of the tasks of wives and mothers, who contribute to stability and progress in the life of the nation."[13]

One is tempted to speculate as to what the result might be if the Roman Catholic, and Protestant churchwomen could start discussing some of the particularly "difficult" questions with which men of the churches are struggling in these days of good will. Perhaps they could approach these "problems" with the avowed purpose of trying to understand each other's points of view rather than with the determination of trying to "convince" each other!

It has been the writer's privilege, on several occasions, to serve on committees or work in groups on which there were representative women of both these major faiths. We have valued this fellowship and the opportunity to speak in unison to bring needed common religious viewpoints into secular situations or programs. Often the degree of mutual confidence has seemed to surprise our secular colleagues. When our conference or committee tasks have been completed, we have often parted with a mutual blessing and a wrench in our hearts, that the witness of religion should be so divided in the world, yet with full appreciation of the practical problems involved in achieving more effective ongoing relationships.

Eastern Orthodox churches emphasize the family concept of the Church, and the women have not been very vocal about any independent role. Recent admission of Orthodox churches to ecumenical groups both nationally and internationally means that the churches that ordain women are in a smaller numerical minority than previously. However, women of the "free" churches are not unmindful of the fact that, so far as the participation of the average woman in the work of the Church is concerned, the deaconess pattern, as practiced in the Episcopal and Lutheran churches, or the Eastern Orthodox pattern which separates the function of the priest and the lay theologian, without downgrading either, suggest avenues for the women of the churches to explore together.

The Jewish Sisterhoods

Vera Weismann, in the Universal Jewish Encyclopaedia, stresses[14] that Jewish women are under the same obligations of the law as men are, except that "since woman was burdened with numerous household duties, she was exempted from the religious obligations for the performance of which a definite time was set . . . and from such other obligations as studying the Torah. . . ." Some women, however, did become Torah scholars. Beruiah is quoted with deference in the Talmud. There were even Torah teachers (separated by a curtain from their pupils). Special translations of the Torah into the vernacular were made for women.

There seems almost no probability that the Conservative or Orthodox branches of Judaism will consider the possibilities of women rabbis in the near future. However, in 1961 the National Federation of Temple Sisterhoods, holding a biennial assembly in Washington, D.C., in conjunction with the Assembly of the Union of American Hebrew Congregations, heard their chief executive urge Reform Judaism to consider at their next assembly the acceptance of Jewish women as candidates for the rabbinate. Miss Jane Evans, the executive secretary of the sisterhoods, was quoted in the U.P.I. news service release as saying that "the time has come for the Sisterhoods to make a definite stand." She asked that the reform seminaries "ordain women as rabbis when they are properly qualified and upon completion of the identical course of study with men."[15]

Chapter 19

CHURCHWOMEN TODAY

From a Folder Crammed with Material about Some of
the Things Women in Religion Are Doing
in the Second Half of the Twentieth Century

These items do not refer to work women are doing specifically *in* their churches, nor specifically *for* their churches, and surely not *outside* their churches (if by that we imply any suggestion that even mild competition to the churches is involved). The items mentioned are rather a small selection of things women are doing *on behalf of* their churches and with full church approval. They seem to indicate that women are willing to lose themselves and their special interests in order that all God's children, together, may find the way a little nearer to their Father's house.

Let us glance briefly at just a few of the activities that are going on across the country, in this spirit, as women's role in religion begins to round out the twentieth century:

Item: In hospitals and institutions thousands of women recruited through their churches are acting as volunteers to bring friendly and needed services to the sick, the physically and mentally handicapped, to the aged and infirm, or to children in trouble, underprivileged, abandoned, orphaned. The extent of this sort of service is incalculable; its value to those who give and to those who receive cannot be put into figures or words, and its scope in service, supplies, love, and trust, freely given and received, can hardly be comprehended. Few churchwomen are not involved one way or another through their gifts of time, talents, and money; but we seldom stop to think of the whole operation in its aggregate.

Item: WICS (Women in Community Service) was incorporated in 1964 by members of the National Council of Catholic Women, National Council of Jewish Women, National Council of Negro Women, and

United Church Women. Working in teams, WICS volunteers seek out girls who would profit from training outside their homes for enrollment in Job Corps residential centers. They help those selected for Job Corps training to find jobs after graduation, and help those not selected to make better adjustment to their ongoing life situations.

Item: Several social-action magazines of various denominations have competent and courageous women editors.

Item: A civil rights worker reports that southern churchwomen, individually and as groups, are a source of main support.

Item: In the Morningside Heights area of New York City, which includes an unusual variety of races, a very wide range of economic levels, institutional and apartment living, and such institutional fortresses as Columbia University, Union and Jewish Theological Seminaries, and various schools, homes, and hospitals, a few churchwomen tackled head on the job of moving toward a "mingling" of the peoples in the neighborhood, setting up various gatherings designed to "establish relationships, deepen knowledge and understanding of each other, and increase readiness to work collectively." Meetings to which clergy and laity were invited have been held in Greek Orthodox, Protestant, and Roman Catholic churches, and in the seminaries.

Item: Thousands of churchwomen are among those working with all their time and talents in church-related peace movements.

Item: Churches in many parts of the country have been recruiting retired teachers from their congregations to participate in voluntary tutoring programs, to help children having difficulties at school, or to supervise study halls which the churches set up in their own buildings to give children of crowded areas a place for quiet study. Churchwomen have worked enthusiastically in the pre-school "Head Start" programs, readying underprivileged children for their first days of school experience.

Item: American churchwomen were among the thirty Roman Catholic, Eastern Orthodox, and Protestants who attended a conference in Rome in October 1965. The women met under the joint auspices of the World Council of Churches, the Vatican Secretariat for Promoting Christian Unity, and the Permanent Committee for International Congresses of the Lay Apostolate. They discussed such matters as the role of women in the world and church of tomorrow, concern for family life, changes in women's status, and the problems of communication between people; also what could be done about the fact that many men of the Church retain an outmoded idea of women's role in society.

Item: At the Church Center for the United Nations during the three fall months of 1965, 743 women attended one- to three-day briefing sessions on the work of the U.N. and the churchwoman's responsibility in this field. Among these were interfaith groups from other states; also seventy-eight state leaders of United Church Women, representing all states, and attending a yearly meeting in New York City. They heard U.N. officials and international affairs leaders from the church organizations speak and visited the U.N. headquarters. Many more groups came for an hour's briefing by staff personnel, before going on their own to visit the U.N. and returning home to tell the U.N. story in their own churches and communities. The Church Center at the U.N. is itself a hope of long standing brought to reality largely by the interest, generosity, and persistence sparked originally by one Methodist churchwoman.

Item: Church and Labor Management has been the assignment of a woman staff member of the National Council of Churches who came from a background of government and political science and is now retiring after eighteen years of distinguished service. She recently edited the official report of the Fourth National Study Conference on the Church and Economic Life, which she titled "The World that Won't Hold Still."

Item: Director of Intergroup Activities at the Jewish Theological Seminary of America (N.Y.C.) is a woman who is also director of the Institute for Religious and Social Studies, a graduate school for religious teachers and clergymen of all faiths (founded by the seminary in 1938); and the Conference on Science, Philosophy and Religion (founded 1940), of which she is executive vice-president.

Item: Women have recently been appointed to top staff positions in the Methodist Church (Board of Missions—their largest board); the Episcopal Church (Religious Education); The United Presbyterian Church in the U.S.A. (Ecumenical Missions and Relations); United Church of Christ (Lay Life and Work).

Churchwomen in the second half of the twentieth century are definitely in orbit. They are not just on the move. They travel various paths, at various speeds, but they know their direction and, above all,

their orientation. They have not solved all their problems, nor overcome all the opposition, but there no longer seems much probability
that they will, in the long run, be overcome by it. And somehow they
know that most men, in their hearts, are glad of it. A person you can
consistently dominate is neither good for you nor very much fun.

In the mid-twentieth century theologians began to talk insistingly
about the renewal and rebirth of the Church; this involved also a re-
appraisal of the role and responsibility of the laity. Most of what they
said was no surprise to the women so far as program and its social application were concerned. However, women were rather suddenly aware
of their own shortcomings in the field of theology. Certainly they may
have had a theology of their own, and quite a valid one, but they had
not bothered to learn to communicate in the traditional theological
terms of the Church. Maybe, some felt, if they had spent more time
worrying over learning to communicate on matters of religion, their
ideas as to religion's practical application would have been better received. Maybe they had been too impatient with the deliberative side
of the Church's existence. Perhaps by excessive activism they had given
the slower-moving male the impression that they were far less responsible than they really were. Maybe the men were no more off the
beam in equating the volatile, sensitive side of women's nature with
flightiness than the women were mistaken in labeling the men's more
deliberative attitude callousness. Maybe, in fact, women's own sense of
slight in the work of the Church, however understandable, had nevertheless been at least as much of a sin as the men's superior attitude had
been. Maybe, indeed, God had a purpose in making people of different sizes, shapes, complexions, eye sets, sexes. And maybe, since we
were all his handiwork, we should stop criticizing each other, bickering
about each other's shortcomings, hugging our own faults and building
them—in our own minds—into virtues.

Maybe it was time for all God's children to get to work, give each
other a helping hand, and start the assigned task of co-operating in the
building of God's Kingdom on earth.

The Social Revolution

To what extent women's new look at their place in the Church and
the churches tied in with the social revolution of the times is impossible
to say. To what extent women's improved status in secular society made
her more ready and psychologically more willing to assume a place of

greater responsibility in the Church, and to what extent it made the Church more ready and willing to accept her, is really immaterial. There she is. And things are happening.

In the exciting new world in which we live, one of the fundamental insights of the Hebrew-Christian faith is man's and woman's need for each other. God apparently never intended man (the male reflection of his image) or woman (the female reflection) to undertake exclusive responsibility for the human race. Men need women; women need men—mentally and spiritually as well as physically. They both— separately and together—need religion, and institutionalized religion needs to recover the concept of the *person*—mankind, male and female —whom it tells us God created in his own image and to whom he gave responsibility for the created world.

It seems clear that men and women together stand at a turning point. The road ahead in religion, as in other phases of their lives, promises to be very different from the one down which we have been traveling.

The borders of the home, for which women traditionally assumed a major responsibility, are no longer the four walls of the house and the fences of the adjoining enclosures. In a day of free-ranging teen-agers, independent-living seniors, and globally mobile populations in general, a woman's concern for even her immediate family relates itself to their bewildering round of daily activities and situations completely different from those which her grandmother had to worry about; it reaches out to parts of the world which, in even her parents' generation, only the most venturesome members of the family might ever visit.

Woman in orbit, as she is today, needs more than ever the guiding, co-ordinating, motivating, and integrating influence of a religion which she understands and loves. She needs the light of a religion upon whose love and truth she can depend, not only as it affects her own life but especially as it will affect her children and her grandchildren, and the world's children and grandchildren. She has a right to—she *must*— examine and help to revise and redefine the socio-religious heritage which she will pass on to her sons as well as her daughters.

In this twentieth century, skills and attitudes developed through thousands of years are suddenly giving way to an economy of automation that involves men and women alike in the need for new technical skills and new work patterns. In these new patterns of life, the wise use of leisure and the building of sound human relationships will take on wholly new importance. Both the restraining power and the motivating power of religion will be more important factors than ever, if mankind is to maintain his balance and sanity and learn to put the pieces of this new age together into a pattern of realized world civilization.

Religion must retain and strengthen its championship of moral and ethical imperatives, and stretch its vision toward the future to balance its concern over traditions of the past. It must come out of the compartments in which it has come to feel too comfortably at home, and be prepared to throw its light on every aspect of human life, to help the human race achieve new patterns of viable existence. If organized religion rises to the present challenge, the centuries ahead may yet turn out to be something more nearly what the Lord had in mind when he took the trouble to create a world and—hopefully—a responsible human race—not two divided and bickering sexes.

As the light of truth permeates the new order which lies ahead of us, we shall all find ourselves called upon to give up cherished misconceptions and prejudices. When we recognize them, we might as well give them up precipitously and with good grace. There is no time for prejudice in any area to wear out gradually and die a natural death. Organized religion simply cannot carry on its increasingly responsible role in the new structure of the world, if it dissipates its strength in intramural power struggles.

One of the best present approaches to the whole question of women in religion is a consideration of diverse ministries, both lay and clerical. Alden D. Kelley, in *People of God*,[1] makes the point that distinction between clergy and laity or between ministries of men and women are out of order if we believe, as we claim, in the priesthood of all believers. Not all men and not all women are at home in the kitchen. Not all women and not all men are effective in the pulpit. Holding that "the Church is ministry," Dr. Kelley counsels a "discreet agnosticism" as to "accepted" ideas about women and their appropriate roles.

Emil Brunner expresses much the same idea: "It is absolutely impossible to put down in black and white as a universal rule, which spheres of activity 'belong' to women and which do not. This can only become clear through experience, and for experience, first of all, the field must be thrown open."[2] Still, experience might get a helping hand at this juncture from increasing free and open discussion—through official channels and for the record. Our "women in orbit" are in a good position to be taken quite seriously.

The ecumenical movement has a fine formula for deliberations between the various branches of the Church. Representatives are committed to "speak the truth in love" to one another. At the same time it seeks, ideally, to "do together whatever things its member churches do not feel they must, for a valid reason, do separately."

The ecumenical movement does not, of course, always live up to these ideals. Yet such stated ideals do help. Men and women, seeking to live up to the same ideals, or even to hold some preliminary discussions based upon them, would have a long history of tensions and misgivings to live down; but we cannot start any sooner than *now*. These proven formulas might be excellent ones upon which to proceed.

The spirit of love and mutuality, the global outlook, the sense of social justice, empathy and understanding are traits with which both science and everyday observation tell us women are richly endowed. They express these qualities in their everyday life and relationships. They hope and expect increasingly to have the opportunity to express these same convictions through the creeds and councils of the Church. They will work loyally, as they have in other fields of more active religious expression, to be worthy of new responsibilities.

Men and women have no cause to blame each other for the fact that religion has never achieved its full potential in the lives of the human race. Nor is it seemly for them to take to themselves—as male or female—credit for such progress as we have made. The appropriate action would seem to be a sincere handshake and a very sincere *mea culpa* in unison.[3]

Chapter 20

TOWARD A FULL PARTNERSHIP

Many circumstances in the twentieth century have contributed to help woman find her place—volunteer or professional—in the field of religion. The same factors have also often prompted men and religious institutions to a new and different appreciation of women's potential in organized religion and its mission to the world.

1. Archaeology and the new light which its findings are throwing upon history and pre-history (for the casual reader as well as the serious student) show up the fallacy of the persistent myth that woman has always been and always will be an inferior sex. Whether or not there were primitive matriarchies (and findings seem to indicate there were), there have certainly been periods when women were accepted as persons and valued for their intrinsic worth.

2. Genetics has proved the fallacy of classifying most traits as linked with one sex or the other. An aptitude for religion (like an aptitude for music, for instance) involves specific combinations of various genes, but it is most improbable that such an aptitude could in any way be related to one sex or the other.

3. Scholarly Biblical study and interpretation—now available to clergy and laity alike—make any reference to the Old Testament creation stories as proof of women's innate inferiority seem little short of sacrilegious. Most New Testament scholars, moreover, now agree that Paul has been misinterpreted and maligned in portraying him as holding women in low esteem. (See ch. 3 above.) Recent interest in church history reveals women's place of equality in the primitive church.

4. Women's record in today's economic world, politics, education, and other professions, as well as the new understanding of her biological inheritance, has done a great deal to bolster her own self-confidence, which must finally carry over into the field of theology. She can no longer honestly dodge serious study of religion on the grounds that it is beyond or foreign to her ability, to comprehend its true and full meaning for individual or communal life.

5. The work market for the present day and the diversity of religious programs afford women increasing opportunities in religion as in other fields. The microphone removes one admitted handicap (the question of some women's ability to be heard when speaking in public). For many kinds of church-related work, woman has long since demonstrated her ability by the way she has handled positions in parallel secular fields.

6. Increasing theological emphasis on the ethic of personal and social responsibility in most major religions has brought home to women that frequently they tend to accept a role of "influencing" others (especially husbands and sons, but sometimes work colleagues, too) instead of standing up and being counted, and working, themselves, for the thing in which they believe. The technique of "influence" has been described as "degrading" to both men and women. "Petticoat rule" (however cute it may seem in fiction) has no place in a healthy community— least of all in religion. The present emphasis on responsible ethics shows it up for what it is.

Such a list as this could be indefinitely extended, but adds up to one finding: As perhaps never before, we have sound facts and statistics— not theories, rumors, and prejudices—about women's ability to give more than lackey service in the field of religion. Women, and increasingly men also, are showing a willingness to face facts and act upon them. Gradually, too, the institutions of religion are accepting the facts and adjusting to them; and, so far, there has been no loud cry to turn back the clock.

It will be some time before women are full partners in the religious life of the world, but their progress toward that status will undoubtedly be a major chapter in the history of religion in the twentieth century.

Lest woman become so encumbered again in the future with prejudice, it seems desirable that biology, psychology, sociology, economics, ecclesiology, and history should all be explored to discover by what strange turns in the road women arrived at their present position. More important, however, would be the willingness of men and women to sit down together and plan for the future, facing candidly all the problems of their relationships in society. The attitude of men must not be grudging, women's attitude not greedy or vengeful. There is no place for recriminations or quarreling; just planning how best to get on together to what needs doing in an age of automation and cybernation, biological explosion and elongation of human life, new leisure that may be creative or destructive of human values, the ethics of movement from moral authoritarianism to responsible freedom, choice between a war of annihilation and finding a road to peace and justice for all peoples.

In this complex and demanding culture, mankind is simply not going to be able to afford the luxury of either men or women retiring into, or being relegated to, the role of observer.

The Female Skills and Gifts

From centuries of experience, women have learned and passed on to their daughters the skills involved in raising a family of diverse ages, talents, and sexes, so that all remain individuals, yet are even more important as individuals because they are members of the family. Today women are challenged to carry these same insights into the fields of community education, national economics, politics, international relations. In our newly global relationships this is the kind of wisdom the nations of the world need most: empathy, mutuality, cohesion, patience, faith; and the ability to get people to work together creatively.

These are the areas of woman's strength, and she must not disparage God's handiwork by belittling her own present potential or allowing others to do so. Rather, she must find ways to make her special gifts available to the modern mechanically oriented world from which, without her contribution, the human virtues may be crowded into woefully short supply. Without her tempering contribution, mankind as a whole may not only be in serious danger of carelessly or recklessly blowing up the globe on which we live, but by repudiating the half of our nature represented by what we usually think of as the female virtues, we shall all be in increasing danger of becoming less and less the full spiritual image of our Creator.

Whether woman's gifts, which we especially need for these days of our lives, come to her through the genetic or cultural inheritance is not the question here. That question and its final answer will continue to be discussed for many years to come, as science explores the evidence and gives us new data. Meanwhile, we accept woman as she is—as her genetic inheritance and cultural environment have made her—trying only to put aside the prejudices, restrictions, taboos, misinformation, propaganda in the guise of history, jealousies inspired by personal ambitions of both men and her fellow women, and other similar and useless burdens that have made the road difficult in the past.

Shared Plans and Responsibilities

This is a book of record, not of prophecy. Just what the record shows, and just what is indicated as to women's role in the future of religion, each reader must judge on the basis of the evidence, which we hope will be augmented by a great deal of competent, objective research in what has been a neglected (at times suppressed or even distorted) field of inquiry. We have tried to collect and report the most accurate available evidence, in compassable space. It is hoped that experts in various fields will augment and supplement and when necessary correct the record as we have found it.

We hope that this work has at least indicated past reasonable doubt that woman, no less than man, may have an aptitude for religion. We also hope that this too brief record of women's accomplishments in this field, through the ages, will encourage present-day women in the churches seriously to appraise their own attitudes and activities to be sure they are giving the best they have to offer.

It is hoped, also, that as the swing of the pendulum brings woman to a perhaps all-time high level of importance in her economic and community relations, she will increasingly see (and be justified in seeing) the Church itself as custodian of many of the values which to her are of utmost importance.

It is hoped that the Church will find the way to offer her opportunity —more than it has in the past—worthily to expend her enthusiasm, creative energy, and religious motivation, through the channels of established religion. Let her religious activity overflow from the Church to permeate the whole world, not be drained off from the Church into secular channels because the Church does not give her room to operate or any voice in formulating the projects she is to carry out.

The Church, and the world the Church serves, needs more than ever the very gifts woman is always eager to offer, and today, especially, her world-mindedness and devotion to the causes of peace and justice. It needs these even more than it needs her practical services. Our present pattern of civilization forces us to consideration of priorities. Woman must give religion the *best* she has to offer.

Woman has never been at her best in situations of war and violence, or where she was trying to dominate someone else. Her tools have been —from her physical and sociological background—those of vision and skill, not force. Interpersonal understanding, developed through family responsibilities, not competition for power and prestige, have been her strength. Increasingly, it may be up to her to keep alive the personal, human factors in a world of mechanics and automation, and to see that civil rights become a way of life, not just entries on the statute books.

Women—all women—must have the courage and self-respect to appreciate and use the special talents with which the Lord has seen fit to endow them, whoever else does or does not think that these talents amount to much. Woman must not underestimate herself or accept any standards that tend to downgrade her God-given abilities in her own eyes. *She must never be tempted to sell herself short.*

Together men and women reflect the Creator-God, and together, under the guidance of the Holy Spirit, there is work for them to do in the world. There is no room for competitive jealousies. For either sex to downgrade the other in or out of the Church is to downgrade half of one's self, and to disparage an important part of God's creation. The people of the Church, especially, must understand this and set an example for the world. And women, who pride themselves on their world-mindedness and devotion to the ecumenical ideal, will try to help men to understand and accept women as full working partners, with shared ideals and much to contribute.

Moreover, the woman must be ready and willing—to the full extent that she *is* accepted on this basis—to make a worthy contribution and not, under guise of meekness and docility, dodge the demands of ecclesiastical responsibility and theological competence.

Men and women of good will must discover new patterns under which they can face the future as friends and co-workers! Surely it is a most important assignment of religion to help them find the way.

Appendix I

WOMEN IN FOUR MAJOR FAITHS OF THE WORLD

A survey of women's part in most major religions clearly indicated that in their origins, or in the ideas of their founders, women almost invariably held an honorable position. The downgrading of that position came in later years as a result of cultural conflicts, power struggles between rival schools for leadership, or wars of conquest waged in the name of religion. We shall touch very briefly on the place of women in Hinduism, Buddhism, the Confucian philosophy, and Islam, suggesting sources which those interested may find starting points for further study. In no case should this material be taken as an evaluation of the particular faith as a whole, or of its cultural impact on society as a whole. We have tried to hold rather strictly to our subject of *Women* in Religion.

Women in Hinduism

Hinduism has been a great religio-cultural dialectic stretching over the centuries of Indian history, vacillating between a fantastic pantheism and a trend toward ethical monotheism. There are the amiable and noble goddesses of the Vedas, and there are the Laws of Manu of the Brahmans, insultingly repressive to women. There is the personal god Vishnu, and his earthly counterpart Krishna; there is also dark Sivaism represented by the goddess Sakti, who appreciates sex excesses. The world is confusingly peopled by nature gods—Varuna (sky), Angi (fire), Surya (sun); also by the popular favorite, Lakshimy, goddess of luck. How can one know what Hinduism really is? And how can we discover the place of woman in Hinduism or evaluate the effect it has had, as a religion, on her place in the Hindu community?

We are not going to presume to try to bring order out of this divine chaos,[1] but only to indicate the picture of women we get from the basic religious documents from successive periods of India's history.

Dharma, the Indian term for Hinduism, means law, yet Hinduism as such has no code or creed. However, the *Vedas*, the *Brahmanas*, the *Upanishads*, the *Laws of Manu*, the *Puranas*, the great epics of the *Mahabharata* and the *Bhagavad-Gita*, and the *Ramayana*, supply a vast literature, from which we shall try to extract some knowledge of women's role in Hinduism.

Dr. Mildreth Worth Pinkham, while living and studying in India, became convinced that these sacred Scriptures have been a determining influence in the social status of Hindu women.[2] Whatever the future of India may be, she is convinced that it will rest on indigenous Hindu culture, and that the place of women in that culture will be significant.[3] Through lack of education in the past, and because reading their own Scriptures was forbidden them, it was possible to make them believe subjugation was the role actually assigned to them by their religion.

The earliest Indian literature known is the charming *Rig-Veda*, usually dated about 1500 B.C., though some scholars place parts of it as early as 2400 B.C. These *Vedas* were the songs of the Aryans, who entered India from an older civilization to the north and gradually absorbed the Dasyu, or original inhabitants of the Punjab.[4] The Aryans were pastoral and agricultural. They had developed a joint family system, in which the women were well protected; their place was secure and honorable, their responsibilities defined. The Aryans—men and women—seem to have drifted into the Punjab as peaceable settlers rather than "invaders."

Among the Aryans, monogamy was the rule, polygamy the exception, exogamy (intermarriage between clans) the custom. There is no reference to child marriages.[5] There is evidence that in the land from which they came a so-called matriarchate had prevailed, with descent reckoned by mothers—a *Mutterrecht*, as found in the pre-Aryan Etruscans, Picts, and Iberians.

As the immigrants settled in the Punjab, the head of the clan, after death, became its protector and promoter of fertility. The oldest and wisest men and women were priests. Father Sky and the Devas (analogous to human society) may be the center of worship, but the whole world is populated with divine powers and phenomena and qualities. Some are male, some female. There is mention of former times when there were priestly families and perhaps a tendency to ethical monotheism. In these Indo-Iranian days, Varuna was similar in some respects to the Persian Ahura Mazdah. Later there was division of labor between the gods and goddesses, but they still lived together fairly harmoniously except for Indra, who after all was a weather god and understandably unpredictable.

The gods are not strictly anthropomorphic, however. Qualities, rather than personalities, are appreciated. Perhaps mankind was taking a forward step in abstract thinking. A goddess may be called a father, and a masculine deity may be called mother. Some goddesses seem feminine by nature—Usas (dawn) and Prithivi (earth) and Ratri (night). Some goddesses personify such qualities as plenty, nourishment, abundance. Some are "just wives of gods."

One of the most interesting deities is Adita, who personifies "boundless freedom"; she can free from sin and suffering those who worship her; she is the mother of the world, or of "common nature"; she is unlimited light and space, yet can also be identified with the unlimited abundance of the earth. Poets praise her without stint, adore her, seek her protection:

> Adita is the sun and air's mid-region.
> Adita is the father, son and mother.
> Adita all the gods and the five Nations.
> We call for help the Queen of Law and Order
> Great Mother of all those whose word is righteous.
> Far-spread, unwasting, strong in her dominion——
> Adita wisely leading, well protecting!
> Let us bring hither, in pursuit of riches,
> Adita, with our word the mighty Mother,
> Her in whose lap the spacious air is lying.
> May she afford us triply guarding shelter!

If, as some think, the Vedic religion was decadent monotheism, Adita may well have been the previous great mother-goddess.

Of Prithivi, earth goddess, they sing:

> Kind, ever gracious be the earth we tread on,
> The firm earth, Prithivi.
> Borne up by order, mother of plants and herbs,
> The all-producer.

There are a number of hymns to Prithivi in connection with Dyaus, the heaven-god, but not a single one to Dyaus alone.

Of special interest is the tall goddess Vac, who represents speech, "found in the worlds from earliest generations." She is the creative word, the means of communication between the gods and men; she it is who brought forth heaven, father of all things, and who holds together all existence.

There are goddesses of prayer and worship, devotion, bounty, welfare and prosperity, pleasantness and gladness, faith, good gifts, lengthened days, children, welfare for the people. Goddesses are teachers, holy ones, worthy of honor, lofty, benevolent, lovely.

Nor does this appreciation of the feminine sex seem to have been reserved for goddesses only. Good home, family, husband and wife relationships are presumed and extolled. Monogamy is preferable to polygamy:

> Between both poles the car-horse goes, pressed closely,
> As in his dwelling moves the double-wedded.

Husband and wife worship together:

> With gifts of sacrificial meal and wealth,
> They satisfy the claim of love,
> And pay due honor to the gods.

They share:

> Whate'er thy wife away from thee makes ready,
> Or what apart from thee thy husband,
> Combine it all! Let it be yours in common
> While you produce one world with joint endeavor.

The women have responsibility for rearing the family, but the men have parallel family responsibilities; one is to be sure good husbands are found for daughters and sisters—an important piece of family business. Mutual assent to the marriage is required.

A bridegroom says:

> I take thy hand in mine for happy fortune
> That thou may'st reach old age with me thy husband
> [The gods] have given thee to be my household's
> mistress.

Or they might say this charm together:

> Sweet are the glances of our eyes.
> Within thy bosom harbor me——
> One spirit dwells within us both.

In the worship service, which is a family custom, it is the woman who prepares the vessels for the offering, and husband and wife come to the altar together.

Occasionally, of course, someone will remark that "hearts of hyenas are the hearts of women," or make some similar disparaging observation, but it takes all kinds to make up any world.

Women seem to have followed independent vocations; there is mention of the female cane-splitter, worker in thorns, laundress, dealer in love charms, ointment manufacturer, dyer, scabbard maker.

Laying herself down beside her dead husband—thus expressing physically her desire to die with him—was appropriate behavior for a widow. But her friends were expected to dissuade her, and she lived to marry again—perhaps her husband's brother.[6]

Certainly there was moral and ethical content in the Vedas:

> If we have sinned against the man who loves us,
> Have ever wronged a brother, friend or comrade,
> The neighbor ever with us or a stranger,
> Varuna, remove from us the trespass.
> If we, as gamesters cheat at play, have cheated,
> Done wrong unwillingly, or sinned of purpose,
> Cast all these sins away like loosened fetters;
> And Varuna, let us be thine own beloved.
>
> (RV 5.85.7.8.)

Our discussion so far will indicate the nature of the Indian woman's true inheritance from the "ancient religions" of India, to which reformers in the ensuing years liked to refer as the basis for their own source of authority. It is an inheritance in which the Indian woman can take pride, coming as it does from the wellspring of true Indian culture. Few Indian women are, however, aware of their inheritance, which has been much obscured during the intervening years, particularly by Brahmanism.

Brahmanism came into vogue in India between the eighth and sixth centuries, B.C., about the same time that the Old Testament sources were taking shape in Palestine. The Brahmanas were the writings representing the formal religion and metaphysics of the priests, in contrast to the more simple nature religion of the Vedas, and one thing the priests apparently felt to be essential was to repress the influence of women, which was so apparent in Vedic days. As new developments in religion took on complicated ritual and sacrifice, the professional priest became imperative. Only such a professional could assure that no mistake would be made. To the priestly class the calling became highly profitable, and they spared no effort to perpetuate their position. Downgrading of women and observance of caste were very important.

Personal salvation became dependent upon the priest and the gifts of the worshiper to him. The priest was one kind of "god": "With oblations one gratifies the gods, the Brahmans who have studied and teach the sacred lore. Both kinds of gods, when gratified, place him in a state of bliss." (SBE 26.341; Satapatha 4.3.4.4.) The old gods are played down. Worship is recommended, far more than in the Vedic literature, as something to do for the worshiper's own benefit.

One of the chief problems in bringing about these changes must have been how to put women in their place; Dr. Pinkham feels that the new priestly class was rather clever in the way they did this (though certainly parallels of their technique can be found in history). They put a tremendous *over*emphasis on the *physical* aspects of womanhood. In their writing, sex takes on a disproportionate importance. Woman's job is to bear sons. "A sonless one cannot attain heaven." A son is necessary for the transmigration of the soul. The extreme emphasis on sex led to child marriages. The woman who, in earlier days, prepared the offering vessels when she and her family came together at the altar in their home is now excluded from religious observances. Men are even forbidden to eat in the presence of their wives. Only so will the man be assured a vigorous son—"Such, indeed, is the divine ordinance." A maiden may, however, go through certain religious rites to get herself a husband. And when a Brahman decides to be a monk, he may take his wife with him to his retreat. Also, "one man has many wives, but one wife has not many husbands. . . . Many wives are a form of prosperity (social eminence)."

Female goddesses are honored, but the worshiper is enjoined to make offerings to the male deity first, then to the female. "He thereby endows the male pre-eminently with power." The ghee [liquid butter] of an offering "is a thunderbolt, and by that thunderbolt, the ghee, the gods smote the wives and unmanned them. Thus smitten and unmanned, they neither owned any self, nor did they own any heritage." (Satapatha 4.4.2.13, SBE 46.366f., quoted WSSH 61.) "He makes women to be dependent; whence women are sure to be attendant upon man." (Satapatha 13.2.2.4, SBE 44.300, quoted, ibid.)

Women, however, never seem to be too long without a champion. The more liberal attitude of those who cherished the idea that women, too, were people is revealed in the *Upanishads*. These writings may very well be evidence that the popular international school of wisdom literature has reached India; maybe it even began there. At any rate, the picture the *Upanishads* give us of the women of India debating theology with Yajanvalkya, chief philosopher of the day, has much to be said for it as compared with the picture of the ideal woman in the Hebrew wisdom literature as presented in Proverbs 31, or with that other less popular female product of the Hebrew wisdom school—Job's wife.

Salvation, says R. E. Hume, is, according to the *Upanishads*, "to be obtained chiefly through one's own philosophic speculation upon a pantheistic Supreme Being."[7] In the *Upanishads*, the women press their arguments hard—skillfully and persistently. Gargi, one of the most admired women, had a way of putting her keenest observations in the form of questions to the great Yajanvalkya, until he finally ends the conversation with, "Gargi, do not question too much lest your head fall off. In truth you are questioning too much about a divinity about which further questions cannot be asked. Gargi, do not overquestion!" Whereupon she obligingly holds her peace, but only for the moment.

Another *Upanishad* tells about conversations with Yajanvalkya's two wives, Maitreyi and Katyayami. The former is described as a "discourser on sacred knowledge," but her sister is described as having "just the usual woman's knowledge of such matters." Certainly their husband does not spare them, intellectually, in his explanation of the Atman and its relation to the human soul.

The *Upanishads* tell us about the creation of man and woman from Primeval Being:

> One alone has no delight. He desired a second. He was, indeed, as large as a man and woman closely embraced. He caused that self to fall into two pieces. Therefrom arose a husband and wife. Therefore this is true: "One-self is like a half fragment . . . therefore this space is filled by a wife."

Another passage says the wife is the man's voice.

Far from daughters not being wanted, we here have a religious ceremony for those who especially want to beget a female child. Rice boiled with sesame and eaten with ghee, by the parents, together, is recommended for those who desire a learned (pandita) daughter.

However, the Brahmans had not been sleeping; their scholars had been codifying their religious convictions (especially, it seems, about women) into the *Laws of Manu*, and it is shocking to read in this document that not even "pure" women are acceptable as witnesses, because the understanding of females is likely to waver, and they need to be guarded against their own evil inclinations by the protecting male. "Through their passion for men, through their mutable temper, through their natural heartlessness, they become disloyal toward their husbands, however carefully they may be guarded (9.15–16). And although admitting the *Upanishad* teaching that man and woman both emerged from the dividing body of primordial being, the *Laws of Manu* decree that no religious ceremony for women should be accompanied by mantras (prayers), since "by these words the rule of right is fixed . . . women, being weak creatures, and having no [share in the] mantras, are false-hood itself" (9.18).

Woman, in her place, is a real asset to her husband (like the goddess of good fortune). In her proper place as a beautiful, loyal, considerate, faithful wife and mother, she is to be duly honored. It is quite possible for a Brahman to choose a wife of any caste, if she pleases him. In the wives of Brahmans, deviations from prescribed regulations can be over-looked.

Of course polygamy is permitted. The bonds of marriage have become indissoluble for the woman but not for the man. A curious law provides that when there are several wives, the son of one is considered the son of all; involved is probably the problem of inheritance, which is be-coming very important. Why shouldn't a son inherit through *all* the women in his father's harem?

No matter what kind of husband a girl gets, she must treat him with respect and consideration: "Though destitute of virtue or seeking plea-sure [elsewhere], or devoid of good qualities, [yet] a husband must be constantly worshiped as a god by a faithful wife" (5.154). She must never be independent. She takes care of her husband's wealth, keeps everything clean, faithfully performs permitted religious duties, prepares food, looks after the household utensils (9.11.12). A bride not found physically sound, as her husband expected, may be returned to her father. A father may not accept a marriage price for his daughter. If the father after three years fails to find his daughter a husband, she can get one on her own if she can. The father should try to get her a distinguished, handsome suitor of equal caste, even if she is not yet of marriageable age (hence, child marriages were condoned even at eight years). Corporal punishment with a whip, cane, or rope may be measured out by the king to women, infants, men of distorted mind, the poor and sick (9.230). Women, the maimed or deformed, the very aged, and barbarians are not to be present when the king holds consulta-tions (9.230; 7.149-50). Abortion, especially of a Brahman embryo, is condemned. So are prostitution and adultery, which tend to cause mix-ture of castes (8.226; 9.41). Sex seems to have become a veritable obsession: "One should not sit in a lonely place with one's mother, sister or daughter, for the senses are powerful and master even a learned man" (2.213-15). A man may not even watch his wife eat, yawn, sneeze, or sit relaxed. A Brahman may not eat food offered by a woman at a sacrifice. Nice women don't remarry; if she remains chaste, through her son or even possibly on her own, a woman can attain heaven and be with her husband through eternity! But she is not to mention the name of another man after her husband's death (5.160–2; 5.156–7).[8]

Lest there be any mistake about the compilers of the *Laws of Manu* fully appreciating the fine, noble qualities of womanhood, we must do them justice by two brief quotes:

> Women must be honored and adored by their fathers, brothers, husbands and brothers-in-law who desire their [own] welfare (3.55).

> Men who seek [their own] welfare should always honor women on holidays and festivals with [gifts of] ornaments, clothes and dainty food (3.59).

Roughly contemporary with the *Laws of Manu* are the *Puranas*, a series of literary tales which emphasize the anti-feminine bias. There is a great deal of widow-burning (with approval). The king in one story has fifty queens. In another, King Kaikayiy has ten daughters, all of whom marry Satrajita. Krishna is reported to have 16,000 queens. Multiple marriages seem to have approval, but whether in the time of writing (first century A.D.) or some romantic past which appealed to the author, we do not know. A woman who frowns at her husband goes to a hell of meteors and torches for as many years as there are hairs on the husband's body. A wife with an incurable disease, one who drinks too much in public, or who is incompatible to her husband may be discarded, but whoever discards a good and chaste wife must give her a third portion of her ornaments before formally effecting the separation (Garuda 95 Dutt. 269ff.). A man should keep his wife in comfort and happiness and be her friend. Marrying within caste is very important, and an unmarried man cannot perform sacrificial duties. A true wife speaks sweetly to her husband, is a clever household manager, should be beautiful, seductive, a light eater, and ever ready to yield to the procreative desires of her lord. That either mate has a bad character is no reason for neglect by the other (Garuda 108 Dutt. 317; 115 Dutt. 350).

A new note is that wives of Brahmans are to be worshiped as well as their husbands and propitiated with suitable gifts.

As for goddesses, there are so many that the atmosphere seems completely permeated with them. One has the feeling of being at some sort of goddess convention. Almost all are beautiful, creative, wise, helpful, protective. Each has more or less her own field of responsibility, but so powerful is each that it must have been impossible to have one's mind at rest—the day would not have been long enough to serve them all, and how could one choose?

The epic literature of the *Mahabharata* and the *Bhagavad-Gita* developed over several centuries (200 B.C.-200 A.D.?), so are not of much value for our "spot check" approach. One interesting contention of the *Mahabharata* is that the Kshatriya (warrior class) women, teaching the children they had raised by Brahman fathers, and instructing them in the *Vedas*, were responsible for saving the culture of India. This sounds interestingly symbolic.

Men, we note, are still clinging to a special dispensation: "There is not sin if falsehood is spoken to a woman" (Drona Parva 7.191.49). But Sri, goddess of prosperity, warns: "I live in those women who are given to truth and sincerity and who adore the gods. . . . By cherishing women one cherishes the goddess of prosperity herself, and by afflicting her one is said to pain the goddess of prosperity" (Anusasana Parva 13.46.5; 13.11.11).

Krishna, Vishnu's earthly counterpart, assures personal salvation to women, as to all persons, even the lowest of castes. He also cautions about the corruption of women as being one of the causes of various social evils and confusions. Krishna, moreover, identifies himself with the female as well as the male aspects of life: "I am the father of the universe, the mother, creator, the grandsire" (B.G. 9:17).

Perhaps the best known of the sacred writings of India (at least the best known to the general public) is the *Ramayana*. It is much quoted, and everywhere in India one sees pictures taken from the story, which concerns Prince Rama's exile (brought on by dissension within his father's multiple household). Rama is followed into exile by his devoted wife Sita, who is kidnaped and held captive, while Rama irritates the Western reader by sitting there contemplating, till he is at last helped in the rescue by miraculous intervention. But Sita, who has loyally resisted her captor, does not receive the welcome back into Rama's arms that she had expected. After what she has been through, he feels that he must consider whether she will be acceptable as his queen. Sita, heartbroken, asks for a funeral pyre and enters the flames, which miraculously do not harm her. Rama's faith in her is now restored—or rather he explains that he has known all along that a miracle of this sort would happen, but that he had to make a demonstration before the onlookers (who have been most sympathetic to Sita all the time) so *they* would know she had been supernaturally exonerated, and that she was, indeed, worthy to be his queen.

This says something about women, but it is hard to tell exactly what. There is a Job-like quality to Sita's sufferings. Certainly the story must have more than the obvious moral that it is the bounden duty of the wife to stick to her husband through thick and thin, no matter what.

It could be advice to women to put trust in their vindication by heaven (through Krishna) rather than men and to make their approach to salvation on their own merits, as individuals, not only as tolerated adjuncts of the male. Or it could be saying that through the love, devotion, and purity and (like Job) the complete integrity of the individual person (and women are persons) that individual and group salvation can be achieved. There may be a reaching back to the earliest Vedas, trying to interpret the role of women in relation to a society of a time when women were people, as they had not been of late. The authors were surely thinking of the savior concept, which had become important with Vishnu. They may just possibly have been saying that even so lowly a creature as a woman can, by a non-self-seeking life of perfect integrity and devotion to all that is best in her heart and consciousness, help to bring salvation not only to herself but to those dear to her and and to the society of which she is a part.

Are we reading things into the story? What sort of a challenge does the new woman of new India find in this fanciful story from some 2000 years ago?

Dr. Pinkham urges that at least some religiously motivated Indian women should have the opportunity to study all of the Indian "sacred" literature to know what their heritage is. They should also have the opportunity to study those sections which refer specifically to women, in an attempt to discover to what extent they represent the writer's personal viewpoint (perhaps of the moment of writing), to what extent they reflect the cultural periods under which they were produced, and to what extent they are, in toto, a religious heritage of the ages, applicable, intelligently interpreted, to the moral and ethical problems of India today. If we can judge by progress in the field of historical and literary criticism made in other countries and other religions, this may be a long and at times discouraging process. The fear of taboo has a stronger hold on men's minds than most of us are ever willing to admit, and it is never more firmly entrenched than when it has laid its cuckoo eggs in the nest of religion.

More extended study of religion in India would take into account the influence of early Buddhism, which is sometimes referred to as a revolt against the Brahmans; of Jainism, with its place for women in the monastic orders; of Mohammedanism, whose influence has now been only partly removed by the creation of Pakistan; of the twelfth-century reformer, Ramanuja, who was especially concerned with elevating the status of women; and Chaitanya, who in the sixteenth century urged better conditions for widows. We should discuss Yoga and the

Tantras, and the persistent appeal of magic to women, and what, if anything, can be done about it.[9]

In modern times the Christian schools and hospitals have had a salutary effect on the education, health, and general status of the Indian woman. The first Minister of Public Health in the Indian government was both a Christian and a woman, the Rajkumari Amrit Kaur. Having her in this position was a great asset to the women of India. She established hospitals, nurses' training, public health workers' courses. More than this, she was a wonderful symbol to the Indian women of their own realizable potential.[10]

Mrs. Renuka Ray was one of the twelve women members of the Indian Parliament who, in the early fifties, was putting up a tremendous fight for the new Hindu Code Bill. James Michener, in *Voice of Asia*, gives a lively account of that great debate as carried on by the Indian public.[11]

Mrs. Ray was especially adamant about the pious "our traditional religion must be upheld" attack on the bill. Brahmans, she indicated, like to weep about a so-called religious custom which is really "nothing but their own caste prejudices as they were foisted on the English conquerors in the eighteenth century."

The English, Michener quotes her as telling him, sought advice from the Brahman priests as to how to rule India in civil and religious affairs. The Brahmans saw their chance. "Consequently, the British pressed down upon the people of India harsh and ridiculously cruel laws, believing these were historical customs in the land. The worst to suffer were the women."

The Hindu Code Bill, Mrs. Ray is quoted as saying, "does nothing but restore to women the rights they held in ancient times, but which were taken away from them by the priests and the British."

Lest anyone think, however, that the women of India have completely won their battle for the right to be first-class citizens, let them listen to Sivaprasad Bhattacharyya, speaking as recently as 1953:

"The sphere of religious observances has been restricted by the Hindu religious code from very old times, for rigor and practice, as well as proper understanding of the mantras to be repeated, can hardly be expected of women. The Hindu woman is nothing more than an accessory and passive participator in her husband's religious practices. . . . Vedic mantras are taboo for a woman, and thus the Vedic course of daily worship is no part of her religious routine. . . . The one sacrament in her life is marriage. In temple worship women are not allowed to touch images, though there is a concession made in the case of Siva. . . . She worships Siva and the clay Siva linga daily if she chooses. . . . [She] has to look to the comfort of every member of the family as a religious duty; she can take her food only after all the members have taken theirs."[12]

There has been a good deal of recent discussion on the subject of renascent Hinduism. P. D. Devanandan sees this as the result of a "desperate need for faith in ultimates."[13]

Many Hindu philosophers are interested in discovering the "One religion which underlies all religions." Others talk about "reform of social institutions which retard the development of the individual person and the realization of justice in social relations."

Strange words for Hinduism!

Welcome words, we feel sure, to Indian women, if women are included!

Women in Buddhism

Buddhism originated in India as a protest movement against the rigid Brahman teachings. It was, however, only briefly accepted there, but found hospitality and appreciation in Korea, China, Japan, Thailand, Burma, Ceylon, Nepal, and Indo-China.

No religious group reports the story of its leader with more resort to magic and phenomena than do the chroniclers of Buddhism, yet Zen Buddhism, as it developed in Japan, is the most non-corporeal of beliefs. Many Christians find a spiritual challenge in the statement of their Zen Buddhist friends that "the god who can be named is not the true God"; or "the prayer that can be prayed with words is not a true prayer." Yet they cringe at the tremendous amount of "magical baggage" that has attached to many forms of Buddhism.

Gautama Buddha—the "Enlightened One"—lived from 563 to 483 B.C. He was born near Benares, India, into a noble and prosperous family of the Kshatriya caste. The legends of his miraculous birth, involving a white elephant, are usually considered apocryphal. Though he was married and had a son, he was closely shielded from the sorrow of the world; but at twenty-nine, on a journey from the palace, he became aware of death, sickness, and old age. He was so profoundly affected that he left his wife and child with his father and became a hermit. He fasted to the point where he was near death.

Then, as he sat under the famous bo tree, a shepherd girl came and offered him rice and milk. He accepted, ate, and became convinced that the "Middle Way" was the way of wisdom. His five male companions were disappointed in him. However, as he sat there under the bo tree, he had the experience of Enlightenment, and, gathering his friends around him, he preached his first sermon. His five comrades became the first Buddhist monks—arahats.

At that time Brahmanism was very popular in India, but Buddhism challenged its rigid rules and ritual, preaching instead a religion of "salvation." From Brahmanism, Buddha accepted the concepts of karma, transmigration, pre-existence. He taught, however, not that man was controlled by his karma but that he made (was making) his own karma.

The four truths which Buddha received at the time of his enlightenment were:

Existence is suffering.

The origin of suffering is desire (craving).

Suffering ceases when desire ceases.

The way to shed desire is by following the eightfold path of enlightenment:

1. Right belief
2. Right resolve (to withstand the temptation of sensual pleasure and to harm no living creature)
3. Right speech
4. Right conduct
5. Right occupation
6. Right effort (to keep mind free from evil and devoted to good)
7. Contemplation (right mindedness)
8. Ecstasy (achieved by trance-like meditation and selfless contemplation)

Buddha seems to have been neither friend nor foe of women. It does not seem to have cost him undue grief to have gone off and left his wife; she was in good hands, and from what snatches of legend we have about her, she was a part of the life he was repudiating. When she saw him going around the city with his begging bowl, she felt disgraced and reported it to her father-in-law. Gautama's father reminded him of his royal lineage, but the son replied that his father's lineage might be royal, but his own was through a long line of Buddhas. It was, in fact, reported that an abandoned type of entertainment in his father's house was the last straw in making Gautama decide he had to leave home.

Women relatives of his companions were among his first followers. Some seem to have distinguished themselves for generosity. Mahapajapati, however, his widowed aunt, insisted on becoming a nun. Refused, she cut off her hair with a sword, got herself a saffron robe, and, with a group of women, followed Gautama wherever he went. When turned away, the women wept outside his door. Then Ananda, the future Buddha's favorite disciple, put the question to his lord: "Is a woman who has gone forth from a house to a houseless life in the doctrine and discipline declared [by Buddha] capable of realizing the fruit of Entering-the-stream, or of the Once-returner, or of the Non-returner or Arahatship?" "A woman is capable," admitted Buddha, and Mahapajapati had won her case. (For clarity we refer to Gautama as Buddha, though actually he was as yet only a Bodhisattva—potential Buddha.) Ananda drew up some rules which assured the men's order always being given precedence, and the women's order was formed, in the fifth year of Buddha's preaching. One legend says Buddha's wife also entered the order, but this is neither well documented nor very important. A discourser on doctrine, an adviser to the king, a poet were among the list of some seventy early nuns.[14] One report is that Buddha sadly remarked that without women the doctrine would have lasted a thousand years; with them it might last 500. He knew not only their weaknesses but the social pressure that their adherence would bring on the order. Theologically, however, he admitted honestly that there was no basis for excluding them. Moreover, his misgivings about the dire results of their presence do not seem to have been justified. Buddhism did last only about 500 years *in India* (the story just repeated was written considerably later and was probably a post-facto remark credited to Buddha). In the long run, however, Buddhism seems to have survived the women in its rank very creditably. Since the acceptability of women as full participants in the religious life of Buddhism is something that would scarcely have been written into the legends during the next few hundred years, it can probably be considered as authentic Buddhist teaching from the beginning.[15]

When the Buddhist Study and Research Center, at Berkeley, California, was consulted about the place of women in the Buddhist religion, the emphatic answer was that in Buddhism a woman can have exactly the same rights as a man. Yet very few of the thousands of persons seen wearing the saffron robes of the priesthood in Southeast Asia are women. In this respect, as in others, there has been adaptation to surrounding cultures.

Even before Buddha's death there seem to have been monks who apparently thought it was high time to present the religion's "dogma" in a more orderly fashion. Some reports say that within a day after his death a council had been called, at which his teachings were recited by the 500 arahats, and corrections made. Ananda, who received enlightenment only the night before the council opened, was one of the best informed, but the older men gave him a bad time. Among other things, he had to "confess" having permitted the Buddha's body to have been saluted first by the women, so that it was "soiled" by their tears. He also had to "confess" that it was on his recommendation that women had been admitted to the order. Perhaps because of his youth he was courageous enough to protest that he couldn't see why he should "confess" to something Buddha himself had approved. One gets the idea that Buddha's decision to admit women was not applauded by all his disciples, and that there may have been considerable dissension.

Buddhism leaves little provocation for sex rivalry. It is the "Middle Way" rather than a dialectical conflict. Non-violence, truth, and service, not ritual, are important, and this makes as much room for women as men.

Buddha's technique of teaching seems to have been to focus on the mentally and spiritually privileged segment of society and depend upon them, one way or another, to spread his message in turn to the mass of humanity. He wanted to reach those who reached others. The person who had it in his power to command a situation might indeed, unless pride, lust, evil thoughts, and ignorance were "extinguished," continue to control his fellow men by war, or through laws of caste, or through a tyrannical priestly cult. On the other hand, he could take a radically different approach and, through forgiveness, love, charity, and truth, and by striving to become a Bodhisattva, help others to help themselves.[16]

A. B. Keith cites what he calls "Buddha's ethic of love for the laity":

Parents love and protect children.

Children honor parents and maintain family traditions.

Teachers instruct children and receive due honor.

Husbands are courteous, faithful, respect wives, give them authority in the home, and provide them with ornaments in return for fidelity and due performance of duties.

Friends show courtesy, generosity, and benevolence to each other, observe the golden rule, keep faith.

Masters give servants just labor, feed, pay, care in sickness, provision for some luxuries and recreation.

The laity show the monks affection by thought, word, and deed, and supply their temporal needs.

The monks teach laymen and restrain them from evil.[17]

"Potential Buddhas" began in time to question whether their personal hope for nirvana was not a selfish desire. Should they not rather stay in (or return to) this world and help their fellow travelers along the path?

The theory of impermanence—of the constant flux and change in the elements which, through the recurring transmigrations, make up the human personality—demanded a corresponding evaluation of women. Who could say, in this existence of impermanence, how the workings of karma might shift the elements, and who, in the next incarnation, might turn up with a preponderance of male or female characteristics? Since sex could change from one incarnation to another, it was no cause for pride.

Buddhism was at its height in India and Ceylon in the third century B.C. Asoka, a convert from Brahmanism (ruler of the huge Maurya Empire during the third century B.C.), sponsored revision of the scriptures, established monasteries, and in many ways—and for good or ill—played for Buddhism a part similar to that played by Emperor Constantine on behalf of Christianity a few centuries later. His son is credited with taking Buddhism to Ceylon, whence it traveled to China in the first century A.D., to Korea and Japan (sixth century A.D.), to Southeast Asia, and back to India. But it has never, since its early years, been a major religion in the country of its birth. Everywhere it took on the elements of the different cultures, demonstrating in itself Buddha's doctrine of flux and impermanence and reincarnation. There were thousands of Bodhisattvas. There were symbolism and magic and mythology according to the soil in which the religion took root. In the Far East monasticism became important. In Tibet, Buddhism became Lamaism. The Mahayana (greater and more inclusive "salvation-for-all" vehicle) broke off from the Hinayana (lesser exclusive vehicle). The images of Buddha (not idols!) crowded the temples of Burma and Thailand, where Buddhism became the state religion. All young men in Thailand were required to take the yellow robe of the monk and spend a certain length of time in monasteries, where they were taught religion and, if they did not know it already, reading.

Emma Hawkridge, in The Wisdom Tree,[18] points out that though some people called Buddha an atheist, he came to be thought of by others as God himself. To still others he was one among many Buddhas who had taken the shape of gods, demons, and practically everything in between. The teacher who had protested against ritual and formal prayer became the center of so much ritual that his devotees couldn't keep up with it; they devised prayer wheels, which could be turned by water power.[19]

Toward the end of the seventh century the Chinese Buddhist scholar

I-Tsing traveled in some thirty countries, observing Buddhist adaptations of the original teachings and bringing home with him some 400 texts of Buddhist books. He also wrote home reports—for instance, on the different dress within the orders, ways of worship, rules for sleeping and eating, and ordination. He goes into considerable detail, for instance, "concerning the Indian mode of wearing religious garments," and it is interesting to note that essentially dress is the same for the religious men and women. In regard to the Indian nuns, however, he raises a question which he thinks needs discussion:

"If one, though a female, has a powerful mind," he tells us, "she need not engage in shuttle and loom, nor do ordinary [household] tasks. Much less does she need to wear many garments. [The women are not supposed to be squeamish about this.] There are some who never think of meditation or reading, ever hastening onward, driven by earthly desires. There are others who make much of ornament and dress, not caring for the precepts. All these persons are liable to an examination by the lay followers. Nuns in India are very different from those in China. They support themselves by begging food, and live a poor and simple life." Now comes the problem!

"Here a question may be asked: The benefit and supply to the female members of the order are very small, and monasteries of many a place have no special supply of food for them. This being the case, there will be no way of living if they do not work for their maintenance; and if they do so, they often act against the Vinaya teaching and disobey the noble will of the Buddha. How should they decide for themselves as to taking one course and rejecting the other? When once one's body is at ease, one's religion prospers. Pray, let us hear your judgment on these points."[20]

The author I-Tsing cannot, however, resist giving his own opinion, that if what you are seeking is detachment, pangs of hunger are no help. Our interest is that we seem to see the "economic squeeze" being put on the women who still persist in trying to be Bodhisattvas in India.

The list of "prohibitions" put upon women at ordination, however, though slightly different from those put on the men, have nothing to do with their spiritual development and participation, nor with their vows, pilgrimages, etc. Insofar as they differ from those of the men, the prohibitions are actually for the protection of the women or related to their special physical problems. They are not to travel alone, touch the body of a man, have the same lodging with a man, act as a matchmaker, or conceal a grave offense committed by a nun. Less important provisions forbid taking gold and silver which does not belong to her, shaving—except the head—digging up uncultivated ground, willfully cutting growing grass or a tree, eating food which is not offered, eating food which has once been touched.[21]

Keith, quoting from the Buddhist literature, tells us that both the Hinayana and the Mahayana monastic orders demanded celibacy. For the laity, the Hinayana vehicle justifies marriage: In spite of the fact that marriage does seem to be yielding to desire, it gives pleasure to the other party. The Mahayana vehicle finds Buddhism very suitable to a family man. A husband and wife have the best possible opportunities to practice the way of the Bodhisattva, since only together are they capable of the supreme act of generosity—the gift of children to the world. Moreover, only the wife can take the typical vow of marital faith —to live with her husband from existence to existence. Each family of believers is one of potential Buddhas (KV 23.1. A and V).[22]

Especially revealing concerning the place of women in the Buddhist order and theology are the *Psalms of the Sisters,* published in 1909 by the Pali Text Society, London.[23] These purport to be poems composed by "certain eminent sisters of the Buddhist order," and preserved through many centuries in the palm-leaf manuscript of the Sutta-Pikata. The oral poems were presumably committed to writing about 80 B.C.; the comments and stories, giving their background, were added in the sixth century A.D. The commentaries give a picture of a highly devout order of at least seventy-one female arahats, conversant with Buddhist doctrine, completely committed to lives of non-attachment, but who have been prying rather deeply into their previous incarnations to account for their present problems. Some of the commentaries take us through many rebirths for the individual—often both male and female incarnations. Mrs. Rhys Davids says in the introduction to her work, "[The nuns] had laid down all social position, all domestic success; they had lost their world. But in exchange they had won the status of an individual in place of being adjuncts, however much admired, fostered, and sheltered they might, as such, have been. 'With shaven head, wrapped in a robe'—a dress indistinguishable, it would seem, from the swathing toga [of the male arahats]—the Sister was free to come and go, to dive alone into the depths of the wood, or climb aloft. Moreover to free mobility she could wed the other austere joy of being recognized, at least by her brother arahats, as a rational being, without reference to sex. As such she breathed the spiritual atmosphere, she shared the intellectual communion of that aristocracy [the Ariyas] with whom she claimed that power of 'seeing all things as they really are' . . . which the Buddhist called being awake."

The author notes with interest that it was not so much a devotion to Buddha, as a person, that brought these particular nuns to arahathood, for much of the loyalty expressed in the poems is to Patacara, whom these nuns hail as their "Sovereign Lady" and to whom they seem to owe their direct allegiance, rather than to Buddha himself.

There are even some stories of dryads, leaning from the confinement of their tree-trunks to hear about this new religious life open to women!

To demonstrate the truly religious outlook of the stanzas, we quote Snagha, apparently a comparative newcomer:

> Home have I left, for I have left my world!
> Child have I left, and all my cherished herds!
> Lust have I left, and ill-will, too, is gone,
> And ignorance have I put far from me.
> Craving and root of craving overpowered,
> Cool am I now, knowing Nirvana's peace.

Another woman, the veteran of many incarnations, sings:

> Though I be suffering and weak, and all
> My youthful spring be gone, yet have I climbed,
> Leaning upon my staff, the mountain crest.
> Thrown from my shoulder hangs my coat, o'erturned
> My little bowl. So 'gainst the rock I lean
> And prop this self of me, and break away
> The wildering gloom that long has closed me in.

The contrast between voluntary and involuntary poverty is brought out in the story of the beggar woman Canda's encounter with Patacara:

> In gracious pity did she let me come—
> Patacara—and heard me take the vows.
> And thenceforth words of wisdom and of power
> She spake, and set before my face
> The way of going to the Crown of Life.
> I heard her and I marked and did her will.
> O wise and clear Our Lady's homily!
> The threefold Wisdom have I gotten now.
> From deadly drugs my heart is purified.[24]

About this time the Chinese Buddhists also seem to have become aware of the need for the "feminine touch" in their religious observances. In about the seventh century, a Hindu god, Avalokitesvara, had some popularity in China and Tibet. His name means "he who looks down," but whether from heaven, a cliff, or his own height is not clear.

(We have often wondered what became of the tall Hindu goddess Vac, so popular in Aryan days.) At any rate, the Hindu deity Avalo-kitesvara seems to have gone through a reincarnation and to have emerged as the goddess Kuan-Yin, the idealization of womanhood. (Change of sex, status, and race was common enough for Bodhisattvas during transmigration. It gave one varied experience. However, the story of one nun who had put in her stint as a fairy is a bit surprising.) In the tenth century Kuan-Yin was considered a fish-goddess, and with the importance of fish as a food in China had an extended cult. A twelfth-century legend makes her the third daughter of a Buddhist king. Upon her, after great earthly sufferings, deity was bestowed; from her "pure dew" vessel, which she carried with her, she bestowed on mankind bountiful mercy; she was a special protector of women. Her abode in Tibet became the home site of the Dalai Lama; in China she took up residence on Puto Island—and at practically every Buddhist monastery—as next to Buddha himself, their most beloved patron.[25]

There were other goddesses, appearing from time to time, apparently without protest. Next to Kuan-Yin in popularity was Maya, who was introduced as one of the celestial beings who had done honor to Buddha and won herself the title of "Mother of all Buddhas" (a title which was, however, not exclusively Maya's).

She was deified by the Tantric Buddhists as Chun-T'i, or Marichi, who has survived through the centuries with her eighteen arms and (sometimes) three eyes.[26]

Among Tibetan Buddhists developed one of the most unusual inter-pretations—the figure of the Yabyum—a wife and husband in embrace within a circle. He is the Yab, she is the Yum. Together they intercede on behalf of mortals for divine favor.[27]

Buddhism does not become less complex, or its gods, cults, sects, and philosophies more easily sorted out, as the centuries advance. Undoubtedly the fact that there are so many special sects to which an adherent can give quite complete devotion without bothering about the over-all picture accounts for some of its numerical success. (Bishop Manikam says a third of the world's population is Buddhist.)

From this bewilderment of gods, goddesses, symbols, rites, demons, and magic, the reformed movements of Cha'an Buddhism in China and Zen Buddhism in Japan emerged, with the message that what the Buddha stands for is not to be found in any of these paraphernalia, but in the hearts of his devotees. It is to be experienced through all of nature, and through art which seeks to understand and re-express nature. In one stone is every incarnation of every Buddha; every blade of grass knows his salvation. It is interesting to note that Zen Buddhism is perhaps making more impact than any other religion on the secular-minded intellectuals of the Western world at the present time. The University of California, listing a special, week-long, "live-in" seminar on "existentialism and zen," refers to zen consistently not as a religion but as a philosophy.

From 1954–1956 the Sixth Buddhist Council met in Burma, celebrating the 1500th anniversary of Buddha's attainment of nirvana. At the same time a fourteen-story building in Hiroshima, Japan, was being built to enshrine Buddhist relics from Ceylon. With greater world awareness of mankind's essential unity, many Buddhists are becoming more conscious of Buddhism's common background. With a world in turmoil, many sects are discovering ancient authority for a new concern over a more orderly approach to social welfare. Especially, perhaps, as a result of their recent experiences with war, and the threat of nuclear war which is staggering to the world, the people of Buddhist lands are becoming aware of their historic peace position, and the responsibility which this puts upon them in view of present world conditions. Many are saying that "Buddhism must be ready to pick up the pieces." With such potential responsibility on their minds, the Buddhists, at Burma, spoke up strongly for the education and reform of the clergy. With better education and opportunities for exploring the real bases of Buddhism, present Buddhist leadership is also experiencing and advocating a new freedom from the superstition and magic which has encrusted it during the past centuries. Buddhists of many lands are saying, with a new understanding, the ancient vow: "I take refuge in Buddha, I take refuge in the Law, I take refuge in the Order." They are interested in research to discover their common Buddhist heritage. Public servants are feeling a new call to act responsibly out of respect to Buddha. Whether they can rid themselves of the "excess baggage" of magic and superstition, whether they can educate the common people fast enough, whether the religious roots, nourished in perhaps excessive tolerance, can withstand the attack and competition of secular state religions, famous for their promises of quick social results without having to wait for the slow and uncertain progress of reincarnation to do its work—these are some of the questions. Buddhism has also, for the first time in many centuries at least, become a missionary religion, preaching world fellowship and embarking on a world mission.

More than in most religions, women and men have been partners in Buddhism. But the women who have been sufficiently educated to play their part at the leadership level have been comparatively few in number. In some countries where Buddhism was religiously strong, it was culturally overpowered by a society which held women to be of very low value and did not try to further the education of girls. Buddhism, while accepting women, was of no mind to go out and fight the government concerning their political and educational rights. And the same could of course be said concerning the men of the lower castes and classes. Buddha's own evaluation of his calling was undoubtedly colored by the fact that he had been born of a royal household. His reason told him that this made no difference, also that religion and education were by no means twins. But his messages were, essentially, to those who avowedly aspired themselves to achieve Buddhahood. Capable women who fit into this category are welcome, and since this is the closest they have come to real acceptance, in any of the four religions under discussion, they are not ungrateful.

Many women, however, with a minimum of education, drift into the cults or state religions, to which they could also give their devotion without violence to their personal allegiance to Buddha, with no necessity for giving up the "fun" of magic, and with the fond hope for personal salvation without self-sacrifice. To what extent Buddhism rises to the challenge it senses in today's world may depend a lot on how seriously it continues to take its women and to what extent it gives them more education, more responsibility, and more opportunity for service within the ranks of Buddhism.

In all this progress, however, we do hope that the gentle, whimsical, helpful, and fun-loving side of Buddhism will not be lost. The world would be far poorer without the doll festivals of Japan or the kite festival of Thailand.

We have not said much about Thailand, with its 134,000 Buddhist monks (50,000 for life), its 25,000 Buddhist temples, its Buddhist king, and its new interest in girls' education. For many traveling Americans it is their "favorite" country, especially, perhaps, if they have been there when the "battle of the sexes" was at its height—in the sky.

Kite-flying is an ancient and honorable sport in Thailand ("land of freedom"). Early in the spring, when the monsoon winds are just right, crowds turn out to watch the contest between the *Chula* male kite and the considerably smaller but agile *Pukpao*, its female counterpart. The king and queen are supposed to open the kite-flying season by tossing up the first kites. The big star-shaped Chula is almost twice the height of a man and has barbs attached to catch little Pukpao. Pukpao is diamond-shaped and fragile-looking, less than half Chula's size. But she is quick and very maneuverable and trails a very efficient hook, with which she tries to snag her boy friend and pull him over the line, to her side of the designated territory. Chula tries to snag and drag off one or more "wives." The cries from both sides are shrill and loud, the betting fast and furious. It seems on the whole to be a friendly fight. But the experts tell us that the betting is always two to one on the side of Chula. What kind of setup is that? You would think they would change the rules, so the girls as well as the boys had a fair chance.

Women in Confucian Philosophy

Many creeds have come and gone in China. Yet it is reasonable to say that the fundamental motivation in her life over the centuries has been Confucian. It has always been recognized that Confucius was a philosopher, not in the common sense of the word a religious leader. It was easy for the Chinese—always a pragmatic race—to accept and digest religion—in just the same way that they have digested and made their own invading cultures. No race has had more faith in herself than the Chinese; and this includes Chinese women.

Confucius was one more of the amazing number of moral leaders who made their contribution to the world in the fifth and sixth centuries B.C.[28] He taught mutual respect, love, and orderliness within the family as the basis of a happy state and nation. He ran into trouble with the fact that the state built on wisdom, mutual trust, and peaceful intent was then, as now, hypothetical, and so to a large extent are similarly endowed families. Confucius the utopian, like many idealists, suffered over the years from having his words misinterpreted and turned against him.

Man being *stronger*, said Confucius, his place was to work outside the home; woman's responsibility was for all things concerned with the home. When a young man married and brought his bride to his ancestral home, she was responsible, so far as the duties in that home were concerned, to the person responsible for the home—her mother-in-law.

We often forget the importance of home activity in the primitive or pioneer society—or even in a highly cultured society before the days of supermarkets, electric gadgets, frozen foods, laundromats, restaurants, automobiles. Or before schools, hospitals, and community social services and recreation.

Confucius did not minimize women's role—he never said they were "just housewives." Nor does it seem likely he would have disparaged the very different demands which modern society puts on the modern woman. It is probably almost never what she has to do that bothers the housewife. It is being told she *has* to do that *particular kind* of work (whatever her natural abilities), then being told in the same breath that it is an unimportant chore, fit occupation only for those with weak minds. And she knows better! Confucius admitted that some work was more fitting for men because they were *stronger*, but he didn't give women their assignment on the grounds that they were *stupid*.

In the volume of Chinese Tradition, of the *Records of Civilization* series,[29] we read that "to be a woman means to submit." Quoted also are a whole list of prohibitions (or regulations) about women sitting on the same mat or eating from the same dish with male members of the family at mealtime, covering their faces when they go out, not exchanging wine cups, etc.; also what the responsibilities of a matchmaker are. But these regulations reflect, as the author points out, the feudal age in which the *Book of Rites* came into circulation. They do not degrade the woman to the status of a female animal owned by her husband, nor do they invent theological arguments to "prove" her inferior status. This was, in short, the kind of decorum calculated to keep a feudal Chinese family smooth-running and happy; these instructions deal with mores, not religion or philosophy.

In 1944 in New York City it was the writer's privilege to have the late Reverend Timothy Tingfang Lew, then a visitor in this country, participate in her ordination and receive from him a gift of *The Basic Teachings of Confucius* in a translation which he, as a scholar, recommended and hoped would prove useful to her in speaking and writing as a Christian minister.[30]

We suggest in the next few pages a few pertinent quotes from that volume to demonstrate that in his admonitions to women Confucius was not being untrue to his principle of the essential dignity of every individual, but was rather trying to find the *right* role for *every* individual in the well-regulated family and state. The educated Chinese is grounded in this Confucian doctrine of the all importance of the state, with a carefully defined role for every individual in relation to the state. This philosophical background undoubtedly accounts for the *ideological devotion* of the Chinese to communism, which in other countries has developed rather as a *pragmatic step* in the revolutionary process.

We must remember, too, that the precepts of Confucius were just that—precepts. They do not pretend to give us a picture of the daily life of his day. Says the foreword to the *Basic Teachings*: "Confucius strove to make human beings good—a good father, a good mother, a good son, a good daughter, a good friend, a good citizen. Though his truths were unpalatable at the time of their enunciation, they have lived to bear good fruit, despite the desperate efforts of Emperor Tsin Shi-hwang to destroy them by fire."

To the quotes specifically about women we add a few others, not dealing directly with women but actually much more significant to the role of women than are the tidbits of advice on etiquette and current custom we frequently hear quoted. Whatever shows Confucius' attitude toward the human family is a significant comment on his attitude toward women, for women were people, their role was a respected and useful one. Here are some of Confucius' comments:

The "superior man," about whom Confucius was so constantly concerned, "must never fail reverently to order his own conduct; and let him be respectful to others and observant of propriety. Then all within the four seas will be his brothers" (Analects 12.5.4).

"The rules instituted by the ancient kings had their radical element and their outward, elegant form. A true heart and good faith are their radical element. . . . Without the radical element they could not have been established; without the elegant form, they could not have been put in practice." The "superior man" is said to hate "those who have valour merely and are unobservant of propriety" (Analects 17.24.1). "Propriety is seen in humbling oneself and giving honours to others" (Li Ki 1.1.1.6.25).

"The love of virtue should balance the love of beauty. . . . The superior man withstands the allurements of beauty, to give an example to the people. Thus men and women, in giving and receiving, allow not their hands to touch; in driving, even with his wife in his carriage, a husband holds forth his left hand; when a young aunt, a sister or a daughter is wed and returns to her father's house, no male relative should sit with her upon the mat; a widow should not lament at night; in asking after a wife who is ill, the nature of the illness should not be referred to"; etc. (Li Ki 27.37).

Confucius and, for centuries before his time, the dominant persons in Chinese society were firm believers in the home as the sphere of woman. Within the home she was supreme; the privacies of her realm should not be revealed without, nor the hardships and worries of the outside world brought within to annoy and terrify her. "Outside affairs should not be talked of inside the home, nor inside affairs outside of it" (Li Ki 1.1.3.6.33 cf. 10.1.12).

"The superior man commences with respect as a bais of love. To omit

respect is to leave no foundation for affection. Without love there can
be no union; without respect the love will be ignoble" (Great Leaning 24.9).

"To evoke love, you must love; to call forth respect, you must show
respect" (Shu King 4.4.2).

"A happy union with the wife and children is like the music of lutes
and harps. When there is concord between brethren, the harmony is
delightful and enduring" (Doctrine of the Mean 15.2.3).

"The female alone cannot procreate; the male alone cannot procreate; and Heaven alone cannot produce a man. The three, collabo-
rating, man is born. Hence anyone may be called the son of his mother
or the son of Heaven" (Ku-Liang's Commentary).

"There has never been a birth without the collaboration of Heaven.
God is the creator of all men" (Many Dewdrops of the Spring and
Autumn, Bk. 70).

A father is proud of his sons, especially those who show merit, but a
mother, "while she is proud of the meritorious, cherishes those who are
not so able. The mother deals with them on the grounds of affection
rather than pride; the father on grounds of pride rather than affection"
(Li Ki 29.29).

"As they serve their fathers, so they serve their mothers, and they love
them equally" (Book of Filial Piety c.5).

"Filial piety is the constant requirement of Heaven, the righteousness
of earth, and the practical duty of man" (ibid., c.7).

There are various passages indicating that women had a definite part
in the ceremony of offerings to the dead, which, with the emphasis on
filial devotion, took on special significance for the "superior" man and
wife in their maturity: "The ruler and his wife take alternate parts in
presenting these offerings, all being done to please the soul of the departed and constituting a union with the disembodied and the unseen"
(Li Ki 7.1.2.). Day-by-day ancestral reverence is also in the province
of the woman of the house.

That the ladies—of any culture—do not always conform to the concept of their life gained from reading the religious literature of the
period, and the difficulties this places in the path of anyone trying to
find causal relationships, has been mentioned. A delightful little book
has recently come to the writer's attention. It is called Typical Women
of China and is a translation by Miss A. C. Safford of an ancient
Chinese work, Records of Virtuous Women of Ancient and Modern
Times. The translation was printed in Shanghai in 1891 in the hope that
it would reveal the "motives by which Chinese women are still actuated

as well as the models which they profess and attempt to follow." The original Chinese document was, it seems, started by Liu Hiang during the Han dynasty—some 2000 years ago. It then contained only a few chapters, but set the style to which there were frequent additions during the following centuries. The Chinese authors introduce it with the admonition that "Girls should learn about Women's Virtues, Women's Words, Women's Deportment and Women's Employments"; we suspect they thought the modern miss was getting out of hand. The lady Tsao tells them, in her "Precepts for Women" (one of the collected "records") that in olden days a daughter, three days after birth, used to be laid under the bed, given a tile to play with, and sacrifices were then offered to the ancestry. Laying her under the bed typified her future helplessness and subjection; the tile was the symbol of a laborious life to be spent in serving her husband; and the sacrifices signified that it would be her duty to perpetuate that husband's ancestral line. "These things are the chief end of a wife's existence." Quite a life for a three-day-old baby to look forward to!

There is also, in this anthology, a Lady Chang, whose "Rites for Women" the male Chinese compiler thought worth quoting; and the ancient "Ritual of Decorum," which tells women: "Be modest and respectful in demeanor. Prefer others to yourself. If you have done good, do not proclaim it, if evil, do not excuse it. Patiently bear insult and obloquy. Continually fear lest you do something wrong. Go to rest late and arise early, dreading not the earliest dawn, before the darkness flees. Be industrious; never refuse one task because it is difficult, or slight another because it is easy. Cultivate thoroughness in all you do, and order everything methodically. Be sedate and modest, exercise self-control, and serve your husband, preparing his wine and food properly, also the ancestral sacrifices in their season. If you thus minutely perform your duties, you need not fear that you will be unknown and unpraised; that you disgrace your name is impossible." (The poor dear wouldn't have time to!) The compiler himself sums it up: "If a woman would live properly, nothing is better for her to cultivate than reverence; if she would escape rough treatment, let her cultivate docility. Reverential obedience is the great duty of a wife. The husband should lead and the wife follow him; this is the correct relation."

Fine theory! But let us have a glimpse at the women themselves. Some of the tales about these "Typical Women" seem a little "tall," but who knows?

There was, for instance, the man from Ch'u who was taken captive by a band of robbers, who were about to kill and eat him. His wife, in tears, implored them, "Only my husband remains of all his family. I beg you to spare his life and take me in his stead. I am fatter, and have a dark complexion, which is said to be more tasty." Sure enough, they obliged her. She was highly honored (unfortunately posthumously) for her loyalty.

There are a variety of stories about women who thus bargained, at the expense of their own lives, for their husbands or fathers or sons— sometimes for the ruler. When a magistrate was unjustly accused and led off in disgrace, he bewailed the fact that, though he had five daughters, there was no son to help him. The youngest daughter followed him in tears. Finally she got up her spunk and wrote a petition to the emperor, telling him the unhappy story of her father's plight and adding, "If he should die from this punishment, he can never live again to serve Your Majesty. . . . Your handmaiden entreats permission to give herself as a public bond slave, that she may redeem her father from his punishment." Of course the emperor exonerated the father and freed them both.

Jealousy between wives and concubines seems to have been a considerable problem in China's earlier history. The Ming empress who wrote "Instruction for the Inner Apartments" suggests that in earlier times the empress and virtuous concubines, "laying aside selfishness, and with all-pervading kindness, sought for the harem of their Lord pure and accomplished ladies. Therefore their descendants in a continuous line were numerous and flourishing and blessed with every good."

Filial loyalty, always commended, still has its limits. Miss Tsi, who from girlhood had a "fine sense of right and wrong," is commended for refusing to marry the wealthy man her mother had picked out for her. She said, "If I marry a man of high aims and pure life, I am willing to serve him, but I am not willing to marry a man merely because he is rich." Instead she married a poor but celebrated classic scholar and lived happily in a thatch hut. Confucius, with all his regard for the proper filial attitudes, maintained more than once that a son had a right to remonstrate with his father where moral principles were involved— even though in the end he had to obey his parent.

Even a king could be defied for reason—and to one's ultimate honor. A woman with a great tumor on her neck was picking mulberry leaves when the king rode by. Everyone else gaped at the monarch, but she kept on working. He asked why. "I was sent," she said, "by my parents to gather mulberry leaves, but I had no instructions to look at you, the great king." "This," said the king to the courtiers, "is a remarkable woman. What a pity she is afflicted with that tumor!" "My duty," said she, "is to cultivate virtue carefully and attend to business diligently. If I am destined to live here and serve in this way, why should a tumor be of shame to me?" The king, amazed at her ability and virtue, told her to follow him to his palace. "I should be a runaway daughter," protested the young lady, "and how then could I serve Your Majesty properly?" So the king, mortified, returned home and sent messengers with the proper betrothal presents and made her his queen.

One woman got very angry with her soldier husband because, his king being killed and the army destroyed, he was still alive. Who, he asked, would take care of her and their sons if he killed himself? "Your wife and sons are selfish private interests," she told him. "I cannot, like you, veil my shame and live an inglorious life." And she killed herself. A neighboring king praised her moral excellence and sacrificed an ox in her honor.

To prove devotion to a dead husband, widows got the idea of cutting off an ear and throwing it into the coffin—a pledge not to marry again. (At least this was preferable to joining a husband on a funeral pyre.)

Many stories are recounted of the lady saying the right thing at the right time and so saving the day. There was, for instance, the case of the man who had worked three years making the king the best bow in the world. When he tried it out, however, the king couldn't hit the target at all. Enraged, he ordered the bowmaker killed. But the bowmaker's wife stepped in and said, "You did not pierce the mark because you are not a skilled archer. To put my husband to death would be a great error." She then proceeds to give the king some lessons in archery, so that he is able to hit the target seven times in a row. The king liberates the husband and presents her with three pounds of gold.

The "Instructions for Women" say that "Words contain the essence of intimacy and estrangement; they can shake the most stable plans; they can produce harmony, or work hatred and excite to revenge; they can throw all the relations of life into confusion. Therefore a true and noble woman cannot be too careful of her words."

The tales under the chapter heading "Women's Deportment" are somewhat boring. Several of the ladies die of grief in not too original circumstances, because of the death of father or husband. Others give up powder and refuse to paint their lips for the rest of their lives. If, in time of war, a woman falls into the hands of lawless men, she might try following the example of a lady who used a poisonous medicine on her face that made her break out into an appearance of smallpox. One lady, captured, assumed boys' clothing and lived among the soldiers.

"Her exalted purity resembled a clear, variegated gem." When the war ended, she returned home and was known for the rest of her life as the "Pure Woman."

The tales about "Women's Employments" give instructions on silk-worm culture, weaving, cooking, spinning hemp, on looking after the husband's comfort, and being a good daughter-in-law. From the princess to the poor little orphan child, they all attain—whatever it is one attains by working diligently and uncomplainingly from morning to night. The prince, seeking a wife, says to a young lady's father, "I invite your pearly daughter to accompany me to my humble home, to assist in the sacrifices of my ancestral temple and help prepare for the sacrifices in the temple of agriculture." This poem gives a glimpse of her duties:

> She gathers the large duck-weed
> By the banks of the streams in the southern valley;
> She gathers the pond-weed
> In those pools left by the floods.
>
> She deposits what she gathers
> In her square baskets and round ones.
> She boils it
> In her tripods and pans.
>
> She sets forth her preparations
> Under the window in the ancestral chamber.
> Who superintends the business?
> It is the reverend young lady.

There is a great deal of discussion as to whether or not women should be taught to read. Some say no, they will get out of hand. Some say yes, but only such moral precepts as we have been discussing here. Some ask why girls should not have the same education as boys. The arguments all sound familiar. Some women, who had the opportunity, became outstanding scholars.

Women were, in real life, it seems, far more free, active, and intelligent than one would suspect from the books of the male writers—even such a liberal-minded philosopher as Confucius. There is more vitality in women's lives and minds than is evident from rules of decorum. Though subjected to male domination, they are not submerged by it. There is actually something rather profound in the little nursery couplet which the Chinese girl was taught by her governess:

> A young lady does *not* go out at night.
> Going out, she takes a light.

Dr. Ping-Ti Ho, professor of Chinese History and Institutions, University of Chicago,[31] makes a particular point of the fact that most Western observations on the Chinese family deal with the period after 1920, or, at the earliest, with the late imperial age; also that they are concerned mostly with the urban rather than the vast rural picture.[32] They usually base their findings, he suggests, on legal and ethical precepts without due regard for the discrepancies between ideals and realities. The Chinese family, for instance, has historically persistently been the *small* family since the fourth century B.C. Western writers have confused the family and the *clan*. Authority within the family is held jointly by father and mother (including grandparents). On this basis it is not surprising to find, throughout Chinese history down to the time of the republic, according to Dr. Ping-Ti Ho, numerous female rulers, and even yet a considerable number of "matriarchs" in high-status families.[33]

He quotes Dr. Hu Shih, whom he considers "the greatest scholar of twentieth-century China," that "woman has always been the despot of the family" and that "no other country in the world can compete with China for the distinction of being a nation of hen-pecked husbands."[34] But customary law, based on the age-old ethical precepts of mutual respect and consideration, and the ingrained ideal of proper self-restraint and decorum of the "superior person" have tempered both the husband's physical strength and the sharpness of the woman's tongue to the point where the Chinese family has proved, through the centuries, one of the most enduring human institutions.

To know how, and in what form, the Chinese family and the Chinese people will survive the Communist regime, we must wait and see.[35] But in whatever type of social structure, and with whatever religion or religious philosophy, China emerges, it is pretty reasonable to expect that the women will have a hand in it, and with no apologies.

Women in Islam

Of the current major world faiths, the beginnings of Mohammedanism have the best historic documentation. Mohammed was born in 570 A.D. in Mecca, until sometime later quite an uncelebrated desert town on the Arabic Peninsula. He was born after his father's death, reared by his mother Aminah (she died when he was six) and by his uncle, Abu Talib, and his grandfather. Talib took him to Syria when he was twelve. Here he came into contact with both Christians and Jews and acquired a great admiration for Abraham, which was important in his later teachings.

At twenty-five, he was working for Hadijah, a rich Meccan widow, fifteen years his senior, managing her Syrian affairs for her. She became his first convert and his wife. During her lifetime he had no other wives.

They had four daughters, but only one, Fatima, had children: two sons, Hasan and Husain. All Mohammed's sons died at birth, so his numerous descendants are all through Fatima.[36]

For his first three years as a prophet, Mohammed made only fifty converts. He was thoroughly discouraged, for it seemed to him that the people of Mecca cared only for magic and miracles, and that they thought of religion in terms of the business brought to the town by visits of neighboring Arabs to see the Great Black Stone (considered sacred) and the opportunity to purchase an idol or a charm.

In 622 A.D., when he was fifty-two, he turned his back on Mecca and went to Medina. This year of "the Flight" is the date from which Mohammedans reckon their time. Mohammed became a judge; and in the name of Allah a lawgiver at Medina. His followers took the sword to establish the faith and confiscated the infidel's goods to recoup the treasury. In 630 Mohammed returned to and conquered Mecca; the idols were destroyed, but the Great Black Stone was spared.

About this time Hadijah died, and Mohammed became betrothed to Aishah, the six-year-old daughter of a friend. At the same time he married a mature widow and thereafter, throughout his life, built up a harem worthy of an eastern potentate. But Aishah became known as "the Beloved." She is reported to have been his only virgin wife, and certainly many of the women the prophet added to his harem were not added for romantic reasons. Some were gifts and some represented political alliances; but he always seems to have had a sense of responsibility toward unfortunate ladies whom he felt needed protection. The only evidence of his ever having a woman executed was when one sang insulting satirical songs about him and caused him to be laughed at in public.

It was with Aishah that Mohammed spent his final days. She lived for fifty years after his death and was a considerable power in the Mohammedan community.[37]

What interests us now is to point out the prophet's own attitude toward women in relation to the social viewpoint of his day, and then see how matters changed when his militant followers began to

quarrel over power after his death.[38] Finally we would like to note
how this has affected the women of Moslem-dominated countries
through the intervening centuries, and then see how one of Aishah's
namesakes, in our own day, took the lead in freeing her sisters from
the intolerable burden which the religion of the male followers of
Mohammed placed upon them.

The stories from Mohammed's own time do not give the impression
that women in general were "downtrodden." Certainly his widowed
mother does not seem to have been in dire distress, and certainly
Hadijah was a woman of considerable wealth and business interests,
who apparently married her young employee because she was really
devoted to him and believed in him.

Tor Andrae tells us that many married women became converts to
the new faith. In fact, Mohammed may have been a victim of the
unfortunate overpopularity with the ladies which has annoyed other
men of religion from time to time.[39] In Sur 60.10, Allah, speaking
through his prophet, makes it known that such women must all be
examined as to the purity of their faith. Only if they pass this examination are they to be accepted as followers. Otherwise they are returned to the unbelievers from whom they came. Umm Habiba was
one of these converts. She later married Mohammed. Mohammed,
says Tor Andrae, sought to control license concerning sex by (1) raising the ethical concept of marriage, (2) by legislation, (3) by giving
married women their legal rights in regard to inheritance, and (4)
especially by teaching, as part of the Moslem faith, that they must
be treated with kindness, friendliness, justice.[40] Modesty in women
was enjoined, but the veil was adopted later from Persian and Syrian
Christians.[41]

During the wars at Mecca, we are told that "a host of women
followed the army in the belief that they would serve to spur the
fighting spirit [of the Mohammedans]. . . . Before the armies met,
the women marched before the army of the Meccans, singing to the
accompaniment of tambourines, withdrawing later behind the host.
Behind the lines they stopped those who were fleeing and urged them
to return to the battle."[42]

Tor Andrae admits that Mohammed's restrictions on the personal
liberty of women (though his wives were by no means closely restricted, according to later standards) and his patriarchal pronouncements sound like retrogression, but insists that he was only trying to
conform to the attitudes of the country's more "civilized" neighbors.
The idea was to make Arabia more acceptable in international circles.

It was true that a man was allowed to beat his wife if she was really refractory, but otherwise he was enjoined to be good to her. Mohammed was, we hope, referring to physical strength when (Sura 4:3) he said that "men are superior to women on account of the qualities with which Allah hath endowed them one above the other, and on account of the outlay they make from their substance for them."[43]

Nabia Abbott in her story of *Aishah, the Beloved of Mohammed*,[44] gives us an outline of some of the different types of marriage prevalent at this time in Arabia: For many people loose ties and polygamy were the rule. Divorce was simple for either party, and remarriage after divorce was approved. "Sex," she tells us, "was nearly an obsession with the entire population, and sex talk, frank among the better element, tended to be indecent and lewd among the worst sort. Mohammed tried to get both the men and women to be more modest (Sura 24:31–34; 33:59). To honor, protect, and keep track of his wives, Mohammed secluded them." The restrictions were not strict, however. Relatives were permitted to visit the women, and the qualifications widely interpreted. When a woman complained that she wished to have a visitor who was not a relative, the prophet is said to have suggested, "Give him some of your milk, and make him a foster son."

In regard to relations with neighboring countries and the desire to conform to their standards of culture, it might be noted that the Christian governor of Egypt sent two lovely Copt girls to Mohammed for his harem. Women who, like Aishah, had no children of their own were permitted to adopt sons of relatives or other members of the harem (without the child giving up any relation to his own mother). Thus all could happily hold the title of "mother" and share in the honor it implied.[45]

Each of Mohammed's wives (there were eight at the time of his death) had her own apartment, adjoining the mosque, and he apparently prided himself on keeping strictly to schedule in his visits and the supplies sent to the apartments. He even seems to have discouraged their natural tendency to gossip to him about each other. Here, some would say, was truly proof of a self-disciplined man! In his last days, however, he asked and was granted permission by the other wives to end his days in Aishah's apartment. She cared for him at the last, and in her apartment he was buried until a place was made ready for him in the mosque itself. Aishah had been popular with the other wives and had often been able to do favors for those with whom she was most friendly. Mohammed had arranged an income for each of them, with use of their apartments as long as they lived.

As the former wives of the great prophet, it was not considered seemly that any of them should marry again. There were no male heirs through these wives, only through his daughter Fatima, born to Hadijah.[46]

No one was really ready to carry on the prophet's work after he died. Aishah, while still only eighteen, may have imagined that she could do something of the sort. But, in the intrigues and battles that followed, she did not have the competence. Her training had not been in that direction.

But though no match for the Moslem men in intrigue and battle, Aishah became a legend for her contribution to the Moslem religion. Women at this time were not debarred from the mosque, and Aishah must have made good use of her opportunities. Her good works and and wisdom won her the title of "Mother of the Believers." She ranks with the leading traditionalists of the Moslems, being credited with 2210 traditions, of which 1210 were direct from Mohammed. Of these, however, the official compilers accepted only 174. She is said to have known the text of the Koran, considerable medicine, and astronomy. Her reputation for wisdom, and the extent to which she was sought out for consultation and advice, was phenomenal. When she died, at sixty-four, she asked to be buried with the other wives—her "sisters." It is said that Orthodox Moslems honor her memory, but some heterodox groups officially curse her.

Mohammed is said to have been anything but a violent person, and wars of conquest were apparently repugnant to him, though the "Holy War" was "necessary." His followers found no one person around whom to unite. They had, moreover, been awaiting the day when they could put into effect the military expansion which they believed was inevitable. By 800 they had taken over West Asia, North Africa, and West China, and the spread extended on into Central Asia, India, Malaya, Russia. Any pretext of theological unity gave way to warring sects. Superstition won over reason. Women, as always seems to happen, lost position and became subservient in proportion as the devotees took to the sword and put their hopes on military might. Before long the only real unity was in a sort of personal loyalty to the prophet and his words—and perhaps in a determination to keep women in their place. Even the extent of the subjugation of women varied greatly from country to country, for with such rapid expansion there was bound to be a great deal of synchronization with local customs.

It has been said that there is too little history in the earliest period of Mohammedanism, too much in the period following his death. Everyone wanted to prove his closeness to the prophet, and probably everybody's story needed to be accepted with a bit of skepticism. The traditions were compiled of practically everything anyone could remember the prophet saying. They were attacked, edited, and used by rival groups to prove their own superiority. The word Fatimite was invented to indicate families who claimed descent through Mohammed's daughter. But Fatima had married Ali, a cousin of Mohammed, whose adherents had their own claims.[47]

Mohammed is said to have told his daughter: "Fatima, continue to be diligent in religious action, for on the Day of Judgment you will not be asked whose daughter you are, you will only be asked how you employed yourself."[48]

He also said: "He who is blessed with a daughter or daughters and makes no discrimination between them and his sons, and brings them up with fondness and affection, will be as close to me in Paradise as my forefinger and middle finger are to each other."

Marriage was not considered an indissoluble sacrament, but a civil contract with mutual obligations. The husband's settlement of dower (4:5) gives the wife property over which she has absolute control. Meditation must precede divorce—meditation on the part of both husband and wife (4:2–22, 4:36, 2:229, 230). At one time Mohammed got disgusted with the bickerings of his wives over some petty jealousy and seriously threatened to divorce the whole lot of them. However, in more normal moments he said that the best garment is that of righteousness and that the husband and wife should try to be such a garment to each other (7:27, 2:229). Married life is the higher state because it means complete and co-ordinated development of the personality (4:4).

It had been easier for the prophet to smash idols than to root out superstition. One of the oldest superstitions and taboos that has dogged women of practically every race has been a certain fear that primitive men feel of her during the un-understandable process of menstruation. Without knowledge of the physiological processes involved, she seems "strange" and to the primitive mind the strange is always to be feared and avoided. The menstruating woman is sent outside the camp of the primitive tribe and must be ceremonially purified before her return. There are vestiges of this primitive superstitious fear in practically every religion, and it is certainly no surprise to find them among the Moslems. For though the Moslem faith was chronologically late in being founded, it came out of a civilization which was still close to the wandering days in the desert. Moreover, the military advance of the Moslem religion came at a time when civilization in the entire West was more or less at low ebb. In the conquered countries, there was little intellectual leavening force.

Here are ten "prohibitions" against women of Islam during the menstrual period. Their origin is not clear, but they undoubtedly came from the period after the prophet's death. It is codes of this kind which may have led Ibadat, in the medieval period, to say that interpretations of the law are not binding unless founded on the Koran itself. A woman during her menstrual period:

> May not pray (otherwise five prayers are required daily from all adults except women recovering from childbirth).
>
> She is excused from the *obligation* of prayer.
>
> She does not fast.
>
> She does not circumambulate holy places.
>
> She does not read the Koran.
>
> She does not touch a copy of the Koran.
>
> She does not remain in the mosque.
>
> She does not have sexual contacts.
>
> She cannot be formally repudiated as a wife.
>
> These days are not to be counted in a period of voluntary continence.[49]

In a handbook of early Mohammedan tradition, we find that conversation with men other than her family is prohibited at any time. Women may not wear their finest clothes for foreigners, nor to the mosque. But they are not to be prevented from visiting the mosque (there was apparently a move in this direction). Their actions in the mosque are regulated.

A women must always use decent speech. She can't dispose of the husband's possessions without his consent, but can take what she wants and needs. She is responsible for his possessions. She must not be guilty of coquetry during her husband's absence. Special prayers are prescribed for women who die in childbirth. A man should not beat his wife as he beats his slave.

A concordance of the early *hadith*, which has been in preparation since 1916, promises to throw considerable light on the early development, and in instances transformation, of the Mohammedan religion, as taught by the prophet himself; and we are told that many modern Moslem women are very much interested in having this volume for study.[50]

Wilfred Smith points out that "where these two parts of life, sexual and religious, overlap and interpenetrate, the psychological resistance to conscious and rational thought, let alone to actual progress, is enormous. The attitudes, categories of thinking, values, etc., of a given sexual code, when sanctified by religion, can be discarded, or even dispassionately considered, only by those who have attained a very unusual degree of mental and emotional emancipation. In the light of modern psychological knowledge, it is not at all surprising that sex should be about the last point on which a religion makes progress."

To quote Iqbal again, who, at the very end of his life, realized that he had been wrong about women:

> I, too, at the oppression of women am most sorrowful. But the problem is intricate: no solution do I find possible.[51]

There are not too many significant stories about Moslem women from this period of the expansion. The ones, like the story of Abassa, are more boring than informative, but unfortunately typical. Abassa, sister of Haroun al Raschid, caliph of the Saracens, 786, was so beautiful and accomplished that her brother thought she was too good for any man. He finally married her to the Vizar Giafar, on condition that she should never be his real wife. But she was, and had twins. Having broken his vow, Giafar was put to death, and Abassa turned out to wander and sing songs of her misfortunes. But before his death Giafar had managed to hide the twins and send them to Mecca to be educated.

Through the centuries, reformers have risen to question the place of women in the Islamic tradition and the detrimental effect of their subjugation on Islamic culture and world status. Appeals have been made to the Koran—both the written book and the "Invisible Koran," of which the theologians said the written book is a symbol, and to which they could always appeal. But the social pressures, backed by the *popular concept* of what the Moslem religion thought of women, were strong against change. The women, subjugated and uneducated, were without the knowledge or the power to help themselves. It was not till the end of the nineteenth century that there were visible signs of improvement which gave promise of a real turn for the better (at least from the women's point of view).

Emile Dermenghem cites the unrelatedness of the literary vocabulary of the Arabic languages to life and the unrealistic attitude toward women in relation to modern society as two factors that have held back Moslem integration into the fullness of modern culture. "Like most Semitic societies, the Muslims have a patriarchal constitution, and have not yet found the point of equilibrium. The situation with regard to woman and the family has created for Muslim society a serious handicap, of which it is more or less aware, which it sometimes tries to deny, and from which it sometimes tries to free itself." The author, however, seems to be protesting symptoms rather than basic cause: "The three main points are polygamy, the right of jabr [marriage of minors without consent being necessary], and unilateral divorce."[52] But are not the general subjugation, the fact that most women have been cut off from educational facilities commensurate with their capacities, the overapproval of sexy sex in the feminine, and the fact that for the most part women have so little participation in or opportunity to study religion itself the essential obstacles? The Moslem woman needs to rediscover a role of which she can be proud.

At the turn of the century Qasim Amin, known as the "father of feminism," wrote his New Woman and was threatened with assassination. Madame Sharawi founded the Women's Union and edited L'Egyptienne in French and Arabic. In Tunisia, Tahir al-Haddad published in 1930 Our Women in Law and Society, maintaining that the literalists were degrading Moslem society. He was apparently officially ignored, but the fat was in the fire. Unhappily, in many ways, the reforms have not come, in most countries, as a result of religious revival in the true sense, so much as because the countries, now forced willy-nilly into the family of nations, have found their representatives culturally embarrassed. In some countries the Christian universities for women have begun to get to the heart of the matter. In Pakistan, shortly after the partition, the writer heard again and again high commendation for some official, with the interesting explanation (since it usually came from a Moslem) that the official worked under a great advantage—his wife—perhaps a Christian or perhaps a Moslem—had had the privilege of attending Kinnaird Christian College. The principal of the school explained that these girls were always in great demand and actually a very influential factor for honesty and diligence in the new government.

The whole country of Pakistan was at that time a strange mixture of old and new. The same woman might wear a bourka (a tent-like, all-covering outside garment) one day, leave it off the next. Girls would fold their bourkas and lay them aside while they practiced sharpshooting, which they had petitioned to have as part of the school curriculum. The energetic woman head of the Women's Moslem League stopped supervising the unloading of a shipment of relief goods from Church World Service to chat with a visitor from America. The writer shared a train compartment with a young movie actress who was "fed up" with all regulations, visited refugee camps and orphanages with a competent young lady who was a trained social worker, went with the wife of a government official to visit the cottage weavers she was organizing throughout the state, and attended a party where refreshments were wonderful pudding topped with curled silver leaf, and the hospitality surely up to the highest tradition of Moslem women. But, from all of them, there came no real insight into how the Moslem woman really feels about her religion, or what part, if any, she has in it. On the holiday when the little boys' nude bodies were painted as tigers to fight for their patrons Husan and Husein, and the young men competed almost violently for the privilege of bearing on their shoulders in the parade the flower-decked coffins in which these religious heroes "really are, though of course they aren't," the writer sat with the ladies on a shuttered balcony and watched.

These Pakistani women were alert and often well-educated Moslems. But there were few answers to questions about the meaning of what was going on in the street below us. Nor was there any real evidence that their religion was helping them, personally, to resolve their problems, or to work out a basis for the women's integration and usefulness in the social and political life of their country. They were extremely eager, in these days just after the partition of the Indian subcontinent, and the setting up of the new Moslem government of Pakistan, to be good Moslems (even if it involved going back to wearing the all-enveloping bourka, which to a Western woman seemed like quite an ultimate mark of devotion). But aside from traditional loyalty to her husband's religion, it is hard for a westerner to understand exactly what the Moslem religion means to a Moslem woman.

One of the very influential women in bringing new freedom and self-respect to modern Moslem women has been, interestingly enough, the namesake of Mohammed's own Aishah, the Beloved. She is the Princess Aisha, the eldest daughter of the late Mohammed, Sultan, and King of Morocco, sister of the present king. In the November 11, 1957 issue of *Time* magazine[53] there was a feature story about her appearing "unveiled and unashamed," some ten years earlier, when she was only seventeen, to speak to a large gathering of her fellow countrymen, asking them to make bold to root out and reject the bad prejudices which had been fastened upon them. "It is essential," she is quoted as saying, "that the women of Morocco participate ardently and usefully in the life of the nation, imitating in this respect their sisters of the East and West, whose great activity contributes to the welfare of their countries." Morocco's women recognized this for what it was, says *Time*—"a call to shake off age-old bondage fastened on them in the name of Mohammed and perpetuated by generations of mullahs [teachers]. Taking courage from this display of feminist leadership from the royal family itself, thousands of women from all over the country forthwith cast aside their veils and began talking briskly of emancipation."

With a nucleus of educated women to give the movement leadership, in one Moslem country after another, during the period since that day in 1947, the rising tide of national independence and the emancipation of women from their age-old subjugation have gone hand in hand. "In ten years," says the *Time* journalist, "Islam's women have achieved a greater change of status than in the preceding ten hundred." Ten years later Princess Aisha admitted that in her youthful naïveté she hadn't the faintest idea of the importance and possible results of what she was saying. Allah, as Mohammed would undoubtedly have agreed, uses his own channels of communication when the occasion arises.

The beautiful young Princess Aisha would seem to have been an appropriate and effective channel. Of course as soon as the royal party had left the city, officials ordered all the women who had appeared in Western dress arrested, and those who resisted had their clothes torn off and were publicly disgraced. But opposition did not stop the princess or the Moslem women of the twentieth century, any more than it had stopped the original Aishah and the Moslem women of her day. The princess found herself not only a national heroine, but a heroine for the progressive-minded women of the whole Moslem world. The French thought she was inflammatory and forbade her to make speeches. The older official Moslem clique ranted till they got the whole royal family sent into exile. Aisha became a pin-up idol for the veiled women of Morocco and elsewhere. And in one of the strangest feminine movements of modern times, thousands of women refused to have sex relations with their husbands on the grounds that they would not risk bringing into the world girl children to live under the present regime.

The royal family's return after two years was a triumph. The Princess Aisha at once began to devote herself to literacy work and social welfare for the women of her country. Her father backed her completely; in fact, the education and discipline he gave his children indicate he wanted it this way. And fortunately he was the religious as well as the temporal ruler of his people. In spite of what any of the old men said by way of interpreting Mohammed's teaching, King Mohammed insisted that if the prophet were alive he would be shocked at the uses to which his words and teachings had been turned by the reactionaries through all these years.

Morocco's Minister of Justice, agreeing, is quoted as saying: "Over the centuries, false interpretations of Islamic law have loaded society with social abuses of many varieties. Nowhere is this more apparent than in the situation of Muslim women. Islam makes woman equal with man, and with the same rights and the same duties."

In country after country there are similar stories to be told, similar names to be mentioned, similar progress to be reported. The course of change runs unevenly, and, sad to say, much of the most persistent resistance comes from the women themselves, who have believed for so long that their subservience is the will of Allah, as revealed through Mohammed, that they are afraid to let themselves believe it possible that their plight is less than "sacred."

The most encouraging factor is the willingness of privileged Moslem women, who have discovered their own freedom as persons, to help other women make the same discovery—through education, social welfare, and a healthy interest in world politics. The leaders of the feminist movement in Islam hope that they can find a middle way of accepting modern culture without a complete break with the traditions of Islam or with the older generations. They hope Moslem women will not try to take freedom without accepting related responsibilities. And some of them feel that the way to accomplish this may be not to argue with the traditionalists of their religion, but to go back to the very beginnings and apply the first fundamentals of Islamic teaching to the life and customs of the twentieth century.

Appendix II

RELIGIOUS CAREERS FOR TODAY'S WOMEN

Religion as a professional career has, for the first time in many centuries, real possibilities for the woman who feels called to this sort of service and has the persistence and fortitude, good humor and devotion that are necessary. In many denominations the formal barriers even to ordination are down, but this does not, by any means, indicate that more subtle barriers do not still exist.

In the churches of the United States, at least, the vocation of religious education is the one which in all its various ramifications is most genuinely open to women. The religious educators have, of course, their own problems of low salaries and often of not being accepted as full members of the ministerial staff of the church. To the extent that they are "downgraded," it is not their pride but their usefulness to the Church as a whole that is the matter of concern. It is also strange that in some churches the director of Christian education is supposed to deal only with children and young people through the high school age. Adult education is taken over by the minister whose appointment was based, primarily, on his ability to preach a good sermon.

There is little point in going through the list of ministries and services women may be well equipped to offer the Church, together with all the obstacles which may confront them as they seek to make their service really creative and offer the Church the best of which they are capable. Each church—each situation—is different and a case in itself.

The church which hires carefully selected well-trained women for various positions, offering opportunities for and expecting continuing growth, rewarding them with adequate salaries comparable to what the same woman could expect in secular work, giving them responsibility and encouragement and dignity, might expect something very special from them in the line of service and would seldom be disappointed.

The calling of the deaconess varies so much between different churches that it is impossible to generalize about either its problems or opportunities. In general the Episcopal and Lutheran churches, which have been very reluctant to ordain women to a preaching ministry, have urged the deaconess calling as a full-time career and have offered specialized training courses in both the United States and European countries. Recently the Methodist Church has been revitalizing its deaconess program; the magazine *Together* issued a special number (Feb. 1963), with a graphic story about the work and the training which entitles a deaconess to serve "through any of the [Methodist] agencies not requiring full clergy rights. . . . She may be a supply pastor, a parish worker, a teacher, a nurse, a housemother, a dietitian, a chaplain, purchasing agent, program director, or a worker on a state university campus."

In the Baptist churches or United Church of Christ, the deaconess is apt to be elected or appointed for a certain term, requiring no specialized training except such as may be given by the ministerial staff. One New England Baptist Church, however, sent us literature showing a most successful parish plan for home visitation, evangelism, sponsorship of new members, service to the housebound and others in need, all built around a large diaconate in which deaconesses and deacons worked together in teams, or as members of subcommittees on baptism, church membership, Communion, devotional life, fellowship fund, non-resident relations, homebound, evangelism, re-enlistment, sponsorship. But in another church, equally liberal in background, the women are a sort of subcommittee of the male diaconate with only two functions—calling on sick women and caring for the Communion materials and utensils. *The Methodist Woman*, on the other hand (Sept. 1962), carries an article on "Deaconesses Explore International Affairs"; an annual workshop at the United Nations in New York is part of their training and includes techniques for making such matters significant to those with whom they will come in contact during their years of service. The Mennonites also emphasize their deaconess training program.

As long as there is such great diversity in the interpretation of what a deaconess really is, recruitment for this office in the churches on either a vocational or a volunteer basis will suffer. The relation between men and women in the diaconate is also confused. In some churches the deaconess is merely the willing helper of the deacon. In others, the board of deaconesses is quite independent and goes its own way. In some few, there is true partnership within a strong diaconate. One Presbyterian Church reported that it had a board of deaconesses and also women members of the board of deacons—not the same women.

In some churches a deacon is on his way to becoming fully ordained clergy; but this is seldom presumed to be true of a deaconess.

In many ways it seems that a very serious and perhaps prolonged ecumenical study of the diaconate, at highest levels, might be rewarding. It should be a subject upon which men and women and various churches could work together in comparative harmony, yet which would be theologically stimulating enough to have real permanent value to the Church. It would fit in well with the World Council's Department on the Cooperation of Men and Women in Church, the Family and Society, the National Council's Department of the Laity, or with a corresponding department or committee within a local Council of Churches.

At present many girls who sincerely want to go into religious work consider the choice between seminary training or a career with the YW. There is little opportunity to get unprejudiced but informed counsel.

Some time ago the National Council of Churches published a small folder listing a series of "Jobs to Be Done":

Church Secretary
Director of Education
Church Social Worker
Parish Music Director
Weekday Church School Teacher
Ordained Minister
College Religious Teacher
University Worker
General Missionary
Specializing Missionary
Church Journalist and Publicist
(Personal and Family Counseling, Financial Secretary, and Worker with Older Adults are among other headings which should surely be added.)

However, probably in a desire to be "realistic" about church starting salaries and probable future, the job descriptions are scarcely inspiring enough to tempt a top-notch college girl away from a promising secular career. We all know churches in which the church secretary is the on-going spiritual dynamo that lasts through changing pastorates and keeps the laity active and enthusiastic over the program of the church, who has studied—or is studying—theology, edits the minister's sermons as she types them, and sends the newspapers well-constructed and significant news stories which do the public relations job they should do in a community. She has a good chance of working into a regional administrative position. Yet we are told in the above pamphlet that the "usual training" for a church secretary is "high school or business school." If there is any office in the church about which many a congregation needs to have its sights lifted, it is the job of the church secretary. Yet it is true that church secretaries are often hired—and paid—primarily on the basis of words per minute they are able to type. It often seems, in fact, that a woman who is a good typist, mimeograph operator, or who has some other special skill, but is not particularly interested in "meddling" with the minister's job of religion, is what is desired for the church.

It is hardly necessary to suggest how improbable it would be to find a list comparable to this one put out for the recruitment of *men* to the service of the Church. The double standards of responsibility, expectations, and pay for church work as between men and women are really shocking anachronisms of which the secular world is well aware; they lower the respect for religion in the eyes of the government bureau, the honest businessman, or the union member. It is often said that the woman going into church work as a professional career needs to be told that she had better be at the top of her class (which she frequently is), work twice as hard, twice as many hours, and demand only half the pay and none of the credit, if she is to succeed. But she *can* hope that as a pioneer she is, even under her present handicaps, opening the way for many women to have the right to serve the Church to the full extent of their highest spiritual as well as technical abilities.

Even more important (because so *many* women are involved) is the challenge to religion to help the woman whose daily work is in the home, school, factory, office, store, or some of current society's many service programs, to discover and pursue, within her daily work, the possibilities for Christian service. Many women are for a certain period of their lives "home and family management experts" in their own domiciles. Many who work prefer occupations which also involve personal relation contacts of one sort or another. For them, especially, the witness of the "Christian in his daily work" offers tremendous possibilities. This is one of the "growing concerns" of the National Council's Department of Church and Economic Life, whose published materials include *Employed Women and the Church* by Cynthia Wedel, and *Report of Consultation on Employed Women and the Church* (including six speeches by church, employment, and educational leaders). Their *New Trails for a New Decade* is a leaflet listing ideas and materials, which seldom fail to acknowledge the existence of both men and women as church assets.

There would be small profit at this point in going into a full-scale discussion of the problems which arise when volunteers and paid church workers perform the same kind of service for the church. Volunteers can have misgivings about doing (free!) the jobs paid church staff find boring and time-consuming, rather than investing their volunteer hours in some creative activity, along a line in which they are competent—perhaps have a high level of experience.

This may become a serious problem in the case of a minister's wife. Is she presumed to be an unpaid but full-time church employee? How much can the church expect of her? Does the denomination offer higher pay to married male ministers on the grounds that the wife is also obligated? What if she takes a job outside the church? One wife may have "put her hubby through seminary" with her stenographic ac-complishments and attended classes on the side so she could help him in his parish work. Another minister's wife may have only the most casual interest in his career of religion. When we come to discussing minister's wives' responsibilities, Solomon himself should be moderat-ing the panel. But, even without Solomon, it would be better to bring such matters into the open. There is also the minister's wife with no experience or training in religion at the professional level who, in her husband's name, "takes over"—and there are often "old-timers" in the congregation who try to stop her, no matter how competent she may be.

A newer problem concerning volunteers is raised by the greatly in-creased number of retired persons in most churches, many of them living on a very meager pension. They are a real asset for the church, and the church has many interesting jobs—at all levels—which they can do competently, some with real inspiration to the rest of the con-gregation. By far the majority of these older persons are women. Many of them, however, can no longer afford the expenses of volunteering. Bus fares, lunches away from home, even suitable clothing can be a problem when one's cash income is less than $100 per month. While Solomon is presiding at our panel, let him tell us what to do about this.

Girls entering our theological seminaries need excellent counseling, not to dissuade them from working for a B.D. degree, but to tell them exactly what is involved, so they can intelligently make up their own minds whether (1) the pulpit ministry or missionary service is for them; (2) they will find a more fruitful avenue of Christian service in one of the specialized ministries of the Church, such as counseling, religious education, deaconess work, or religious journalism; or (3) they will be at their best in some secular calling such as teaching, social welfare work, or nursing, in which a distinctive Christian witness is needed. A young woman contemplating a career in religion will need counseling by someone who fully understands and can help her to understand the meaning of "the priesthood of all believers," and who will point out that the role of the laity bearing a Christian witness through daily work can be as challenging as the role of the minister in the pulpit.

For the girl who, in the full knowledge of the facts and the probable difficulties and discrimination she may encounter, still feels the call to the pulpit ministry, there should certainly be more opportunities for contact with other women in the ministry, both during her seminary days and during her days in her first church, which can be, professionally, very lonely indeed. Women in the ministry, or those in denominational offices, should do a much better job of encouraging our younger sisters, helping them over the first hurdles, or at least being available when they need a hand. The young woman minister had had in the past almost none of the job companionship she would have had in, for instance, nursing or teaching; or that the male minister finds in colleagues from among the male ministers of his own or other denominations.

Denominational and interdenominational executives can do a great deal to see that she is introduced and invited to ministerial meetings and put on committees that bring her in touch with civic affairs. They can keep a watchful eye to see that she is not being exploited because, in her anxiety to have a chance to serve, she does not protect her own financial interests. None of these matters are "asking for special privileges"—which is usually the last thing a newly ordained woman wants; they represent only the concern of the responsible and established person for the newcomer and the minority, making sure she receives the normal welcome which should be extended to *any* new minister.

Oddly enough, some of the best statements concerning women's right to full participation in the life and work of the Church have come from members of the Anglican clergy. Canon Charles E. Raven of Liverpool was for many years a vigorous and scholarly advocate of women's full participation. In his *Women and Holy Orders* (Hodder and Stoughton, 1928) he set the tone on this solid footing:

The admission of women to Holy Orders on an equality with men is inherent in the teachings of Jesus and necessitated by a true understanding of the nature of the Church; and my experience of their spiritual fitness and of the needs of the time confirms this conclusion. . . . It is a matter of theological principle, even more than of justice and expediency." As examining chaplain to three bishops, he assures us that he knows "literally dozens of women far more fit for ordination than the majority of the men now being accepted; and this is not because the men are of poor quality, but because the women are better. . . . It is really tragic that the Church's work should be starved because we refuse to recognize and accept the offering of the new womanhood.

Other excellent material on this whole subject is contained in the *Report of the Archbishop's Commission on the Ministry of Women* (Church House, Westminster S.W. 1, 1935).

More recently, Donald Noor, Archbishop of York, has stated in a letter published in the *Diocesan Leaflet* (Dec. 1962):

There took place a vigorous debate at Church House, Westminster. The occasion was the Church Assembly. The theme was the work of women in the Church. The report under discussion was entitled "Gender and Ministry." The subject under debate was *not* whether women should be ordained, though some persons brought that issue in. It is an acknowledged fact that too few women are devoting their gifts full-time to the work of the Church. . . . Many who are well trained for this work are seeking their life-work elsewhere. . . . There is an ethic of finance which must be attended to. Why should a competent, fully-trained woman worker receive less than a man of similar qualifications? (Moreover) a woman worker in a parish should be accorded the courtesies which belong to the curate.

Attention should be given to the training of specialists for various kinds of work in the Church. In addition to parochial workers, I think, among a multitude of activities which call for a woman's gifts, of divinity specialists in colleges and schools (with time in their programme for individual and group counseling); of lecturers in theological colleges (there are able women theologians who could lecture at men's colleges, and why should women be trained, in all parts of their work, apart from men?); of women chaplains in the universities; of women chaplains in hospitals and factories; of women in charge of Bible study and discussion groups. . . .

A conservatism which leaves little room for the operation of the Holy Spirit, and a fear which deprives the Church of a great source of strength waiting to flow into it through the proper use of its godly and able women is wholly to be deprecated.

A stirring of conscience, some hard thinking and praying, and swift and costly action are called for.

Appendix III

THE WORLD PICTURE

Ordination

The World Council made a survey of women's ordination in 1958 and again in 1963. Not all churches or countries reported, and there were the inevitable differences in the definition of "ordination," "theologian," etc., but the answers, and subsequent reports, show interesting trends. Churches established as missions are apt to follow the example of the mother church, but may be more liberal. United churches seldom debar from ordination women if they have been accepted by one of the uniting churches. The "Plan of Union in North India" was probably lost because in it the Methodist women would have lost their right of ordination, and Bishop Sunderam warned that "if the women lose their rights now, it will be a century or more before they can get back those lost privileges" (*Christian Century*, 9-25-63).

The following is a summary (updated) of the present status of ordination for women in churches which replied to the W.C.C. questionnaire:

Within the *Orthodox* and related *Eastern churches*, there is no ordination of women to the priesthood. However, the Mar Thoma Church of Malabar (South India) has been studying the Scriptures on the subject and says they are not yet ready to come to a conclusive answer.

Of the *Anglican churches*, only one, in China, has ever ordained a woman, Miss Li Tim Oi. This ordination, directed by urgent wartime need of her services, was later "deplored" by the Lambeth Conference as "a most unwelcome unilateral act," and she was asked not to take advantage of it. There is in England, however, a vigorous minority movement for the ordination of women, and quite a few women study theology. As of October 1963, a lay reader may preach, teach, read parts of the Communion service, but may not administer the sacraments. The Protestant Episcopal Church in the United States granted women similar rights in 1961. However, in 1964 the Episcopalians once more refused to grant women representation in the House of Deputies. The clergy had overwhelmingly approved the proposal, submitted for the fourth time at successive triennial sessions. The vote of the laymen defeated it. However, the Episcopal Church in the United States did recently appoint a woman as head of its very important national Department of Christian Education. A recently (1966) appointed national committee will study the proper place of women in the churches' ministry.

Among the *Lutheran* churches, those in America, Estonia, Iceland, Rumania, and Poland say no to women's ordination. The Lutheran Church in America—largely at the insistence of its seminaries—has authorized (1966) a "comprehensive study" of the advisability of ordination of women as clergy. Czechoslovakia and Denmark were ordaining women in 1958, but only in 1964 did the clergy association of the Lutheran Church of Norway admit a woman to membership. Finland and Sweden, where many women study theology, now accept women as lectors or pastors, but the fact that these countries have state churches complicates the matter and adjustment is slow. It has sometimes been hard to find a bishop willing to ordain a qualified woman, and it has recently been proposed that such unwillingness should disqualify a priest for appointment as a bishop. A woman ordained in Norway does not conduct marriages or funerals. French Lutherans have ordained women, but a woman must give up her parish if she marries. Augsburg of Strasbourg specifies, however, that a woman may resume her ministry if she becomes a widow or is divorced. The Lutheran Church of Hanover now accepts women as pastors; they preach and administer the sacraments. The Evangelical Lutheran Church of the Netherlands has given women full ordination rights since 1929. The Slovak Lutheran Church has for years ordained women as assistants to male pastors. They have now ordained a woman to full charge of a bilingual (Slovak and Magyar) church. Austria makes a nice distinction: they voted in 1956 "on theological grounds" that women have equal *worth* but not equal *nature!* They demonstrated what they meant by putting women *theologians* on an equal financial footing with pastors.

The *Methodist* Church in the United States, which for some time has ordained women, but without any assurance of appointment, in 1956 gave them full clergy rights. As of 1963, there were 380 ordained women, but only a few were ministers in churches. In South America women have had the same rights as men since 1960. Methodists in England and Australia do not ordain women to the ministry—their reluctance is on "pragmatic grounds." The English churches do ordain deaconesses, who may serve the sacraments, and women can and do sit on the committee which examines male candidates for the ministry. Methodists of Ireland have fully ordained women ministers. Korea, New Zealand, and South Africa offer no official discrimination. Dr. Ivy Chou is president of a Methodist Theological Seminary established in 1955 in Sarawak. The Reverend Gusta Robinett is district superintendent of the Methodist Church in North Sumatra Chinese District.

Baptist churches traditionally ordain women.

Congregational churches, and usually those with whom they unite, ordain women. This includes the United Church of Christ (Congregational-Christian-Evangelical-Reformed) in the United States.

The United *Presbyterian* Church in America has ordained women since 1956. The Presbyterian Church in the United States (Southern) voted in 1964 to ordain women as ministers, deacons, and elders. Two weeks later for the first time a woman was elected to the session of a local church of this denomination (*Christian Century,* 7–15–64, p. 916). Ghana ordains women ministers and elders, as do Thailand and, as of 1966, Canada (*Christian Century,* 7–20–66). In many of the younger churches, the question has not come up.

English Presbyterians do not object to women "in principle," but seem to prefer to make good use of their 553 women elders (ordained since 1921). Holland's Presbyterians removed all discrimination in 1958. Australia still says no. The Presbyterian Church of Formosa has ordained women ministers and elders and claimed (1958) that one in four theological students was a woman. The United Free Church of Scotland proudly proclaims that it is the only Presbyterian Church in the world that has a woman as general secretary.

The *Reformed* Church in America does not ordain women, but its theologians have officially found that there is no Scriptural reason against it. The Reformed Church of France has said a limited yes since 1949; all restrictions were removed in 1965. In Czechoslovakia, fifteen women have been ordained since 1953; all are ministers or assistant ministers. In France and Switzerland custom varies from synod to synod.

The *Evangelical Church* of Germany ordains women as vikarin: their ministry is limited, but they can administer the sacraments. In some German churches ordination of women is called "consecration." In February 1963 the *Evangelical Church* in the Rhineland authorized the ordination of thirty-five women theologians; they are all assistant pastors, and the church is encouraging others to study for similar appointment (*EPS,* 2–8–63). Full ordination of women pastors was approved in

West Berlin Church of Berlin-Brandenburg in December 1963. The women will receive the same salary as men pastors. The Church's eastern region had taken similar action in February 1963 (*EPS*, 12–19–63). The *Evangelical Reformed Church* of the canton of Berne, Switzerland, will appoint a qualified woman theologian, where there is already a man pastor. She may be ordained on the same basis as a man pastor.

The *Evangelical United Brethren* say yes without restriction.

The *Evangelical churches* of Brazil and Tanganyika say no. The *Evangelical Protestant churches* of Belgium voted in 1964 to admit women to full ordination from which they had been barred "not by ecclesiastical statutes but by long tradition." The Grossmünster Church of Zurich in 1963 ordained twelve women assistants or acting pastors to full ministerial standing (*EPS*, 11–22–63).

The *Disciples of Christ* in the United States and Canada "make no distinction." Australian *Disciples* ordain women for the mission field. Great Britain *Disciples* do not ordain women and in New Zealand they simply report that they "have no woman ministers."

Mennonites of Germany do not ordain women, but the *General Mennonite Society* of the Netherlands does ordain and makes them members of the presbytery.

The *Moravian Church* says they are encouraging women to train and apply for ordination as a potential "great service to the Church."

The *Brethren* have ordained women since 1960.

The *Old Catholic* churches do not ordain women.

The *Liberal* (Unitarian and Universalists) churches do.

In the Remonstrance Brotherhood of the Netherlands "every church office is open to women."

The United Church of Canada and the United Church of Japan both give full ordination; Japan reports over 100 ordained women. The United Free Church of Scotland removed all restrictions in 1929. The Philippine Independent Church has not yet decided. The Church of South India and the United Church of Northern India and Pakistan have not ordained women, but the latter has accepted ordination of women ordained in America. The Church of South India has an "order of lay women in addition to the deaconesses."

The *Salvation Army* International says all offices are open alike to both sexes. The Army is run on a basis of complete equality.

The *Friends* have "no concept of special ordination for men or women," but "boast a little" of "equal status both programmed and pastoral and a lively history in mission and ministry from the Friends' beginning."

This sampling, with all allowances for differences in ways of reporting, terminology, and time lag, indicates what seems to be an undeniable trend. The prohibitions against women in the ministry are giving way. But there is the long road ahead of winning full acceptance and approval.

For a comprehensive survey of the world picture, see Madeleine Barot's *Cooperation of Men and Women in Church, Family and Society* (World Council of Churches, 150 route de Ferney, 1211 Geneva 20, Switzerland, or 475 Riverside Drive, New York, N.Y. 10027). See also "Ordination of Women, an Ecumenical Problem," "Basic Considerations," "Christian Women in Africa Share in Responsibility," "Partnership," and other related documents (same address). Same address for *Ecumenical Press Service*.

See also roundup of current developments, *Christian Century*, 4-20-66, p. 502.

Representation

It is very difficult to get most member churches of the World Council of Churches to appoint women delegates to the General Assembly. It is next to impossible to get most of them to confirm appointments of women to the Central Committee. Competition for the 100 or so places is very keen, and few women, whatever their qualifications, have a chance with their own churches. The World Council can do nothing about the fact that, of the 160 voting delegates sent by the United States churches to the Third World Council Assembly in 1961, just sixteen were women. (For list see *Church Woman*, Jan. 1962.) Neither did the World Council have any control over the fact that there was only *one* woman delegate (she was from Britain) to the Fourth World Conference on Faith and Order at Montreal in 1963.

The Montreal conference had the grace to be quite self-conscious over the matter. Some of the delegates asked, "Aren't the women part of our one household?" or "Why is only half the Church represented?" Perhaps the point was made by the almost complete absence of women more forcibly than it could have been made in any other way. It became evident that some of the world's most profound theologians (their own status very sure indeed!) agree that the question needs serious top-level discussion, with plenty of the time for ecumenical dialogue. The study section dealing with "relevant ministry" sought to put the "ordained" ministry in the larger context of *corporate* ministry "of the whole people of God" and to relate it to the work of the Council's Departments on the Laity and Evangelism. In this context the section urged a study of women "in the ministry and ministries"— "a subject on which the traditions of the churches vary sharply." They said, "It is of great importance to insure that there should be a real ecumenical dialogue on the subject." The study, they insisted, should include church law and practice, Biblical and doctrinal examination, and sociological and psychological factors. Professor J. D. McCaughey, Presbyterian of Australia, was the chairman of this section of the conference (*EPS*, 8–2–63).

Attending the important Consultation of Church Union's fifth session, held at Dallas (May 1966) were over seventy churchmen from eight major United States denominations. Except for Rachel Henderlite of Austin Presbyterian Seminary, the women were all from the growing fellowship of *writing* ministers—Margaret Frakes, associate editor, *Christian Century*; Dorothy McConnell, editor of Methodist *Outlook*; Helen Baker, for many years editor of *Church Woman*; Janet Harbison, staff of *Presbyterian Life*.

NOTES AND BIBLIOGRAPHY

Introduction

Background References

S. Faber and R. Wilson, *Potential of Women* (New York: McGraw-Hill, 1963). The report of the papers given at the University of California conference; authoritative scientific background from various disciplines.

Alva Myrdal and Viola Klein, *Women's Two Roles* (London: Routledge and Kegan, 1956).

Marion Turner Sheehan, ed., *The Spiritual Woman* (New York: Harper, 1955).

Betty Friedan, *Feminine Mystique* (New York: Norton, 1962).

Morton Hunt, *Her Infinite Variety* (New York: Harper and Row, 1962).

Simone de Beauvoir, *The Second Sex*, tr. by H. M. Parshley (New York: Knopf, 1953).

Ashley Montagu, *Natural Superiority of Women* (New York: Macmillan, 1953). An unfortunate title for a good book.

John Henry Cutler, *What about Women?* (New York: Ives Washburn, 1961). A popular presentation of some general facts and statistics comparing men and women.

Margaret Mead, *Male and Female* (New York: Morrow, 1949).

———*Continuities in Cultural Evolution* (New Haven: Yale University Press, 1964).

E. W. Sinnott, *Matter, Mind and Man* (New York: Harper, 1957). A beautiful exposition of the light botany can contribute to our discussion.

Lynn White, Jr., ed., *Frontiers of Knowledge* (New York: Harper, 1956). Chapter I by Theodosius Dobzhansky, re genetics.

Julian Huxley, *Evolution in Action* (New York: Harper, 1953).

Russell Prohl, *Women in the Church* (Grand Rapids, Mich.: Eerdmans, 1957): "The church has a vast reservoir of latent talent in her devoted and highly qualified women. To keep this treasure in storage is poor stewardship."

D. Heinz-Dietrich Wendland, "Partnership," a paper prepared for the 1955 Kirchentag at Frankfurt, Germany. Available through the World Council of Churches. "Neither human society nor the Christian community can exist without this di-unity of man and woman."

William Douglas, "Women in the Church: Historical Perspectives and

Contemporary Dilemmas" in *Pastoral Psychology*, June 1961. Excellent
background for our discussion.

Columbia Encyclopedia (New York: Columbia University Press, 1950).

Webster's Biographical Dictionary (Springfield, Mass.: G. and C. Merriam
and Co., 1943). Used, in general, for spellings and dates.

Catholic Encyclopaedia (New York: Appleton, 1907).

Jewish Encyclopaedia (New York: Funk and Wagnalls, 1904).

Holy Bible, Revised Standard Version.

Concerning the Orante

W. Lowrie, *Monuments of the Early Church* (London: Macmillan, 1901).

H. D. M. Spence-Jones, *The Early Christians in Rome* (New York: John
Lane, 1911).

Jack Finegan, *Light from the Ancient Past* (Princeton: Princeton University Press, 1947).

Chapter 1: The Awakenings

1. Some scholars will say it was to keep an eye on them—prevent them
from hurting the living. This is possible at certain times and places, but
in general the idea seems unnecessarily cynical.

2. Fire was undoubtedly the most striking and comprehensive religious
symbol of primitive man. The god who revealed himself in lightning or
in the raging flames sweeping the forest was powerful indeed. There were
also, however, the warm, life-bringing rays of the sun—certainly akin to
fire. And there was the welcoming fire of the hearth outside the cave that
guided the hunter home, made the family food tastier, kept wild animals
away, and provided warmth through the night or on cold days. The flame
was the most cherished family possession, yet had no corporeal existence.
It flickered and crackled, cast strange shadows, and gave off a very savory
smell, especially when chunks of wild boar were being roasted. It involved
man, also, with his first real challenge (aside from procreation) for co-
operative and ongoing response to the physical universe in which he was
learning to live. The fire had to be *tended*, faithfully. It was the woman
who, home with the children, learned to tend the mysterious flame which,
through the ages, was to set man apart from even his closest relatives in the
animal kingdom.

3. Perhaps the discovery of agriculture was the most truly creative act
in man's history. Strangely, Greece made Diana goddess of the hunt,
Apollo god of verdure.

4. Perhaps the breaking through of the Atlantic to flood the populated
and abundant Mediterranean valley and turn it into a sea?

5. Gerald Heard has made a great deal of the gregarious basis of religion. *Social Substance of Religion* (New York: Harcourt, Brace, 1931).
In later books he asks whether the aim of religion is, basically, to make the
individual able to recover his symbolic relationship to his fellows. Of course
there is no record of man ever living in flocks or herds. Could the primitive

social break which Heard perceives be the spiritual and cultural break between the sexes? Heard also points out, as other sociologists have, that primitive man is not at all "wild," being more receptive than aggressive, more sensitive than imposing. In earliest burials the only weapons found were those for hunting food. *Source of Civilization* (New York: Harper, 1937), pp. 15f., 112f. H. G. Wells, in *Outline of History* (Garden City: Garden City Publishing Co., 1949), has a lengthy discussion of developing religious patterns. He thinks that "fear of the old man" is basic to primitive thought—one must not touch his spear or his women, even after his death (p. 120). But this is hardly in the most primitive society. Wells also mentions that among settled peoples gods have wives and families, but "the gods of the nomadic semites were not of this marrying disposition. Children were less eagerly sought by inhabitants of the food-grudging steppes" (p. 209).

Edvard Westermarck, in *Origin and Development of the Moral Ideas* (New York: Macmillan, 1906), says that in primitive society women's place was by no means that of subjugation; she could be man's equal or superior. He gives pages of examples in fine print. (See ch. IV, note 16. In first edition only!)

6. Religion is the way of compliance and co-operation; magic the way of using compulsion in regard to the spiritual forces of the universe.

7. Re fertility cult background see Samuel Noah Kramer, ed., *Mythologies of the Ancient World* (Garden City: Doubleday, Anchor Book, 1961), especially chapter on "Canaanite Mythology" by Cyrus H. Gordon, p. 183. (See note 13, below.)

Edwin O. James, in *Comparative Religion* (New York: Barnes and Noble, 1961, University Paperbacks), says we may have been too harsh on early fertility religions, judging them by their perversions and excesses. One looks to God, he reminds us, as the source of all good, and, for primitive man, "good" is symbolized by sufficient food. Sex, he says, plays an insignificant part in primitive religion, taking sharp issue with Freud's idea that family life was disrupted by the son's slaying of the father to get the women for himself. Sigmund Freud, *Totem and Taboo*; (New York: Moffett, 1918). Cf. Branislaw Malinowski, *Sex and Repression in Savage Society* (New York: Harper, 1927). Also E. D. James, *Cult of the Mother Goddess* (New York: Barnes and Noble, 1961) and William James, *Varieties of Religious Experience* (New York: Longmans, Green, 1902).

8. See ch. 2, section on Old Testament religion.

9. Re Moloch, see Arnold Toynbee, *An Historian's Approach to Religion* (London: Oxford University Press, 1956), pp. 36–42. Re Moloch and war, pp. 61f.

10. See A. M. Hocart, *Kingship* (London: Oxford University Press, 1927); also J. G. Fraser, *The Golden Bough* (New York: Macmillan, 1907–15).

11. Toynbee's idea of the parochial community seems more comprehensible to the writer from the point of view of the king-dominated group superimposing its culture on a formerly fertility-minded community. See

his discussion of polytheistic nature worship in *An Historian's Approach to Religion* (London: Oxford University Press, 1956), pp. 33f.

12. Charles Mills Gayley, *Classic Myths* (Boston: Ginn, 1911).

13. *Mythologies of the Ancient World*, Samuel Noah Kramer, ed., (Garden City: Doubleday, Anchor book, 1961), presents ten papers of the 1959 annual meeting of the American Anthropological Association and American Folklore Society, on myth in Egypt, Sumer, and Akkad, the Hittite kingdom, Canaan, Greece, India, Iran, China, Japan, and Mexico. The chapter on ancient Iran, by M. J. Dresden, reveals development of a very male-centered religion as described in the Avesta, but this is of comparatively late date. It is generally ascribed to Zoroaster (sixth century B.C.) and reflects the dualistic point of view, with women notably on the wrong side. The author points out that records are completely absent for the time when the Indo-Iranian unity was breaking up and the great migrations starting. (Other authorities make this a 500-year period around 1500 B.C.) This is the very material we should like to have. It seems likely that these materials were intentionally destroyed, because Zoroaster's new religion was a definite protest against former female power in this area. These anti-feminine sentiments were absorbed also by the Semites to some extent and were certainly strengthened by the era of great migrations. We have already noted that male gods and male rulers tend to dominate migratory peoples. The militarism of the Persians and the invasion at a later date by the military cult which had taken over Mohammedanism did women no good in either religion or society in general in this part of the world.

However, Dr. Stilson Judah has pointed out to the writer that although Zoroastrianism in the early Avesta seems to reflect the dominance of the male, in the fifth century B.C., Anahita (originally one of the forms of Ishtar) became one of the most worshiped deities in Persia. Artaxerxes II erected images of her in Babylon, Susa, Damascus, and other cities, and one of the Yashts of the Avesta refers to her as the goddess of the waters let down from heaven to fructify the earth.

There were many changes of name, and confusions of identities were common among the writing of classic scholars, as well as among those who today try to unravel the affairs of the classic gods and goddesses. One school of thought tries to identify the changing names, in particular, with successive waves of invasion. After all, there was nothing factual about a goddess. She was what her admirers made her, and both her name and her character might change according to what a new generation, or a new wave of immigration, required of her.

14. Cf. Gen. 6:1–6.

15. Kramer, *op. cit.*

16. For superstitions about Lilith, see the *Jewish Encyclopaedia*. It is worthy of note that a people's cultural judgments and the semantic implications of their vocabularies perpetuate—in myth—both valid and invalid ideas. The antiquity of a myth does not guarantee that the idea behind it is acceptable. It might have been artificially perpetrated by those who found it useful or convenient for their own purposes. This may be particularly true where myth deals, as early myth often does, with sex.

There was no corrective from the field of science. And even in these early, less inhibited days, there was relatively little opportunity for the mutual correction and understanding which come from open discussion.

17. Kramer, *op. cit.*, Rudolph Anthes on "Mythology in Ancient Egypt."

18. Toynbee, *Study of History* (London: Oxford University Press, 1954), vol. X, p. 143:

"Mother Mary, Mother Cybele, Mother Ishtar, Mother Kwanyin. . . . By whatever name we bless thee for bringing our Savior into the world. . . . Omnes Sancti et Sanctae Dei, intercidite pro nobis. . . ."
See Toynbee index under "Great Mother."

19. Edwin Diller Starbuck, "Female Principle," in *Hastings Encyclopedia of Religion and Ethics.* He quotes G. A. Barton following W. R. Smith in *Religion of the Semites,* who found the early Semites, before their dispersion, had a polyandrous social organization. "The chief deity of the clan was a goddess, and so far as any male deity played any considerable part, he was her son and reflex." (*Semitic Origins,* London: 1902, p. 106.) Starbuck refers also to Johann Bachofen, *Das Mütterecht* (Stuttgart: Krais and Hoffman, 1861), who, it seems, makes a case for primitive *Amazons.* (These books not consulted by the writer.) Ishtar, says Starbuck, rose to a position independent of any male god and "the highest religious and ethical thought attained by the Babylonians." Cf. Jastrow, *Religion of Babylonia and Assyria* (quoted) and E. J. Payne, *History of the World Called America,* vol. I, p. 462 and II, p. 480, re the goddess Tonantzin and her relation to Our Lady of Guadalupe; also E. Westermarck, *op. cit.,* chapter on "Subjugation of Wives."

See: Claude Bragdon, *Delphic Woman* (New York: Knopf, 1936); Edward Norbeck, *Religion in Primitive Society* (New York: Harper, 1961). For modern scientific background, read Laura Thompson, *Toward a Science of Mankind* (New York: McGraw-Hill, 1961); for a popular treatment, see George A. Dorsey, *Man's Own Show: Civilization* (New York: Harper, 1931).

Chapter 2: The Old Testament

1. We are trying, however, from all the evidence available, to discover God's appraisal of women, not the appraisal of one writer or group of writers or priests or temple officials at any given time in the world's history. The way in which unwarranted patterns perpetuate themselves is demonstrated from a usually reliable reference volume published in 1962. We find, under the heading "Woman," such generalizations as:

"Woman's position in the Bible is largely that of subordination to her father and husband." The astonishing references for this wide-sweeping statement are Gen. 2:24–25; 3:8; 3:17; 4:1; 4:17. However, says this authority, she does have freedom to act. As proof of this, see Gen. 19:31–35; 16:2; I Sam. 25; II Kings 4. Still searching for a "Biblical view of women," we find that she "makes herself sexually available to her husband for his pleasure and reproductive purposes." This seems hardly an adequate "Biblical view" of the reason for woman's place in God's creation. Would the author accept the reverse statement as to God's plan and design for the male? Even if he would, the discussion seems somewhat limited.

Those who have tried to delve into the matter of women in the Scriptures have found little help from concordances or most textbooks. When women are not ignored completely, the references are often very casual and misrepresentations are perpetuated, apparently without checking the sources, probably on the ground that nobody cares about women anyway —at least theologically. A scholar who would like to treat the subject fairly doesn't have much chance. Dr. W. L. Bevan, writing in the four-volume, 3667-page *Smith's Bible Dictionary* (Cambridge: Houghton Mifflin, Hackett's 1889 edition) was apparently assigned almost three-quarters of a page to discuss "Women"—interestingly enough almost exactly the same amount of space that was assigned to another writer for the word "Worm"! Realizing that this might seem to be slighting the ladies, readers were, however, referred to Deaconesses (1 page), Dress (7½ pages), Hair, Marriage, Slave, Veil, Widow (1 page each). Dr. Bevan used what space was allotted him to emphasize the "ish-ishah" (he-she) relationship as "exact correlatives" capable of "receiving and reflecting thoughts and affection from and to each other."

2. The Biblical student will ask, among other questions: To what time in Hebrew history does the passage *refer?* When was the passage *written?* Has the passage been re-edited one or many times? By a disinterested person? Could the author be expected to know from his own experience, or is he using sources—oral or written? Is the author (quite humanly) presuming that certain conditions of his own time have *always* been the same?—e.g., that women have *always* been subordinate? Does the author *expect* us to think that what he has written is *historically* true, or is it rather a statement in terms of his own day and culture, of a great religious truth as he understands it, without pretending to conform to historic or statistical fact?

3. We are, for instance, only just beginning to unravel the Hittite records of northern Palestine—the pantheon of El and Noah and Astarte; and the patriarchal traditions of Shechem, with its altars to many gods, outside the city gates. These may be very significant for Biblical study.

4. See Gen. 6:1–6 for a fragment of one almost wholly discarded myth.

5. Adam and Eve were a couple naturally to capture the imagination of any primitive people, and the stories about them persisted through the years and became the subject of a considerable popular literature about the time of Christ. Some of these non-canonical writings were quite different from the Biblical version. One, for instance, tells of Eve's penitence over all the trouble for which she was blamed. She tells Adam that she is going to do some penance. Adam says, swaggering, "Thou can'st not do as much as I . . . I will spend forty days fasting. But do you go to the Tigris, and lift up a stone in the water and stand on it in the water up to thy neck. . . . Let no speech proceed out of thy mouth, since we are unworthy to address the Lord . . . and do thou stand in the water of the river for

thirty-seven days. But I will spend forty days in the water of the Jordan."
He then goes and stands in the Jordan up to the hairs of his head, while all
God's creatures gather round to sympathize. But poor Eve, alone in the
waters of the Tigris, and feeling as abused as any wife might under similar
circumstances, is found, on the eighteenth day, alone and weeping. She is
found by the devil, who assumes the appearance of an angel and weeps
with her, saying, "Come out of the water, Eve. The Lord hath heard the
prayer of me and all us angels, and hath sent me to you, that thou mayst
come out of the water." However, Eve suspects duplicity and stands stead-
fast till Adam, his own penance finished, sees the devil's footprint in the
sand and, suspecting the truth, comes to her rescue.

For all intertestament material, consult R. H. Charles, *Apocrypha and
Pseudepigrapha* (New York: Oxford University Press, 1913): also Edgar J.
Goodspeed, *Story of the Apocrypha* (Chicago: University of Chicago Press,
1939).

6. Theodor Reik, *Creation of Woman* (New York: Braziller, 1960), sub-
titled *A Psychological Inquiry into the Myth of Eve*. He concludes: "Letting our thoughts drift from the primordial world to our own, and to this
age of reason, we might wonder at ourselves, and at our own stupid and
stubborn pride. Vanity of vanities! The white man imagines that he is made
of nobler dust than the Negro. The Gentile of more valuable earth than
the Jew. The human male animal finds reason for higher self-esteem in the
thought that he will crumble into better dust than the female." In his
postscript he adds: "Looking back at the Yahwistic report of Eve's creation, the impression remains that it was conceived in a spirit of hostility
to women. Our sketchy survey of the rabbinical and early Christian commentaries show that the misogynous attitude toward Eve prevailed until
the end of the Middle Ages, rarely interrupted by flickers and flashes of
friendlier feeling . . . [but] the last word has not yet been spoken. Everybody knows that inevitably woman has the last word" (pp. 147–149).
Appropriately, Reik dedicates the study to his daughter.

We must remember, of course, that the story we are reading in Gen. 2 is
neither a documentary history of the creation, nor even an original primitive myth, as it was first told, perhaps around the campfire, outside the
cave. It is the story as told and retold, generation after generation, modified
to achieve what man considered more essential validity from generation to
generation, and finally edited into the *J* source document, and from there
into the Pentateuch; translated and retranslated many times.

7. Edith Deen, *All the Women of the Bible* (New York: Harper,
1955), furnishes some helpful lists; her interpretations are traditional. See
also her *Great Women of the Christian Faith* (New York: Harper, 1959).
Lee Anna Starr, *Bible Status of Women* (New York: Revell, 1926), is
recommended as "traditional in scholarship, liberal in viewpoint."

8. The Hammurabi Code (c. 2000 B.C.?) indicates that this early civilization out of which the patriarchs came was generally favorable to women.

9. The Exodus material is a very much edited account combining the
main northern (*E*), southern (*J*), priestly (*P*), and several special strands.
A too close analysis is probably futile except for the most specialized

scholars with a good knowledge of Hebrew. However, it is important for *all* of us to understand how the Scriptures as we know them grew. The priestly scholars had the last word, many years after the events, carefully adding footnotes that rationalized the institutions of their own era. It is most unfortunate that the priesthood, in their desire to purify the Hebrew religion, threw out the women along with the fertility cult, with which, from their limited surroundings, they probably honestly more or less identified them. The temple harlot was condemned, and along with her all her sisters, who were by no means all harlots. The identification of woman as a "sinful vessel" made her services, aside from minor chores, anathema to many religious circles for centuries. In many clerical minds the concept of the Mother-goddess, the temple harlot, and the modern role of women with *"Kinder und Kücke"* is all mixed up. But this is *not* the Christian, nor the modern Jewish tradition.

10. Concerning circumcision, see Gen. 17:14, 21:4; Ex. 4:24–26, 12:48; Lev. 12:3; Josh. 5:2–9, *et al.* The references in the earliest stories are suspected of being the work of later priestly redactors, intent on establishing the fact that the custom was vital to Hebrew religion from the very beginning. If, as Ex. 4:26 suggests, in earlier times a circumcised male was referred to as a "bridegroom in blood," it opens the way for interesting speculation that the *original* deity of the Semitic people may have been a *female* goddess, demanding male devotees to do her fighting for her. The fact that circumcision came to be thought of as the mark of the covenant certainly perverted religious thought and excluded women from full citizenship. In spite of the fact that woman's one hope of salvation came to be thought of in terms of bearing sons, the birth of a child demanded a "sin offering" before a woman could be "clean."

The affair of Cozbi, the Midianite woman slain in relation to a plague (Nu. 25:8–18), has no special significance for us; the Israelite man with her was also slain. Whether it was the fact that she was a Midianite or that she threatened the health of the Hebrew community that caused the commotion is not quite clear.

11. It is sometimes claimed that women always had a place in Jewish religious worship, but their place was certainly not that of a full participant. Three times a year, only the *males* were required to visit a sanctuary (Deut. 16:14). Women were specifically included in the Feast of Booths or harvest festival (which became the Christian Pentecost), but this was the one Jewish festival at which children and resident aliens were also specifically included (Deut. 14:29). Joshua read the whole law to the people—including women and resident aliens (Josh. 8:3). In Jeremiah's time the women do seem to have been allowed to be official "wailers" (Jer. 9:17).

12. These two schools of thought during the exile are well covered by R. H. Pfeiffer, *Introduction to the Old Testament* (New York: Harper, 1941). This is a very complete and scholarly treatment. See especially pp. 260ff., 470ff.

Concerning women's possible participation, cf. the Pythagorean school of the sixth and fifth centuries B.C. in Greece, where women philosophers flourished. See "Pythagoras" in William Smith's Dictionary of Greek and

Roman Biography and Mythology (London: John Murray, 1902). Pythagoras' wife and daughters were all scholars, philosophers, and writers; their writings, like those of all members of the group, were ascribed to the founder. See "Mystery Religions" in *Cambridge Ancient History* (New York: Macmillan, 1923-1927), vol. 4, ch. XV, esp. p. 545.

13. Read the Book of Malachi, who certainly tried to point out what was going on. R. H. Pfeiffer, *op. cit.*, p. 615, describes Malachi (460 B.C.) as "invaluable as the picture of a dying church and the beginning of the movement giving it a new birth and energy. . . ."

14. C. C. McCown, *Genesis of the Social Gospel* (New York: Knopf, 1929), pp. 268ff.

Other References:

Georgia Harkness, *Toward Understanding the Bible* (New York: Scribners, 1954).

Bernard Anderson, *Rediscovering the Bible* (New York: Association Press, 1951).

Mary Ellen Chase, *Life and Language of the Old Testament* (New York: Norton, 1955).

Edmund Wilson, *Scrolls from the Dead Sea* (Toronto: Oxford University Press, 1955).

Martin Hopkins, O.P., *God's Kingdom in the Old Testament* (Chicago: Regnery, 1964).

For the stories of Judith, Susanna, and Tobit and other intertestamental writings, see Charles, *op. cit.*, note 5 above.

Additional References in the O.T.

A. Additional references from the book of Genesis (mentioned in genealogies):
Milcah, wife of Nahor (11:29)
Iscah, Milcah's sister (11:29)
Reumah, Nahor's concubine (22:24)
Judith and Basemath, Esau's wives (26:34) cf.
Adah, Oholibamah, Basemath (36:2)
Timna, Eliphaz' concubine (36:12; cf. 36:40)
Mehetabel, wife of Hadar (36:39)
Serah, daughter of Gad (46:17)

The story of Tamar, who plays harlot to teach Judah a lesson, is out of the main narrative and is probably a propaganda story for the new law that if a husband dies, his nearest available kin is to marry the widow and raise his family (ch. 38). The stories of Lot, his wife, and two daughters (ch. 13 and ch. 19) are what are frequently called "imbedded legends"; they seem to have no special significance for our discussion.

B. See I Chronicles, ch. 2, 3, 4, 7, 8 for a listing by tribes; forty-three women are named, far the largest proportion from the northern tribes.

In II Chronicles are only two references to women: Maacah, daughter of Absalom, is Rehoboam's favorite of his eighteen wives and sixty concubines (11:18); and Jehoram's wife was Ahab's daughter—consequently, Jehoram did evil (21:6).

C. Additional women mentioned in Samuel and Kings:

Saul's daughters Merab and Michal, his wife Ahinoam (I Sam. 14:49f.)

Witch of Endor (a kindly soul) (I Sam., ch. 28)

Rizpah, Saul's concubine. His son is accused of having relations with her. Her two sons are hanged. (II Sam. 21:8)

Tamar, Absalom's beautiful daughter (II Sam. 14:27)

A woman hides Ahimaaz and Jonathan (II Sam. 17:19–20)

Abigail, daughter of Nahash (II Sam. 17:25)

Wise woman of Abel-Beth-maacah (II Sam. 20:16ff.)

The rival mothers before Solomon (I Kings 3:16)

Taphath, Solomon's daughter (I Kings 4:11)

Tahpenes, Queen of Egypt—her sister marries Hadad (I Kings 11:19–20)

Zeruah, mother of Jeroboam the rebel (I Kings 11:26)

Naamah, wife of Rehoboam (I Kings 14:21, 31)

Maacah, mother of Asa, worshiped Asherah (I Kings 15:10, 13)

From here on only mothers are mentioned:

Maachah (mother of Abijam) I Kings 15:2; Azubah (Jehoshaphat) I Kings 22:42; Zibiah (Jehoash) II Kings 12:1; Jehoaddin (Amaziah) II Kings 14:2; Jecoliah (Azariah) II Kings 15:2; Jerusha (Jotham) II Kings 15:33; Abi (Hezekiah) II Kings 18:2; Hephzibah (Manasseh) II Kings 21:1; Meshullemeth (Amon) II Kings 21:19; Jedidah (Josiah) II Kings 22:1; Zebidah (Jehoiakim) II Kings 23:36; Hamutal (Jehoahaz and Zedekiah) II Kings 23:31 and 24:18; Nehushta (Jehoiachin) 24:8.

D. References from the Prophets:

Israel as a faithless wife: Is. 1:21; 54:6; 57:3ff.; Jer. 3:20; 4:14; 5:7ff.; Ezek. 16; 23:1–49; 36:17ff.; Hos. 2:2ff.; 4:12ff.; 5:3; ch. 9.

Woman as a symbol of wickedness: Zech. 5:7.

"Daughter of Zion": Is. 62:11; Jer. 4:30–31; 6:2–14; 31:22; Micah 4:10.

"Sons and daughters": frequent in Jer., Ezek.; Joel 2:28 ("sons and daughters will prophesy") (cf. Acts 2:17, 18).

Russell Prohl, in *Women in the Church*, p. 66, calls attention to Adam Clark's translation of Is. 40: "O *daughter* that bringest good tidings to Zion. . . . O daughter that bringest good tidings to Jerusalem. . . ." Also Ps. 68:11: "The *women preachers* were a great host."

E. References from the Law:

The Commandments enjoin respect equally for father and mother. The curse of Deut. 27:16 for those who dishonor either parent is the same. Soothsayers, magicians, and sorcerers are to be killed without discrimination as to sex (Lev. 20:27, Deut. 18:10–11), and there is the same penalty for "burning" a son or a daughter. But cf. witches, Ex. 22:18, Deut. 18:10—witches had probably not yet become almost exclusively female.

There is frequent recognition of the fact that woman's physical strength puts limitations on her activities. E and Deuteronomy both display a certain humanitarian frame of mind, from which women of the northern kingdom profited. Ex. 21:7–11 provides that "when a man sells his daughter as a slave, she shall not go out as the male slaves do. If she does not please her master who has designated her for himself, then he shall let her be redeemed; he shall have no right to sell her to a foreign people, since he hath dealt faithlessly with her. If he designates her for his son, he shall deal with her as with a daughter. If he takes another wife to himself, he shall not diminish her food, her clothing or her marital rights. And if he does not do these three things for her, she shall go out for nothing without payment of money." This is often cited as evidence of the kind treatment of women, but it is a very severe deterioration from our picture of patriarchal days. See:

Marriage: Ex. 19:21; Lev. 18:6ff.; 19:29; 21:7–13; Deut. 20:10–ch. 28 (passim)

Sexual practices: Lev. ch. 18–20; Nu. 5:11

Ritual uncleanliness: Lev. 12:2ff.; 15:19ff.; Nu. 31:17

Trial for unfaithfulness: Nu. 5:12, 14; Deut. 22:14

Commandments: Ex. 20:17ff.; Deut. 5:21ff.

Veil as evidence of harlotry: Gen. 38:15–16

Vows do not bind if husband objects: Nu. 36:8

Rahab's privileges (as innkeeper?): Josh. 2:1; 6:22

See Elizabeth Mary MacDonald, *Position of Women as Reflected in the Semitic Codes of Law* (Toronto: University of Toronto, 1931).

We have made no attempt in this survey to deal with such obviously non-historic books as Proverbs, Psalms, or the Song of Songs.

Chapter 3: Women in the New Testament

1. The basic background for this chapter is:

E. D. Burton and E. J. Goodspeed, *Harmony of the Synoptic Gospels* (New York: Scribner, 1920) and *The Interpreter's Bible* (New York and Nashville: Abingdon Cokesbury, 1952–1957).

2. Jesus' attitude of acceptance of women was much more radical than a comparable attitude would be today. The interest in celibacy in the first century tended to reinforce the identification of women as "sinful vessels" —an attitude that went back to the time when temple prostitutes were in vogue in many countries and religions.

3. Acts 1:14 shows women accepted as part of the early church at Jerusalem. Peter, preaching his famous sermon (Acts 2:17) on the first Christian Pentecost, pointedly quotes the prophet Joel: "Your sons and daughters shall prophesy . . . on my manservants and maidservants I will pour out my spirit. . . ." For other references to women at work in the Church during this early era, see Acts 6:1–2 (deacons); 5:1–11 (Sapphira's responsibility); 9:39, 9:44 (Tabitha and the saints and widows); 12:12,

12:14 (John Mark's mother's "church in her house" and Rhoda the door-keeper).

4. Louise Seymour Houghton, "Women's Work in the Church," in the *New Schaff-Herzog Encyclopaedia of Religious Knowledge* (New York: Funk and Wagnalls, 1912 edition).

5. The time span during which the major New Testament literature came into being is probably somewhat less than fifty years (c. 50–100 A.D.). Some of the source material for the Gospels was somewhat earlier. The pastoral epistles may be as late as 175 A.D.

6. Paul himself warned that spurious letters were already being written and circulated in his name and made a point of how his own signature could be identified. This was quite different from the ancient practice of a person writing in the name and under the aegis of a teacher or admired predecessor and trying anonymously to perpetuate his views. Sometime before 175 A.D. a theologian borrowed Paul's name and, in a manner that was hardly "cricket," used this device to put some quite un-Pauline sentiments into Paul's mouth, while propagandizing for the new organizational structure into which the Church was being molded. The letters purportedly written by Paul to his younger colleague Timothy display a love for the Church as the second-century author knew it and as he saw its future. As generation after generation of young theologians have grown up over the years, each one seems to have heard Paul speaking to himself through those letters. Yet today practically all Biblical criticism agrees that they could not possibly be Pauline. But one of the things those letters tell the young theologian is where women's place is, and that it is not in any significant position in the Church. However, to make any pretense of scholarly approach to Biblical study, yet continue to attribute the passages in these letters concerning women to Paul, is not possible. We cannot hold to literal interpretation of the Bible when it suits our purposes unless we are ready to repudiate the entire approach of historic and literary criticism. We must be honest about this.

7. The fact that, at a time when it was by no means customary, Priscilla's name usually preceded Aquila's is generally considered significant. Some think that Aquila may have been a freed man. Evidence from the catacombs suggests that Priscilla was from one of the distinguished families of Rome. See Walter Lowrie, *Monuments of the Early Church* (London: Macmillan, 1901). There is a church named for Priscilla at Rome, possibly on the site of the church house where she lived and where she conducted services.

8. Compare Paul with the non-Pauline rewrite found in Ephesians 5:21ff., usually dated about 100 A.D.

Additional References to Women

Paul's sister's son saves his life (Acts 23:16)
Philip's four prophetess daughters (Acts 21:9)
Felix and Drusilla (Acts 24:24)
Agrippa and Bernice (Acts 25:23)

Women as symbols (Rev. 12:1; 17:3)

Eph. 5:21—"Women be subject to your husbands" is considered by almost all scholars as not Pauline, but from about 100 A.D.

Titus 2:45 and I Peter 3:1-3 are probably from Rome in the second century, certainly not Pauline.

Consult

C. F. D. Moule, *Birth of the New Testament* (New York: Harper, 1962).

K. S. Latourette, *The First Five Centuries* (Vol. I of *History of the Expansion of Christianity* (New York: Harper, 1937).

M. Scott Enslin, *Ethics of Paul* (New York and Nashville: Abingdon, 1962).

H. D. Spence-Jones, *Early Christians in Rome* (New York: John Lane and Co., 1911) (esp. re Priscilla, her family, the catacombs, etc.).

A. C. McGiffert, *History of Christianity in the Apostolic Age* (New York: Scribner, 1914); also "Apostolic Age" in Hastings (*HERE*).

Jean Danielou, S.J. (Glen Simon, tr.), *Ministry of Women in the Early Church* (London: Faith Press, 1961). Quoted in *People of God*; not seen.

Margaret Crook, *Women and Religion* (Boston: Beacon, 1965).

Madeline Southard, *Attitude of Jesus toward Women* (New York: Doran, 1927).

Elizabeth Achtemeier, *Feminine Crisis in Christian Faith* (New York-Nashville: Abingdon, 1965).

Chapter 4: The Early Church

1. J. Langdon-Davies, *Short History of Women* (New York: Viking, 1927), ch. 4. The author has assembled a choice collection of such verbal abuse. Check context, etc., before quoting; he is not exactly objective.

2. For extensive bibliography, see Latourette, *First Five Centuries*. He mentions (pp. 3–27) some rival religions: (I) Stoics (a religion of the aristocrats); equality of men by divine right—including slaves; all entitled to share good things of life. (II) Cynics (religion of the common people) denounced idols, divination, pretense, and ostentation. (III) Neoplatonists; belief in one transcendent God; mysticism. (IV) Popular religion of gods, demons, spirits. (V) The mystery religions from Egypt, Babylonia, Persia, and Greece; highly emotional; exclusive, concerned with individual security in a shifting world; sacramental drama, great appeal to women. (VI) The Great Mother cult; had become dramatic and often excessive, with self-mutilation; mystic marriage of the deity; bathing in blood of sacrificed bull, etc. (VII) The cult of Isis, founded on the system of Egyptian myths. (VIII) The Mithraism of Persia; usually for men only; ethical, dualistic; baptism and the sacramental meal.

Mithraism is said to have been the most powerful rival of Christianity. It would be interesting to know to what extent Christianity borrowed, in its organizational phase, its ideas about women from this "soldiers' religion" from the East. Hermeticism and Gnosticism (from Egypt) were rivals of the main-line Christian development, especially in the second and third centuries.

Latourette says (*op. cit.*, pp. 260ff.): "While some prominent Christians assented to the custom of the times in regarding woman as 'the weaker vessel' none of the church fathers acknowledged that differences in sex affected salvation. Men and women might equally be heirs to eternal life." He quotes I Pet. 3:7; Eph. 5:23. See also Chrysostom, *Hom. 13 on Eph.*; also Schmidt, *Social Results of Early Christianity*—cf. Gal. 3:28; Augustine, Sermon CXC par. 2; S. J. Case, *Social Origins of Christianity* (Chicago: University of Chicago, 1923), VII 263.

3. Latourette, *op. cit.*, pp. 333ff. (and all of ch. 7 and 8 concerning effects of environment on the early Church).

4. Usually dated at the end of the first century are Timothy and Titus (95 A.D. or later), Hebrews (between 80 and 110), I John 90–115, Gospel of John (100), I Peter (95–115), Ephesians (100?), Jude (before 150), II Peter (before 150). A date as late as 175 A.D. has been suggested for the Pastorals.

5. Iraneus dates the papacy from Peter and Paul; Origen from the "Rock" (all with faith like Peter's); Tertullian from Peter personally; Cyprian says authority was to *all* the apostles (stressing the importance of the episcopate): "The Church is the Bishop and the Bishop is the Church." Some say that Leo I (440) was the "first real Pope." The edict of Valentinian III (445) sets forth the claim of the Bishop of Rome to be supreme head of the Western Church.

6. Latourette, *op. cit.*, pp. 94f.

7. *Ibid.*, p. 252.

8. Houghton, *op. cit.* In the *Testament of Our Lord* widows have precedence over deaconesses, but in the *Apostolic Constitutions* it is the opposite: widows must *obey* deaconesses. The *Constitutions* pretend to be words of the apostles themselves; but they speak of fourth-century events.

9. A. C. McGiffert, "Apostolic Age," in *HERE*. McGiffert points out that "the idea of social service and the desire to promote the spirit of brotherhood in the world at large had little place among the early Christians. Rather to gather out of the world a company of holy men, heirs of the promised Kingdom—this was their great aim. (Didache 9.10) . . . [Love] commonly takes the form of love for the Christian brethren, which is to be manifested in charity, hospitality, sympathy, concord, forbearance, tenderheartedness, forgiveness, humility, etc. . . ." The place of supremacy given to it by Christ and after him by Paul is not common to other writers of the age. The fathers were more interested in "confronting" Marcion and the gnostics.

10. Latourette, *op. cit.*, ch. 6.

11. Cyril C. Richardson (ed.), in *Early Christian Fathers* (Philadelphia: Westminster, 1953), gives a very readable account of the developing power of the church organization, with the comments of early writers, e.g., "Sub-

mit to the Bishop as to God's law," or "Pay attention to the Bishop so that God will pay attention to you." Until we have a complete and objective check of the church fathers in the original tongues, it is hard to tell how the laudatory remarks about women weigh against those which are less complimentary. The best scholars are apt to report from sources that uphold their own position, and this is not a field which seems to have attracted many women scholars. Augustine Rössler, writing in the *Catholic Encyclopaedia*, tells us that the great church fathers praise not only their mothers and sisters, but speak of Christian women in general in the same terms of respect as the Gospel. "The alleged contempt of the Christian Fathers for women," he reports, "is a legend that is kept alive by the lack of knowledge of the Fathers." On the other hand, he quotes Aristotle as referring to woman as an incomplete or mutilated man (II/3d ed. Berol, 773 a). In the centuries that followed, this idea rather than the Gospel viewpoint seems to have survived. See Cyril Richardson, "Women in the Ministry," *Christianity and Crisis*, xi–21, Dec. 10, 1951.

12. Richardson, *Early Christian Fathers*, p. 16. There is no mention of deaconesses in Pope Cornelius' list of Roman clergy (251). *Apostolic Church Order* (third-century Egyptian?) discusses "a ministry for women," apparently in regard to someone seeking an appointment for a woman. The answer is that the woman's ministry can only be "a ministry of succor to needy fellow-women." See R. W. Stewart, "Apostolic Constitutions" in *Dictionary of the Apostolic Church*, James Hastings, ed. (New York: Scribner, 1916).

13. John Foster, *Beginning in Jerusalem* (London: World Christian Books, Lutterworth Press, 1956), p. 17.

14. Latourette, *op. cit.*, p. 108, refuses to guess what proportion of the people in the Roman Empire were Christians at this time, but cites estimates that range from one-twentieth to one-eighth to one-half. Christians included all classes, from slaves to the emperor's household. From personal accounts, evidence in the catacombs, etc., it would appear that a large proportion of the believers were women. It is quite possible that the women, having less to lose in the empire, felt more free to embrace and propagandize for the new belief. "The 4th and 5th centuries saw the transition of Christianity from the position of a minority religion, well organized and vigorous but persecuted, to the faith of the majority of the Mediterranean basin" (p. 237).

15. By the fourth century the teaching office in the Church had generally been taken away from women.

16. Michael Gough, *The Early Christians* (New York: Praeger, 1961).

17. A. C. McGiffert, "Apostolic Age" in HERE.

18. *Letter to Diognetus* (quoted in C. Richardson, ed., *Early Christian Fathers*): "Now then, clear away all the thoughts that take up your attention, and pack away all the old ways of looking at things that keep deceiving you. You must become like a new man from the beginning since, as you yourself admit, you are going to listen to a really new message" (pp. 213ff.).

19. Most biographic statistics and spellings are from the *Columbia Encyclopedia*. Interesting popular sketches of women "from the Garden of Eden to the twentieth century" are found in *Woman*, William C. King, ed. (Springfield, Mass.: King Richardson, 1902). Hardly for scholarly research today, but an interesting check list.

20. Irene (752–803) should be mentioned for the in-between years. Constantine noticed her, an orphan, and married her to his son, Leo. She was much distressed to have to give up the images with which she was familiar in the Greek Church. When her husband died and she became regent for their ten-year-old son, she immediately began a move to restore the images and called a church council at Constantinople and then one at Nice, which declared images agreeable to Scripture and reason, and to the fathers and councils of the Church. There was a struggle for power between Irene and her son. After his death she ruled with vigor for five years, establishing good relations with Charlemagne. For her influence in re-establishing the use of images in worship, she was made a saint in the Greek Church.

21. *Special Note on the Catacombs:* The record of the catacombs throws considerable interesting light on our subject. We have spoken in the introduction of the little feminine figures of the Orans (praying one) which seem in the art of the catacombs to represent the souls of the departed praying for those who remain. Considerable activity aside from burials seems to have gone on in these underground rooms, but authorities by no means agree in their reconstruction of some of the history represented. One of the most famous crypts was that of Priscilla, the noble lady for whom the Priscilla of Acts was probably named. The older Priscilla's son, Pudens, seems to have been a man of considerable wealth and authority, and may have been Paul's sponsor and host when he came to Rome. He had two daughters, Prudentia and Prassedia. His house became the church of Prudentia. The cemetery of Priscilla was established on the same property. The Biblical Priscilla (Prisca) was very likely a relative, and it could have been this family who built the church in which she preached when she returned to Rome during the tolerant years during the second half of the first century A.D. We would like to know more about this lively and courageous family of Christians. We should like to know, too, about Petronilla, to whom altars were apparently erected in various churches, and who has been described as the "spiritual daughter" of Peter. Most of all, we should like to know more about the average, unheralded Christian women of the day, who accomplished so much against such great odds. "But why?" the historians of that day—or today—might ask. "They were just women."

For a description of what the catacombs can tell us, see:

Jack Finegan, *Light from the Ancient Past* (Princeton: Princeton University Press, 1946).

W. Lowrie, *Monuments of the Early Church* (London: Macmillan, 1901).

H. D. M. Spence-Jones, *The Early Christians in Rome* (New York: Lane, 1911).

Chapter 5: Finding New Channels of Service

1. For a general overview of the flow of history, see Rand-McNally's "Histomap of History" and "Histomap of Religion" (180,000 years!). This does not imply complete agreement as to details on the chart. For instance, there should be more recognition of awe, gratitude, love, and faithfulness factors in primitive religion.

2. Augustine's aged mother, Monica, to whom he was so devoted, was treated quite shamefully, it seems, by the bishop of her home church in Africa. She was in the habit of coming to the church and talking with worshipers, distributing to them small cakes and sips of wine from a tiny glass she carried with her. The bishop, apparently provoked because it had been Monica, not the bishop himself, who had "saved" Augustine from following the Manichaean doctrine, told the doorkeeper to stop her distribution of these festive foods and if necessary to shut her out of the church. He said her sips of wine might make drunks drunken. Augustine found it necessary to defend her (Confessions Book VI.). His mother, he said, was brought up in a Christian family and had Christian instruction from her father's ancient nurse. "The charge of her master's daughters was entrusted to her, to which she gave diligent heed, restraining them earnestly, when necessary, with holy severity, and teaching them with grave discretion." They were refused water to drink when they were thirsty so that when they grew up and had the keys to the wine cellars of their homes they would be temperate.

It seems that someone at this time must have raised the question of women's immortality, though that was supposed to have been settled long since. Augustine says, "To me they seem to think most justly who doubt not that both sexes shall rise again." He admits they will be changed and women will be less seductive in the next life. Apparently bored by the citing of precedents by his clerical brethren, Augustine says (Book VII), "When God commands a thing to be done, against the customs and compact of any people, though it were never by any of them done heretofore, it is to be done; and if intermitted, it is to be restored; and if never ordained, it is now to be ordained."

3. *Dictionary of Christian Biography and Literature to the Sixth Century A.D.* (Boston: Little, Brown, 1911) (DXBL).

4. George Hodges, *Early Church* (Boston, New York: Houghton Mifflin, 1915), ch. 4.
R. C. Prohl, *Women in the Church* (Grand Rapids, Mich.: Eerdmans, 1957), p. 74.
L. A. Starr, *Bible Status of Women* (New York: Revell, 1926), p. 203.

5. Houghton, *op. cit.*

6. Toynbee, *Study of History*, pp. 6, 155–156.

7. Houghton, *op. cit.* See also Alden D. Kelley, *People of God* (Greenwich, Conn.: Seabury, 1962).

8. Latourette, *op. cit.*, vol. II, *Thousand Years of Uncertainty* (New York: Harper, 1938), pp. 85ff., esp. p. 95.

9. See Latourette, *op. cit.*, I, *First Five Centuries*, p. 393, for a bibliography re effect of Christianity on family and status of women and children.

Chapter 6: Eleventh-Century Revival

1. Etienne Gilson, *Heloise and Abelard* (Ann Arbor, Mich.: University of Michigan: Ann Arbor Paperback, 1960). This could be the best all-time discussion of the psychology of romantic love. Abelard is the successful young teacher of theology, interested in pride of scholarship, money, fame. Heloise, who starts out with position and education, loses her head, to say the least. But Gilson points out that it is her "sin" against Abelard, not against God, that obsesses her. "God knows," she says, "I never wanted anything from you but yourself. . . . No doubt the name of wife is stronger and more sacred, but I have always preferred that of mistress or concubine and prostitute. For the more I degrade myself for you, the more did I hope to find favor with you." Even forgetting that this is *romantic* love, we can see that female point of view cropping out. If only poor Heloise could have remembered to respect *herself!* If only all women could!

2. Henry Adams, *Mont-Saint-Michel and Chartres* (Garden City: Doubleday, Anchor Book, 1959). See also Amy Kelly, *Eleanor of Aquitaine and the Four Kings* (Cambridge: Harvard, 1950). Martin Schmidt is recognized as an authority on the eleventh to thirteenth centuries; most of his available works are in German.

3. Adams, *op. cit.*, chs. 5–10.

4. Quoted, *ibid.*, p. 216 from *Social State of France during the Crusades*.

5. *Ibid.*, p. 217.

6. *Ibid.*, pp. 271–272. The author of the article on "Women" in the *Catholic Encyclopaedia* says, "Next to the clergy, the women in the medieval era were more representative of learning and education than the men."

7. Adams, *op. cit.* See all of ch. XI, esp. pp. 218, 223.

8. The story of her life was written by Georgiana Buckler in 1829, but no copy of the work was available.

9. Latourette, *Thousand Years of Uncertainty*, ch. VIII, esp. pp. 360f. re women.

10. Voluntary celibacy is a way of life which has always been open to men or women. The decision is completely personal and may arise from a sense of vocation—religious or otherwise—which is so overpowering that it leaves no time or interest for family or extramarital relationships. This seems, in general, to have been the attitude of the ancient hermits of most religious faiths—or at least their apologia for the celibate life which they espoused. Repudiation of social responsibility, psychological or even physical ineptness, or, in the case of the monasteries, a willingness on the part of some unscrupulous characters to accept life security in exchange for the vows that could be, after all, occasionally circumvented all enter into the

picture. Only the celibate himself knows his motives, and these are between himself and God, and, in the case of a religious order, between himself, his God, and the group through which he makes his vows. Some religions insist that their priesthood "renounce the world," including the responsibilities of marriage and family. Others say that the priesthood is a symbol of the relation of humanity as a whole to God and insist that their priesthood be married. Though not couched in these terms, something of this feeling undoubtedly enters into the Protestant preference for the married minister with a "suitable" wife—often as well trained as himself, who is expected to serve the parish full time without salary. It enters also into the encouragement of the missionary dynasties and the educational scholarships traditionally available to missionaries' and ministers' children. The Catholic Church, on the other hand, draws upon the community through the well-imbued obligation of each religiously devoted family to give at least one of its sons or daughters to the service of the Catholic Church, and, through the Church to the community.

Through the discovery of the Dead Sea Scrolls and related material, we have been learning a good deal recently about some of the "separatist" communities which were part of the Palestine culture at the beginning of the Christian era. Some of these may have been celibate communities, but others were groups of families; withdrawal from the press and strains of Roman domination and its headlong economic splurge could be desired for one's children as well as for one's self.

Considering the amount of argument that has gone on in the Christian Church concerning the question of celibacy, it is strange that we find no particular advocacy for or against it in the Gospels. (See Matt. 19, which seems to make chastity, rather than celibacy, imperative.) Some of the older prophets had been married, and the rabbinical school followed this tradition. We simply do not know about the apostles. At the time the Scriptures took their final form, male dominance in the Church was strong, and, as we have seen, women got short shrift in the reporting.

The position of Jesus himself was of course unique. God the Son, God the Father, and God the Holy Spirit were individually and collectively complete wholeness. The idea of making the Holy Spirit the female aspect of the Trinity was quickly abandoned by the theologians. God is God—not man, not woman; not black, not white; not soft, not harsh; not a realist nor a mystic nor a neo-orthodox; neither East nor West. If we had been as diligent to understand Paul in this basic theological premise as we have been to generalize his advice on the isolated matter of procedure in a local church dispute, the Church through the years might have better deserved its designation as "the body of Christ," and more effectively have manifested the Holy Spirit in the Father's created world.

Paul's ideas on celibacy are sketchy. See I Cor. 7:25. Since the end of the world was expected in the almost immediate future, it seemed to him better, perhaps, to devote one's thoughts to that, rather than to marriage, but this was a personal decision. Perhaps he would have given a different opinion if he had been thinking of generations to come. He emphasizes that he claims no special wisdom on the subject. Marcion, on the other hand, who was in Rome in 140 A.D., was extreme in his insistence on celibacy and founded widespread colonies. He had a dualistic point of view which put sex and procreation thoroughly on the side of the devil. Latourette finds it difficult to understand how—with procreation forbidden—Marcionism could endure and spread as it did. Yet so strong was it that some scholars find opposition to Marcionism the basis for parts of the Apostles' Creed, and say the canon of the New Testament was influenced by this same rivalry.

The second-century Gnostics, Montanists, and other groups preached ascetic practices, including celibacy—as special groups have before and since that time. By what process the celibacy of the monastery was taken over and became the rule for all clergy in the Western Church is not clear, but by the fourth century it was the rule in Rome. See Latourette, *First Five Centuries*, p. 354. Latourette quotes and recommends Workman, *Evolution of the Monastic Ideal* (not seen).

Pope Hildebrand campaigned for "sacerdotal celibacy" in the monasteries, but was vigorously opposed by those clergy who were openly living with their wives. This continued till the thirteenth century, but whether the monks of the time thought it "immoral" or believed the vow of celibacy was archaic is not clear. The morals involved in the bishop's accepting a fee for allowing a parish priest to keep a concubine seem fairly clear. However the monks felt about such matters at the time, celibacy was accepted and in due course was enforced within reason. But its very enforcement as a *rule*, to be obeyed and debated, took the emphasis off the very reason for celibacy in the first place. Celibacy was admonished in the beginning so a religious devotee could devote himself undividedly to religion. When a monk began to advocate celibacy *per se*, woman became once more a sinful vessel—the Eve who tempted the holy man to disobedience. This must have had considerable influence on the downgrading of the place of women in society and in the Church, just as the institution of temple prostitutes had downgraded the place of women in the early Hebrew temples. It would seem that not only is the woman always to blame, but that the woman who is to blame is somehow always taken as typical of her sex! The universal popularity of the Eve stories is easily explained on the basis of universal validity.

11. A general time schedule would indicate: fourth century—monasteries in Gaul; fifth century—preaching and teaching monasteries in Ireland; sixth century—Benedict of Nursia sets Western monastic pattern: work, care for the poor, preserve manuscripts, serve as isles of security, provide exemption from military service, economic security; 910—Cluny reforms; 1084—St. Bruno, Carthusian order, very cloistered; 1098—Cistercian order goes back to St. Benedict's ideas; St. Bernard; twelfth-fifteenth centuries—Monks too numerous, monasteries too rich, many abuses; thirteenth century—Dominicans (founded 1216) not cloistered; Dominic preached to Albigensians in South France. Franciscans (not cloistered), Poor Clares, Third Order (lay men and women). In 1228 the Dominicans, very popular with the women, refused to receive nuns—"too much responsibility for the

men"; in 1257 they changed their minds; sixteenth century—Henry VIII suppresses monasteries in England; 1540—Jesuit order founded.

See Augustus Jessopp, *Coming of the Friars* (London: Unwin, 1889).

For a charming historical novel, read Alfred Duggan, *Cunning of the Dove* (New York: Pantheon, 1960), a story of Edward the Confessor, as told—presumably—by one of his household.

For purposes of reference, we shall mention a few of the scholastics: Anselm (1034–1109); Abelard (1079–1142)—and never say we mentioned him without Heloise; Albertus Magnus (1193?–1280); Thomas Aquinas (1225–1274); Duns Scotus (1265–1308)—a Scottish Franciscan; William Occam (1280–1349).

12. Patrick Cowley, *Franciscan Rise and Fall* (London: Dent, 1933). One must search the sources if one wishes to discover the part the women's orders had in this day and to what extent the story of their activity has been repressed—or should we say overlooked?—by many church historians. If the result of such oversight was simply that women did not get their just desserts, the matter could be excused. The real problem is that today's women, with competence in so many fields, search in vain for evidence that women have had much of anything to do with the whole story of religion; and today's woman may despair, unless her call to the vocation of religion is clarion clear, from venturing into a field which she has been told in no uncertain terms is none of her business and never has been.

13. Fr. Cuthbert, *Life of St. Francis of Assisi*, is the source book for most we know about Francis and Clare. Good modern "Lives" include: Ernest Gilliat-Smith, *St. Clare of Assisi* (New York: Dutton, 1914); Michael de la Bedoyere, *Francis* (New York: Harper and Row, 1962); Maria Sticco, *The Peace of St. Francis*, tr. by Salvator Attanasio (New York: Hawthorn, 1962).

Chapter 7: Search for Meaning

1. Latourette, *Thousand Years of Uncertainty*, pp. 365ff.

Anna Seeholtz, *Friends of God* (New York: Columbia University, 1934), pp. 17f.

J. T. McNeill, *Makers of Christianity* (New York: Holt, 1937).

Catholic Encyclopaedia, "Beguines."

2. A. C. McGiffert, *History of Christian Thought* (New York: Scribner, 1933), pp. 65–67; 395ff. See also:

W. Nigg, *The Heretics* (New York: Knopf, 1962).

H. A. Oberman, *Harvest of Medieval Theology* (Cambridge: Harvard, 1963).

Rufus Jones, *Flowering of Mysticism* (New York: Macmillan, 1939).

W. E. Flemming, *Mysticism in Christianity* (Westwood, N.J.: Revell, 1913).

Evelyn Underhill, *Mystics of the Church* (New York: Doran, 1925).

Latourette, *Thousand Years of Uncertainty*, pp. 352, 358f., 434.

C. F. Kelley, tr., *Book of the Poor in Spirit* (New York: Harper, 1954), intro., p. 288.

Susanna Winkworth, tr., *Theologia Germanica* (London: Macmillan, 1874).

Jeanne Ancelet-Hustache, *Master Eckhart and the Rhineland Mystics*, tr. by Hilda Graef (New York: Harper Torchbook, 1957), esp. pp. 18ff.

Chapter 8: The Renaissance

1. G. F. Renard, *Guilds of the Middle Ages*, quoted by Mary Beard, *Woman as a Force in History* (New York: Macmillan, 1946), pp. 226ff.

2. J. E. Staley, *Guilds of Florence and Dogaresses of Venice* (quoted *ibid.*).

3. George G. Coulton, ed., *Life in the Middle Ages* (London: Cambridge University Press, 1910), 4 vols. of resource material from original documents; excellent material from many sources. Medieval life as it was lived.

4. Most dates and biographical information in this section are from the *Columbia Encyclopedia*.

5. From the end of the fourteenth century, copies of the Wyclif translation had been available and portions used extensively, especially by the Lollards, a free-wheeling group in which the women participated fully. See next chapter.

6. Latourette, vol. III—*Three Centuries of Advance*, p. 5.

Chapter 9: The Reformation

1. For concise background and readings re Luther and other Reformation leaders, see Harry Emerson Fosdick, *Great Voices of the Reformation* (New York: Random House, 1952).

It would indeed be interesting to study the lives of—for example—Erasmus (1469?–1536) and Zwingli (1484–1531), as well as Luther (1483–1546) and Calvin (1509–1564), to discover what relationships to women in their personal history gave direction to their lives. We know that Erasmus owed his early training to the education-minded Brethren of the Common Life; Zwingli had done battle against the idea of clerical celibacy and, though a priest, had married.

For fiction, read Charles Reade, *The Cloister and the Hearth*, a delightful story of Erasmus' parents (New York: Harper, 1890).

2. Georgia Harkness, *John Calvin, the Man and his Ethics* (New York: Holt, 1931), pp. 153ff.

3. James Anderson, *Ladies of the Reformation* and *Ladies of the Covenant* (Edinburgh: Blackie and Son, 1855).

John Knox (1558) wrote a pamphlet on "The First Blast of the Trumpet against the Monstrous Regiment of Women"; for comment, see Toynbee,

Study of History (London: Oxford University, 1954), vol. VIII Annex D, p. 651. Women have been suffering ever since from the feelings of the time brought on by "Bloody Mary."

Quoted by Anderson: Strickland, *Queens of England;* Stowe, *Great Chronicles of England;* Vaughn, *Life of Wicliff;* Rymer, *Foedera;* Lewis, *English Biblical Translations;* Foxe, *Acts and Monuments;* Froissart, *Chronicles of England;* Krasinski, *Reformation in Poland;* Crull, *Antiquities of St. Peter;* Baker, *Chronicles.*

4. See biography of Matthaus Zell by A. Erickson (o.p.).

5. For other Catholic reformers, see Latourette, III *Three Centuries of Advance,* pp. 19f.

6. Pertinent references will be found in these bibliographies:
Roland Bainton, *Bibliography of the Continental Reformation* (American Society of Christian History, 1935); Shirley Jackson Case, *A Bibliographical Guide to the History of Christianity* (University of Chicago, 1931).

7. Mary Beard, *Woman as a Force in History* (New York: Macmillan, 1946), p. 247.

Chapter 10: Witches

1. Ex. 22:18–20 (some say added by a much later editor, 450 B.C.); Deut. 18:11–12; Lev. 20:27. See also Kings 28.

2. Latourette, II *Thousand Years of Uncertainty,* pp. 360f.

3. *Ibid.,* p. 374.

4. Herbert Thurston, "Witchcraft" in *Catholic Encyclopaedia.*

5. The story of Faust, in its many ramifications, is the perfect example of "pact."

6. Charles Williams, *Witchcraft* (New York: World, 1941; Meridian, 1946).

R. H. Robbins, "Salem Witch Trials" in *Encyclopaedia of Witchcraft and Demonology* (New York: Crown, 1959).

George L. Kittredge, *Witchcraft in Old and New England* (Cambridge: Harvard, 1929).

7. The last recorded execution for witchery in England was in 1685. There was an isolated execution in Russia in 1796, and a peasant community in Russia is said to have burned a person as a witch in 1881.

Chapter 11: Puritans and Pietists, Methodists, Too

1. Mary Taylor Blauvelt, *Oliver Cromwell* (New York: Putnam, 1937), introductory quote.

2. Rufus Jones, *Mysticism and Democracy* (Cambridge: Harvard, 1932), p. 25; see also *Flowering of Mysticism* (New York: Macmillan, 1939).

3. Vernon Noble, *The Man in Leather Breeches* (New York: Philosophical Library, 1953). See also:

H. H. Henson, *Puritanism in England* (London: Hodder and Stoughton, 1912).

H. W. Clark, *History of English Nonconformity* (London: Chapman and Hall, 1911).

W. A. Shaw, "Commonwealth and Protectorate" in *Cambridge Modern History* (New York: Macmillan, 1906), vol. IV, ch. XV.

4. Sewel, an eighteenth-century historian, quoted, Noble, *op. cit.*, p. 191.

5. Noble, *op. cit.*, p. 193.

6. Ruth Rouse and Stephen Neill, *History of the Ecumenical Movement* (Philadelphia: Westminster, 1954), p. 100.

7. *Ibid.*, pp. 83, 100, 105.

8. The Methodists were already emphasizing numbers! They claim 11,000,000 members in the U.S.A.

See also:

Charles Franklin Potter, *Faiths Men Live By* (New York: Prentice-Hall, 1940), ch. 18.

J. T. McNeill, *Modern Christian Movements* (Philadelphia: Westminster, 1954); ch. 1 on English Puritanism, ch. 2 on German Pietism.

William Haller, *Rise of Puritanism* (New York: Columbia, 1938).

Chapter 12: Missions

1. The *Columbia Encyclopedia* has generally been used for spelling of names and dates in this chapter, unless otherwise indicated.

2. James Hill, *Immortal Seven* (Philadelphia: American Baptist Pub. Soc., 1903).

3. Margaretta Burr Wells, *Journey Among Friends* (Thailand and New York: Board of Foreign Missions, Presbyterian Church in the U.S.A., 1950).

4. Interviews, Vellore, 1949.

5. H. P. Van Dusen, *World Christianity* (New York: Friendship Press, 1947), pp. 124ff.

6. Richard Baird, United Presbyterian Church, U.S.A., interview, 1964.

7. Latourette, *op. cit.* IV, *The Great Century: in Europe and the U.S.A.*, p. 318.

C. M. Drury, ed., *First White Women over the Rockies* (Glendale, Calif.: A. H. Clark, 1963; 2 vols.). Diaries and letters of Marcus and Narcissa Whitman and other Oregon missionaries.

T. C. Elliott, *Coming of the White Women* (Portland: Oregon Historical Society, 1937; essentially the same material as in the Drury volumes; a centennial publication of the original 1836 materials.

8. Joseph B. Clark, *Leavening the Nation* (New York: Baker and Taylor, 1903), ch. 19.

9. Although missionary work was done largely by women, and women raised much of the money to keep the mission program operating, it is notable that the top direction has almost always been in the hands of the men. Women have, however, made creditable records at the executive level

on both the International Missionary Council (now one with the World Council of Churches) and the (U.S.) Foreign Missions Conference (now part of the National Council of Churches), as well as in a few of the denominational boards.

10. *Amanda Smith's Own Story* (Chicago: Meyer and Bro., 1893). For a general overview of missions up to the middle of the twentieth century, see John C. Thiessen, *Survey of World Missions* (Inter-Varsity Press, 1955); 500 packed pages summarizing the findings of questionnaires sent to 300 mission boards; ten-page bibliography.

W. H. Milburn, *Rifle, Axe and Saddlebags* (Derby and Jackson, 1857). A minister's account of the background for early home missions; see ch.3 re "Women, Society, and Moral Issues." There are many good fictionalized accounts from the foreign field, e.g., Brian O'Brien, *She Had a Magic* (New York: Dutton, 1959); re Mary Slessor in Nigeria. *Mary McLeod Bethune* by Rackham Holt (Garden City: Doubleday, 1964) tells of a Negro woman's determination to help her own people, and how she became one of the country's great educators.

Chapter 13: Women and Causes

1. John T. McNeill, *Modern Christian Movements*, reviews the contributions of modern Protestant thought of the English Puritans, German Pietists, the Evangelical movement, Tractarianism, Anglo-Catholicism, the Ecumenical movement, and modern Roman Catholicism. Good bibliography. Not much specifically about *women*, but interesting background of religious trends.

2. Eleanor Flexner, *Century of Struggle* (Cambridge: Belknap Press, Harvard University, 1959), p. 15. CoS is the source for much of the material in this chapter. Abigail Adams had realized the full significance of the cry "taxation without representation is tyranny." See *Familiar Letters* (of John and Abigail Adams), Charles F. Adams, ed. (Boston: Houghton Mifflin, Riverside Press, Cambridge, 1898); also Tom Paine, in *Penn. Magazine* (August 1775, p. 363, quoted by Flexner). Abigail's and John's son was also a great help to the ladies (*CoS*, p. 51). When it was suggested that since the ladies did not have the right to vote, they certainly did not have the right to petition, he is reported to have inquired of the gentlemen at the meeting, "What makes you so sure they haven't the right to vote?" Paine was right to be concerned; the divine right of kings had given way to the divine right of males. In country after country in Europe and state after state in America, suffrage for *males over 21*, with representation in an all-male legislature, became the rule. See *Cambridge Modern History*, (New York: Macmillan, 1909) vol. VI—*18th Century*: article by Arthur Lionel Smith on "Passive Obedience," pp. 801–806, for a most penetrating discussion of the political philosophy of this period.

3. *CoS*, p. 16.

4. *CoS*, p. 17. See Susan B. Anthony's speech (1873), "Are Women

Persons?" in *Treasury of Great American Speeches*, Chas. Hurd, ed. (Englewood Cliffs, N.J.: Hawthorn, 1959).

5. See several articles in *nexus 19*, the twenty-fifth anniversary edition of the alumni magazine of Boston University, 1964.

6. *CoS*, p. 26.

7. *Ibid.*, pp. 27, 44, 105.

8. *Ibid.*, passim. See note on Woman, the Law, and the Church (below).

9. Also see *CoS* passim and bibliography, pp. 341–345; also see G. H. Barnes and D. L. Drummond, *Letters of T. D. Weld* [and Grimke sisters] (New York: Appleton-Century, 1934).

10. Women's wages in 1833 for work in the home were as little as $1.25 per week (*CoS*, pp. 53ff.). When men and women did piecework in a garment factory, the man would be paid two or three times as much for making the same garment. The cotton and woolen mill hours were usually sunup to sundown. Women and children went to work at 4:30 A.M. and worked as long as they could see. Women got three dollars per week and paid $1.50 to $1.75 for board in a company boardinghouse.

11. Re education, see article by Robert S. Fletcher, "Education of Women," in *Americana Encyclopedia*; also *Saturday Review*, May 18, 1963, special issue on women's education. Also *CoS*, pp. 32ff. and passim.

H. G. Wells, *Outline of History* (Garden City: Garden City Publishing Co., 1949) quotes Napoleon as saying, "I do not think we need trouble ourselves with any plan for instruction of young females. They cannot be better brought up than by their mothers. Public education is not suitable for them because they are never called upon to act in public. Manners are all in all to them, and marriage is all they look to." Napoleon is also quoted as saying, "Society cannot exist without inequality of fortunes, which cannot endure apart from religion. When a man is dying from hunger, near another who is ill of surfeit, he cannot resign himself to this difference unless there is an authority which declares God wills it thus" (p. 937).

Note on: *Women, the Law, and the Church*

In the Doomsday Book (listing property deeds under very early English law) we learn that the woman Asa holds her land free from any power of her husband and can keep it when she leaves him. There is apparently also inheritance through females. There seems to be no question whatever that woman "exists" as a person under the law, whether married or unmarried. Under early law, also, if a man was killed, the killer must pay the family, not just the male heirs. Blood money was due both maternal and paternal relatives. If a woman was murdered, indemnity went to her kin, not to her husband.

The period of Roman law in Britain tended to make the married woman a copartner with her husband, so far as property rights were concerned. The idea of the woman as liege of her lord-husband was a feudal idea that entered England with the Norman Conquest. The wife was the feudal vassal. This idea won immediate popularity in the male-dominated courts.

Blackstone (1723–1780) followed this feudal concept as reflected in the "common law" (based on the precedent of decisions in the courts) rather than the earlier law concerning women. He held in his *Commentaries* (1765) that by common law (i.e., law based on the precedent of court findings in similar cases) a woman's legal existence was suspended when she married. Her husband had to support her, pay her debts (even premarital ones), and her bills for necessities. A husband could not enter into a contract with his wife, since this would presume she had "existence"; however, he could if he wished remember her in his will, for after his death she would legally exist again. So she could inherit. It was his right to "chastise" her to promote discipline. However, with the "age of courtesy" under Charles II, the right of corporal punishment "began to be doubted." All the restrictions placed on women, says Blackstone, were for their own protection, "so great a favorite is the female sex of the laws of England."

Unfortunately the general public at the time of Blackstone were inclined to accept the word of a great jurist at face value. His statements were, moreover, quoted, repeated, exaggerated, oversimplified, and glibly mouthed in court to establish one more "precedent." There is considerable question whether Blackstone really cared if he was misunderstood on this point. He never *said* his interpretation of the law about married women having no legal existence applied also to unmarried women. If people would misread and oversimplify and generalize, was it his fault?

If Blackstone did not especially like women, he did not understand them either, or he would have known that the *femmes couvertes* and all the ladies who hoped some day to be in this happy married state, and all their sisters, would raise a battle cry. If you are non-existent, you can lose nothing by protesting. Mary Wollstonecraft (1792) in her *Vindication of the Rights of Woman* (published together with John Stuart Mill's and Harriet Mill's *Subjugation of Women*, with an appropriate introduction by Pamela Frankau in Everyman's Library ₦825) raised the hue and cry for "natural rights" as opposed to the "divine rights of husbands." She also challenged Rousseau's advice to the ladies that they attain feminine rule by tricks and subterfuge; to govern by sex charm, she told the women, was below their human dignity, and very bad for the men, playing up to their passions, arrogance, and prejudices.

Actually it was the Church that came to the woman's legal rescue, though her status after marriage had already been considerably modified in England by contract agreements entered into at the time of marriage, as part of the ceremony itself. The Church came to women's rescue through equity. Equity was originally a petition to the king, through his chancellor (a religious office), begging extraordinary privileges and consideration "for the love of God and in the way of Charity." (It was a little like the custom of sending "hardship" cases in our modern military forces to "see the chaplain.") So many people came to see the chancellor to seek help and relief from the harshness and inadequacy of the English common law that a special court of equity was established to deal with their cases. Thus chancery became a court in the fifteenth century, concerning itself with justice rather than usage, however well established under the common law. It drew heavily upon the civil law of Rome; and the civil law of Rome had made men and women partners. The court of chancery found many ways to relieve injustices to women.

The United States inherited the common law from England, but it has largely been modified by codification of the laws of the states. In 1836 Mrs. Ernestine Rose, recently from Poland, presented to the New York Legislature the first petition, with a few signatures, for a Married Women's Property Law. By 1850 most states had legislation allowing women to hold property. Lawyers also discovered how to get around inheritance problems by the use of trust funds. One man was so harassed by all the problems of being deprived of his "rights" that he struck back, suing his wife's mother's estate for the wife's wages for the time she had spent caring for her mother.

See Mary Beard, *Woman as a Force in History* (New York: Macmillan, 1946), for something less than appreciation of Blackstone and his views on women. Pertinent also are F. W. Maitland, *Constitutional History of England* (London: Cambridge University Press, 1931), and *Roman Canon Law in the Church of England* (London: Methuen, 1898); also G. Ferrero, *Women of the Caesars* (New York: Century Co., 1911).

Chapter 14: The "Prospector" Groups

1. Stilson Judah, Pacific School of Religion, President, American Theological Library Assn., manuscript, 1964.

In general see: Frank S. Mead, *Handbook of Denominations* (New York and Nashville: Abingdon Cokesbury, 1951). Good background material on early roots from which some of our nineteenth-century movements grew. Also Elmer T. Clark, *Small Sects in America* (Nashville: Abingdon Cokesbury, 1937, rev. 1949).

H. P. Van Dusen estimated there is a "third force" of American Christendom, numbering 4,350,000 members of churches between the "traditional" and the "fringe" groups (*Life*, 6-9-58). In some of the "third force" churches, women play a significant role.

Of interest is Vittorio Lanternari's *Religions of the Oppressed* (Italy, 1960; New York: Knopf, 1963). Chapter II concerning the "Peyote Woman" presents intriguing variations on the "savior concept" common in one way or another to many religions.

2. Donald Meyer, *The Positive Thinkers* (Garden City: Doubleday, 1965). The whole book is pertinent to our subject in this chapter.

3. See discussion of William James' contribution, Meyer, *op. cit.*, Postscript I. Meyer points out that the idea of "mind cure" was nothing especially new to religion, but had a special attraction for what are sometimes called the "dispossessed," whereas "historians generally write about one minority of people—adult males."

4. Judah, *op. cit.*

5. Meyer, *op. cit.*, ch. 2. See also ch. 3 on "The Troubled Souls of Females," for one interesting analysis of cultural forces in society which made women susceptible to the influx of cults. Meyer is inclined to think this susceptibility came from a recognition of their own weakness; we have

taken the position that their interest was a result of the women recognizing their potential strength. There is undoubtedly some truth in both viewpoints.

6. Extra-sensory perception. Of course other universities have also been studying in this field. Duke's studies came early and were popularized on radio programs.

Chapter 15: The Cause of Youth

1. W. E. Garrison, *March of Faith* (New York, Harper, 1933), ch. x.

2. Rouse and Neill, *History of the Ecumenical Movement*, pp. 327, 599n., 605, 607. For a history of the YWCA read Mary S. Sims, *The YWCA —an Unfolding Purpose* (New York: Women's Press, 1950) and Grace H. Wilson, *The Religious and Educational Philosophy of the Young Women's Christian Association* (New York: Teachers' College, Columbia University, 1933); also files of *World's YWCA Monthly*. For a study of cooperation between the YM and YW in recent years, see Dan W. Dodson, "The Role of the YWCA in a Changing Era" (New York: National Board, YWCA, 1960—reprint from 22d National Convention Yearbook). Some twenty-five per cent of the YM membership in the United States is girls and women. Leaders say a major problem is to "guard against accepting women as a minority in a man's movement." To guard against this, they stress family and community relations and the need for women's leadership. YM-YW relationships is a subject for ongoing discussion over the years.

Chapter 16: At the Heart of the Matter: Woman in Her Church

1. *Yearbook of the American Churches* (New York: National Council of Churches); consult current issue.

2. *Woman, Some Aspects of Her Role in the Modern World* (Loveland, Ohio: Grailville pamphlet, 1960).

3. *Commonweal*, 12–20–63.

4. *New York Times*, 11–28–63. See *America*, 11–23–63 for review of Cardinal Suenens' *Nun in the World*; 11–14–64 correspondence about "Mind in Woman" as related to Phyllis McGinley's *Sixpence in Her Shoe*; 10–17–64 re recruitment of women for religious vocation in the Catholic Church.

Also see: Hendrik Kraemer, *Theology of the Laity* (Philadelphia: Westminster, 1949); Georgia Harkness, *The Church and Its Laity* (Nashville: Abingdon, 1962); Cynthia Wedel, *Employed Women and the Church* (New York: Department of United Church Women and Department of Church and Economic Life, National Council of Churches, 1959).

Chapter 17: The Coming of the Councils

1. See report of Joint Consultation on Employed Women and the Church held at Greenwich, Connecticut, 1958 (National Council of Churches).

Many competent churchwomen have been reading with interest—and drawing appropriate analogies for the churches—from the recent report of the President's Commission on the Status of Women. In December 1961, President Kennedy established a commission of twenty-six leading citizens "to indicate what remains to be done to demolish prejudices and out-moded customs which act as barriers to full participation of women in our democracy." The commission was concerned with employment practices, social insurance, tax laws, labor conditions, political and civil rights, family relations, counseling service, education, especially in relation to the changing social and industrial scene. The United Church Women and National Council staff were represented on this commission, as were the National Council of Jewish Women and the National Council of Catholic Women. *American Women,* the commission report (October 1963), stressed among other matters that women in any field must not shy away from top-rung responsibility. Reports of various commissions, as well as the over-all report, are available from the Superintendent of Documents, Washington, D.C., or regional U.S. offices.

One of the valuable services rendered was to hold a consultation (3-19-63) on "The Portrayal of Women by Mass Media." The thirty-three participants, nationally known in various fields of writing and broadcasting, took themselves seriously to task for accepting too readily two "stereotypes" of women: either the courtesan (or "bunny girl") or the "uniform, shallow, even grotesque image" of the housewife in commercials. It was suggested that the mass media had a responsibility to show pluralistic images of women, relating the image to such problems as women's aspirations, motivations, standards of performance, interest in lifelong education, career planning, attitudes of employers. Lack of any inspiring image of the Negro woman in the general media was especially deplored. One participant thought that to a certain degree mass media do reflect the middle-class homebound housewife with children, but to an "uncondonable degree" they neglect such very large minorities as the full-time working wife, the woman head of the family, the single career girl, the professional intellectual.

Some persons will feel that the image of women for which the churches are responsible might well be subjected to similar diagnosis, repentance, and a will to update and diversify the concept of "woman" which the churches present to the world. This is especially important if the concept being held up—explicitly or implicitly—is something of a motivating image of what the woman should ideally be. Much of the material in the various reports of the commission and commissions can be interpreted to have considerable significance for the churches.

Re women's interest in council work, see Mossie Wyker, *Church Women in the Scheme of Things* (St. Louis: Bethany Press, 1953); Grace Gilkey Calkins, *Follow Those Women* (New York: United Church Women, 1961), and files of *The Church Woman*, published by United Church Women, 475 Riverside Drive, New York.

2. *Ecumenical Press Service* (Geneva, Switzerland), 2–13–64.

3. See Appendix III for world results of a survey by the World Council of Churches Department of Cooperation of Men and Women in Church, Family and Society.

Chapter 18: Preaching, Teaching, and Other Occupations

1. *The Bridge* (Unitarian-Universalist Women's Federation, June 1963), quoted, Mary Brackenridge Crook, *Women in Religion* (Boston: Beacon, 1964).

2. The writer has in her possession a small autograph album presented to her grandmother, Celestia Moore Streeter, by a Sunday-school class which she taught in a small Nebraska town during a stopover en route to California. Like many a woman, Celestia Streeter carried her family Bible with her, studied it as the wagon rolled across the plains, and read from it to her seven children. When the family decided to stop for a short time, Grandpa, who had become a Methodist preacher, started out on horseback to visit the neighboring settlements and isolated settlers. Grandma would "stay put" and call the women together in one of their homes, or a hall, or a barn. She held Sunday-school classes and got folks used to using their Bibles again. The Bible class included everybody, from the old folks to the babies. Sometimes a little service was arranged for persons who had died and been buried without benefit of a "real" funeral. Grandpa might come back to preach now and then, but it was Grandma who kept things going. If it had been the first century A.D., there would certainly have been Biblical references to "the church that meets in Celestia's house."

3. Jeanette E. Newhall, "There Were Giants in Those Days" in *nexus*, VII–1, Nov. 1963. This 125th anniversary number from Boston University contains a great deal of interesting material about women in the Church.

4. *nexus*, VII–1.

5. Winfred Ernest Garrison, *March of Faith* (New York: Harper, 1933).

6. In the discussions of ordination it is hard to distinguish between objections that demand respectful attention, even though we may not agree, and those which are simply excuses based on rationalizations and prejudice. The following arguments have sometimes been set forth against ordination of women:

Jesus was a man; his representative on earth should be a man. (But surely we think of the Trinity as supra-sexual.)

Paul commanded women to be silent. (See ch. 3, supra.)

Peter established the apostolic succession—a physical laying on of hands which has been unbroken. . . . (Most ministers would be reluctant to accept this as a test of their own ordination.)

Jesus did not choose female apostles. (Might he not, today? Again, see the New Testament record in ch. 3. Chrysostom refers to Junias as a notable female apostle. Priscilla has also been called an apostle. How many were omitted by male scribes and priestly editors?)

In favor of ordaining women, people say:

Male dominance in the churches is a hold-over from patriarchal Judaism.
In the Protestant churches, opposition to women is a protest against Mariolotry.
Our traditions have come down to us through male scribes and monks, who have ignored women's contribution to the Church.
The Church has paid too little attention to the doctrine of the Holy Spirit, which comes to women as well as to men—no one can compel it.
Women's contribution is needed for the renewal and wholeness of the Church.
We need to recapture the doctrine of the (responsible) priesthood of all believers. There has been too much of a gulf between the role of the clergy and laity, with *all* women traditionally classified as laity.
There are also problems, though none of us like to mention them, of the Church conforming, historically, to a male-dominated pattern of society, glorification of the military organizational pattern, entrenched institutionalism.
We seldom hear today the argument frequently brought forth in the past, of woman's strength not being equal to the task, her mind not up to the challenge.

Concerning the ongoing controversy on ordination, refer to:
Maude Royden, *Church and Woman* (London: J. Clarke, 1924).
C. E. Raven, *Women and Holy Orders* (London: Hodder and Stoughton, 1928).
Report of the Archbishop's Commission on the Ministry of Women (London: Church House, Westminster, 1935).
Kathleen Bliss, *Service and Status of Women in the Churches* (London: Student Christian Movement, 1952).
Max Zerbst, *Office of Women in the Church*, tr. by A. G. Markens (St. Louis: Concordia, 1955).
M. E. Thrall, *Ordination of Women to the Priesthood* (New York: Student Christian Movement, 1958).
Helen Turnbull, *Ministry of Women* (Geneva: World Council of Churches, 1958).
Madeleine Barot, "Women in Ministry" in *Laity* #9 (Geneva: W.C.C., 7–60).

7. Benson Landis, *Religion in the United States* (New York: Barnes and Noble, 1965).
See also the National Council of Churches' *Information Service* (3–6–54) and *Yearbook of the American Churches*, 1963 and current issue.

8. Margaret Henrichsen, *Seven Steeples* (Boston: Houghton Mifflin, 1952).

9. *Christian Century*, 6–5–63, 8–28–63.

10. In general, see *Official Catholic Directory* (New York: P. J. Kenedy). Also *National Catholic Almanac* (Garden City, New York: Doubleday).

11. *Ecumenical Press Service*, 9–9–65. See frequent reports in *Commonweal*.

12. Cardinal Suenens, *Nun in the World* (Westminster, Md.: Newman, 1963).
Arthur McCormack, "A New Era for the Nun in the World" (*Catholic World*, 6–64).

13. Religious News Service, New York, 3-21-56.

14. Vera Weismann, "Woman," in *Universal Jewish Encyclopaedia* (New York, 1943).

15. See Max I. Dimont, *Jews, God and History* (New York: Simon and Schuster, 1962) for a liberal Jewish view of Jewish history.

Note on the American Association of Women Ministers, et al.

The American Association of Women Ministers, founded in 1919 under the leadership of the Reverend Madeline Southard, publishes *Woman's Pulpit*, which provides news of the association and its members, and other pertinent material. The Reverend Hazel Foster has for several years provided a very useful report on "The Ecclesiastical Status of Women" as a feature of this publication, reporting the work and achievements of women ministers in the United States and elsewhere.

Marquis' *Who's Who in American Women* (listing over 20,000 names) has two pertinent categories: Club/Religious/Civic Leaders (2850 names, or 14.4 per cent of the total listings) and Religious Workers, career (eighty-seven names, or .4 per cent).

At the time of the Evanston World Council of Churches Assembly (1954), the World Council U.S. office listed 132 women participants in all categories, including forty-seven women from the United States.

The whole question of birth control, and its religious, economic, and sociological implications, is beyond the scope of the present discussion, but one which women of various faiths need to face together in the light of religion.

Neither can we go into the question of sainthood, about which there is abundant material, especially in the U.S., in connection with canonization of Mother Cabrini and the beatification of Mother Elizabeth Ann Seton.

Chapter 19: Churchwomen Today

1. Alden D. Kelley, *People of God* (Greenwich, Conn.: Seabury, 1962), contains a good bibliography on the place of the laity in the Church.

2. Emil Brunner, *The Divine Imperative*, tr. Olive Wyon, (Philadelphia: Westminster, 1947), p. 376.

3. As this is written, a joint assembly of United Church Men and United

Church Women (National Council of Churches) is being planned for Purdue, 1967.

See Cox van Heestra, *Christian Women in Africa* (Geneva, W.C.C., 1963); and listings under ch. 18.

Appendix I: Women in Four Major Faiths of the World

Women in Hinduism

1. Schaff-Herzog and *Hastings Encyclopaedia of Religion and Ethics,* "Hinduism" for basic facts.

Generally pertinent to this and the following sections are:

M. Eliade, *Patterns of Comparative Religion,* R. Sheed, tr. (London: Sheed and Ward, 1958); Emma Hawkridge, *The Wisdom Tree* (Boston: Houghton Mifflin, 1945); Ruth Cranston, *World Faith* (New York: Harper, 1949); Lin Yutang, *Wisdom of China and India* (New York: Random House, 1942).

2. Mildreth Worth Pinkham, *Women in the Sacred Scriptures of Hinduism* (New York: Columbia, 1941). This section is based largely on Dr. Pinkham's material. Her 200-page volume offers a sixteen-page bibliography, text citations, good index. See also, *passim,* F. Max Mueller, *History of Ancient Sanskrit Literature,* which she freely quotes.

3. Pinkham, *op. cit.,* p. xi.

4. The Dasyu religion is described as crude sex-related magic.

5. H. D. Griswold, *Religion of the Rig-Veda* (quoted Pinkham, *op. cit.,* p. 3). Some scholars believe that at a somewhat earlier period polyandry was practiced either in India or by the immigrants in their previous homeland (*ibid.,* p. 34). HERE says: "It is possible that mother-right once widely prevailed in India, as is indicated by the common rule of inheritance through females, the position of the paternal uncle at marriages, and the priestly function assigned to the sister's son." Hindu home life (especially where the joint family system prevails) is characterized by "good sense, benevolence, self-control, self-abnegation, active charity and kindliness."

6. See E. Thompson, *Suttee,* p. 18, quoted Pinkham, *op. cit.,* p. 43. If widow sacrifice had previously been a custom, it was now in abeyance.

7. R. E. Hume, *World's Living Religions,* pp. 24ff., quoted Pinkham, *op. cit.,* p. 63.

8. Not until 1856 was marriage for all widows in India legalized. However, the law prohibiting marriage was not always observed by the lower castes, as witnessed by the many tales extolling the virtue of women who did *not* remarry. How such a repressive social law can operate to correct itself was illustrated from the visit the writer paid to a community housing development in Bombay a few years ago. Women were arriving home from the near-by factory, with children who had been cared for in the company crèche while their mothers worked. The women were calling to one another, arguing, singing. "There," said my guide, "you see the hope of India. These women were formerly untouchables. They have learned to look out for themselves and their children. Now restrictions of generations are being

removed. They can say anything, do anything; they have nothing to lose. Keep your eye on them!" See Pinkham, *op. cit.*, ch. 6, and J. J. Meyer, *Sexual Life in Ancient India*, quoted.

9. Of course not all the Indian goddesses are the kind and helpful nature deities we meet in the *Rig-Veda*. Some are, in fact, quite weird. Many of these are related to the worship of the active female principle, *prakrite*, as manifested in one or the other of the various forms of the consort of Siva.

10. Concerning Christian influence in recent years, consult Rajah Manikam, ed., *Christianity and the Asian Revolution* (New York: Friendship Press, 1954). This is a joint effort of a number of reliable scholars.

11. James Michener, *Voice of Asia* (New York: Random House, 1951), chapter on India: see "Defense of the New Woman" and "Case against the New Woman."

12. Kenneth W. Morgan, ed., *Religion of the Hindus* (New York: Ronald Press, 1953), ch. 5.

13. Paul Devanandan, *Gospel of Renascent Hinduism* (New York: Friendship Press, 1959). See also Edw. W. Hopkins, *Great Epic of India* (New York: Scribner, 1902).

Women in Buddhism

14. Edward J. Thomas, *Life of Buddha* (New York: Knopf, 1927), ch. 8.

15. See Mrs. Rhys Davids, *Psalms of the Sisters*, Part I of *Psalms of the Early Buddhists* (London: Pali Text Society, 1909).

16. Cranston, *op. cit.*, ch. 2.

17. A. B. Keith, *Buddhist Philosophy in India and Ceylon* (London: Oxford, 1923), DM 3.18off.; Suttanipata 2.4.14.

18. Hawkridge, *op. cit.*, part 3, ch. 2.

19. *Ibid.*

20. I-Tsing, *A Record of the Buddhist Religion as Practiced in India and the Malay Archipelago*, tr. by J. Takakusu (London: Oxford, 1896), p. 80.

21. *Ibid.*, p. 98. Also Keith, *op. cit.*, p. 133.

22. Keith, *op. cit.*, p. 296.

23. *Psalms of the Sisters*, Introduction, *passim*, and pp. 20, 27.

24. *Ibid.*, p. 76.

25. R. F. Johnston, *Buddhist China* (London: John Murray, 1913), pp. 285–290.

26. *Ibid.*, pp. 278ff.

27. Hawkridge, *op. cit.*, part 3, ch. 2.

See also Mabel Bode, *Women Leaders of the Buddhist Reformation* (London: Royal Asiatic Society, 1893); L. B. Horner, *Women under Primitive Buddhism* (New York: Dutton, 1930); A. Getty, *Gods of Northern Buddhism* (New York: Clarendon, 1914); Nancy Ross, ed., *World of Zen* (New York: Random House, 1960); Aelred Graham, *Zen Catholicism* (New York: Harcourt, Brace and World, 1963).

Women in Confucian Philosophy

28. E.g., II Isaiah, Socrates, and Buddha. Dates usually assigned to Confucius are 551–479 B.C.

29. See William T. DeBary, Wing-Tait Chan, and Burton Watson, *Sources of Chinese Tradition* (New York: Columbia, 1960), pp. 816f.

30. Miles Meander Dawson, *Basic Teachings of Confucius* (New York: Random House, 1942). Unless otherwise noted, quotes in this section are from this source.

31. Dr. Ping-Ti Ho is author of *Ladder of Success in Imperial China*, 1368–1911, and *Studies on the Population*, 1368–1953 (New York: Columbia, 1962).

32. Lecture, University of California Medical Center, San Francisco, 1964.

33. See Lien-sheng Yang, "Female Rulers in Imperial China," in *Harvard Journal of Asiatic Studies*, XXIII, 1960–1961.

34. See Dr. Hu Shih, *Chinese Renaissance* (Chicago: University of Chicago, 1934).

35. See Dr. Denis Lasure, "Cheerful Children of Red China's Communes" in *MacLean's Magazine*, 3–11–61, quoted by Ping-Ti Ho.

Also see T. de Lacouperie, *Silk Goddess of China* (London, 1891) (not seen).

Women in Islam

36. See Dorothy Van Ess, *Fatima and Her Sisters* (New York: John Day, 1961). She points out (p. 178) that in earlier days a wife had been called Aqila, "tethered one"—an interesting commentary on the desert background of the Arabs. Mohammed changed the word to Karina, "joined." Subordination and restriction from the mosque were, Van Ess insists, not Mohammed's idea, nor is it the idea of the modern Arab woman.

37. *Schaff-Herzog Encyclopaedia*. Also Nabia Abbott, *Aishah, the Beloved of Mohammed* (Chicago: University of Chicago Press, 1943)—highly recommended by competent authorities.

38. The Arab expansion was finally stopped by Charles Martel in 732.

39. Tor Andrae, *Mohammed, the Man and His Faith*, T. Menzel, tr. (Paris, 1945; New York: Harper, 1960).

40. *Ibid.*, pp. 90ff.

41. Wilfred Cantwell Smith, *Modern Islam in India* (London: Gollancz, 1946), p. 75, remarks, however, that some authorities insist Mohammed put woman on a pedestal, but wanted her veiled while she was admired. Also "that men and women should enjoy each other's company is thought to be obscene." These would seem to be the ideas of Mohammed's followers, rather than of the prophet himself. The observation about "the chivalry which the Arabs gave to Europe but forgot to keep for themselves" also has more of the *bon mot* than historic value.

42. Tor Andrae, *op. cit.*, p. 149.

43. *Ibid.*, p. 79.

44. Abbott, *op. cit.*, pp. 16ff., 22ff., 6off.; see also 80, 81, 91ff. and *passim.*

45. W. C. Smith points out that segregation of women, whether in Indian or Moslem culture, is actually based on social function "If women were taking part in the productive activities of society, they would soon have that economic independence without which they cannot be truly free, and with which they will necessarily find freedom." (*Op. cit.*, p. 80 and *passim.*)

46. Although there was no limit set on the number of wives the prophet could have, other Moslem men could have only four, and then only if they could provide for all of them and treat them without partiality. In the recent enthusiasm of Pakistan to be "the most Moslem of the Moslem states," the men began reading and quoting the provision about the number of wives to the women. But the women had been reading the Koran on their own and gave that provision back to the men in context. The men said they were only joking anyway—who would *want* more than one wife?

47. E. Dermenghem, *Muhammad and the Islamic Tradition*, J. M. Watt, Jr., tr. (New York, Harper, 1958), p. 47, states that "certainly the attitude of the Prophet as regards women has weighed heavily on the Muslim civilization, for the examples and principles were forcibly warped by the natural tendency of men to seek their own advantage. He certainly improved women's lot in the Arabia of his day. He prohibited infanticide and prostitution of slave women. He established the rights of women to inherit (a half share). He proclaimed that 'Paradise is at a mother's knees,' that married couples have reciprocal duties and rights, and that women ought to be educated. . . . Daughters could not be married without their own consent. . . ." It was a good beginning, but Dermenghem points out that "Instead of taking advantage of these rules to move in a more liberal and progressive direction, jurisprudence and morals have, on the contrary, made [restrictions on women] more rigid."

48. Zafrulla Kahn, *Islam* (New York: Harper and Row, 1962), p. 142.

49. John A. Williams, *Islam* (New York: Braziller, 1961), p. 99.

50. A. J. Wensinck, *Handbook of Early Muhammadan Tradition* (University of Leiden, 1960).

51. W. C. Smith, *op. cit.*, pp. 78, 140.

52. Dermenghem, *op. cit.*, p. 77.

53. *Time* magazine, 11–11–57.

See Ruth F. Woodsmall, *Women of the Near East* (Middle East Institute, 1960).

Appendices II and III

In general, for current Protestant materials mentioned, write to departments indicated at the National Council of Churches or World Council of Churches, New York office, both at 475 Riverside Drive, New York, N.Y. 10027. Geneva address of the World Council is 150 route de Ferney, 1211, Geneva, 20, Switzerland.

For denominational and interdenominational organizations and personnel in the U.S.A., consult current issue of *Yearbook of the American Churches* (N.C.C., above address); National Catholic Almanac (Yearbook) (Garden City, N.Y.: Doubleday); Official Catholic Directory (New York: P. J. Kenedy); or American Jewish Yearbook (annual) (American Jewish Committee and Jewish Publication Society of America, 165 E. 56 St., New York, N.Y. 10022).

INDEX OF PROPER NAMES

H